MODERN CURRICULUM
PHONICS

A complete phonics and word study program in 7 levels: K, A-F

This program has helped 50 million children learn to read. It can help your students, too.

ALL photographic picture clues

MCP "Plaid" Phonics
A Complete Program Newly Revised

A+ FOR MCP PHONICS

"Every year I have a range of students in my class. I need a flexible program that gives me a way to provide each child what he or she needs to become a reader. MCP Phonics teacher edition has enough variety to reach children of all levels in each lesson."

Carol Sibila
Third Grade Teacher
St. Joseph School
Cuyahoga Falls, Ohio

— **has an unparalleled track record of student success.**

— **is the standard** by which every other program is measured.

— **has lots of practice with kid-appeal!** In phonics, practice really does make perfect. **MCP Phonics** packs practice into lots of fun riddles, rhymes, games, puzzles, and activities that challenge students to read aloud, write, review, and check their work.

— **is flexible. MCP Phonics** is tailor-made for classes that represent a wide range of ability levels. It helps all students become successful readers through multiple approaches that reach visual, auditory, and kinesthetic learners.

Call MCP "Plaid" Phonics at
800-321-3106

MCP Phonics has helped more than 50 million kids learn to read in the past 40 years.

It can help your students, too.

— **is research-based.**
MCP Phonics has been continuously revised to reflect the latest classroom research and to maintain a relevance for each generation of students and teachers.

— **is systematic and explicit.**
Studies show that most students benefit from explicit phonics instruction. Like training wheels on a bike, **MCP Phonics** provides the systematic, intensive support children need to become independent readers.

— **earns a teacher's trust, year after year.**
The method is sound; the materials are first-rate. Reading trends may come and go — **MCP Phonics** steers students on a steady course to success.

TEACHERS!
DO YOU HAVE A GREAT *"PLAID" PHONICS* IDEA TO SHARE WITH OTHER TEACHERS?

ANNOUNCING
"PLAID" PHONICS PARTNERS GRANTS!
MCP is awarding grants to teachers who want to create a phonics workshop using *MCP Phonics*. Grants include a $400 stipend in money and materials. For an application, write to:

Modern Curriculum Press
attn. Marketing Dept.
299 Jefferson Road
Parsippany, NJ 07054

or call
800-321-3106
Share your teaching strategies with others!

Ten key features in MCP Phonics

1 Easy-to-use Teaching Plan with all you need at point of use

▶ This teaching plan is the easiest ever! **Quick-scan lesson plans** put everything you need at your fingertips. No confusion, no page flipping, no losing your place.

MCP Phonics' Teaching Plan includes...

- simple step-by-step lesson plans
- strategies to help every learner
- lesson objectives that serve as a guide to informal assessment
- spelling practice that flows from phonics
- quick and easy curriculum connections

Lessons begin with phonemic awareness activities (Levels K, A, B).

Find approaches for auditory, visual, kinesthetic, ESL, gifted, and those who need extra support in every lesson.

Lesson 40

Pages 85–86

Short

a

INFORMAL ASSESSMENT OBJECTIVES

Can children

✓ identify picture names and words that contain the short sound of *a*?

✓ write words that contain the short sound of *a* to complete sentences?

Lesson Focus

PHONEMIC AWARENESS

Say a word that begins with the short *a* sound. Have children say the word, repeating /a/ twice before the word. For example, children would respond *a-a-apple*. Use these words: *alligator, accident, ant, animal, ax, apple*.

SOUND TO LETTER

- Write these words on the board and read each one: *cat, cab, fan, map, dad, ham, bag, sad, can*. Call on volunteers to use colored chalk to underline the letter *a*. Have children name the sound in each word.
- Give children an opportunity to name other words that contain the short *a* sound. Write the words on the board as they are suggested.

USING THE PAGES

- Help children identify the pictures on pages 85 and 86.
- **Critical Thinking** Read aloud the Think! question at the bottom of page 85 and discuss answers with the children.

85

▶ Look at the picture. Circle the word that will finish the sentence. Print it on the line.

1. Max is my ___cat___
   (cat) / sat / can

2. He licks my ___hand___
   land / (hand) / ham

3. Max sits on my ___lap___
   pad / rap / (lap)

4. He likes my ___dad___
   sad / (dad) / bad

5. He plays with a ___bag___
   bat / rag / (bag)

6. Max takes a ___nap___
   (nap) / cap / cab

THINK! Why does the girl like Max?

Lesson 40 — Short vowel a: Words in context — 85

FOCUS ON ALL LEARNERS ✳ ◦ ◆ ■ ◦◦

ENGLISH LANGUAGE LEARNERS/ESL
Before beginning page 85, have children talk about pets they have or would like to have.

VISUAL LEARNERS
SMALL GROUP Materials: paper bag, index cards or slips of paper

Have each child in the group write three short *a* words on separate cards or slips of paper and place the words in the bag. Ask children to take turns picking a card, reading the word aloud and using it in a sentence.

KINESTHETIC LEARNERS
SMALL GROUP Have children say a sentence leaving out a short *a* word which they can pantomime for others to guess. They might suggest *cat, sat, nap, lap, pan,* or *man*.

Teacher Resource Guide, page 85, Level A

---

2 Approaches you need to reach every learner

▶ The Focus On All Learners supports students' **preferred learning styles** while also helping them develop other ways to learn.

▶ Say the name of each picture. Print the letter for its beginning sound. Then print the letter for its ending sound.

1	2	3	4
c a t	p □ n	t □ g	h □ m
5	6	7	8
m □ p	d □ d	r □ m	r □ t
9	10	11	12
h □ t	b □ g	c □ n	b □ t
13	14	15	16
m □ n	c □ p	v □ n	f □ n

 Lesson 40
Short a words: Spelling

Ask your child to read the story on page 85.

AUDITORY/KINESTHETIC LEARNERS

Materials: fingerpaints; paper

Have children listen to words and paint a picture for each one with a name that contains a short *a*. They can write *a*'s under the pictures. Use: *apple, ant, dog, cat, dad.*

GIFTED LEARNERS

Challenge children by having them write a song that contains short *a* words, using a familiar tune. Encourage them to perform their songs.

LEARNERS WHO NEED EXTRA SUPPORT

Materials: Letter Cards

Use Letter Cards to make groups of words with the same phonogram. For example, use cards to spell *bat*. Ask children to change the *b* to *c* to make *cat*, the *c* to *f* to form *fat*, the *f* to *h* to make *hat*, and so on. See Daily Phonics Practice, page 312.

CURRICULUM CONNECTIONS

SPELLING

Write the List Words *bag, can, cat, fan, ham,* and *map* on the chalkboard and read them with children. Give clues for each word such as *It is food.* Have volunteers touch and spell the word that goes with the clue.

WRITING

Portfolio — Have the children reread the story about Max on page 85. Then suggest that they write and draw their own stories that tell more about Max. Brainstorm a list of short *a* words and write them on the board for children to use in their stories. Invite volunteers to share their stories with the class.

MATH

Invite children to name pets they have or would like to have. List the kinds of pets, such as gerbils, fish, cats, and dogs. Record the names of children who have or would like to have each kind of pet on a chart under the pet name. Have children count the names to determine which pets are the most popular and which are the most unusual.

Technology — **AstroWord** Short Vowels: *a, i.* ©1998 Silver Burdett Ginn Inc. Division of Simon & Schuster.

Book Corner

PHONICS CONNECTION

Riley, Kana. *That Fly.* Ready Readers. (Modern Curriculum Press, 1996). A girl unwittingly gets a fly to stop bothering her.

THEME CONNECTION

Michelson, Richard. *Animals Ought to Be: Poems About Imaginary Pets.* (Simon & Schuster, 1996). This collection of short poems tells about such animals as the Roombroom and the Channel Changer.

86

Teacher Resource Guide, page 86, Level A

Curriculum Connections include suggestions for integrating phonics with a range of content areas. The writing activities make great additions to student portfolios.

New! References appear for technology phonics practice.

Book Corner suggests favorite titles to reinforce the lesson's phonics / thematic connection (Levels K, A, B, C).

"I look for ease of use in a teaching plan with quick tips and ideas for reaching all learners. I find that in MCP Phonics. If I were a beginning teacher, I'd really appreciate the step-by-step approach MCP Phonics presents."

Karen Gordon
First Grade Teacher
Alimacani Elementary
Jacksonville, Florida

No more confusion! Page numbers align! The page number you see in the student edition is the one you'll find in the teaching plan.

3 The only program with all photographic picture clues

In MCP Phonics you'll find page after page of **powerful photography** — all easy for students to identify.

In MCP Phonics, picture clues are...
- easy and fun to identify
- representative of our nation's diversity
- kid-tested

Take-Home Books with powerful photography engage young readers in nonfiction.

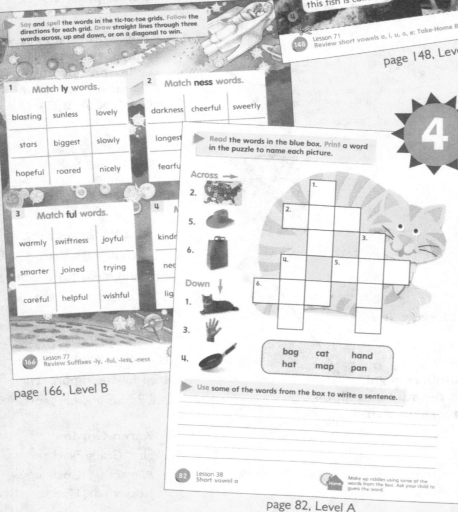

Think about fish. Fish are amazing!

Can you tell what this fish is called?

148 Lesson 71
Review short vowels a, i, u, o, e: Take-Home Book

page 148, Level A

Say the name of each picture. Circle its name.

1 bat bad ban	2 ant wax ax	3 nap can cat
4 cab cap nap	5 man bag band	6 tag rag tap
7 fat fan tan	8 had hand land	9 tap lap lamp
10 van had ran	11 bad cab dad	12 pat pan ran

Short vowel a: Picture-text match
Lesson 38
81

page 81, Level A

Say and spell the words in the tic-tac-toe grids. Follow the directions for each grid. Draw straight lines through three words across, up and down, or on a diagonal to win.

1 Match ly words.

blasting	sunless	lovely
stars	biggest	slowly
hopeful	roared	nicely

2 Match ness words.

darkness	cheerful	sweetly
longest		
fearfu		

3 Match ful words.

warmly	swiftness	joyful
smarter	joined	trying
careful	helpful	wishful

4		
kindr		
nec		
lig		

166 Lesson 77
Review Suffixes -ly, -ful, -less, -ness

page 166, Level B

Read the words in the blue box. Print a word in the puzzle to name each picture.

Across →
2.
5.
6.

Down ↓
1.
3.
4.

bag	cat	hand
hat	map	pan

Use some of the words from the box to write a sentence.

82 Lesson 38
Short vowel a

Make up riddles using some of the words from the box. Ask your child to guess the word.

page 82, Level A

---

4 A variety of fun formats provide practice galore!

Now you'll find an even **greater variety** of exercise formats.

MCP Phonics practice pages...
- feature photographs and realistic up-to-date illustrations
- motivate students with kid-friendly puzzles, games, and quizzes
- provide for a range of levels and learning styles
- make phonics learning FUN!

5 Skills presented in kid-friendly, thematic contexts

> MCP Phonics introduces **every skill in context** to help students apply their phonics learning to their reading.

MCP Phonics features...

- popular unit themes kids love (and teachers love to teach!)
- interest-grabbing openers with lots of ways for kids to apply phonics skills
- engaging rhyme, rhythm, and repetition so essential in building phonics skills

You'll find lots of "let's recite" and "read-again rhymes" throughout MCP Phonics.

page 29, Level A

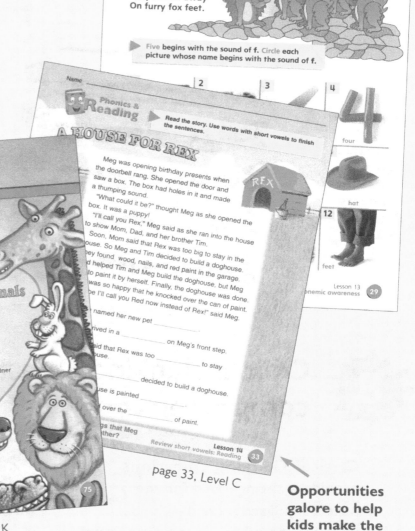

Five furry foxes
Fanning in the heat.
They all run away
On furry fox feet.

Five begins with the sound of f. **Circle** each picture whose name begins with the sound of f.

Name

Phonics & Reading

Read the story. Use words with short vowels to finish the sentences.

A HOUSE FOR REX

Meg was opening birthday presents when the doorbell rang. She opened the door and saw a box. The box had holes in it and made a thumping sound.
"What could it be?" thought Meg as she opened the box. It was a puppy!
"I'll call you Rex," Meg said as she ran into the house to show Mom, Dad, and her brother Tim.
Soon, Mom said that Rex was too big to stay in the house. So Meg and Tim decided to build a doghouse. They found wood, nails, and red paint in the garage. Dad helped Tim and Meg build the doghouse, but Meg was to paint it by herself. Finally, the doghouse was done. Meg was so happy that he knocked over the can of paint. "Maybe I'll call you Red now instead of Rex!" said Meg.

named her new pet _____.

rived in a _____ on Meg's front step.

id that Rex was too _____ to stay
use.

_____ decided to build a doghouse.

use is painted _____.

over the _____ of paint.

gs that Meg
ther?

Review short vowels: Reading
Lesson 14
33

page 33, Level C

four

hat

feet

12

Lesson 13
onemic awareness
29

Opportunities galore to help kids make the phonics/reading connection.

UNIT 3

Initial Consonant Sounds
Theme: Eyes on Animals

Read Along

Always Be Kind to Animals

Always be kind to animals,
Morning, noon, and night;
For animals have feelings too,
And furthermore, they bite.

John Gardner

THINK! Why is it important to treat animals kindly?

Directions: Ask children to name all the animals pictured on the page. Then talk about what people can do to be kind to animals.
Unit 3 • Introduction

75

page 75, Level K

A variety of unit openers include poems, songs, and activities that provide context and foster discussion.

6 Clear, concise directions and rules for students

> MCP Phonics pages win loud praise from teachers **for easy-to-follow directions** for students.

In MCP Phonics student pages...

- directions are boxed and easy to find
- key words "pop" in bold, red type
- directions for students are highlighted in yellow

page 89, Level B

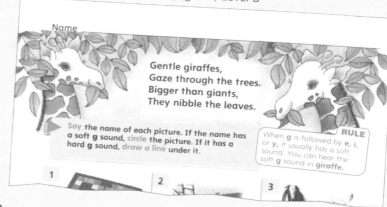

Name

Gentle giraffes,
Gaze through the trees.
Bigger than giants,
They nibble the leaves.

Say the name of each picture. If the name has a soft g sound, **circle** the picture. If it has a hard g sound, **draw a line** under it.

RULE
When g is followed by e, i, or y, it usually has a soft sound. You can hear the soft g sound in giraffe.

1   2   3

7 Purposeful writing and spelling connections

MCP Phonics helps children see the phonics / reading / spelling / writing connection. Phonics **builds decoding skills** which helps students in their reading. Spelling **develops encoding skills** which helps them in their writing.

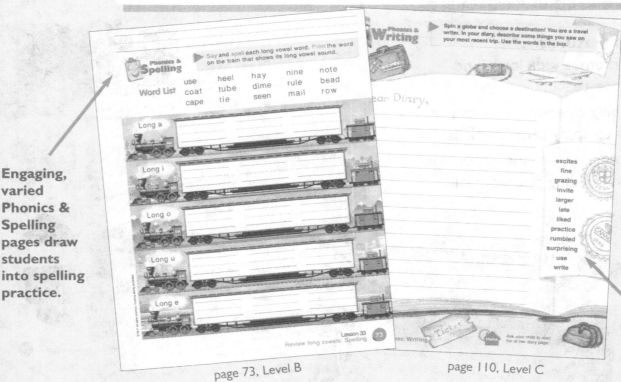

Engaging, varied Phonics & Spelling pages draw students into spelling practice.

page 73, Level B

page 110, Level C

Students apply newly learned phonics skills to their writing.

8 Critical Thinking Questions develop comprehension

Critical Thinking Questions provide a springboard for the necessary discussion that helps students **develop vocabulary, oral language**, and **comprehension**. Critical Thinking Questions appear in unit openers, sentence practice pages, and story pages.

This Critical Thinking Question prompts discussion that checks students' understanding.

page 225, Level B

page 76, Level A

Home Letter

Dear Family,
The sounds that short vowels make are what we will be learning about in the next few weeks. Here are some examples.

a — cat
e — hen
i — pig
o — dog
u — duck

As you can see, many animal names contain short vowel sounds. In this unit we will be learning about all kinds of animals.

At-Home Activities
Here are some simple, fun activities you and your child can do at home to practice short vowel sounds.

▶ Ask your child to draw a picture of an animal that she or he considers amazing and to give the animal a special short vowel name.

▶ Make a collage of animals whose names have a short vowel sound. Cut pictures from old magazines or newspapers and glue them on paper, one sheet for each vowel. You can make the collage into a mobile by hanging the pages from a wire hanger with string or yarn.

Book Corner
You and your child might enjoy reading these books together. Look for ... ... r local library.

90 Lesson 42
Review short vowel a: Writing

Ask your child what he or she might like to do on a camping trip

page 90, Level A

9 Fun, effective ways to foster reinforcement at home

With MCP Phonics, you always have an answer for parents who ask how they can **help their child** develop phonics skills.

Make a stronger Home Connection with...
- Home Letters that include suggested books to read (no need to copy, just send them home!)
- colorful, "just the right level" Take-Home Books

Workbook pages include simple tips for sharing at home to make it easy for parents to follow phonics learning in the classroom. (Levels K, A, B, C).

page 89, Level E

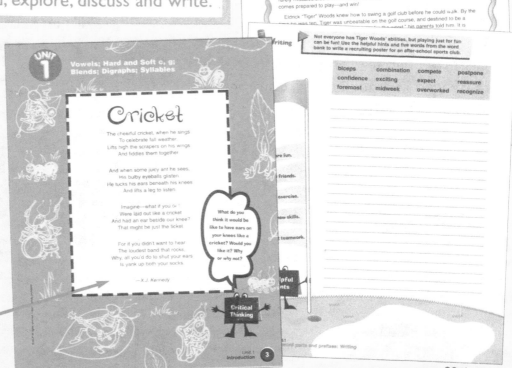

10 Big word strategies for big kids!

MCP Word Study levels D, E, and F provide **word study** and more **challenging structural analysis** for older students. They offer lots of opportunities to read, explore, discuss and write.

MCP Word Study levels D, E, and F provide review and prepare students for...
- multi-syllable words
- base words
- roots
- more difficult prefixes
- suffixes
- dictionary skills

Each unit opener shows words in context, in a playful, appealing way.

UNIT 1 Vowels; Hard and Soft c, g; Blends; Digraphs; Syllables

Cricket

The cheerful cricket, when he sings
To celebrate fall weather,
Lifts high the scrapers on his wings
And fiddles them together.

And when some juicy ant he sees,
His bulby eyeballs glisten
He tucks his ears beneath his knees
And lifts a leg to listen.

Imagine—what if you or I
Were laid out like a cricket
And had an ear beside our knee?
That might be just the ticket.

For if you didn't want to hear
The loudest band that rocks,
Why, all you'd do to shut your ears
Is yank up both your socks.

— X.J. Kennedy

What do you think it would be like to have ears on your knees like a cricket? Would you like it? Why or why not?

Critical Thinking

Unit 1
Introduction 3

page 3, Level D

page 90, Level E

MCP Phonics and Stories Libraries
Four levels of books make it easy and fun for students to apply decoding skills to reading for comprehension.

Level K

Consonants

Level A

Consonants
Short Vowels
Long Vowels
Consonant Blends
Consonant Digraphs

Level B

Short Vowels
Long Vowels
Hard, Soft g
Consonant Blends
Consonant Digraphs
r-Controlled Vowels
Contractions
Plurals
Suffixes
Endings
Variant Vowels
Prefixes

Level C

Short Vowel Review
Long Vowel Review
Consonant Blends
r-Controlled Vowels
Contractions
Plurals
Endings
Diphthongs
Vowel Pairs
Suffixes/Prefixes
Syllabication
Synonyms
Multiple-meaning Words

20 different books in each Library!

Phonics Power Packs

Available at Levels K, A, B

Complement instruction with posters, audio cassettes, picture cards, word cards and more! Packaged in a pocket-chart storage bag. Each component is also available separately.

AstroWord

The first and only multimedia program that provides comprehensive reading skills and strategies instruction for students of all ages!

17 individual CD-ROMs for Macintosh or Windows. Modules available separately or as Lab Packs.

Call 800-321-3106 for more information

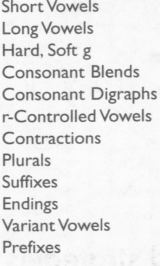

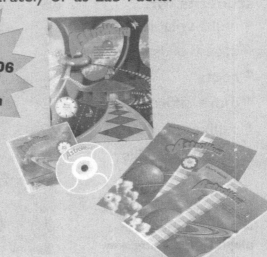

A research-based scope and sequence for student success

MCP Phonics Program Scope and Sequence of Skills

LEVELS	K	A	B	C	D	E	F
Alphabetic Awareness	•	•	•	•			
Auditory Discrimination	•	•					
Compound & Two-Syllable Words			•	•	•	•	•
Consonant Blends			•	•	•	•	•
Consonant Digraphs			•	•	•	•	•
Consonant Letter-Sound Associations	•	•	•	•			
Consonant Variations					•	•	•
Consonant-Vowel-Consonant Blending		•					
Contractions			•	•	•	•	•
Critical Thinking	•						•
Dictionary Skills					•	•	•
Inflectional Endings			•	•			
Letter Identification	•	•					
Listening & Speaking Skills	•	•	•	•	•	•	•
Listening Comprehension Strategies	•	•	•	•	•	•	•
Long Vowel Letter-Sound Associations			•	•			
Motor Skills	•						
Multiple-Meaning Words						•	•
Orthographic Awareness	•	•	•	•			
Phonemic/Phonological Awareness	•	•	•	•			
Plurals			•	•	•	•	•
Possessives, Apostrophe					•	•	•
Prefixes			•	•	•	•	•
Print Awareness	•	•	•				
R-Controlled Vowels			•	•	•		
Reading Comprehension Strategies	•	•	•	•	•	•	•
Roots					•	•	•
Short Vowel Letter-Sound Associations	•	•	•	•			
Silent Letters					•	•	•
Sounds of Hard & Soft c, g			•	•	•	•	•
Suffixes			•	•	•	•	•
Syllabication			•	•	•	•	•
Synonyms, Antonyms, Homonyms			•	•	•	•	•
Visual Discrimination	•	•					
Vowel Diphthongs			•	•	•	•	•
Vowel Pairs, Vowel Digraphs			•	•	•	•	•
Y as a Vowel		•	•	•			

MCP Phonics Program Features

LEVELS	K	A	B	C	D	E	F
Home Letters	•	•	•	•	•	•	•
Literature selections, Songs, Activity Pages	•				•	•	•
Phonics & Reading; Reading & Writing Pages		•	•	•	•	•	•
Phonics & Spelling Pages			•	•	•		
Phonics & Writing Pages		•	•	•			
Take-Home Books	•	•	•	•			

FREE CORRELATIONS! *to any existing reading programs*

☎ (800) 321-3106

Request your **FREE** Teacher Resource Guide for each 20 Student Editions of the same level ordered

MODERN CURRICULUM PRESS
WORD STUDY

ELWELL • MURRAY • KUCIA

TEACHER ADVISORY BOARD

Robert Figueroa
Cheektowaga, NY

Jackie Fonte
Gretna, LA

Karen Gordon
Jacksonville, FL

Tim Hamilton
Hermitage, TN

Sr. Denise Lyon, I. H. M.
Philadelphia, PA

Rachel Musser
Jackson, NJ

Sr. Mary Jean Raymond, O. S. U.
Cleveland, OH

Gloria Tuchman
Santa Ana, CA

ACKNOWLEDGEMENTS

EXECUTIVE EDITOR
Ronne Kaufman

EDITORIAL DEVELOPMENT
Brown Publishing Network

COVER DESIGN
Bill Smith Studios

PRODUCT MANAGER
Christine A. McArtor

PRODUCTION
Julie Ryan, Helen Wetherill

CREATIVE DIRECTOR
Doug Bates

ART DIRECTORS
Rosanne Guararra, Elaine Sandersen

ELECTRONIC PUBLISHING DIRECTOR
Sandy Kerr

IMAGE SERVICES MANAGER
Sandy Gregg

PROJECT EDITORS
Leslie Feierstone-Barna, Nancy Ellis,
Beth Fernald, Donna Garzinsky, Betsy Niles

MANUFACTURING & INVENTORY PLANNING
Karen Sota, Danielle Duchamp

COMPOSITION
Desktop Media, Devost Design, Hester Hull Associates, Caragraphics

LAYOUT AND PRODUCTION
Deena Uglione, Terri Shema
Larry Berkowitz, Peter Herrmann, Rachel Avenia-Prol, Pat Carlone, Diane Fristachi, Mary Jean Jones,
Chris Otazo, Andrea Schultz, Nancy Simmons, Dave Simoskevitz, Melinda Judson, Diana Rudio,
Murray Levine, Johanna Moroch, Sarah Balogh, Ruth Leine, Jennifer Peal

DESIGN
Michele Episcopo, Denise Ingrassia, Aggie Jaspon, Diedre Mitchel,
Karolyn Necco, Ruth Otey, Siok-Tin Sodbinow, Terry Taylor, Deborah Walkoczy

ILLUSTRATION CREDITS
Jim Connolly: p.4; Terry Taylor: p. 31o, 91o, 135o, 161o, Claude Martinot: p. 32; Bill Bossert: p. 61o;
Mary Keefe: p. 62; Elise Mills: p. 92, 136; Jerry Smath: p. 162; Peter Fasolino: bulletin board frames

PHOTO CREDITS
All photographs by Silver Burdett Ginn & Parker/Boon Productions for Silver Burdett Ginn.

IMAGE SERVICES
Barbara Haugh
Photographers: John Paul Endress; Michael Gaffney, Michael Provost;
Image Research: Leslie Laguna, Betsy Levin
Digital Photographers: John Serafin, Bob Grieza, Douglas Carney; Stylists: Judy Mahoney, Debbie Gaffney

Alphabet Font Copyright © 1996 Zaner-Bloser

ISBN 0-7652-0028-7 (Teacher Resource Guide)   ISBN 0-7652-0027-9 (Two Color Edition-Pupil)
Printed in the United States of America

7 8 9 10   V3CR   13 12 11 10   09

Modern Curriculum Press

Pearson Learning Group

1-800-321-3106
www.pearsonlearning.com

CONTENTS

Consonant Variants, Letter Combinations, Syllables

Student Performance Objectives 3a

Assessment Strategy Overview 3c
Formal Assessment • Informal Assessment •
Portfolio Assessment • Student Progress
Checklist 3c
Administering and Evaluating the Pretest
and Posttest .3d
Assessment Blackline Masters 3e

Spelling Connections 3j
Spelling Blackline Master 3k

**Word Study Games, Activities, and
Technology** 3l
Activity Blackline Master 3o

Home Connection 3p
Spanish Home Letter Blackline Master . .3q

LESSON PLANS
Unit Opener 3
Unit Focus
Unit Opener Activities
Bulletin Board Suggestion
Home Connections
Curriculum Connections

Lessons 1-13 5-30
Informal Assessment Objectives
Lesson Focus
Focus on All Learners
English Language Learners • Visual Learners •
Kinesthetic Learners • Auditory Learners •
Gifted Learners • Learners Who Need
Extra Support
Curriculum Connections

Vowel Pairs, Digraphs, Diphthongs, Syllables

Student Performance Objectives 31a

Assessment Strategy Overview 31c
Formal Assessment • Informal Assessment •
Portfolio Assessment • Student Progress
Checklist 31c
Administering and Evaluating the Pretest
and Posttest .31d
Assessment Blackline Masters 31e

Spelling Connections 31j
Spelling Blackline Master 31k

**Word Study Games, Activities, and
Technology** 31l
Activity Blackline Master 31o

Home Connection 31p
Spanish Home Letter Blackline Master . .31q

LESSON PLANS
Unit Opener 31
Unit Focus
Unit Opener Activities
Bulletin Board Suggestion
Home Connections
Curriculum Connections

Lessons 14-27 .33-60
Informal Assessment Objectives
Lesson Focus
Focus on All Learners
English Language Learners • Visual Learners •
Kinesthetic Learners • Auditory Learners •
Gifted Learners • Learners Who Need
Extra Support
Curriculum Connections

Units of Meaning in Words, Prefixes

UNIT 3

Student Performance Objectives 61a

Assessment Strategy Overview 61c
Formal Assessment • Informal Assessment •
Portfolio Assessment • Student Progress
Checklist 61c
Administering and Evaluating the Pretest
and Posttest 61d
Assessment Blackline Masters 61e

Spelling Connections 61j
Spelling Blackline Master 61k

**Word Study Games, Activities, and
Technology** 61l
Activity Blackline Master 61o

Home Connection 61p
Spanish Home Letter Blackline Master . .61q

LESSON PLANS
Unit Opener 61
Unit Focus
Unit Opener Activities
Bulletin Board Suggestion
Home Connections
Curriculum Connections

Lessons 28-41 63-90
Informal Assessment Objectives
Lesson Focus
Focus on All Learners
English Language Learners • Visual Learners •
Kinesthetic Learners • Auditory Learners •
Gifted Learners • Learners Who Need
Extra Support
Curriculum Connections

Roots, Compounds, Possessives, Contractions, Syllables

UNIT 4

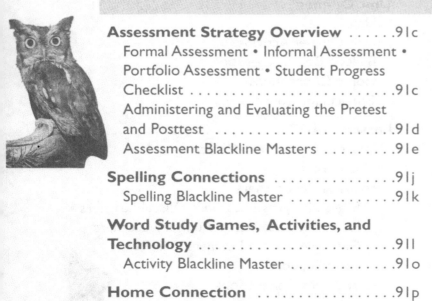

Student Performance Objectives 91a

Assessment Strategy Overview 91c
Formal Assessment • Informal Assessment •
Portfolio Assessment • Student Progress
Checklist 91c
Administering and Evaluating the Pretest
and Posttest 91d
Assessment Blackline Masters 91e

Spelling Connections 91j
Spelling Blackline Master 91k

**Word Study Games, Activities, and
Technology** 91l
Activity Blackline Master 91o

Home Connection 91p
Spanish Home Letter Blackline Master . .91q

LESSON PLANS
Unit Opener 91
Unit Focus
Unit Opener Activities
Bulletin Board Suggestion
Home Connections
Curriculum Connections

Lessons 42-50 93-110
Informal Assessment Objectives
Lesson Focus
Focus on All Learners
English Language Learners • Visual Learners •
Kinesthetic Learners • Auditory Learners •
Gifted Learners • Learners Who Need
Extra Support
Curriculum Connections

Suffixes

Student Performance Objectives 111a

Assessment Strategy Overview 111c
Formal Assessment • Informal Assessment •
Portfolio Assessment • Student Progress
Checklist 111c
Administering and Evaluating the Pretest
and Posttest 111d
Assessment Blackline Masters 111e

Spelling Connections 111j
Spelling Blackline Master 111k

**Word Study Games, Activities, and
Technology** 111l
Activity Blackline Master 111o

Home Connection 111p
Spanish Home Letter Blackline Master . .111q

LESSON PLANS
Unit Opener 111
Unit Focus
Unit Opener Activities
Bulletin Board Suggestion
Home Connections
Curriculum Connections

Lessons 51-61 .113-134
Informal Assessment Objectives
Lesson Focus
Focus on All Learners
English Language Learners • Visual Learners •
Kinesthetic Learners • Auditory Learners •
Gifted Learners • Learners Who Need
Extra Support
Curriculum Connections

Suffixes, Plurals, Syllables

Student Performance Objectives 135a

Assessment Strategy Overview 135c
Formal Assessment • Informal Assessment •
Portfolio Assessment • Student Progress
Checklist 135c
Administering and Evaluating the Pretest
and Posttest 135d
Assessment Blackline Masters 135e

Spelling Connections 135j
Spelling Blackline Master 135k

**Word Study Games, Activities, and
Technology** 135l
Activity Blackline Master 135o

Home Connection 135p
Spanish Home Letter Blackline Master . .135q

LESSON PLANS
Unit Opener 135
Unit Focus
Unit Opener Activities
Bulletin Board Suggestion
Home Connections
Curriculum Connections

Lessons 62-73 .137-160
Informal Assessment Objectives
Lesson Focus
Focus on All Learners
English Language Learners • Visual Learners •
Kinesthetic Learners • Auditory Learners •
Gifted Learners • Learners Who Need
Extra Support
Curriculum Connections

Alphabetizing, Dictionary, Multiple-meaning Words

UNIT 7

Student Performance Objectives 161a

Assessment Strategy Overview 161c
Formal Assessment • Informal Assessment •
Portfolio Assessment • Student Progress
Checklist 161c
Administering and Evaluating the Pretest
and Posttest .161d
Assessment Blackline Masters 161e

Spelling Connection 161j
Spelling Blackline Master 161k

**Word Study Games, Activities, and
Technology** 161l
Activity Blackline Master 161o

Home Connection 161p
Spanish Home Letter Blackline Master . .161q

LESSON PLANS
Unit Opener 161
Unit Focus
Unit Opener Activities
Bulletin Board Suggestion
Home Connections
Curriculum Connections

Lessons 74-79 163-174
Informal Assessment Objectives
Lesson Focus
Focus on All Learners
English Language Learners • Visual Learners •
Kinesthetic Learners • Auditory Learners •
Gifted Learners • Learners Who Need
Extra Support
Curriculum Connections

Daily Word Study Practice 178

Contents

UNIT I RESOURCES

Assessment Strategies	3c
Overview	3c
Unit 1 Pretest	3e–3f
Unit 1 Posttest	3g–3h
Unit 1 Student Progress Checklist	3i
Spelling Connections	3j–3k
Word Study Games, Activities, and Technology	3l–3o
Home Connection	3p–3q

TEACHING PLANS

Unit 1 Opener		3–4
Lesson 1:	Words with the *k* or *kw* Sound and the Sounds of *ch* and *kn*	5–6
Lesson 2:	The Sounds of *c* and Words with the *g* or *j* Sound	7–8
Lesson 3:	Words with the *f* Sound and the Sounds of *gh*	9–10
Lesson 4:	The Sounds of *s*	11–12
Lesson 5:	The Sounds of *wh* and Words with the *sh* Sound	13–14
Lesson 6:	The Sounds of *th* and *sc*	15–16
Lesson 7:	Review Consonant Variants, Letter Combinations	17–18
Lesson 8:	Words with *gn*, *tch*, and the *r* Sound	19–20
Lesson 9:	The Sounds of *ear*	21–22
Lesson 10:	Words with the *air* Sound and with *ild*, *ind*, *ost*, *old*	23–24
Lesson 11:	Syllables	25–26
Lesson 12:	Review Consonant Variants, Letter Combinations, Syllables	27–28
Lesson 13:	Unit 1 Checkup	29–30

Student Performance Objectives

In Unit 1, students will be introduced to two types of word-study elements: consonants having more than one sound; and various consonant and vowel combinations and the sounds for which they stand. As students learn to apply these concepts, they will be able to

◆ Associate words that contain /k/ or /kw/ with the letters that stand for those sounds

◆ Associate the letters *c, g,* and *s* with the sounds for which they stand

◆ Identify the letters that can represent /f/ and /j/

◆ Associate the letter combinations *ch, gh, wh, th, sh,* and *sc* with the sounds for which they stand

◆ Associate the letter combinations *kn, gn, tch,* and *wr* with the sounds for which they stand

◆ Associate the vowel combinations *air* and *ear* with the sounds for which they stand

◆ Associate the letter combinations *ild, ind, ost,* and *old* with the sounds for which they stand

◆ Identify the number of syllables in words

3b

Assessment Strategy Overview

Throughout Unit 1, assess students' ability to read and write words with consonant variants, consonant combinations, and vowel combinations. There are various ways to assess students' progress. You may also want to encourage students to evaluate their own work and participate in setting goals for their own learning.

FORMAL ASSESSMENT

The Unit 1 Pretest on pages 3e–3f helps to assess a student's knowledge at the beginning of the unit and to plan instruction.

The Unit 1 Posttest on pages 3g–3h helps to assess mastery of unit objectives and to plan for reteaching, if necessary.

INFORMAL ASSESSMENT

The Reading & Writing pages and Unit Checkup in the student book are an effective means of evaluating students' performance.

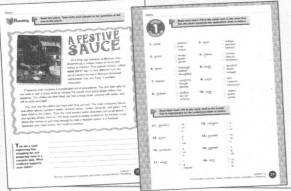

Skill	Reading & Writing Pages	Unit Checkup
/k/ or /kw/	17–18	29–30
ch and *kn* words	17–18	29–30
Sounds of *c*	17–18	29–30
/g/ or /j/	17–18	29–30
/f/	17–18	29–30
Sounds of *gh*	17–18	29–30
Sounds of *s*	17–18	29–30
Sounds of *sh, th, wh*	17–18	29–30
Sounds of *sc*	17–18	29–30
gn and *tch* words	27–28	29–30
/r/	27–28	29–30
Sounds of *ear*	27–28	29–30
/air/	27–28	29–30
Sounds of *ild, ind, ost, old,*	27–28	29–30
Syllables	27–28	29–30

PORTFOLIO ASSESSMENT

Portfolio This logo appears throughout the teaching plans. It signals opportunities for collecting students' work for individual portfolios. You may also want to collect the following pages:

❖ Unit 1 Pretest and Posttest, pages 3e–3h

❖ Unit 1 Checkup, pages 29–30

❖ Reading & Writing pages, 17–18, 27–28

STUDENT PROGRESS CHECKLIST

Use the checklist on page 3i to record students' progress. You may want to cut the sections apart to place each student's checklist in his or her portfolio.

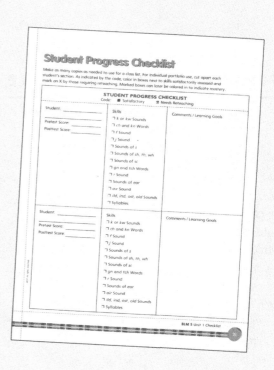

Administering and Evaluating the
Pretest and Posttest

DIRECTIONS

To help you assess students' progress in learning Unit 1 skills, tests are available on pages 3e–3h. Administer the Pretest before students begin the unit. The results of the Pretest will help you identify each student's strengths and needs in advance, allowing you to structure lesson plans to meet individual needs. Administer the Posttest to assess students' overall mastery of skills taught in the unit and to identify specific areas that will require reteaching.

PERFORMANCE ASSESSMENT PROFILE

The following chart will help you identify specific skills as they appear on the tests and enable you to identify and record specific information about an individual's or the class's performance on the tests.

Depending on the results of the tests, refer to the Reteaching column for lesson-plan pages where you can find activities that will be useful for meeting individual needs or for daily word study practice.

PERFORMANCE ASSESSMENT PROFILE

Skill	Pretest Questions	Posttest Questions	Reteaching Focus on All Learners	Daily Word Study Practice
k, ck, que /k/; qu /kw/	3, 7, 26	1, 4, 26	5–6, 17–18	180–183
ch /k/ /sh/; kn /n/; c /k/ /s/	1, 2, 8	3, 7, 18	5–8, 17–18	180–183
g, /g/; g, dge /j/	4, 9, 10	2, 16, 17	7–8, 17–18	180–183
f, ff, ph, gh /f/	13, 16	8	9–10, 17–18	180–183
s /z/ /s/ /sh/ /zh/	12, 15, 34	12	11–12, 17–18	180–183
wh /h/ /hw/; thin; then	6, 14, 23, 24, 27, 28	9, 14, 23, 24, 27, 28	13–14, 15–18	180–183
sh, ci, ce, ti /sh/	11	10	13–14, 17–18	180–183
sc /sk/ /s/ /sh/	17	11	15–18	180–183
gn /n/; tch /ch/; rh, wr /r/	5, 18, 21, 22, 29	5, 6, 13, 15, 21, 22, 29	19–20, 27–28	180–183
ear /ear/ /air/ /ur/	20, 25	20, 25	21–22, 27–28	180–183
are, air /air/	19	19, 34	23–24, 27–28	180–183
ild /ild/; ind /ind/;	32, 33	32, 33	23–24, 27–28	180–183
ost /ost/; old /old/	30, 31	30, 31	23–24, 27–28	180–183
Syllable Recognition	35–40	35–40	25–28	195

▶ Read the first word in each line. Fill in the circle next to the word that has the same sound as the underlined letters in the first word.

1.	k<u>n</u>eel	○ carpeting	○ knowledge	○ keyhole
2.	<u>ch</u>arade	○ scene	○ carton	○ chef
3.	<u>k</u>ing	○ kangaroo	○ stage	○ queen
4.	ri<u>dge</u>	○ ranch	○ dodge	○ gallop
5.	wa<u>tch</u>	○ shady	○ champion	○ chorus
6.	<u>th</u>ick	○ thunder	○ celery	○ these
7.	anti<u>que</u>	○ queen	○ physique	○ quit
8.	<u>c</u>ucumber	○ century	○ chance	○ copper
9.	dra<u>g</u>on	○ giant	○ garden	○ jewel
10.	ma<u>g</u>ic	○ page	○ guitar	○ bag

▶ Read each word. Fill in the circle below the sound that is represented by the underlined letters.

11.	par<u>ti</u>al	s ○	sh ○	z ○	15.	<u>s</u>ugar	s ○	sh ○	z ○
12.	noi<u>s</u>y	s ○	sh ○	z ○	16.	triump<u>h</u>	f ○	sh ○	no sound ○
13.	tou<u>gh</u>	f ○	g ○	h ○	17.	<u>sc</u>enery	s ○	sh ○	sk ○
14.	<u>wh</u>irl	h ○	w ○	hw ○	18.	<u>wr</u>ite	w ○	r ○	no sound ○

Go to the next page. →

BLM 1 Unit 1 Pretest: *k, r, f* sounds; sounds of *sh, th, wh, s, sc*; *gn* and *tch* words; *ch* and *kn* words

3e

> ▶ Read both words and decide if the underlined letters stand for sounds that are the same or different. Fill in the circle next to the correct response.

19. f<u>air</u>, b<u>ear</u>   ○ same   ○ different

20. sm<u>ear</u>, c<u>are</u>   ○ same   ○ different

21. <u>wr</u>estle, <u>r</u>est   ○ same   ○ different

22. <u>wr</u>ist, <u>rh</u>ombus   ○ same   ○ different

23. <u>th</u>istle, <u>th</u>at   ○ same   ○ different

24. Ma<u>tt</u>hew, <u>Th</u>ursday   ○ same   ○ different

25. w<u>ea</u>ry, p<u>ea</u>rl   ○ same   ○ different

26. techni<u>que</u>, <u>qu</u>arrel   ○ same   ○ different

27. <u>wh</u>ittle, <u>wh</u>ither   ○ same   ○ different

28. <u>wh</u>om, <u>h</u>airy   ○ same   ○ different

29. rei<u>gn</u>, desi<u>gn</u>   ○ same   ○ different

30. c<u>ost</u>, h<u>ost</u>   ○ same   ○ different

31. h<u>old</u>er, t<u>old</u>   ○ same   ○ different

32. gr<u>ind</u>, c<u>ind</u>er   ○ same   ○ different

33. m<u>ild</u>, m<u>ild</u>ew   ○ same   ○ different

34. trea<u>s</u>ure, lei<u>s</u>ure   ○ same   ○ different

> ▶ Read each word in the list. Then divide the words into syllables using slash marks.

35. object   **37.** petal   **39.** visit

36. reward   **38.** sentence   **40.** nasal

Possible score on Unit 1 Pretest is 40. Number correct _____

BLM 2 Unit 1 Pretest: *k, kw, r, air, ild, ind, ost, old* sounds; sounds of *s, sh, th, wh, ear; gn, tch* words; syllables

3f

▶ Read the first word in each line. Fill in the circle next to the word that has the same sound as the underlined letters in the first word.

1. <u>k</u>ick   ○ know   ○ kite   ○ center

2. wa<u>g</u>er   ○ guard   ○ dagger   ○ giraffe

3. <u>ch</u>ord   ○ chemist   ○ shadow   ○ challenge

4. bou<u>tique</u>   ○ quilt   ○ bouquet   ○ quiet

5. <u>wr</u>eck   ○ rhyme   ○ water   ○ while

6. ki<u>tch</u>en   ○ gather   ○ chorus   ○ chick

7. <u>c</u>ookie   ○ cents   ○ chapter   ○ copy

8. <u>ph</u>ony   ○ pencil   ○ follow   ○ heavy

9. ga<u>th</u>er   ○ think   ○ talon   ○ feather

10. por<u>ti</u>on   ○ shore   ○ cheese   ○ party

▶ Read each word. Fill in the circle below the sound that is represented by the underlined letters.

11. <u>sc</u>ent	s ○	sk ○	sh ○	15. si<u>gn</u>	g ○	gh ○	n ○
12. ea<u>s</u>y	s ○	sh ○	z ○	16. bri<u>dge</u>	d ○	j ○	g ○
13. <u>rh</u>yme	h ○	r ○	no sound ○	17. wa<u>g</u>on	g ○	j ○	gn ○
14. <u>wh</u>ole	w ○	h ○	hw ○	18. <u>kn</u>owledge	n ○	k ○	no sound ○

Go to the next page. →

> ▶ Read both words and decide if the underlined letters stand for sounds that are the same or different. Fill in the circle with the correct response.

19. st<u>air</u>, p<u>ear</u>   ○ same   ○ different

20. g<u>ear</u>, st<u>are</u>   ○ same   ○ different

21. <u>w</u>ren, <u>r</u>elief   ○ same   ○ different

22. <u>wr</u>ing, <u>rh</u>ythmic   ○ same   ○ different

23. <u>th</u>ough, <u>th</u>irty   ○ same   ○ different

24. bro<u>th</u>er, <u>th</u>reat   ○ same   ○ different

25. h<u>ear</u>se, sp<u>ear</u>   ○ same   ○ different

26. qui<u>z</u>zical, my<u>s</u>tique   ○ same   ○ different

27. <u>wh</u>ether, <u>wh</u>eelbarrow   ○ same   ○ different

28. <u>w</u>holesale, <u>h</u>earty   ○ same   ○ different

29. mali<u>gn</u>, consi<u>gn</u>   ○ same   ○ different

30. fro<u>st</u>, po<u>st</u>   ○ same   ○ different

31. g<u>old</u>, unf<u>old</u>   ○ same   ○ different

32. m<u>ind</u>, w<u>ind</u>ow   ○ same   ○ different

33. w<u>ild</u>cat, gu<u>ild</u>   ○ same   ○ different

34. sc<u>are</u>, rep<u>air</u>   ○ same   ○ different

> ▶ Read each word in the list. Then divide the words into syllables using slash marks.

35. rotate   **37.** punish   **39.** famous

36. lemon   **38.** bison   **40.** pities

Possible score on Unit 1 Posttest is 40. Number correct _____

BLM 4 Unit 1 Posttest: *k, kw, r, air, ild, ind, ost, old* sounds; sounds of *s, sh, th, wh, ear; gn, tch* words; syllables

3h

Student Progress Checklist

Make as many copies as needed to use for a class list. For individual portfolio use, cut apart each student's section. As indicated by the code, color in boxes next to skills satisfactorily assessed and mark an X by those requiring reteaching. Marked boxes can later be colored in to indicate mastery.

STUDENT PROGRESS CHECKLIST

Code: ■ Satisfactory   ☒ Needs Reteaching

| Student: _____ _____

 Pretest Score: _____
 Posttest Score: _____ | Skills
 ❑ *k* or *kw* Sounds
 ❑ *ch* and *kn* Words
 ❑ *f* Sound
 ❑ *j* Sound
 ❑ Sounds of *s*
 ❑ Sounds of *sh, th, wh*
 ❑ Sounds of *sc*
 ❑ *gn* and *tch* Words
 ❑ *r* Sound
 ❑ Sounds of *ear*
 ❑ *air* Sound
 ❑ *ild, ind, ost, old* Sounds
 ❑ Syllables | Comments / Learning Goals |
| Student: _____ _____

 Pretest Score: _____
 Posttest Score: _____ | Skills
 ❑ *k* or *kw* Sounds
 ❑ *ch* and *kn* Words
 ❑ *f* Sound
 ❑ *j* Sound
 ❑ Sounds of *s*
 ❑ Sounds of *sh, th, wh*
 ❑ Sounds of *sc*
 ❑ *gn* and *tch* Words
 ❑ *r* Sound
 ❑ Sounds of *ear*
 ❑ *air* Sound
 ❑ *ild, ind, ost, old* Sounds
 ❑ Syllables | Comments / Learning Goals |

Spelling Connections

INTRODUCTION

The Unit Word List is a comprehensive list of spelling words drawn from this unit. The words are grouped by skill. To incorporate spelling into your word study program, use the activity in the Curriculum Connections section of each teaching plan.

The spelling lessons utilize the following approach for each set of words.

1. Administer a pretest of the words that have not yet been introduced. Dictation sentences are provided.

2. Provide practice.

3. Reassess. Dictation sentences are provided.

A final test is provided on page 30.

DIRECTIONS

Make a copy of Blackline Master 6 for each student. After administering the pretest for the sounds of the various letters and combinations, give each student a copy of the appropriate word list.

Students can work with a partner to practice spelling the words orally and identifying the appropriate sound in each word. They could also create letter cards to use to form the words on the list. You may want to challenge students to identify other words that have the same sound variant or combination. Students can write words of their own on *My Own Word List* (see Blackline Master 6).

Have students store their list words in envelopes or plastic zipper bags in the back of their books or notebooks. Alternatively, you may want to suggest that students keep a spelling notebook, listing words with similar patterns. You could also invite students to build word-wall displays in the classroom. Each section of the wall can focus on words with a single word study element. The walls will become a good spelling resource when students are writing.

UNIT WORD LIST

Words with *k* or *kw*; *ch*, *kn*; Sounds of *c*; Words with *g* or *j*; Words with *f*; Sounds of *gh*; Sounds of *s*

quiet

tickle

chorus

knee

silence

bridge

telephone

laugh

pleasure

sugar

wh, *sh*, *th*, *sc*, *gn*, and *tch*; *r*, *ear*, *air*; *ild*, *ind*, *ost*, *old*; **Syllables**

whispered

special

thousand

science

design

kitchen

rhythm

pearl

despair

children

Name _____

**S**pelling

UNIT 1 WORD LIST

Words with k or kw; ch, kn; Sounds of c; Words with g or j; Words with f; Sounds of gh; Sounds of s

quiet	bridge
tickle	telephone
chorus	laugh
knee	pleasure
silence	sugar

wh, sh, th, sc, gn, and tch; r; ear, air; ild, ind, ost, old; Syllables

whispered	kitchen
special	rhythm
thousand	pearl
science	despair
design	children

My Own Word List

Word Study Games, Activities, and Technology

The following collection of ideas offers a variety of opportunities to reinforce word study skills while actively engaging students. The games, activities, and technology suggestions can easily be adapted to meet the needs of your group of learners. They vary in approach so as to consider student's different learning styles.

● PHONEME BINGO

Provide students with blank bingo game boards (containing either 9 or 16 squares) and markers for covering squares. Select an appropriate number of consonants, consonant combinations, and consonant-vowel combinations from the unit. Have students randomly write these phonemes in the spaces on the boards. To play, call out a word slowly. Students can cover the square containing the sound heard in the word. Play until someone has bingo.

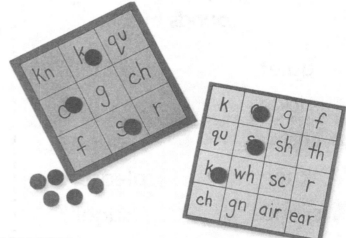

▲ CLASSIFYING THE PARTS OF AN AUTOMOBILE

Write the words *body, cabin,* and *chassis* on the chalkboard. Explain that the body is the outer shell of an automobile, the cabin is the interior in which people ride, and the chassis is the frame and all the moving parts. Invite students to identify various parts of a car and suggest under which classification each belongs. As you write the words on the chalkboard, ask volunteers to identify letters and letter combinations from this unit. As new ideas become more difficult, allow students to consult magazines or an encyclopedia. Examples include: *body*– trunk, hood, bumpers, fenders; *cabin*– steering wheel, brake, gearshift, dashboard, turn signal, radio; *chassis*– engine, transmission, carburetor, spark plug, radiator, generator, shock absorber.

◆ WORD PYRAMIDS

Arrange students in groups of three or four. Write one of the letters or letter combinations discussed in this unit on the chalkboard. Tell the students that they are going to build word pyramids, starting from the top down. Each group should write a four-letter word containing the assigned phoneme at the top of a sheet of paper. On the line below they should write a five-letter word containing that phoneme, and so on, adding one letter at a time. You might allow them to consult a classroom dictionary. Tell students to arrange their lines to form the shape of a pyramid. The group forming the highest pyramid wins. Alternatively, you might have groups build four- to eight-letter pyramids using different phonemes. The group completing the most pyramids in a designated time wins. Afterward, consider combining all the different words in one "great pyramid" on a word wall.

■ MAPPING OUT SOUNDS

Display a large map of your state for the students to examine. Have partners work together to identify and list words on the map that contain letters or letter combinations discussed in this unit. They should include cities and towns as well as physical features such as mountains and rivers. After students have completed their work, use this as the basis for a class discussion. Ask each set of partners to point out two locations on the map and pronounce the names. You might guide students with the correct pronunciation of unfamiliar terms.

✳ PLAN A TRIP

You might have students plan a trip from their home to another location in your state. They might use the information from the lists they developed previously to identify points of interest they would like to see. Suggest that they identify letters and letter combinations discussed in the unit that appear in place names on their itinerary.

● MIME TIME

After completing a lesson, you might suggest that students play charades. Print each of the letters and letter combinations on one side of different sheets of posterboard. Hold one up for the class to see. Tell students to write a word that contains this sound and that they think could be acted out in mime. Ask volunteers to write their words on the opposite side of the posterboard at your desk so their classmates do not see the words. Have the class repeat the sound. Each volunteer can then act out clues to his or her word as others try to guess it. Suggest that students use the charade symbol for "sounds like" (tugging on an earlobe). Continue until a word has been mimed and guessed for each sound in the unit.

▲ SOUNDS OF THE ANIMAL WORLD

Discuss with the class that animals make a variety of sounds and that language uses phonemes to create words that mimic these sounds. Provide some examples, such as *bark, chirp, roar*. Call on different students to spell these words as you write them on the chalkboard, underlining letters and letter combinations discussed in this unit. Then brainstorm with the class to list and spell as many animal sounds as possible, identifying relevant phonemes. You might suggest that students first think of animals and then try to recall words that imitate the sounds they make. Students may enjoy illustrating "conversations" between various animals producing these sounds.

◆ PEOPLE I ADMIRE

Have individual students develop a list of friends, relatives, and others (teachers, scientists, athletes, entertainers) that they admire. Tell each student to select one person from his or her list and write a paragraph explaining why he or she admires that individual. Encourage students to underline any letters or letter combinations discussed in the unit in their final draft.

■ PHONETIC LOCOMOTIVE

Select six letter combinations discussed in this unit. Arrange students in groups of four. Provide each group with a 12"-x-12" sheet of posterboard. Have the groups create a standard game board similar to that used in Monopoly and other games. Each of the four sides should contain six spaces, with a different letter combination printed in each space. Suggest students print the sound under each letter combination. The four corner spaces can be free, roll-again spaces. Provide each student with two index cards. Explain that each member should draw, trace, or cut out a locomotive on one card and a boxcar on the second.

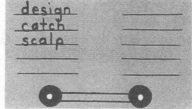

Students take turns rolling a number cube and moving that number of spaces. When they land on a space, they must say that sound, identify a word containing the letters, and write the word in the boxcar. The first to have ten words in his or her boxcar wins.

✳ BE A CITY PLANNER

Make enough copies of Blackline Master 7 to distribute one to each student. Tell students to imagine that they have been hired to plan the development of a new neighborhood in a growing city. Explain that each rectangle represents a city block. They might develop (1) a downtown area with office buildings and other skyscrapers, (2) a shopping area with a variety of stores, (3) a residential area with homes and parks, or (4) a cultural area with museums, theaters, and other attractions. Students should divide each block into smaller rectangles to represent building lots, indicate the types of buildings and other features that they are placing on each lot, and label the streets and buildings, underlining letters and letter combinations discussed in this unit.

● A FRIENDLY LETTER

Have students write a friendly letter to a relative or acquaintance. Challenge them to include words from the Unit Word List. Some examples are *quiet, special, silence, telephone, laugh, pleasure, design, children, thousand,* and *science.*

Technology

The following software products are designed to provide practice in spelling.

Word City   Students (grades 3–9) can develop their skills in vocabulary, spelling, and reading comprehension while exploring themes such as sports, science, and favorite tales.
****Sanctuary Woods
  1825 South Grant Street
  San Mateo, CA 94402
  (800) 943-3664

Word Attack 3   A "vocabulary builder" for students (ages 10 to adult), this product encourages students to engage in crossword puzzles and arcade games to master definitions, spellings, and pronunciations of thousands of new words,

each categorized by subject and level of difficulty.
****Davidson & Associates, Inc.
  19840 Pioneer Avenue
  Torrance, CA 90503
  (800) 545-7677

Spell Dodger   Teachers can create customized word lists for this arcade game designed to help children practice spelling words.
****Davidson & Associates, Inc.
  19840 Pioneer Avenue
  Torrance, CA 90503
  (800) 545-7677

Name _____

Home Connection

HOME LETTER

A letter is available to be sent home at the beginning of Unit 1. This letter informs family members that students will be learning to read and write words containing consonant variants, consonant combinations, or vowel combinations. The suggested home activity revolves around the poem "Lost." This activity promotes interaction between child and family members while supporting the student's learning of reading and writing words with the targeted word study skills. A letter is also available in Spanish on page 3q.

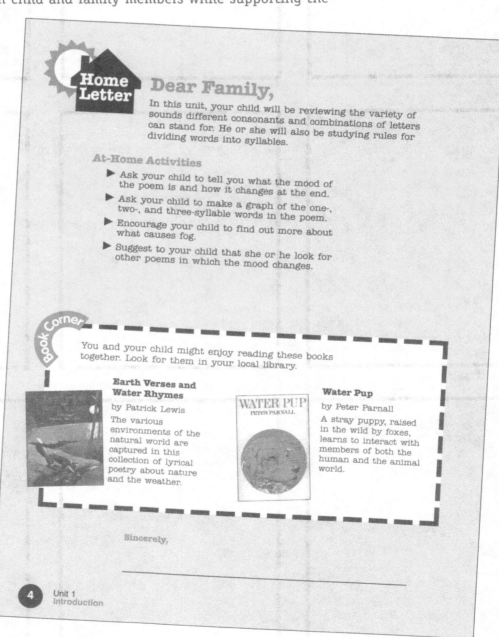

Home Letter

Dear Family,

In this unit, your child will be reviewing the variety of sounds different consonants and combinations of letters can stand for. He or she will also be studying rules for dividing words into syllables.

At-Home Activities

► Ask your child to tell you what the mood of the poem is and how it changes at the end.

► Ask your child to make a graph of the one-, two-, and three-syllable words in the poem.

► Encourage your child to find out more about what causes fog.

► Suggest to your child that she or he look for other poems in which the mood changes.

Book Corner

You and your child might enjoy reading these books together. Look for them in your local library.

Earth Verses and Water Rhymes
by Patrick Lewis
The various environments of the natural world are captured in this collection of lyrical poetry about nature and the weather.

Water Pup
by Peter Parnall
A stray puppy, raised in the wild by foxes, learns to interact with members of both the human and the animal world.

Sincerely,

_____

4 Unit 1
Introduction

Carta para la casa

Estimada familia,

En esta unidad, su hijo/a va a repasar la variedad de sonidos que representan las consonantes y las combinaciones de letras en inglés. También estudiará las reglas para dividir las palabras en sílabas.

Actividades para hacer en casa

▶ Pídanle a su hijo/a que lea el poema de la página 3 y que les diga cuál es el ambiente del poema y cómo cambia al final.

▶ Pídanle a su hijo/a que haga una gráfica de las palabras de una, dos y tres sílabas que aparecen en el poema.

▶ Animen a su hijo/a a averiguar más acerca de lo que causa la niebla.

Rincón del libro

Su hijo/a y ustedes pueden disfrutar juntos de la lectura de estos libros. Búsquenlos en la biblioteca de su localidad.

Earth Verses and Water Rhymes
por J. Patrick Lewis

Los diversos entornos del mundo natural son captados en esta selección de poesía lírica acerca de la naturaleza y del clima.

Water Pup
por Peter Parnall

Un cachorrito perdido, criado por zorros en el monte, aprende a relacionarse con miembros del mundo humano y del mundo animal.

Atentamente, _____

Unit 1

Consonant Variants, Letter Combinations, and Syllables

ASSESSING PRIOR KNOWLEDGE

To assess students' prior knowledge of the consonant variants, letter combinations, and syllables covered in this unit, use the pretest on pages 3e–3f.

Unit Focus

USING THE PAGE

- Read aloud the poem "Lost" on page 3, conveying the frightening mood of the situation. Then encourage students to read the poem aloud.

- Invite students to share their reactions to the poem and its surprise ending.

- Ask students what "wet paint" situations they have ever been in or seen (perhaps in cartoons or movies).

- **Critical Thinking** Read aloud the question and ask students to share their opinions about the trick the poet plays.

BUILDING A CONTEXT

- Remind students that some consonants can have different sounds in different words. Write *once* and *could* on the board. Ask what sounds the letter *c* stands for in the words. (/s/, /k/)

- Write *where* and *these* and ask students what consonant pairs spell the beginning sounds in the words. *(wh, th)*

- Write *signpost* and ask students to name the silent consonant in it. *(g)*

- Remind students that certain letter combinations, like *ost* appear often in words. Use the words *lost* and *post* from the poem to show how the vowel sound can vary.

- Ask students to name words with one, two, and three syllables in the poem.

UNIT 1 Consonant Variants, Letter Combinations, Syllables

LOST

In a terrible fog I once lost my way,
Where I had wandered I could not say,
I found a signpost just by a fence,
But I could not read it, the fog was so dense.
Slowly but surely, frightened to roam,
I climbed up the post for my nearest way home,
Striking a match I turned cold and faint,
These were the words on it, "Mind the wet paint."

—James Godden

This poem starts with a mysterious, frightening mood and ends with a silly surprise. How does the poet trick the reader?

Critical Thinking

Unit 1 Introduction 3

UNIT OPENER ACTIVITIES

LOOKING AT HUMOR

Reread "Lost" together. Explain that the humor or joke of the poem is based on a misunderstanding. Have students share occasions in their lives when they were puzzled or lost. How did the situation feel at the time? Did the experience make a funny story afterward? Why?

RETELLINGS

Have students present the chain of events described in "Lost" in different formats. They might mime the events, create a comic strip showing it as a series of scenes, describe the events in a humorous monologue, or write a short narrative.

PAINT EFFECTS

Have students investigate arts and craft books and home-decorating magazines for interesting painting techniques, such as stenciling, sponging, ragging, and combing. Students may enjoy trying new techniques on paper, cardboard boxes, or simple unpainted wooden items they may have.

Home Letter

Dear Family,

In this unit, your child will be reviewing the variety of sounds different consonants and combinations of letters can stand for. He or she will also be studying rules for dividing words into syllables.

At-Home Activities

▶ Ask your child to tell you what the mood of the poem is and how it changes at the end.

▶ Ask your child to make a graph of the one-, two-, and three-syllable words in the poem.

▶ Encourage your child to find out more about what causes fog.

▶ Suggest to your child that she or he look for other poems in which the mood changes.

Book Corner

You and your child might enjoy reading these books together. Look for them in your local library.

Earth Verses and Water Rhymes
by Patrick Lewis
The various environments of the natural world are captured in this collection of lyrical poetry about nature and the weather.

Water Pup
by Peter Parnall
A stray puppy, raised in the wild by foxes, learns to interact with members of both the human and the animal world.

Sincerely,

_____

Unit 1
Introduction

4

BULLETIN BOARD

As students progress through the unit, encourage them to add jokes and riddles to a bulletin board entitled "Just Joking Around." Students can fold their paper and write questions or clues on the outside and hide punch lines inside. Students can search the board for sounds studied in this unit.

HOME CONNECTIONS ✳

● The Home Letter on page 4 is intended to acquaint families with the word study skills students will be studying in this unit. Students can tear out page 4 and take it home. Suggest that they read the poem, complete the activities with a family member, and look in the library for the books mentioned on page 4 to share at home.

● The Home Letter can also be found on page 3q in Spanish.

CURRICULUM CONNECTIONS ✳

SCIENCE

Have students find facts about fog in science texts or nonfiction library books or articles. Invite them to add one or two different ideas to "Fog Fact Sheets" attached to a clipboard in the center.

HEALTH

Assemble clean, empty containers (or the labels) from several household supplies including at least one type of paint or paint-related product if possible. Have students read the usage instructions and warnings on the containers and create a list of health and safety guidelines for using these products.

READING

Share poems from writers known for their humor, such as Jack Prelutsky or Shel Silverstein. Have each student choose a humorous poem that particularly tickles his or her funny bone. Invite each student to memorize or prepare a reading of all or part of the poem. Plan time for a group poetry reading when students can present their favorites and listen to classmates' choices.

4

Lesson 1

Pages 5–6

/k/ and /kw/;
Sounds of ch and kn

INFORMAL ASSESSMENT OBJECTIVES

Can students

✔ identify the letters that can represent /k/ and /kw/?

✔ recognize the sounds that *ch* and *kn* can represent in words?

Lesson Focus

INTRODUCING THE SKILLS

● On the board write the words *antique, quiet, notice, checkers, queen, kettle, knead, quill,* and *knowledge.* Have students read the words and rewrite them in three groups according to a sound that is common to the words. (/k/: *antique, checkers, kettle;* /kw/: *quiet, queen, quill;* /n/: *notice, knead, knowledge*)

● Ask students to underline the letters that represent the sound in each group. (/k/ *qu, ck, k;* /kw/ *qu;* /n/ *n, kn*)

● Then write *character, challenge, chauffeur, chef, chameleon,* and *charcoal.* Ask students to identify the words in which *ch* stands for /ch/ (*challenge, charcoal*), /sh/ (*chauffeur, chef*), and /k/ (*character, chameleon*).

USING THE PAGES

Have students apply the rules to the words from the previous activity. When students have completed the pages, summarize what they learned about letter sounds.

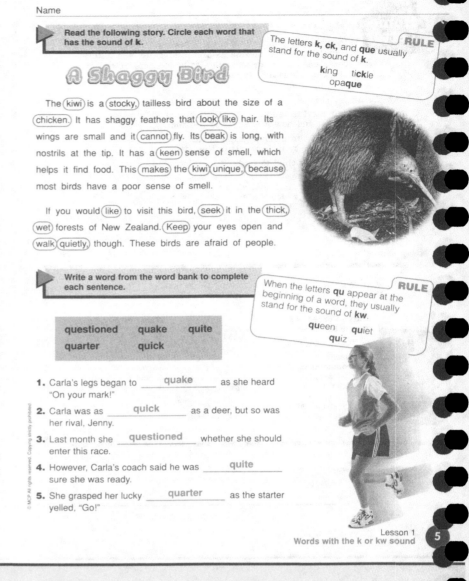

Name _____

▶ Read the following story. Circle each word that has the sound of **k**.

RULE
The letters **k, ck,** and **que** usually stand for the sound of **k**.

king   ti**ck**le
opa**que**

A Shaggy Bird

The (kiwi) is a (stocky,) tailless bird about the size of a (chicken.) It has shaggy feathers that (look)(like) hair. Its wings are small and it (cannot) fly. Its (beak) is long, with nostrils at the tip. It has a (keen) sense of smell, which helps it find food. This (makes) the (kiwi)(unique,)(because) most birds have a poor sense of smell.

If you would (like) to visit this bird, (seek) it in the (thick,) (wet) forests of New Zealand. (Keep) your eyes open and (walk)(quietly,) though. These birds are afraid of people.

▶ Write a word from the word bank to complete each sentence.

RULE
When the letters **qu** appear at the beginning of a word, they usually stand for the sound of **kw**.

queen   **qu**iet
quiz

questioned	quake	quite
quarter	quick	

1. Carla's legs began to _____quake_____ as she heard "On your mark!"

2. Carla was as _____quick_____ as a deer, but so was her rival, Jenny.

3. Last month she _____questioned_____ whether she should enter this race.

4. However, Carla's coach said he was _____quite_____ sure she was ready.

5. She grasped her lucky _____quarter_____ as the starter yelled, "Go!"

Lesson 1
Words with the k or kw sound

5

FOCUS ON ALL LEARNERS

ENGLISH LANGUAGE LEARNERS/ESL

Before beginning the story on page 5, have students locate New Zealand on a world map or globe. Have partners use encyclopedias to locate facts and photographs about New Zealand.

VISUAL LEARNERS

SMALL GROUP

Materials: dictionaries, writing paper

Ask students to use dictionaries to locate words that fit the sounds and spelling patterns in the lesson. Have each group choose a recorder who will list the words in categories. Groups can check other groups' work and compare words.

KINESTHETIC LEARNERS

INDIVIDUAL

Materials: magazines, art paper, scissors, glue

Have students cut words with /k/, /kw/, *ch*, and *kn* from the magazines. Suggest that they make sentences with the words, gluing them on paper and writing in other words they need.

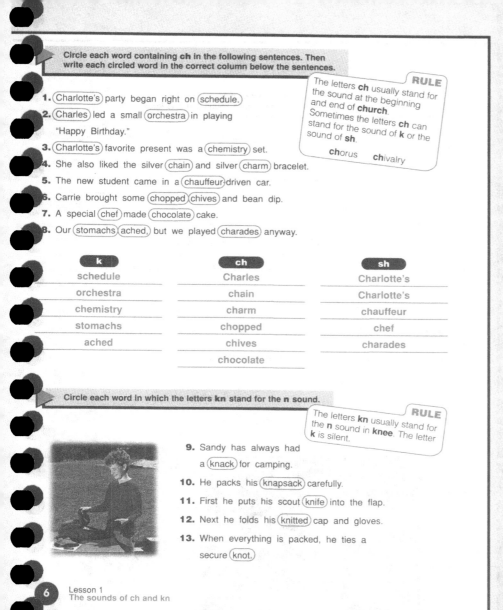

Circle each word containing **ch** in the following sentences. Then write each circled word in the correct column below the sentences.

RULE
The letters **ch** usually stand for the sound at the beginning and end of **church**. Sometimes the letters **ch** can stand for the sound of **k** or the sound of **sh**.

chorus   **ch**ivalry

1. (Charlotte's) party began right on (schedule.)
2. (Charles) led a small (orchestra) in playing "Happy Birthday."
3. (Charlotte's) favorite present was a (chemistry) set.
4. She also liked the silver (chain) and silver (charm) bracelet.
5. The new student came in a (chauffeur)-driven car.
6. Carrie brought some (chopped) (chives) and bean dip.
7. A special (chef) made (chocolate) cake.
8. Our (stomachs) (ached,) but we played (charades) anyway.

k	ch	sh
schedule	Charles	Charlotte's
orchestra	chain	Charlotte's
chemistry	charm	chauffeur
stomachs	chopped	chef
ached	chives	charades
	chocolate	

Circle each word in which the letters **kn** stand for the **n** sound.

RULE
The letters **kn** usually stand for the **n** sound in **knee**. The letter **k** is silent.

9. Sandy has always had a (knack) for camping.
10. He packs his (knapsack) carefully.
11. First he puts his scout (knife) into the flap.
12. Next he folds his (knitted) cap and gloves.
13. When everything is packed, he ties a secure (knot.)

Lesson 1
The sounds of ch and kn

6

CURRICULUM CONNECTIONS ✴ ● ◆ ■ ◆ ●

SPELLING

Use the following words and dictation sentences as a pretest for the first group of spelling words in Unit 1.

1. **quiet**   It is **quiet** in the library.
2. **tickle**   Don't **tickle** the baby while she's eating.
3. **chorus**   The **chorus** members walked onto the stage.
4. **knee**   Put an ice pack on your swollen **knee**.
5. **silence**   The **silence** was broken by a ringing telephone.
6. **bridge**   Turn right after you cross the **bridge**.
7. **telephone**   Dad bought an antique **telephone**.
8. **laugh**   It is mean to **laugh** at someone's mistake.
9. **pleasure**   It's a **pleasure** to help someone you care about.
10. **sugar**   The recipe calls for one cup of **sugar**.

WRITING

Portfolio Ask students to imagine they are going on a six-month camping trip to a remote mountain area. Everything they take, except for food and shelter, must fit into their knapsacks. Have students write a paragraph listing ten items they will pack and the reason for their choices.

SCIENCE

Tell students that, while it may seem strange that there are birds that do not fly, the kiwi is not the only bird that can't. Encourage students to discover what classifies an animal as a bird. (feathers, two feet, beak) Invite them to research other flightless birds, such as the ostrich.

SOCIAL STUDIES

Point out that because of New Zealand's geographic isolation, it has native plants and animals found nowhere else in the world. Prompt students to learn more about an aspect of New Zealand's animals and plants, geography, history, or culture. Ask them to write a brief informative report. Challenge students to find any /k/, /kw/, *kn*, or *ch* words in their completed reports.

6

Lesson 2
Pages 7–8

Sounds of c, g, and j

INFORMAL ASSESSMENT OBJECTIVES

Can students

✔ distinguish the hard and soft sounds of *c* and *g* in words?

✔ read words with /j/ spelled *dge*?

Lesson Focus

INTRODUCING THE SKILLS

● Write these words on the board and have students read each row aloud.

camp	cone	cubic
gallop	gone	guess
cent	civil	cymbal
germ	giant	gym
ridge	dodge	wedge

● As students read the words aloud, invite them to apply the rule from page 7 or 8 to each set of words to focus on the sounds represented by *c*, *g*, and *dge*.

USING THE PAGES

● Help students as necessary to complete pages 7 and 8, and then discuss what they have learned about *c*, *g*, and *dge*.

● **Critical Thinking** Encourage students to answer the questions that relate to the passages on pages 7 and 8.

Name _____

> Underline each word in the sentences that contains the letter **c**.
> Then write **k** or **s** above each **c** to show which sound it stands for.

RULE

When the letter **c** comes before **a, o,** or **u,** it usually stands for the **k** sound. When **c** comes before **e, i,** or **y,** it usually stands for the **s** sound.

coat   silen**c**e

1. For centuries, people have wanted to comprehend outer space.

2. A Russian satellite named *Sputnik I* circled the earth in 1957.

3. This was a major advance in the conquest of space.

4. The first person to travel into space was cosmonaut Yuri Gagarin.

5. In 1969 the world celebrated when U.S. astronauts Armstrong and Aldrin landed on the moon.

6. Today, space shuttles take off from the Kennedy Space Center, in Florida.

7. There, audiences anticipate the countdown as spacecraft are sent into space.

8. In the cabin, astronauts rely on computers to control the blastoff.

9. During a mission, astronauts carry out many complicated procedures and experiments.

10. People seem to welcome the excitement of facing the unknown.

What is the main idea of this passage?

Critical Thinking

FOCUS ON ALL LEARNERS

ENGLISH LANGUAGE LEARNERS/ESL

Build background about the history of space exploration. Show photographs related to the U.S. and Russian space programs. Have students discuss what they see and know. Play videotapes of recent space shuttle and space station events.

VISUAL LEARNERS

PARTNER Have pairs of students make columns on a sheet of paper with the headings /k/, /s/, /g/, and /j/. Challenge them to write as many words as possible under the appropriate headings.

AUDITORY LEARNERS

LARGE GROUP Invite students to take turns saying sentences that include words with the sounds of *c*, *g*, and *j* spelled *dge*. Volunteers can identify the noted sounds and spell the words.

Read each word below. Write g in the blank if the word has the hard g sound. Write j if the word contains the j sound.

1. region ___j___
2. gentle ___j___
3. giant ___j___
4. stage ___j___
5. gobbled ___g___
6. endangered ___j___
7. largest ___j___
8. gorillas ___g___
9. range ___j___
10. pledge ___j___
11. edge ___j___
12. disgust ___g___

Write the word from the list above that completes each sentence. Use each word only once.

13. We met on the school ___stage___ to build the set for the play.
14. Our play is about saving the wild ___gorillas___.
15. Gorillas are the ___largest___ of all the apes.
16. They look a bit scary, but actually they are quite ___gentle___.
17. These ___giant___ apes live in groups of 30 animals or more.
18. Each group has a territory that will ___range___ from 5 to 15 miles.
19. We decided to make the stage look like a ___region___ of the rain forest where the gorillas live.
20. Gorillas are ___endangered___, mostly because people are cutting down the rain forests.
21. We soon stopped for lunch, but Harry had ___gobbled___ all the sandwiches.
22. "Act your age," snapped Marla in ___disgust___.
23. After working hard, we sat on the ___edge___ of the stage and rested.
24. We decided to ___pledge___ some of the money from the play to a wildlife fund.

What are some other ways to let people know about endangered animals?

Critical Thinking

8 Lesson 2
Words with the g or j sound

AUDITORY/KINESTHETIC LEARNERS

SMALL GROUP

Write the letters c, g, and dge on the board. Divide the group into small teams. Ask a member of each team to write on the board a word in which c represents /k/. Award points for words with the correct sound and spelling giving one point per letter. Alternate requests for words with soft c and hard and soft g.

GIFTED LEARNERS

Materials: dictionaries

Challenge students to find words that have a word from the lesson as a base word. Encourage students to write sentences with the different forms of the words.

LEARNERS WHO NEED EXTRA SUPPORT

Materials: large index cards

Ask students to write g on one side of their cards and dge on the other side. Read /j/ words from page 8 and have students show the card face with the correct spelling for the sound. **See Daily Word Study Practice, pages 180-183.**

CURRICULUM CONNECTIONS

SPELLING

Read aloud each phrase and have students write it down. Ask student pairs to exchange papers and check each other's spelling. Then challenge students to use the phrases in sentences.

1. a quiet room
2. tickle gently
3. the chorus of the song
4. bend your knee
5. an awkward silence
6. over the bridge
7. uses of the telephone
8. laugh all the time
9. with pleasure
10. without sugar

WRITING

Portfolio After reading the information about gorillas on page 8, have students work in pairs to research and write a radio documentary about these giant apes. Remind students to work in script format, showing dialogue and sound effects. Invite students to present their radio shows for the class.

SCIENCE

The first landing on the moon took place in 1969. Encourage students to learn about the specifics of this achievement, the technical advances that made it possible, and the scientific knowledge that resulted from it.

SOCIAL STUDIES

Gorillas and other apes are popular subjects for books and movies. Encourage students to go on a library hunt to discover some of the appearances great apes have made in such children's books as *Koko's Kitten* and *The Escape of Marvin the Ape* and such movies as *King Kong* and *Planet of the Apes*. Suggest using the library's subject index as a starting point.

Lesson 3
Pages 9–10

The f Sound; Sounds of gh

Lesson Focus

INTRODUCING THE SKILLS

- As you say the following words, invite students to write them on the board: *cliff, cough, telephone, phantom,* and *fear.* Ask volunteers to circle the letters that stand for /f/. Lead students to conclude that the sound can be represented by *ff, gh, ph,* and *f.*

- Ask students to write the words *laugh, ghetto,* and *sigh,* underlining *gh* in each word.

- Ask them to identify the word in which gh stands for /g/ (*ghetto*), /f/ (*laugh*), and is silent (*sigh*).

USING THE PAGES

Read the rules on pages 9 and 10 with students and have them apply the rules to the words on the board. Read and discuss the definition of *analogy.* After students have completed the pages, invite them to discuss what they learned about letters that represent /f/ and the sounds of *gh.*

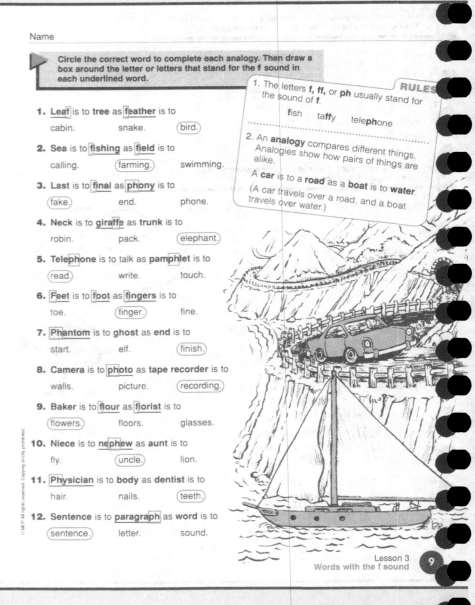

Name _____

Circle the correct word to complete each analogy. Then draw a box around the letter or letters that stand for the f sound in each underlined word.

RULES

1. The letters **f, ff,** or **ph** usually stand for the sound of **f.**

   fish   taffy   telephone

2. An **analogy** compares different things. Analogies show how pairs of things are alike.

   A **car** is to a **road** as a **boat** is to **water.** (A car travels over a road, and a boat travels over water.)

1. **Leaf** is to **tree** as **feather** is to
   cabin.   snake.   (bird.)

2. **Sea** is to **fishing** as **field** is to
   calling.   (farming.)   swimming.

3. **Last** is to **final** as **phony** is to
   (fake.)   end.   phone.

4. **Neck** is to **giraffe** as **trunk** is to
   robin.   pack.   (elephant.)

5. **Telephone** is to **talk** as **pamphlet** is to
   (read.)   write.   touch.

6. **Feet** is to **foot** as **fingers** is to
   toe.   (finger.)   fine.

7. **Phantom** is to **ghost** as **end** is to
   start.   elf.   (finish.)

8. **Camera** is to **photo** as **tape recorder** is to
   walls.   picture.   (recording.)

9. **Baker** is to **flour** as **florist** is to
   (flowers.)   floors.   glasses.

10. **Niece** is to **nephew** as **aunt** is to
    fly.   (uncle.)   lion.

11. **Physician** is to **body** as **dentist** is to
    hair.   nails.   (teeth.)

12. **Sentence** is to **paragraph** as **word** is to
    (sentence.)   letter.   sound.

Lesson 3
Words with the f sound   **9**

FOCUS ON ALL LEARNERS

ENGLISH LANGUAGE LEARNERS/ESL

Explain that an analogy shows how pairs of things are related. Help students to work with the analogies on page 9, reading the words and discussing how the items are related to each other. Also, remind native Spanish speakers that in English /f/ in *telefono* is spelled with *ph.*

AUDITORY LEARNERS

PARTNER   Have pairs of students compose humorous sentences, riddles, or jokes, using words from the lesson. Partners can share their material with the class.

VISUAL/KINESTHETIC LEARNERS

SMALL GROUP   **Materials:** index cards

Ask students to work individually to compose an analogy and write the four words from it on separate cards. In small groups, ask students to shuffle all the cards, then take turns drawing cards and sequencing them to form analogies.

Read each sentence and underline the word or words containing **gh**. Then write each gh word in the correct column at the bottom to show which sound, if any, it stands for.

> **RULE**
> The letters **gh** can stand for the **g** sound or the **f** sound.
> Sometimes **gh** is silent and stands for no sound.
>
> **gh**ost   lau**gh**   nau**gh**ty

1. I hoped we would have <u>enough</u> food for our community party.
2. I <u>sighed</u> as I realized I had practically <u>bought</u> out the grocery store.
3. I had gotten bread and rolls, olives, and <u>gherkin</u> pickles.
4. I had gotten lean meat so it wouldn't be <u>tough</u>.
5. Some of the <u>neighbors</u> were making salads and desserts.
6. I <u>thought</u> about the terrible party we had during a blizzard last year.
7. It was a <u>ghastly</u> day.
8. Everyone had a <u>rough</u> time getting to our house.
9. The snow-covered guests arrived looking like <u>ghosts</u>.
10. It seemed that everyone was <u>coughing</u> and sneezing.
11. The howling wind made a <u>ghostly</u> sound in the chimney.
12. Someone's <u>daughter</u> wrote a news article about the party.
13. Afterward, everyone <u>laughed</u> about it.

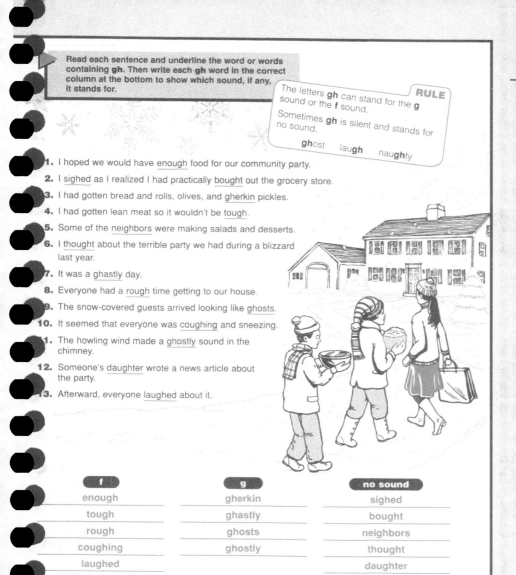

f	**g**	**no sound**
enough	gherkin	sighed
tough	ghastly	bought
rough	ghosts	neighbors
coughing	ghostly	thought
laughed		daughter

10   Lesson 3
The sounds of gh

VISUAL/AUDITORY LEARNERS

SMALL GROUP   Invite group members to fold a sheet of paper to make 16 squares and write a word with *gh* in each square. Then students take turns choosing a word to read, identify the sound of *gh*, and give another word with the same *gh* sound. Students can cover words as they are used.

GIFTED LEARNERS

Encourage students to find out how to say and spell one or more words from the lesson in another language.

LEARNERS WHO NEED EXTRA SUPPORT

Help students identify the relationship between the first word pair in the analogies before asking them to find the word that completes the second pair. For example: *a leaf is part of a tree; a nephew is the male counterpart of a niece.* **See Daily Word Study Practice, pages 180-183.**

CURRICULUM CONNECTIONS

SPELLING

On the board list the spelling words *quiet, tickle, chorus, knee, silence, bridge, telephone, laugh, pleasure,* and *sugar*. Invite students to stand when they are able to fill in the missing spelling word to each of the following sentences as you read them aloud. The student who stands first may repeat and complete the sentence.

1. Please be _____ while the baby is napping. (*quiet*)
2. Does the feather _____ your skin? (*tickle*)
3. Sing the _____ of the song more loudly than the verses. (*chorus*)
4. Wash and bandage your scraped _____. (*knee*)
5. Jake whistled to break the _____ of the woods. (*silence*)
6. A rope _____ stretches across the stream. (*bridge*)
7. By the time I reached the _____, it had stopped ringing. (*telephone*)
8. I was in a bad mood, but the jokes made me _____. (*laugh*)
9. Mom smiled with _____ when we brought dinner home. (*pleasure*)
10. The pie has too much _____ in it. (*sugar*)

WRITING

Portfolio Propose that students play the role of advertising copywriters for a shopping mall. Ask them to develop store names and write window advertisements that would attract customers to a bakery, camera shop, telephone or electronics store, flower shop, walk-in medical office, or pet store. Encourage students to proofread their copy, especially for correct spelling of words containing the phonics elements from the lesson.

SCIENCE

Invite students to learn about the invention of the telephone. Have them compare the first telephone with the advanced technology of today.

MATHEMATICS

Direct partners to conduct a survey to identify each classmate's favorite and least favorite board, computer, and card game. Pairs can then present their findings in bar graphs or circle graphs.

Lesson 4

Pages 11–12

Sounds of s

Lesson Focus

INTRODUCING THE SKILL

- On the board, write the words *solve*, *insure*, *enclosure*, and *husband*. Ask students to read the words and identify the sounds *s* stands for.(/s/, /sh/, /zh/, /z/)

- Say the words *measure*, *positive*, *sugar*, and *discover*. Invite volunteers to write these words under the words on the board that have the same sound for *s*. Encourage students to continue by adding words of their own to each group.

USING THE PAGES

Have students read the rule at the top of page 11 and apply it to the words on the board. Ask volunteers to read and explain the directions for pages 11 and 12. When reviewing the pages, have students read the passages from page 12 in correct order.

Name

> Write each word in the word bank on the line beside its definition. Then write **s**, **z**, **sh**, or **zh** to show the sound that **s** stands for in that word.

> **RULE**
> The letter **s** usually stands for the **s** sound you hear at the beginning of **silent**. Sometimes the letter **s** can stand for the **z**, **sh**, or **zh** sound.
>
> ea**s**y   **s**ugar   trea**s**ure

harvest	hasten	insurance	leisure
measure	miser	noisy	research
reservoir	result	similar	usual

1.	leisure	zh	free time
2.	reservoir	z	a place that holds an extra, or reserve, supply; often a lake where water is collected
3.	research	s	careful investigation of something
4.	usual	zh	ordinary or customary
5.	noisy	z	full of loud and unusually unpleasant sounds
6.	measure	zh	find the size or amount of something
7.	similar	s	almost, but not exactly, the same
8.	miser	z	a greedy or stingy person who doesn't want to spend money
9.	insurance	sh	a contract that pays money to a person if, for example, something the person owns is stolen
10.	harvest	s	gathering of a crop
11.	hasten	s	to speed up; to move or act swiftly
12.	result	z	what happens because of something; the outcome

Lesson 4
The sounds of s

11

FOCUS ON ALL LEARNERS

ENGLISH LANGUAGE LEARNERS/ESL

Remind students that, in English, many letters stand for more than one sound. Have students make cards for the *s* words on their pages and sort them by matching sounds.

AUDITORY/VISUAL LEARNERS

LARGE GROUP

Have students form teams to represent /s/, /z/, /sh/, and /zh/. As you say words from the lesson, invite the teams to claim their words and write them on a section of the board.

AUDITORY/KINESTHETIC LEARNERS

SMALL GROUP

Have students make up a dance or an exercise composed of four simple steps. Ask them to write the steps in order. Have classmates try the steps once after hearing the directions read and once again after seeing a demonstration.

11

The sentences in the paragraphs below include words that contain the letter **s**. The sentences are not in the correct order. Number the sentences within each group to show the correct order. Then underline each letter **s** that stands for the **s** sound and circle each letter **s** that stands for the **z** sound.

1

3   This is because Sally enjoys making others laugh.

2   However, her sad mood doesn't often last long.

1   Sometimes Sally Simpson feels unhappy.

4   Here is what happens. Sally puts a plastic crimson rose between her teeth and vigorously hums a song.

5   When other people are happy, suddenly Sally isn't sad any more.

2

3   The combination of drums, saxophone, and horns was too much.

4   After two "For Sale" signs appeared overnight, my parents suggested that we play one of their favorite songs—"Far, Far Away.

1   I've always loved music, so one day I decided to compose some songs.

2   When I succeeded in writing several pieces, I invited my friends Sally, Susan, and Sam over to play them.

Choose five words containing the letter **s** from the sentences above and use them in original sentences of your own.

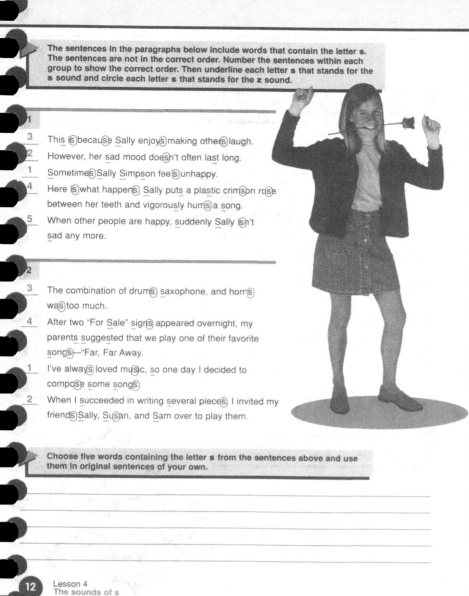

_____

_____

_____

_____

_____

_____

AUDITORY LEARNERS

 LARGE GROUP

Invite students to name steps for a familiar task or a simple story, putting one step or sentence out of order. Have students identify the mistake and explain how to correct it.

GIFTED LEARNERS

Challenge students to write sentences that have at least one word for each of the sounds of *s* in them.

LEARNERS WHO NEED EXTRA SUPPORT

Have students write down directions for a simple task they know well (such as giving a dog a bath). Have them cut apart the steps, exchange with a partner, and re-order each other's steps. Then discuss the *s* sounds in words students used. **See Daily Word Study Practice, pages 180–183.**

CURRICULUM CONNECTIONS

SPELLING

Use the following words and dictation sentences as a posttest for the first group of spelling words in Unit 1.

1. **quiet**   The lights dimmed and the theater got **quiet**.

2. **tickle**   Jen says her wool sweater does not **tickle**.

3. **chorus**   The sixth grade **chorus** gave a concert.

4. **knee**   Pam twisted her **knee** playing soccer.

5. **silence**   I can't study unless there is **silence**.

6. **bridge**   The tall ship could not pass under the **bridge**.

7. **telephone**   We are not allowed to use the **telephone** after nine o'clock at night.

8. **laugh**   John makes us **laugh** with his jokes.

9. **pleasure**   Some people take **pleasure** in hard work.

10. **sugar**   Have you seen **sugar** cane growing in fields?

WRITING

 Portfolio Invite students to write a story titled "The Mystery of the Missing Museum Treasure." Encourage them to use the words *hasten, usual, miser, surely, insure, solid, result, wise, answer, person, inside, treasure* and other words with the sounds of *s*. Call on volunteers to read their completed stories to the class. Ask listeners to evaluate the logical sequence of the stories.

SCIENCE

Prompt students to find out how and why reservoirs are created. Challenge them to determine where the nearest reservoir is and how it helps the surrounding area.

SOCIAL STUDIES

Remind students that reservoirs are dependent on rainfall. Have them research rainfall statistics for their state or region. Suggest that they look in U.S. or state almanacs. Encourage them to check recent rainfall statistics for their area in a newspaper or on the Internet.

Lesson 5

Pages 13–14

Sounds of wh;
Words with /sh/

INFORMAL ASSESSMENT OBJECTIVES

Can students

✔ recognize the sounds that *wh* can represent in words?

✔ identify the letters that represent /sh/ in words?

Lesson Focus

INTRODUCING THE SKILLS

- On the board, write the words *whom*, *whittle*, *whinny* and *whoever*. Say the words and ask students to sort them by initial sounds.

- Have volunteers find the phonetic respellings of the words in a dictionary to write on the board to conclude that *wh* can stand for /hw/ and /h/ in words.

- Write *shout*, *special*, *ocean*, and *action* on the board and read the words aloud. Ask students to name the sound common to all the words. (/sh/)

- Call on volunteers to underline the letters that represent /sh/ in the words. (*sh, ci, ce, ti*)

USING THE PAGES

Invite students to read the rules on pages 13 and 14 and apply them to the sample words shown. After students have completed the pages, discuss what they have learned about the sounds of *wh* and the letters that stand for /sh/ in words.

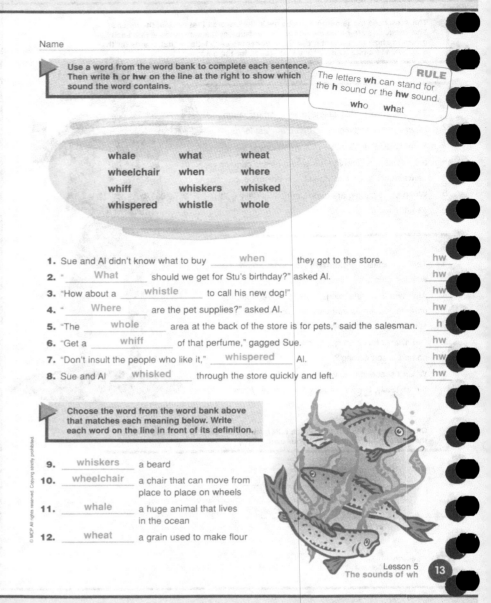

Name _____

Use a word from the word bank to complete each sentence. Then write **h** or **hw** on the line at the right to show which sound the word contains.

> **RULE**
> The letters **wh** can stand for the **h** sound or the **hw** sound.
> wh**o**   **wh**at

whale	what	wheat
wheelchair	when	where
whiff	whiskers	whisked
whispered	whistle	whole

1. Sue and Al didn't know what to buy _____ **when** _____ they got to the store. hw
2. " _____ **What** _____ should we get for Stu's birthday?" asked Al. hw
3. "How about a _____ **whistle** _____ to call his new dog!" hw
4. " _____ **Where** _____ are the pet supplies?" asked Al. hw
5. "The _____ **whole** _____ area at the back of the store is for pets," said the salesman. h
6. "Get a _____ **whiff** _____ of that perfume," gagged Sue. hw
7. "Don't insult the people who like it," _____ **whispered** _____ Al. hw
8. Sue and Al _____ **whisked** _____ through the store quickly and left. hw

Choose the word from the word bank above that matches each meaning below. Write each word on the line in front of its definition.

9. _____ **whiskers** _____ a beard
10. _____ **wheelchair** _____ a chair that can move from place to place on wheels
11. _____ **whale** _____ a huge animal that lives in the ocean
12. _____ **wheat** _____ a grain used to make flour

Lesson 5
The sounds of wh   **13**

FOCUS ON ALL LEARNERS ✱ · ◆ · ■

ENGLISH LANGUAGE LEARNERS/ESL

Before beginning the lesson, have students suggest sounds in their first languages that are spelled with letter combinations. Write down examples they mention. Then practice reading the words on the pages that use letter combinations.

VISUAL LEARNERS

INDIVIDUAL   **Materials:** dictionaries

Have students check the respellings of *wh* words in the dictionary to find those beginning with /h/. Have them write the words they find in sentences.

KINESTHETIC LEARNERS

PARTNER   **Materials:** index cards

Challenge students to create a word card game. Have partners write several words with *wh* and /sh/ on cards. Then have them create the rules for playing a game.

Read each word in the word bank. Then write it on the line beside its definition.

special	fashion	Oceania	election

1. _fashion_   popular or up-to-date style
2. _election_   the process of voting for candidates or issues
3. _Oceania_   the lands of the central and south Pacific
4. _special_   distinctive, unusual, or unique

As you read the story, circle each word that has the **sh** sound. Then write the words you circled in the correct columns below. Write each word only once.

LEARNING ABOUT OCEANS

Since the days of the (ancient) Greeks and (Phoenicians,) people have been interested in exploring the vast (oceans) that surround us. For a long time, people have been fed by the wide variety of (fish,) mammals, and (crustaceans) that inhabit the waters of the earth.

Through (patient) (exploration,) we have learned basic (information) about the (oceans,) but there is much left to find out. The study of the sea is called (oceanography,) and the scientists who study it are called (oceanographers.) These scientists spend some of their time working on research (ships.) They study many different things. Some study waves and tides. Some study how the (ocean) floor is (shaped) and how (shores) are formed. Others study the living creatures of the sea. Some scientists have found (offshore) oil deposits with the (potential) to help us maintain a (sufficient) supply of fuel.

ce	ti	sh	ci
oceans	patient	fish	ancient
crustaceans	exploration	ships	Phoenicians
oceanography	information	shaped	sufficient
oceanographers	potential	shores	
ocean		offshore	

14   Lesson 5
Words with the sh sound

LARGE GROUP

AUDITORY/VISUAL LEARNERS

Materials: dictionaries

Start by naming words that contain /sh/ and begin with *a*, such as *action* or *accomplish*. Assign each student a letter of the alphabet. Students can use dictionaries to find words that begin with their letters and include /sh/. Compile a class list.

GIFTED LEARNERS

Challenge students to do the alphabetical *sh* activity described above, but make it more difficult by designating one spelling of /sh/, such as *ti*, to use each time.

LEARNERS WHO NEED EXTRA SUPPORT

Have students collectively write a story, using as many words that contain *wh* and /sh/ as possible. **See Daily Word Study Practice, pages 180-183.**

CURRICULUM CONNECTIONS

SPELLING

Use the following words and dictation sentences as a pretest for the second group of spelling words in Unit 1.

1. **whispered**   The girls **whispered** in the museum.
2. **special**   We like **special** sauce with our chicken.
3. **thousand**   Five **thousand** people attended the concert.
4. **science**   We study weather in **science** class.
5. **design**   The winning **design** will be used on a poster.
6. **kitchen**   Our guests chatted in the **kitchen**.
7. **rhythm**   This song has a tricky **rhythm**.
8. **pearl**   The **pearl** fell out of her ring.
9. **despair**   We groaned with **despair** when our team lost.
10. **children**   Some **children** are in the wedding party.

WRITING

Portfolio   Brainstorm a list of words that contain the letters *wh* or /sh/. Have students write riddles that either have these words as the answers or as part of the clues.

SCIENCE/GEOGRAPHY

The word *ocean* comes from the Greek word *Okeanos*. The ancient Greeks thought Okeanos was an enormous river that stretched around the entire earth. Have students research and record facts about the world's oceans and use these facts to invent a trivia game to play with classmates.

HEALTH

Challenge students to compile a list of the foods that come from the ocean. Make sure they include seaweed as well as various kinds of fish and shellfish. Have students research nutrients provided by these foods and health concerns posed by some items. One example is mercury contamination of fish.

Lesson 6

Pages 15–16

Sounds of th and sc

Lesson Focus

INTRODUCING THE SKILLS

- Write the following words on the board, underlining the letters *th* or *sc* in each word: *conscious, authentic, luscious, scarecrow, worthy, beneath, scallop, scenery, them, thumb, scent, muscle, mother, thirty, scandal, clothing.*

- Ask a volunteer to read each word aloud and use it in a sentence.

- Ask students to determine if each word contains the *th* sound as in *thin* or the *th* sound as in *then.* (*th* as in *thin*: *authentic, beneath, thirty, thumb*; *th* as in *then*: *clothing, worthy, them, mother*)

- Have students identify the sounds that the letters *sc* stand for in the *sc* words. (/s/: *scent, muscle, scenery*; /sk/: *scallop, scandal, scarecrow*; /sh/: *luscious, conscious*)

USING THE PAGES

Give students help as needed to complete pages 15 and 16. After completing the pages, encourage students to summarize what they have learned about the sounds of *th* and *sc.*

15

Name

The sentences in the paragraphs below include words that contain the letters **th.** The sentences are not in the correct order. First number the sentences in each group to show the correct order. Then underline each **th** as in **thin** and circle each **th** as in **then.**

> **RULE**
> The letters **th** can stand for the **th** sound as in **thin.** The letters **th** can also stand for the **th** sound as in **then.**

1

3 Then Mother heard that running is healthful, so she and I joined in.

1 Father really started something when he began to run.

2 First, my brother Matthew began to run with Dad.

4 Now my whole family is so enthusiastic about running that we will enter a marathon on Thursday.

2

2 "I'd rather go out myself," thought Kim, but she thawed a thick pizza to eat.

1 Mom asked Kim to baby-sit for her baby brother while her parents went to the theater.

4 "Thank you a thousand times, Kim," said her mother when they returned. "You're a faithful sister."

3 Later she threw a ball for her brother Seth, who got enthusiastic each time the ball went farther. •

Choose two words containing the letters **th** from the sentences above and use them in original sentences of your own.

_____

_____

_____

FOCUS ON ALL LEARNERS

ENGLISH LANGUAGE LEARNERS/ESL

Work with students to help them discriminate between the two pronunciations of *th* in the words on page 15.

VISUAL LEARNERS

INDIVIDUAL **Materials:** dictionaries

Have students do a dictionary search for ten words that begin with *th* or *sc.* Ask them to check the phonetic respelling of each entry and write the words and respellings on paper.

KINESTHETIC LEARNERS

SMALL GROUP **Materials:** dictionaries

On the board write dictionary spellings for words with *th* and *sc.* Invite students to write the word for each spelling and then verify using a dictionary.

Underline each word in which you see the letters **sc**. Then write **sk, s,** or **sh** above each word you underline to show the sound that **sc** stands for in that word.

> **RULE**
> The letters **sc** can stand for the **sk, s,** or **sh** sounds.
> **sc**alp   **sc**ientist
> con**sc**ience

1. At the art museum we <u>sk</u> <u>scanned</u> the <u>landscapes</u> first.

2. In one <u>s</u> <u>scene</u> a farmer held a huge <u>s</u> <u>scythe</u>.

3. Another painting showed a <u>sh</u> <u>luscious</u> <u>sk</u> <u>scarlet</u> sunset.

4. In one room we were <u>sh</u> <u>conscious</u> of the <u>s</u> <u>scent</u> of paint.

5. A man on a tall <u>sk</u> <u>scaffold</u> <u>sk</u> <u>scowled</u> at us.

6. Throughout our visit, Amy took <u>sh</u> <u>conscientious</u> notes.

7. I paid <u>sk</u> <u>scant</u> attention to the paintings about wars.

8. Many <u>s</u> <u>scenes</u> in the modern art section seemed straight from <u>s</u> <u>science</u> fiction.

9. I <u>sk</u> <u>scampered</u> into the <u>sk</u> <u>sculpture</u> room to see if they had any work by the <u>sk</u> <u>sculptor</u> Michelangelo.

Choose a word from those you underlined above to fit each definition.

conscientious	showing care
scanned	glanced at or looked over
scampered	moved quickly
scent	smell
landscapes	pictures of natural inland scenery
scowled	frowned

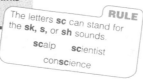

CURRICULUM CONNECTIONS ✳ ● ◦ ■ ◆ ○

SPELLING

Challenge pairs of students to create crossword puzzles featuring the spelling words *whispered*, *special*, *thousand*, *science*, *design*, *kitchen*, *rhythm*, *pearl*, *despair*, and *children*. Pairs of students can trade puzzles to solve.

WRITING

Portfolio Encourage students to think of a field of science that they are enthusiastic about and write about it to share with the group.

ART

Display photographs of Michelangelo's works. Explain that Michelangelo, who lived from 1475 to 1564, was a great Italian sculptor, painter, and architect. At the age of 23, he created his first important sculpture, *Pietà*.

PHYSICAL EDUCATION

Have students research the physical and psychological benefits of running or jogging. Prompt them to talk with their physical education teacher about the national standard for how long it should take students their age to run a mile, and determine whether or not they can meet this standard.

AUDITORY LEARNERS

LARGE GROUP Challenge students to write tongue twisters featuring words with *sc* and *th*. Begin with *Thirty thousand enthusiastic marathon runners thundered through the streets on Thursday.*

GIFTED LEARNERS

Have students research the word histories of words that begin with *th* and *sc* to discover from what languages the words come.

LEARNERS WHO NEED EXTRA SUPPORT

Invite students to read aloud the sentences from pages 15 and 16 to reinforce word recognition. **See Daily Word Study Practice, pages 180–183.**

Lesson 7
Pages 17–18

  **Reading** **Writing**

Reviewing Consonant Variants and Letter Combinations

Lesson Focus

READING

- Write these words on the board, underlining the indicated consonants: *chef, chicken; unique, kitchen; cook, sauce; measures, seeds, raisins; garlic, range; thick, then.*

- Ask students to compare the sounds the underlined consonants make.

- Tell students that the article they will read tells about Mexican food and uses words that contain these and other consonant sounds. After reading the article on page 17, have students respond to the premise at the bottom of the page.

WRITING

- Provide students with samples of restaurant advertisements and discuss the language writers use when describing restaurants to make them sound appealing.

- Read together the directions and the words in the word bank on page 18. Review the ideas for information to include.

17

Name _____

Reading ▶ Read the article. Then write your answer to the questions at the end of the article.

 # A FESTIVE SAUCE

At a long-ago banquet, a Mexican chef dreamed up a unique sauce to serve with turkey or chicken. This special mixture, called **mole** [MOH' lay], is very different from the usual sauces served in Mexican American restaurants. For one thing, it contains chocolate!

Preparing mole involves a complicated set of procedures. The first step calls for the cook to use a sharp knife to remove the seeds from some whole chilies (hot peppers). The chilies are then fried, put into a large bowl, covered with water, and left to soak overnight.

The next day the chilies are fried until they are soft. The cook measures cloves and other spices, pumpkin seeds, sesame seeds, raisins, almonds, and garlic, and adds them to the chilies. Then the cook breaks some chocolate into small pieces and quickly whisks them in. The mole sauce is slowly cooked on the kitchen range. When the mixture is just thick enough to coat a wooden spoon, it is finished. Spooned over roast turkey, the result is luscious.

You are a cook explaining that shopping for and preparing mole is a complex task. What evidence supports your claim? _____
_____
_____
_____
_____
_____

Lesson 7
Review consonant variants and letter combinations: Reading **17**

FOCUS ON ALL LEARNERS

ENGLISH LANGUAGE LEARNERS/ESL

To help students understand the article on page 17, discuss basic cooking and recipe terminology such as *sauce, measure, fry,* and *whisk*.

 ### VISUAL LEARNERS

PARTNER Have partners list words with the sounds of *ch, kn, gh, wh, sh, th* and *sc* and use the words to write a poem.

 ### VISUAL/KINESTHETIC LEARNERS

SMALL GROUP **Materials:** poster board, dice, game markers

Encourage students to create board games, featuring words from Lessons 1-6. Groups can teach one another how to play their games.

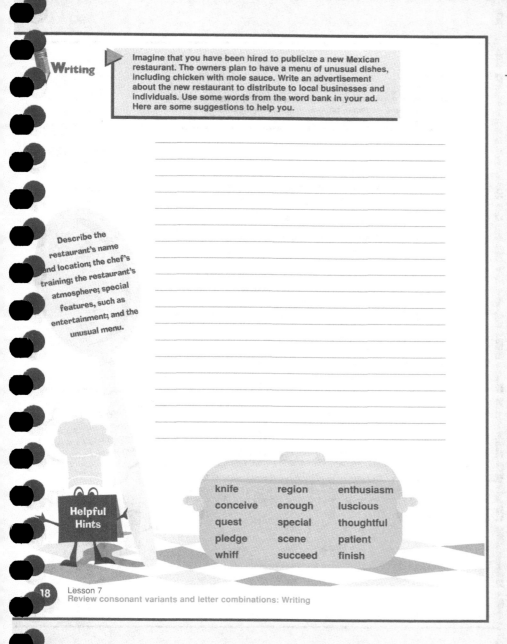

Writing

Imagine that you have been hired to publicize a new Mexican restaurant. The owners plan to have a menu of unusual dishes, including chicken with mole sauce. Write an advertisement about the new restaurant to distribute to local businesses and individuals. Use some words from the word bank in your ad. Here are some suggestions to help you.

Describe the restaurant's name and location; the chef's training; the restaurant's atmosphere; special features, such as entertainment; and the unusual menu.

Helpful Hints

knife	region	enthusiasm
conceive	enough	luscious
quest	special	thoughtful
pledge	scene	patient
whiff	succeed	finish

Lesson 7
Review consonant variants and letter combinations: Writing

AUDITORY/VISUAL LEARNERS

LARGE GROUP Say pairs or groups of words that have the same sound, spelled differently. Try these: *recipe, serve; opaque, stocky, kiwi; chef, sufficient, luscious; fudge, storage.* Then have volunteers write the words on the board to show that, although sounds may be the same, spellings can be different.

GIFTED LEARNERS

Have students find as many words as possible in the article on page 17 that illustrate the consonants and consonant combinations covered in Lessons 1–6. Encourage students to list the words by letter or sound patterns.

LEARNERS WHO NEED EXTRA SUPPORT

Review these concepts: 1) A consonant or combination of consonants can make more than one sound. 2) A sound can be spelled in various ways. Have students list and explain examples from the unit for each idea. **See Daily Word Study Practice, pages 180-183.**

CURRICULUM CONNECTIONS

SPELLING

Call out each of the spelling words *whispered, special, thousand, science, design, kitchen, rhythm, pearl, despair,* and *children.* After each word, have a volunteer write on the board a two-word phrase using the spelling word along with another word with the same number of syllables. For example: *whispered secrets.*

HEALTH

Have students collect recipes for their favorite Mexican dishes and arrange them in a binder. Discuss the nutritional value of ingredients found in the recipes and ways the dishes can be prepared in the most healthful or low-fat ways. Provide copies to be used at home.

SOCIAL STUDIES

Encourage students to find out which foods were first grown in the Americas and later transported to Europe, Africa, and Asia. Challenge them to also find crops from Europe or Africa that were brought to America.

MATH

Have students decide on a simple recipe from their Mexican favorites that can be prepared at school. Have them examine the recipe for ingredients and utensils needed. Students can determine how to multiply the recipe to provide enough servings for the class. You may wish to invite school aides or parents into the classroom for this project or to help with in-kitchen work that must be done.

Lesson 8
Pages 19–20

Words with gn, tch, and the r Sound

Lesson Focus

INTRODUCING THE SKILLS

- Write these words on the board: *gnaw, write, gnarl, catch, ditch, fetch, rhino, rhubarb, rhyme, wren, cologne, wrap.*

- Tell students that each word contains one of the consonant combinations *gn, tch, rh,* and *wr.* Write the letters on the board.

- As volunteers read the words aloud, have them identify the sounds represented by these consonant combinations.

USING THE PAGES

- Have students read aloud the rules in the boxes on pages 19 and 20 and discuss how the rules apply to the sample words. Later, have students check their work to assess what they learned about the letter combinations covered in this lesson.

- **Critical Thinking** Encourage students to respond to the question on page 19 by discussing strategies for political campaigns.

Name _____

> Read the words in the word bank. Underline each word that contains the letters **gn** and circle each word that contains the letters **tch**. Then use the words to complete the sentences below.

RULE
The letters **gn** can stand for the **n** sound. The letters **tch** can stand for the **ch** sound.

gnat   si**gn**
ma**tch**   ki**tch**en

Word Bank:
resign   watch
assign   catching
stitching   batches
design   pitchers
kitchen   campaign

My aunt was in charge of the mayor's reelection __campaign__. She had to ____assign____ tasks to the other volunteers. She asked people to bake __batches__ of cookies and make __pitchers__ of iced tea for neighborhood meetings. She found an artist to __design__ election posters. My cousin helped by __stitching__ a banner to hang in the center of town.

It was a difficult campaign. One candidate was demanding that the mayor __resign__ before the election! My aunt kept a close __watch__ on the election polls. At first the mayor seemed to have a good lead. Then the polls showed that another candidate was __catching__ up. In the end, however, the mayor won the election. And my aunt had run the whole campaign from her __kitchen__.

> **What aspect of the campaign do you think played the most important part in the mayor's reelection?**

Critical Thinking

Lesson 8
Words with gn and tch   **19**

FOCUS ON ALL LEARNERS

ENGLISH LANGUAGE LEARNERS/ESL

Before beginning page 19, remind students that many English words contain silent letters. Ask students if they can provide any examples of such words. Practice reading words from this lesson that include silent letters.

VISUAL LEARNERS
PARTNER   Ask students to look up the meaning of *gnome* in the dictionary. Invite partners to write a poem about a gnome, using words that contain *gn, tch, rh,* and *wr.* Remind them that poems do not always rhyme.

KINESTHETIC LEARNERS
PARTNER   **Materials:** dictionaries

Suggest that students write definitions for words with *gn* and *tch* and ask a partner to identify and write the word for each definition. Locate the words in a dictionary to verify.

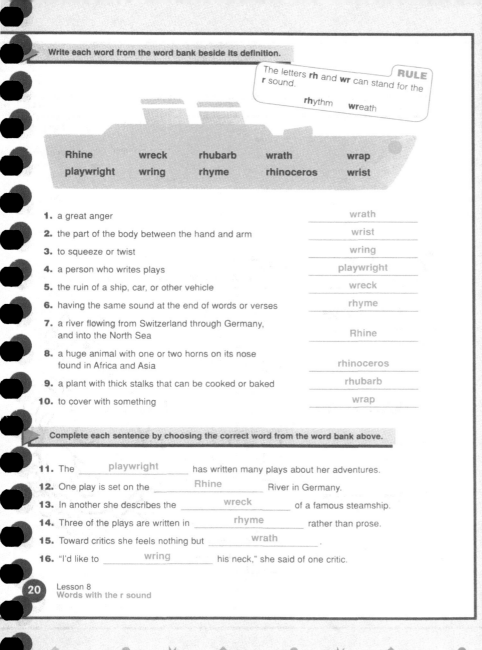

Write each word from the word bank beside its definition.

RULE The letters **rh** and **wr** can stand for the **r** sound.

rhythm   **wr**eath

Rhine	wreck	rhubarb	wrath	wrap
playwright	wring	rhyme	rhinoceros	wrist

1. a great anger — wrath
2. the part of the body between the hand and arm — wrist
3. to squeeze or twist — wring
4. a person who writes plays — playwright
5. the ruin of a ship, car, or other vehicle — wreck
6. having the same sound at the end of words or verses — rhyme
7. a river flowing from Switzerland through Germany, and into the North Sea — Rhine
8. a huge animal with one or two horns on its nose found in Africa and Asia — rhinoceros
9. a plant with thick stalks that can be cooked or baked — rhubarb
10. to cover with something — wrap

Complete each sentence by choosing the correct word from the word bank above.

11. The _____playwright_____ has written many plays about her adventures.
12. One play is set on the _____Rhine_____ River in Germany.
13. In another she describes the _____wreck_____ of a famous steamship.
14. Three of the plays are written in _____rhyme_____ rather than prose.
15. Toward critics she feels nothing but _____wrath_____.
16. "I'd like to _____wring_____ his neck," she said of one critic.

AUDITORY/VISUAL LEARNERS

SMALL GROUP

Materials: magazines, newspapers, scissors

Have students cut out words from newspapers and magazines that contain the consonant combinations featured in this lesson. Encourage them to create original sentences using the words.

GIFTED LEARNERS

Have pairs of students use the dictionary to make lists of words that contain the target consonant clusters. Invite them to try to stump each other on how to spell the words.

LEARNERS WHO NEED EXTRA SUPPORT

Have students write sentences that leave out words from the lesson. Invite them to trade papers with a partner and find the words to complete each other's work. **See Daily Word Study Practice, pages 180–183.**

CURRICULUM CONNECTIONS

SPELLING

Write the spelling words on slips of paper: *whispered, special, thousand, science, design, kitchen, rhythm, pearl, despair,* and *children.* Give one word to a pair of students. As you call out the following definitions, each pair should decide if they hold the matching word. If so, one student should spell the word aloud and the other should use the word in a sentence. Use the definitions: said quietly (*whispered*), unusual (*special*), ten hundreds (*thousand*), the study of how things work (*science*), a pattern (*design*), a room for cooking (*kitchen*), musical beat (*rhythm*), jewel from an oyster (*pearl*), deep sorrow (*despair*), sons and daughters (*children*).

WRITING

Portfolio Have students create persuasive campaign posters. Each poster should contain a brief list of the credentials and achievements of a candidate, plus a short, powerful slogan. Encourage use of words from the lesson.

SOCIAL STUDIES

Ask students to locate Europe on a map or a globe, then track the Rhine River as it flows from the Swiss Alps to the North Sea. Have students name the countries the river flows through or between.

MATH

Have students look up the length of the Rhine River in miles. Next, have them convert the measurement into kilometers (approximately 0.62 mile), first using mental math to estimate, then using paper and pencil to calculate more exactly.

Lesson 9

Pages 21–22

Sounds of ear

INFORMAL ASSESSMENT OBJECTIVE

Can students

✔ recognize the sounds that *ear* can represent in words?

Lesson Focus

INTRODUCING THE SKILL

- On the board write the words *fear, yearly, learn, pear, wear, smear, yearn, pearl, weary,* and *beard.* Ask students to name the letter combination that all the words have in common. (*ear*)

- As students pronounce the words, ask which words have the same vowel sound as *ear* (*fear, yearly, smear, weary, beard*) as *bear* (*pear, wear*) and as *earth* (*learn, yearn, pearl*).

- Invite students to add other *ear* words to the board.

USING THE PAGES

Direct attention to the rule box on page 21. Have students read and apply the rule to the words *appear, pear,* and *pearl.* Ask students for any questions they may have about the exercises. After students have completed the pages, encourage them to discuss what they learned about the letter combination *ear.*

Name _____

 Write **ear, pear,** or **pearl** to show which sound the letters **ear** stand for.

RULE
The letters **ear** can stand for the **ear** sound, the **air** sound, or the **ur** sound.

app**ear** ear   p**ear** air
p**earl** ur

1. weary	ear	2. earnest	pearl
3. spear	ear	4. earth	pearl
5. tear	pear or ear	6. clear	ear
7. gears	ear	8. learn	pearl
9. bearer	pear	10. smear	ear
11. beard	ear	12. earrings	ear

Think of a word that fits each definition and has the sound of **ear** shown for each section. Write the word in the boxes at the right. Some of the words may come from the list above, but others will not.

ear as in ear

13. a feeling of terror or fright — f e a r
14. opposite of **far** — n e a r
15. 12 months — y e a r
16. to listen to sounds — h e a r

ear as in pear

17. a large mammal with thick fur — b e a r
18. to have on the body — w e a r
19. to become torn — t e a r
20. a person or thing that carries — b e a r e r

ear as in pearl

21. listened to — h e a r d
22. to look for — s e a r c h
23. to gain knowledge — l e a r n
24. the planet we live on — e a r t h

Lesson 9
The sounds of ear   **21**

FOCUS ON ALL LEARNERS

ENGLISH LANGUAGE LEARNERS/ESL

Before beginning page 21, remind students that, in English, the same combination of letters can often represent different sounds. Read the words aloud before students begin the exercises.

VISUAL LEARNERS

SMALL GROUP Have students create word puzzles featuring *ear* words that follow the model of those on page 21. Groups can then exchange puzzles to solve.

KINESTHETIC LEARNERS

LARGE GROUP Have teams of students play *ear* charades. Each team writes clue words containing *ear* on pieces of paper and teams exchange words. Students take turns acting out clue words as their teammates guess the answers.

Write a word from the word bank that fits each definition.

Word bank:
- rehearsal
- bearded
- earthenware
- yearling
- bearing
- research
- spearmint
- forebears
- rainwear

1. a plant used for flavoring — **spearmint**
2. a one-year-old animal — **yearling**
3. practice for a play or speech — **rehearsal**
4. clothes for wet weather — **rainwear**
5. people who lived before us; ancestors — **forebears**
6. dishes or jars made from baked clay — **earthenware**
7. a careful investigation to find information — **research**
8. having hair growing on the lower part of the face — **bearded**
9. a part of a machine that helps another part to move — **bearing**

Write the letter of the phrase that completes each sentence. Then circle each word that contains the letters ear and write the word in the correct column.

10. This (year) we will go — a. a (bear.)
11. We'll pack our (gear) and decide — b. what to (wear.)
12. In case of bad weather we should take — c. if we don't (tear) our clothes?
13. During our last trip we (heard) — d. our (rainwear.)
14. We (learned) to stay quiet, — e. to the (Earth) Trails Campground.
15. Will we (earn) any points — f. so we had no (fear.)

ear as in appear	ear as in wear	ear as in search
year	bear	heard
gear	wear	learned
fear	tear	earn
	rainwear	Earth

SPELLING

On the board write the spelling words *whispered, special, thousand, science, design, kitchen, rhythm, pearl, despair,* and *children.* Have a team of three students stand with their backs to the board. Invite a classmate to call out one spelling word. The team must spell the word, with each team member giving one letter until the word has been spelled correctly. If any member makes a mistake, the classmate who called the word says, "Stop." The next team member can then correct the mistake. Continue until all students have participated and all words have been spelled.

WRITING

Portfolio Have students write a short story about an encounter with a bear during a camping trip. Challenge them to use at least six *ear* words in their story.

SCIENCE

Invite students to create encyclopedia articles on the following subjects: earthenware, spearmint, bears, or pearls.

HEALTH

Have students research how the human ear functions. Encourage them to prepare a report that includes a diagram showing the different parts of the ear. Some students may want to extend their research into how to detect and prevent common hearing problems.

AUDITORY LEARNERS

LARGE GROUP Provide each student with an *ear* word. Invite one student to begin telling a story, using the *ear* word that was given. The next student continues the story and must include his or her *ear* word, and so on.

GIFTED LEARNERS

Suggest that students write a story about a rehearsal for a musical production. Ask them to use words containing the different sounds of *ear* in their story.

LEARNERS WHO NEED EXTRA SUPPORT

Materials: index cards, markers

Have students write *ear* words on individual index cards. Have students color-code the cards according to the sound *ear* stands for in each word. Use the cards to create word games. **See Daily Word Study Practice, pages 180-183.**

Lesson 10
Pages 23–24

Words with the air Sound; Words with ild, ind, ost, old

✶ ⋅ ⋅ ◆ ⋅ ■ ⋅ ⋅✶ ⋅ ⋅ ◆ ⋅ ⋅ ● ⋅

INFORMAL ASSESSMENT OBJECTIVES

Can students

✔ identify the letters that can represent the *air* sound in words?

✔ recognize the sounds that *ild, ind, ost,* and *old* can represent in words?

Lesson Focus

INTRODUCING THE SKILLS

● Write *pair, pare, flair,* and *care* on the board. Ask a volunteer to read the words aloud. Elicit that each word contains the *air* sound. Ask how the sound is spelled. *(air, are)*

● Write these sentences on the board. Ask volunteers to read each sentence and identify the vowel sound in each underlined word.

Do you <u>mind</u> a <u>mild</u> winter?

The <u>post</u> office will <u>hold</u> my mail.

Did you <u>find</u> the <u>most</u> answers?

● Help students recognize that words ending in *ld, nd,* and *st* and preceded by *i* or *o* can have the long vowel sound.

USING THE PAGES

● Have students read the directions for the exercises on pages 23 and 24. Later, have them share what they have learned about words with the *air* sound and words with *ild, ind, ost,* and *old.*

● **Critical Thinking** Encourage students to answer the question on page 24.

23

Name _____

▶ Use the words from the word bank to complete the rhymes.

repair	Clare	fair	rare	declare	scare
Blair	flair	despair	mare	care	air

1. There once was a brave girl named _____ Clare _____ .
   Who loved to ride her pet _____ mare _____ .
   The horse ran quite fast,
   And as they flew past,
   They gave everybody a _____ scare _____ .

2. There was a sad girl in _____ despair _____ .
   Who wanted to go to the _____ fair _____ .
   She got there by noon,
   And then very soon,
   She felt like she hadn't a _____ care _____ .

3. There once was a young boy named _____ Blair _____ .
   Who one day was heard to _____ declare _____ .
   "I'll inflate a balloon,
   While I'm singing a tune!"
   Was young Blair just full of hot _____ air _____ ?

4. There once was a man with a _____ flair _____ .
   Who could do any kind of _____ repair _____ .
   He fixed odds and ends,
   For all of his friends.
   They agreed that his talent was _____ rare _____ .

Lesson 10
Words with the air sound   **23**

FOCUS ON ALL LEARNERS ✶ ⋅ ● ◆ ■

ENGLISH LANGUAGE LEARNERS/ESL

Review with students the difference between short and long *i* and *o* vowel sounds. Point out that in this lesson, they will learn about some special letter combinations that represent long vowel sounds.

VISUAL LEARNERS

PARTNER Invite pairs of students to write a letter to each other, using words with the letters *are, air, ild, ind, ost,* and *old.* Have students exchange letters and circle all these letter combinations.

KINESTHETIC LEARNERS

SMALL GROUP Challenge students to expand on the story from page 24 and rewrite it as a script for a short skit. Then invite students to perform the skit for the group.

Fill in the circle beside the word that completes each sentence.

The day dawned sunny and not very _____ on our farm.
- ○ cost
- ● cold
- ○ mold

We planned to _____ a large birthday party that evening.
- ● host
- ○ ghost
- ○ most

Grandma was 70 years _____.
- ○ told
- ● old
- ○ kind

Then the _____ weather grew violent.
- ○ kind
- ○ hold
- ● mild

A _____ blizzard blew in and snow covered the land.
- ○ wind
- ● wild
- ○ gold

"There will be no letters from the _____ office today," said Grandma.
- ○ find
- ○ fold
- ● post

7. "No, the carrier would get _____ in the snow and wind," replied Grandpa.
- ● lost
- ○ most
- ○ mind

8. "How will people _____ us for the party?" asked Katya.
- ○ hind
- ● find
- ○ grind

9. "I doubt anyone will get through," Grandpa _____ her.
- ● told
- ○ bold
- ○ sold

"We will _____ another party in the spring," laughed Mother.
- ○ mold
- ○ cold
- ● hold

Next morning, _____ of the high winds had stopped.
- ● most
- ○ ghost
- ○ mild

Katya thought the bright sun might _____ her.
- ○ sold
- ○ child
- ● blind

24 Lesson 10
Words with ild, ind, ost, old

How do you know the family was not upset about the blizzard that canceled the party?

Critical Thinking

SPELLING

Call out the spelling words *whispered, special, thousand, science, design, kitchen, rhythm, pearl, despair,* and *children*. For each word, have a volunteer name two other words that would fit in the same category. For example: *ten, hundred, thousand*. Then invite them to write the three words on the board.

WRITING

Portfolio Have students write limericks such as those on page 23. Challenge them to end lines 1, 2, and 5 or lines 3 and 4 with a word with the *air* sound or with a word that contains *ild, ind, ost,* or *old*.

SCIENCE

Have students investigate the mechanics of how a hot-air balloon works. Have them prepare diagrams labeled with explanatory captions and share them with the rest of the class.

SOCIAL STUDIES

Ask students to identify a region of the United States that regularly suffers from severe winter weather. What effect has the winter weather had on the history of the region? Encourage students to find accounts of famous blizzards.

● ◆ ■ ● ◆ ● ○ ✳ ● ● ■ ● ◆ ● ✳ ● ◆ ■ ◆ ●

LARGE GROUP

AUDITORY LEARNERS

Invite volunteers to read aloud the limericks on page 23, placing emphasis on words with the *air* sound.

GIFTED LEARNERS

Challenge students to think of homophones (words that sound the same but are spelled differently) that contain the *air* sound and have one syllable. (Possible answers: *hair, hare; pair, pare, pear; stair, stare*)

LEARNERS WHO NEED EXTRA SUPPORT

Have students create six columns on paper with the headings *air, are, ild, ind, ost,* and *old*. Have them write words from the lesson under each heading and then add words of their own. **See Daily Word Study Practice, pages 180–183.**

Lesson 11
Pages 25–26

Syllables

Name

Read each word in the list. On the line in front of the word, write how many syllables it has. Then write the word in the correct column below.

RULE
If you hear one vowel sound in a word, the word has one syllable. If you hear two vowel sounds, the word has two syllables, and so on.

1. _2_ appear
2. _1_ share
3. _3_ repairing
4. _2_ thunder
5. _1_ calm
6. _2_ binder
7. _1_ flair
8. _4_ sympathetic
9. _2_ earring
10. _4_ celebration
11. _1_ youth
12. _4_ astonishment
13. _3_ accomplish
14. _3_ poisonous
15. _4_ mathematics
16. _3_ carefully

One Syllable
share
calm
flair
youth

Two Syllables
appear
thunder
binder
earring

Three Syllables
repairing
accomplish
poisonous
carefully

Four Syllables
sympathetic
celebration
astonishment
mathematics

Lesson 11
Syllables 25

INFORMAL ASSESSMENT OBJECTIVES

Can students

- ✔ identify the number of syllables in words?
- ✔ divide words with one consonant between two vowels into syllables?
- ✔ divide words with two consonants between two vowels into syllables?

Lesson Focus

INTRODUCING THE SKILL

- Ask students to tell how many syllables they hear in the following words: *wear, trees, shadow, unfairly, cauliflower, trinket, impulsively, moon.*
- Write these words on the board.

  1. *letter, outdoor, bigger, permit*

  2. *never, river, rapid, honest*

  3. *polar, razor, nation, humor*

  4. *zebra, ticket, bother, digraph*

  Ask students to identify which of the four rules of syllabication on page 26 each group of words illustrates.

USING THE PAGES

Assist students with the directions for pages 25 and 26. After they have completed the pages, encourage them to tell why it is important to know the syllabication rules.

FOCUS ON ALL LEARNERS

ENGLISH LANGUAGE LEARNERS/ESL

Make sure that students understand the words used in the syllabication rules (e.g., consonant, vowel, digraph, blend, etc.).

VISUAL LEARNERS
INDIVIDUAL **Materials:** poster board

Suggest that each student create an attractive poster to show the four rules of syllabication. Display the posters as a reminder.

KINESTHETIC LEARNERS
SMALL GROUP **Materials:** index cards, scissors, stopwatch

Have students write several two-syllable words from the lesson on index cards. Have them cut apart the words between syllables and mix the cards. Have the group members time one another to see how quickly the words can be reassembled.

Study the rules. Then divide the words into syllables using vertical lines.

RULES

1. When a single consonant comes between two vowels in a word, the word is usually divided after the consonant if the first vowel is short.

nev/er   Phil/ip
shad/ow   rap/id

2. When a single consonant comes between two vowels in a word, the word is usually divided before the consonant if the first vowel is long.

po/lar   na/tion
ra/zor   hu/mor

3. When two or more consonants come between two vowels in a word, the word is usually divided between the first two consonants.

bet/ter   wes/tern
per/mit   big/ger

4. When a consonant blend or consonant digraph comes between two vowels in a word, the word is usually divided after the blend or digraph if the first vowel is short, or before the blend or digraph if the first vowel is long.

moth/er   tick/et
di/graph   ze/bra

1. earnest	ear/nest	2. shiver	shiv/er
3. nectar	nec/tar	4. comic	com/ic
5. sentence	sen/tence	6. either	ei/ther
7. object	ob/ject	8. rhubarb	rhu/barb
9. cheetah	chee/tah	10. cricket	crick/et
11. shoulder	shoul/der	12. quiver	quiv/er
13. reward	re/ward	14. brother	broth/er
15. photo	pho/to	16. cabin	cab/in
17. jacket	jack/et	18. cartoon	car/toon

26 Lesson 11
Syllables

SPELLING

Call out each of the spelling words *whispered*, *special*, *thousand*, *design*, *kitchen*, *rhythm*, *pearl*, *despair*, and *children* and have students write them in syllables.

WRITING

Portfolio Encourage students to write syllable cinquain poems.

Line 1: title (2 syllables)
Line 2: description of title (4 syllables)
Line 3: action (6 syllables)
Line 4: feeling about the title (8 syllables)
Line 5: synonym for title (2 syllables)

GEOGRAPHY

Have students use a map to identify the fifty states of the United States. Have them write the state names and divide the names into syllables. Which state name has the most syllables? Which has the fewest?

SOCIAL STUDIES

Encourage students to research important celebrations in different cultures and in different parts of the world. Challenge them to find pictures of these celebrations to share with their classmates.

TECHNOLOGY

AstroWord Multisyllabic Words.
©1998 Silver Burdett Ginn Inc.
Division of Simon & Schuster.

AUDITORY LEARNERS

LARGE GROUP Create two teams. Have one team call out a number of syllables. See how quickly the other team can call out a word with that number of syllables and spell each syllable of the word.

GIFTED LEARNERS

Challenge students to write "same syllable sentences" in which every word in the sentence has the same number of syllables.

LEARNERS WHO NEED EXTRA SUPPORT

Give students lists of words with different numbers of syllables. Help them determine which syllabication rule applies to each word, then have them draw lines between the syllables. **See Daily Word Study Practice, page 195.**

Lesson 12

Pages 27–28

 **Reading**  **Writing**

Reviewing Consonant Variants, Letter Combinations, Syllables

INFORMAL ASSESSMENT OBJECTIVES

Can students

✔ read an article which contains words of one or more syllables with consonant variants and letter combinations?

✔ write a newspaper review of a play?

Lesson Focus

READING

- Write *playwright* and *roles* on the board. Ask students how the *r* sound is spelled in each.

- Write *wear* and *weary* on the board. Ask the students how the letters *ear* are pronounced differently in the two words. Ask if anyone can give examples of words with a third pronunciation for *ear*. (*pearl, earth, yearn, earn*)

- Write the words *host, cold, child,* and *find* on the board to review long vowel sounds in words ending with the consonant combinations *ld, nd,* and *st.*

- Have students read the article on page 27 and discuss their responses to their career selection.

WRITING

Explain that on page 28 students will write a review of a play. Read the tips provided on page 28. Encourage students to use words from the word bank in their writing.

27

Name _____

Reading ▶ Read the article. Then answer the question at the end of the story.

Lights! Camera! Action!

Before the first ticket is sold for a new play, many individuals have already acted out their own behind-the-scenes drama. It takes the time, talent, and energy of many different people with a variety of skills to put on a show.

The playwright must create the story. He or she must dream up an original plot, create believable characters, and write interesting dialogue.

The producer handles the business—finding a theater to host the new production and money to fund the show. The director must find actors to play the roles. Meanwhile, costume designers make sketches of the kinds of clothes the characters will wear, and carpenters build the set. The actors struggle to learn their lines and make the characters come alive.

As opening night draws near, everyone is nervous and weary. The director is in despair—certain that the audience won't even stay to watch. The playwright feels as if the play is a beloved child being sent out into the cold, cruel world before it is ready. The producer is sure the show will lose money.

On opening night, excitement builds, and suddenly everyone is eager for the show to begin. The audience is buzzing. Then a hush comes over the theater as the curtain slowly rises.

If you wanted a career in the theater, which of the jobs described above would best fit your personality? Analyze the skills and the qualities needed for the job, and explain why you think you could perform it well.

_____
_____
_____
_____
_____
_____

Lesson 12
Review consonant variants, letter combinations, syllables: Reading 27

FOCUS ON ALL LEARNERS

ENGLISH LANGUAGE LEARNERS/ESL

To help students comprehend the review, activate any prior knowledge they may have about the importance of the characters, plot, and actions in a play.

VISUAL LEARNERS

INDIVIDUAL Encourage children to use words from Lessons 8-10 to write analogies. For example: *Cookie is to batch as pear is to bushel. Fair is to fare as a pear is to pare.*

KINESTHETIC LEARNERS

SMALL GROUP **Materials:** index cards

Have students write words from Lesson 8-10 on index cards and create a game to play with the word cards.

Imagine that you are a newspaper reporter assigned to write a review of a play that has just opened in your town. Use some of the words in the word bank in your review. Below are some questions to help you.

catching	wrath	beard	learn	fair
declare	ghost	old	wild	kind
despair	heard	design	rhyme	assignment

What is the name of the play? In what theater is it playing? Where does the story take place? Who are the main characters? What is the plot? Is the play successful? Why or why not?

Helpful Questions

28

Lesson 12
Review consonant variants, letter combinations, syllables: Writing

---

CURRICULUM CONNECTIONS

SPELLING

You may use the following words and dictation sentences as a posttest for spelling words in Lessons 8–12.

1. **whispered** Lily **whispered** that she felt ill.
2. **special** Jan has a **special** winter hat with bells.
3. **thousand** A **thousand** homes lost electricity.
4. **science** To do **science** experiments, you must be accurate.
5. **design** The **design** of the house is not practical.
6. **kitchen** We want to remodel our **kitchen**.
7. **rhythm** The drummer kept a steady **rhythm**.
8. **pearl** A real **pearl** should have a soft glow.
9. **despair** Don't **despair** over your lost report.
10. **children** Two **children** were tossing a ball on the beach.

MATH

Have students calculate how many seats in a 1500-seat theater would be sold if the theater was 90% full. (1,350) What if it was 75% full? (1,125)

FINE ARTS

Give students some collections of famous plays or famous monologues. Have them find a monologue that contains some of the sounds and letter combinations covered in this unit. Have them memorize their monologues and perform them for the class.

TECHNOLOGY

AstroWord Multisyllabic Words. ©1998 Silver Burdett Ginn Inc. Division of Simon & Schuster.

AUDITORY LEARNERS

LARGE GROUP

Read aloud words that demonstrate the four syllabication rules on page 26. Have students listen carefully, spell each syllable of the word, and identify the rule.

GIFTED LEARNERS

Have pairs of students copy and number the syllabication rules on page 26. Have them take turns calling out the number of a rule and having their partner call out a word that demonstrates that rule.

LEARNERS WHO NEED EXTRA SUPPORT

Work with small groups of students to create sentences using words with the sounds of *ear*, *air*, *ild*, *ind*, *ost*, and *old*. Then circle the words and discuss the sounds these letter combinations make.
See Daily Word Study Practice, pages 180–183, 195.

Lesson 13

Pages 29–30

Unit Checkup

Reviewing Consonant Variants, Letter Combinations, and Syllables

INFORMAL ASSESSMENT OBJECTIVES

Can students

✔ distinguish among the sounds made by consonant variants and letter combinations?

✔ apply syllabication rules to determine how many syllables given words contain?

Unit Focus

PREPARING FOR THE CHECKUP

- Write /k/, /kw/, /f/, /sh/, and /r/ on the board. Ask students to give examples of words with letters that stand for these sounds.

- Write the letters *ch, c, g, gh, s, wh, th, sc, gn,* and *tch* on the board. Ask students to give examples of words in which the letters stand for different sounds.

- Write the letter combinations *ear, air, are, ild, ind,* and *ost* on the board. Ask for some words that contain these combinations and discuss how the words are pronounced.

USING THE PAGES

Review the directions on pages 29 and 30 and be sure students understand them. When students have finished, discuss the completed pages.

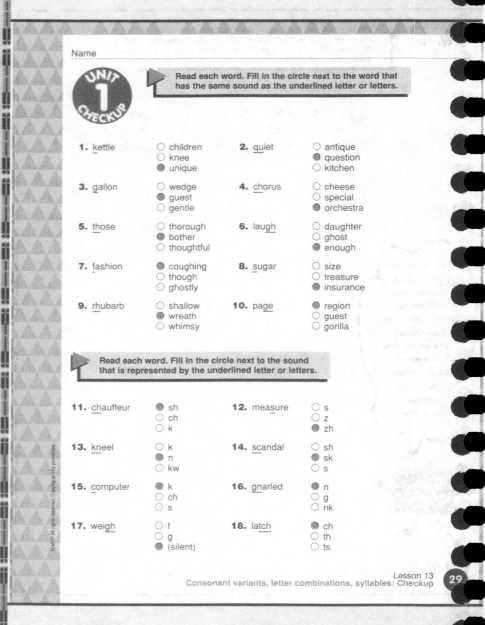

Name _____

UNIT 1 CHECKUP

▶ Read each word. Fill in the circle next to the word that has the same sound as the underlined letter or letters.

1. <u>k</u>ettle
   - ○ children
   - ○ knee
   - ● uni<u>q</u>ue

2. <u>qu</u>iet
   - ○ antique
   - ● question
   - ○ kitchen

3. <u>g</u>allon
   - ○ wedge
   - ● guest
   - ○ gentle

4. <u>ch</u>orus
   - ○ cheese
   - ○ special
   - ● orchestra

5. <u>th</u>ose
   - ○ thorough
   - ● bother
   - ○ thoughtful

6. lau<u>gh</u>
   - ○ daughter
   - ○ ghost
   - ● enough

7. fa<u>sh</u>ion
   - ● coughing
   - ○ though
   - ○ ghostly

8. <u>s</u>ugar
   - ○ size
   - ○ treasure
   - ● insurance

9. <u>rh</u>ubarb
   - ○ shallow
   - ● wreath
   - ○ whimsy

10. pa<u>g</u>e
    - ● region
    - ○ guest
    - ○ gorilla

▶ Read each word. Fill in the circle next to the sound that is represented by the underlined letter or letters.

11. <u>ch</u>auffeur
    - ● sh
    - ○ ch
    - ○ k

12. mea<u>s</u>ure
    - ○ s
    - ○ z
    - ● zh

13. <u>kn</u>eel
    - ○ k
    - ● n
    - ○ kw

14. <u>sc</u>andal
    - ○ sh
    - ● sk
    - ○ s

15. <u>c</u>omputer
    - ● k
    - ○ ch
    - ○ s

16. <u>gn</u>arled
    - ● n
    - ○ g
    - ○ nk

17. wei<u>gh</u>
    - ○ f
    - ○ g
    - ● (silent)

18. la<u>tch</u>
    - ● ch
    - ○ th
    - ○ ts

Lesson 13
Consonant variants, letter combinations, syllables: Checkup **29**

FOCUS ON ALL LEARNERS

ENGLISH LANGUAGE LEARNERS/ESL

After students have completed the Checkup pages, review with them any errors they made or questions they have about specific items, words, sounds, and/or spellings.

 VISUAL LEARNERS

PARTNER Have students pick the two words that share the same sounds from items 1–6 and use them in an original sentence.

 VISUAL/KINESTHETIC LEARNERS

LARGE GROUP After students have completed the Checkup, have them pick five to ten items and one by one turn to the lesson page that is relevant to each and point to the rule that applies.

Read each sentence. Circle the word that contains the same sound as the underlined sound.

1. What are those girls (whispering) about, and who are they?
2. They are Jen and Mia, and Jen is muttering breathlessly about her new ski (clothing.)
3. Last year Jen wore her sister's shabby old ski (gear,) but this winter she'll wear a great new outfit on the slopes.
4. She is sure that the other skiers will stare in envy at her new (pair) of boots and her fuzzy purple ear warmers.
5. Her ski pants have a wild pattern, as if someone (childishly) spilled red paint on a black background.
6. Even in blinding snow and driving wind, people will be able to (find) Jen on the mountain.
7. Jen keeps searching the sky, (yearning) for snow to fall soon this year.
8. Mia says that she ordered the most beautiful white ski jacket, but it makes her feel like a (ghost) in the snow.
9. She says she will phone the company to see if they have any (photographs) of jackets in other colors.
10. Mia says that it is unusual for her to return things, but she is sure she will find another that she will (treasure) just as much.

Write each word that you circled above. Next to the word, write the number of syllables it contains.

11. whispering — 3   12. clothing — 2
13. gear — 1   14. pair — 1
15. childishly — 3   16. find — 1
17. yearning — 2   18. ghost — 1
19. photographs — 3   20. treasure — 2

30
Lesson 13
Consonant variants, letter combinations, syllables: Checkup

AUDITORY LEARNERS

LARGE GROUP

Assign different subgroups from the class particular sounds covered in this unit. Then read aloud a random passage from a book or newspaper and ask each group to listen for its sound.

GIFTED LEARNERS

Have students create their own test for this unit. Make sure they cover all the skills.

LEARNERS WHO NEED EXTRA SUPPORT

Team learners who need extra support can work with supportive partners to review the Unit Checkup together and discuss any problems. **See Daily Word Study Practice, pages 180–183, 195.**

ASSESSING UNDERSTANDING OF UNIT SKILLS ✳ • • ◆ ▪ ◆ •

Student Progress Assessment You may wish to review the observational notes you made as students worked through the activities in this unit. Your notes will help you evaluate the progress students made with consonant variants, letter combinations, and syllables.

Portfolio Assessment Review the materials students have collected in their portfolios. Talk with students individually to discuss their written work and the progress they have made since the beginning of the unit. As you review students' work, evaluate how well they use the unit word study skills.

Daily Word Study Practice For students who need additional practice with any of the topics in this unit, quick reviews are provided on pages 180–183, 195 in Daily Word Study Practice.

Word Study Posttest To assess students' mastery of skills covered in this unit, use the posttest on pages 3g–3h.

SPELLING

Use the following dictation sentences to review the spelling words in Unit 1.

1. **quiet**   The audience was **quiet**.
2. **chorus**   A **chorus** of birds was singing.
3. **knee**   Put ice on Emma's swollen **knee**.
4. **silence**   The chess players demanded **silence** in the room.
5. **bridge**   The wooden **bridge** needs repairs.
6. **laugh**   Emily has a squeaky **laugh**.
7. **pleasure**   My cat gives me **pleasure**.
8. **whispered** Lena **whispered** to Ben that it was Rachel's birthday.
9. **thousand**   That castle is almost a **thousand** years old.
10. **science**   Hanna always gets good grades in **science**.
11. **design**   That car has an elegant **design**.
12. **rhythm**   The dancers followed the **rhythm** of the drums.
13. **pearl**   This **pearl** necklace is quite expensive.
14. **despair**   Molly is in **despair** because she can't go on the field trip.

Teacher Notes

Student Performance Objectives

In Unit 2, students will review and extend their familiarity with vowel pairs, vowel digraphs, diphthongs and syllables. As students apply these concepts, they will be able to

◆ Recognize the various sounds represented by the vowel pairs *ai, ay, ee, ei, oa, oe,* and *ow*

◆ Recognize the various sounds represented by the vowel digraphs *ea, ie, ei, ey, au, aw, ui,* and *oo*

◆ Recognize the sounds represented by diphthongs *oi, oy, ou, ow,* and *ew*

◆ Apply the rules of syllabication to words containing vowel digraphs and diphthongs

◆ Recognize that the number of syllables in a word is determined by the number of vowel sounds, not by the number of vowels

Contents

UNIT 2 RESOURCES

Assessment Strategies	31c
Overview	31c
Unit 2 Pretest	31e–31f
Unit 2 Posttest	31g–31h
Unit 2 Student Progress Checklist	31i
Spelling Connections	31j–31k
Word Study Games, Activities, and Technology	31l–31o
Home Connection	31p–31q

TEACHING PLANS

Unit 2 Opener	31–32
Lesson 14: Vowel Pairs *ai, ay*	33–34
Lesson 15: Vowel Pairs *ee, ei*	35–36
Lesson 16: Vowel Pairs *oa, oe,* and *ow*	37–38
Lesson 17: Vowel Digraph *ea*	39–40
Lesson 18: Vowel Digraph *ie*	41–42
Lesson 19: Vowel Digraphs *ei, ey* and Vowel Digraphs *au, aw*	43–44
Lesson 20: Vowel Digraph *oo*	45–46
Lesson 21: Vowel Digraph *ui*	47–48
Lesson 22: Review Vowel Pairs, Vowel Digraphs	49–50
Lesson 23: Diphthongs *oi, oy*	51–52
Lesson 24: Diphthongs *ou, ow*	53–54
Lesson 25: Diphthong *ew* and Syllables	55–56
Lesson 26: Review Vowel Pairs, Vowel Digraphs, Diphthongs, Syllables	57–58
Lesson 27: Unit 2 Checkup	59–60

31b

Assessment Strategy Overview

Throughout Unit 2, assess students' ability to read and write words with vowel pairs, vowel digraphs, and diphthongs. There are various ways to assess students' progress. You may also want to encourage students to evaluate their own work and participate in setting goals for their own learning.

FORMAL ASSESSMENT

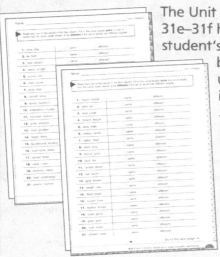

The Unit 2 Pretest on pages 31e–31f helps to assess a student's knowledge at the beginning of the unit and to plan instruction.

The Unit 2 Posttest on pages 31g–31h helps to assess mastery of unit objectives and to plan for reteaching, if necessary.

INFORMAL ASSESSMENT

The Reading & Writing pages and Unit Checkup in the student book are an effective means of evaluating students' performance.

Skill	Reading & Writing Pages	Unit Checkup
Vowel Pairs *ai, ay*	49–50	59–60
Vowel Pairs *ee, ei*	49–50	59–60
Vowel Pairs *oa, oe, ow*	49–50	59–60
Vowel Digraph *ea*	49–50	59–60
Vowel Digraph *ie*	49–50	59–60
Vowel Digraphs *ei, ey*	49–50	59–60
Vowel Digraphs *au, aw*	49–50	59–60
Vowel Digraph *oo*	49–50	59–60
Vowel Digraph *ui*	49–50	59–60
Diphthongs *oi, oy*	57–58	59–60
Diphthongs *ou, ow*	57–58	59–60
Diphthong *ew*	57–58	59–60
Syllables	57–58	59–60

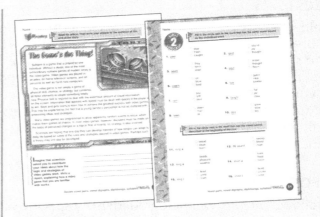

PORTFOLIO ASSESSMENT

Portfolio This logo appears throughout the teaching plans. It signals opportunities for collecting students' work for individual portfolios. You may also want to collect the following pages.

❖ Unit 2 Pretest and Posttest, pages 31e–31h

❖ Unit 2 Reading & Writing, pages 49–50, 57–58

❖ Unit 2 Checkup, pages 59–60

STUDENT PROGRESS CHECKLIST

Use the checklist on page 31i to record students' progress. You may want to cut the sections apart to place each student's checklist in his or her portfolio.

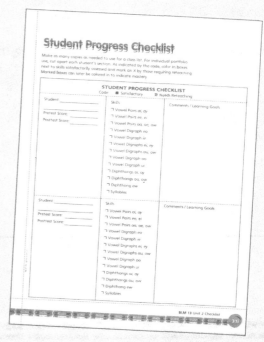

Administering and Evaluating the
Pretest and Posttest

DIRECTIONS

To help you assess students' progress in learning Unit 2 skills, tests are available on pages 31e–31h. Administer the Pretest before students begin the unit. The results of the Pretest will help you identify each student's strengths and needs in advance, allowing you to structure lesson plans to meet individual needs. Administer the Posttest to assess students' overall mastery of skills taught in the unit and to identify specific areas that will require reteaching.

PERFORMANCE ASSESSMENT PROFILE

The following chart will help you identify specific skills as they appear on the tests and enable you to identify and record specific information about an individual's or the class's performance on the tests.

Depending on the results of the tests, refer to the Reteaching column for lesson-plan pages where you can find activities that will be useful for meeting individual needs or for daily word study practice.

PERFORMANCE ASSESSMENT PROFILE

Skill	Pretest Questions	Posttest Questions	Reteaching	
			Focus on All Learners	Daily Word Study Practice
Vowel Pairs /ā/ ai, ay	1, 14, 22, 28	1, 14, 22, 28	33–34, 49–50, 57–58	183–186
Vowel Pairs /ē/ ee, ei	4, 31	4, 31	35–36, 49–50, 57–58	183–186
Vowel Pairs /ō/ oa, oe, ow	7, 13, 18, 19, 26, 32, 42	7, 13, 18, 19, 26, 32, 42	37–38, 49–50, 57–58	183–186
Vowel Digraphs /e/, /ē/, /ā/, /ī/ ea, ie, ei, ey	2, 3, 5, 8, 14, 17, 23, 24, 27, 29, 30, 33, 34, 38	2, 3, 5, 8, 14, 17, 23, 24, 27, 29, 30, 33, 34, 41	39–44, 49–50, 57–58	183–186
Vowel Digraphs /o/ au, aw	16, 37	16, 37	43–44, 49–50, 57–58	183–186
Vowel Digraph /oo/, /o͞o/, /u/ oo	6, 11, 15, 20, 41	6, 11, 15, 20, 39	45–46, 49–50, 57–58	183–186
Vowel Digraph /i/, /o͞o/, ui	9, 39	9, 38	47–50, 57–58	183–186
Diphthongs /oi/ oi, oy	10, 18, 40	10, 18, 40	51–52, 57–58	183–186
Diphthongs /ou/ ou, ow	12, 36	12, 36	53–54, 57–58	183–186
Diphthong /oo/ ew	21, 25, 35	21, 25, 35	55–58	183–186
Syllables	43–45	43–45	55–58	195

Name _____

> Read each set of two words in the first column. Fill in the circle beside **same** if a set of words has the same vowel sound, or by **different** if the set of words has different sounds.

1. mayor, explain	○ same	○ different
2. yield, pie	○ same	○ different
3. neat, creak	○ same	○ different
4. breeze, leisure	○ same	○ different
5. obey, reign	○ same	○ different
6. moose, stood	○ same	○ different
7. tiptoe, moan	○ same	○ different
8. skein, prey	○ same	○ different
9. biscuit, juice	○ same	○ different
10. spoil, toy	○ same	○ different
11. tycoon, bloom	○ same	○ different
12. owl, found	○ same	○ different
13. goal, thrown	○ same	○ different
14. weight, stay	○ same	○ different
15. flood, blood	○ same	○ different
16. caught, thaw	○ same	○ different
17. feather, thread	○ same	○ different
18. towel, groan	○ same	○ different
19. goes, bowl	○ same	○ different
20. nook, wood	○ same	○ different
21. shrewd, views	○ same	○ different

Go to the next page. →

BLM 9 Unit 2 Pretest: Vowel pairs, vowel digraphs, diphthongs

Name _____

> ► Read each word in the first column. Fill in the circle by the vowel sound that matches the sound of the underlined letters.

22. str<u>ai</u>n	○ short **a**	○ long **a**	○ short **i**
23. conv<u>ey</u>	○ long **e**	○ long **a**	○ short **e**
24. retr<u>ie</u>ve	○ long **i**	○ long **e**	○ short **i**
25. ask<u>ew</u>	○ long **u**	○ long **e**	○ short **e**
26. gr<u>ow</u>n	○ long **a**	○ long **o**	○ short **o**
27. w<u>ei</u>ght	○ short **e**	○ short **i**	○ long **a**
28. pl<u>ay</u>wright	○ short **i**	○ short **a**	○ long **a**
29. ph<u>ea</u>sant	○ long **e**	○ long **a**	○ short **e**
30. <u>ea</u>gle	○ long **a**	○ long **e**	○ short **e**
31. prot<u>ei</u>n	○ short **e**	○ long **e**	○ short **i**
32. thr<u>oa</u>t	○ long **a**	○ long **o**	○ short **o**
33. appl<u>ie</u>d	○ long **e**	○ long **i**	○ short **i**

> ► Read the words in the box. Write each word in the correct column. Then circle the vowel pair, vowel digraph, or diphthong in each word.

34. wheat	37. thesaurus	40. decoy
35. withdrew	38. treason	41. waterproof
36. however	39. juice	42. boast

One Syllable	Two Syllables	Three Syllables
43. _____	44. _____	45. _____
_____	_____	_____
_____	_____	_____

Possible score on Unit 2 Pretest is 45. Number correct _____

BLM 10 Unit 2 Pretest: Vowel pairs, vowel digraphs, diphthongs, syllables

Name _____

> Read each set of two words in the first column. Fill in the circle beside **same** if a set of words has the same vowel sound, or by **different** if the set of words has different sounds.

1. tailor, play	○ same	○ different
2. tie, field	○ same	○ different
3. treat, bleach	○ same	○ different
4. sweet, receipt	○ same	○ different
5. survey, vein	○ same	○ different
6. room, brook	○ same	○ different
7. oboe, loan	○ same	○ different
8. conceit, whey	○ same	○ different
9. quiver, nuisance	○ same	○ different
10. embroidery, voyage	○ same	○ different
11. monsoon, snooze	○ same	○ different
12. growl, astound	○ same	○ different
13. toast, crowbar	○ same	○ different
14. freight, delay	○ same	○ different
15. bloodhound, flooding	○ same	○ different
16. automobile, shawl	○ same	○ different
17. spread, bead	○ same	○ different
18. coast, trowel	○ same	○ different
19. mistletoe, elbow	○ same	○ different
20. hook, understood	○ same	○ different
21. pewter, nephew	○ same	○ different

Go to the next page. →

> Read each word in the first column. Fill in the circle by the vowel sound that matches the sound of the underlined letters.

22. drain	○ short **a**	○ long **a**	○ short **i**
23. obey	○ long **e**	○ long **a**	○ short **e**
24. grief	○ long **i**	○ long **e**	○ short **i**
25. blew	○ long **u**	○ long **e**	○ short **e**
26. shown	○ long **a**	○ long **o**	○ short **o**
27. reindeer	○ short **e**	○ short **i**	○ long **a**
28. spray	○ short **i**	○ short **a**	○ long **a**
29. pleasant	○ long **e**	○ long **a**	○ short **e**
30. beast	○ long **a**	○ long **e**	○ short **e**
31. seizure	○ short **e**	○ long **e**	○ short **i**
32. roast	○ long **a**	○ long **o**	○ short **o**
33. notified	○ long **e**	○ long **o**	○ long **i**

> Read the words in the box. Write each word in the correct column. Then circle the vowel pair, vowel digraph, or diphthong in each word.

34. beagle	37. dinosaur	40. employ
35. strewn	38. bruise	41. threat
36. powerful	39. schoolmaster	42. floated

One Syllable	Two Syllables	Three Syllables
43. _____	44. _____	45. _____
_____	_____	_____
_____	_____	_____

Possible score on Unit 2 Posttest is 45. Number correct _____

Student Progress Checklist

Make as many copies as needed to use for a class list. For individual portfolio use, cut apart each student's section. As indicated by the code, color in boxes next to skills satisfactorily assessed and mark an X by those requiring reteaching. Marked boxes can later be colored in to indicate mastery.

STUDENT PROGRESS CHECKLIST

Code: ■ Satisfactory   ☒ Needs Reteaching

Student:_____
_____

Pretest Score: _____

Posttest Score: _____

Skills

❒ Vowel Pairs *ai, ay*
❒ Vowel Pairs *ee, ei*
❒ Vowel Pairs *oa, oe, ow*
❒ Vowel Digraph *ea*
❒ Vowel Digraph *ie*
❒ Vowel Digraphs *ei, ey*
❒ Vowel Digraphs *au, aw*
❒ Vowel Digraph *oo*
❒ Vowel Digraph *ui*
❒ Diphthongs *oi, oy*
❒ Diphthongs *ou, ow*
❒ Diphthong *ew*
❒ Syllables

Comments / Learning Goals

Student:_____
_____

Pretest Score: _____

Posttest Score: _____

Skills

❒ Vowel Pairs *ai, ay*
❒ Vowel Pairs *ee, ei*
❒ Vowel Pairs *oa, oe, ow*
❒ Vowel Digraph *ea*
❒ Vowel Digraph *ie*
❒ Vowel Digraphs *ei, ey*
❒ Vowel Digraphs *au, aw*
❒ Vowel Digraph *oo*
❒ Vowel Digraph *ui*
❒ Diphthongs *oi, oy*
❒ Diphthongs *ou, ow*
❒ Diphthong *ew*
❒ Syllables

Comments / Learning Goals

Spelling Connections

INTRODUCTION

The Unit Word List is a comprehensive list of spelling words drawn from this unit. The words are grouped by phonetic element. To incorporate spelling into your word study program, use the activity in the Curriculum Connections section of each teaching plan.

The spelling lessons utilize the following approach for each set of words.

1. Administer a pretest of the words that have not yet been introduced. Dictation sentences are provided.

2. Provide practice.

3. Reassess. Dictation sentences are provided.

A final test is provided in Lesson 27 on page 60.

DIRECTIONS

Make a copy of Blackline Master 14 for each student. After administering the pretest for the sounds of the various letters and combinations, give each student a copy of the appropriate word list.

Students can work with a partner to practice spelling the words orally and identifying the appropriate sound in each word. They can also make and use letter cards to form the words on the list. You may want to challenge students to identify other words that have the same sound variant or combination. Students can write words of their own on *My Own Word List* (see Blackline Master 14).

Have students store their list words in an envelope or plastic zipper bag in the back of their books or notebooks. Alternatively, you may want to suggest that students keep a spelling notebook, listing words with similar patterns. You could also invite students to build word-wall displays in the classroom. Each section of the wall can focus on words with a single word study element. The walls will become a good spelling resource when students are writing.

UNIT WORD LIST

ai, ay; ee, ei; oa, oe, ow; ea; ie

acquaintance
delay
proceed
ceiling
groan
tiptoe
outgrow
sweater
yield
cried

ei, ey; au, aw; oo; ui; oi, oy; ou, ow; ew

vein
obey
autumn
lawyer
juice
moist
enjoy
mountain
vowels
newspaper

Name _____

 **S**pelling

UNIT 2 WORD LIST

ai, ay; ee, ei; oa, oe, ow; ea; ie

acquaintance	tiptoe
delay	outgrow
proceed	sweater
ceiling	yield
groan	cried

ei, ey; au, aw; oo; ui; oi, oy; ou, ow; ew

vein	moist
obey	enjoy
autumn	mountain
lawyer	vowels
juice	newspaper

My Own Word List

Word Study Games, Activities, and Technology

The following collection of ideas offers a variety of opportunities to reinforce word study skills while actively engaging students. The games, activities, and technology suggestions can easily be adapted to meet the needs of your group of learners. They vary in approach so as to consider students' different learning styles.

● THE SUPERMARKET GAME

Have partners create a circular game board with 12 spaces on which to land. Tell them to print one of the following words on each space: *bread; chowder; flounder; beef; cheese; peas; cauliflower; honeydew; cantaloupe; strawberries; pie; juice.* Partners take turns rolling a number cube or die and moving that number of spaces. A player landing on a space "buys" the item by identifying the vowel combination and saying the word. (Identifying both combinations in *cauliflower* gains an extra turn.) Play continues until one player has filled his or her "shopping cart" with every item. Invite partners to find other appropriate names for supermarket items that can be used to play again.

▲ WHAT'S THE ANSWER?

Have the class play "What's the answer?" Explain that you are going to ask some questions, and that the answers should be words that contain the vowel pairs *ai, ay, ee, ei, oa, oe,* or *ow.* For example, the word *boat* can answer the question "What kind of vehicle do people use to ride on the water?" Create questions based on these answers: *crayon, steed, arrow, blackboard, doe, holiday, breeze, rain,* and *protein.* As each answer is given, write it on the chalkboard and ask a volunteer to circle the vowel pair. Challenge students to add original questions and answers to the list.

◆ PHONEMIC TRACK MEET

Provide each student with a sheet of paper titled "Track Meet" and three rows headed *Marathon, 60-yard Dash, 400-meter Hurdle.* Explain that the marathon is a long race, the dash is a short race, and the hurdle race has its own special feature—runners must jump barriers as they run. Tell students that you are going to pronounce a series of words from the unit. When they hear a word with a long vowel sound (such as *obey*), they should write it in the *Marathon* row. When they hear a word with a short sound (such as *bread*), they should write it beside *60-yard Dash.* A word with a special sound all its own (such as *caught*) belongs with *400-meter Hurdle.*

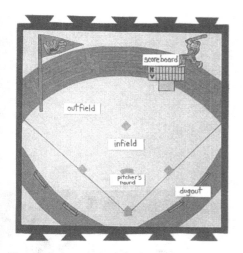

■ TAKE ME OUT TO THE BALL GAME

Have students draw and decorate a diagram of a baseball park. Tell them to imagine that they are watching a game. On their diagram they can list appropriate people, places, and things they see whose names contain vowel pairs, digraphs, and diphthongs. Examples are *diamond, infield, outfield, dugout; players, scoreboard, peanuts, pitcher's mound*.

Variation: Adapt this activity to football, basketball, skating, gymnastics, or any other sport.

✳ A WALK IN THE COUNTRY

Distribute to the class printed copies of the paragraph at right, including the words in parentheses. Have individuals underline the vowel pairs, vowel digraphs, and diphthongs and indicate whether the sound in each is long (L), short (S), or special (SP). Alternatively, you could leave blanks, list the words below the paragraph, and challenge partners to insert the listed words in appropriate places.

> The (w<u>ea</u>ther) was (bl<u>ea</u>k). It had been a (r<u>aw</u>), (r<u>ai</u>ny) (d<u>ay</u>). A (b<u>oy</u>), weary from a day of (t<u>oi</u>l) in the (f<u>ie</u>lds), walked (sl<u>ow</u>ly) home. As night fell, he (appr<u>oa</u>ched) a (w<u>oo</u>ded) area. A (l<u>ou</u>d) (n<u>oi</u>se) made his (bl<u>oo</u>d) run cold. A (h<u>au</u>nted) (f<u>ee</u>ling) (s<u>ei</u>zed) him. His (m<u>oo</u>d) changed abruptly as an (<u>ow</u>l) (fl<u>ew</u>) from a (tr<u>ee</u>) and (sw<u>oo</u>ped) (l<u>ow</u>) over his (h<u>ea</u>d). He (l<u>au</u>ghed) as he (r<u>ea</u>lized) the (s<u>ou</u>nd) he had heard was the (q<u>ui</u>vering) of the bird's wings as it hunted for (pr<u>ey</u>).

● I AM THINKING OF A WORD

Have students play "I am thinking of a word." Write each of the answers to the clues below on an index card. Hold the card to your forehead (with the word hidden). Before you give the hints, explain that each answer is a word that contains the same vowel sound as that of *boy*. When the correct answer is given, look at the card and say, "Right again."

1. I am thinking of a word that names a piece of stamped metal used as money. (*coin*)

2. I am thinking of a word that names a long journey, especially one taken on a boat. (*voyage*)

3. I am thinking of a word that names a substance that can cause illness or death. (*poison*)

4. I am thinking of a word that names the rank or power of a king or queen. (*royalty*)

Write the following words on the board and continue the game with the diphthongs *ou* and *ow*: *town, mountain, shout, plow, blouse, hound, mouse, growl, owl, round, snout, brown, mouth.* As you give hints, tell students to write each answer on a card, which they can hold to their foreheads as they respond.

▲ LISTEN! DO YOU HEAR?

Tell students to close their eyes and imagine that they are sitting on a porch in the middle of a warm sunny afternoon. They should think of the sounds in the environment that they might hear and write a list as they come to mind. Challenge students to include as many words as possible that include vowel pairs, vowel digraphs, and diphthongs.

Variation: Have students imagine that they have just awakened in the middle of the night.

◆ GRAND OPENING: MY CLOTHING STORE

Tell students to imagine that they have purchased a clothing store with a partner. Before the grand opening they want to conduct an inventory—make an itemized list—of their goods. The purpose is to ensure that their store carries whatever customers might want in the clothing line, including footwear. Have student partners work together to list different kinds of clothing and underline all the vowel combinations in the various words. You might suggest that partners draw a floor plan and organize their wares. For example, they can decide which articles they would group together, which items they would place near front windows to attract passersby, and which objects they would place in middle aisles or along walls. (You might combine this activity with Blackline Master 15 by suggesting students create clothed mannequins for their store.)

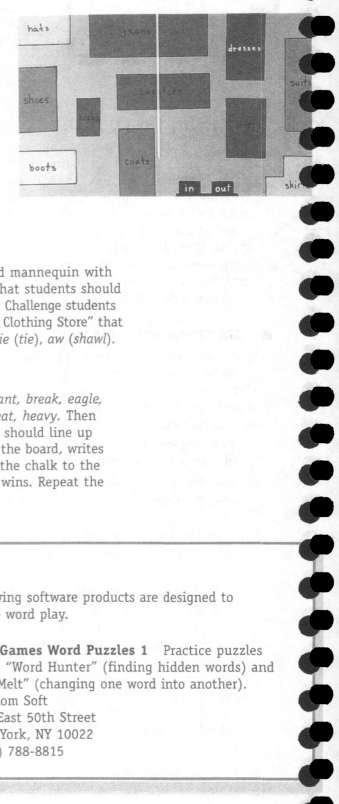

■ PHONEME ANATOMY

Distribute copies of Blackline Master 15, which illustrates a child mannequin with incomplete words indicated under appropriate headings. Explain that students should complete each word with vowel combinations discussed in this unit. Challenge students to draw new lines and add articles of clothing from the activity "My Clothing Store" that include examples of these sounds: long *e* in *ea* (*sneakers*), long *i* in *ie* (*tie*), *aw* (*shawl*).

● CHALK RELAY RACE

Write these words on the board: *squeal, feather, seal, leash, pleasant, break, eagle, spread, treasure, neat, east, steak, bread, team, healthy, clean, great, heavy.* Then invite teams of six students to have a chalk relay race. Each team should line up ten feet from the board. At a signal the first team member goes to the board, writes one word from the list with *ea* that stands for long *e*, then takes the chalk to the next player. The first team to write six long *e* words from the list wins. Repeat the game with words with *ea* standing for the short *e* sound.

Technology

The following software products are designed to encourage word play.

Merriam-Webster's Dictionary for Kids   Students can use this online dictionary to find the meanings of 20,000 words and play a variety of word games.
**Mindscape
  88 Roland Way
  Novato, CA 94945
  (800) 234-3088

Smart Games Word Puzzles 1   Practice puzzles include "Word Hunter" (finding hidden words) and "Word Melt" (changing one word into another).
**Random Soft
  201 East 50th Street
  New York, NY 10022
  (800) 788-8815

Phoneme Anatomy

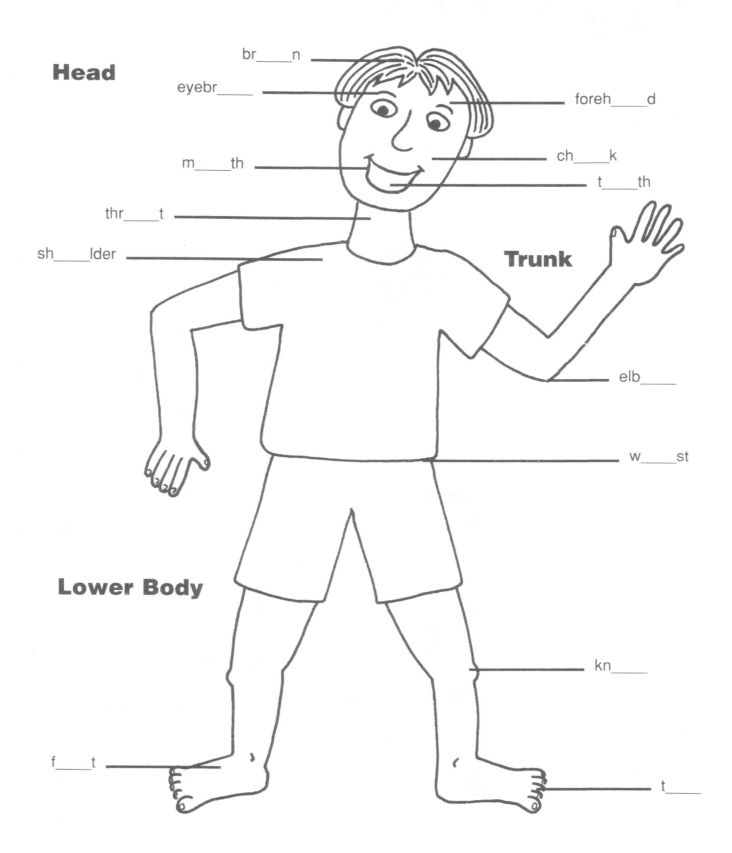

Head

br____n

eyebr____

foreh____d

m____th

ch____k

t____th

thr____t

sh____lder

Trunk

elb____

w____st

Lower Body

kn____

f____t

t____

Home Connection

HOME LETTER

A letter is available to be sent home at the beginning of Unit 2. This letter informs family members that students will be learning to read and write words containing vowel pairs, vowel digraphs, and diphthongs. The suggested home activity revolves around discovering words containing these vowel combinations in newspapers, magazines, and homework papers. This activity promotes interaction between child and family members while supporting the student's learning of reading and writing words with the targeted word study skills. A letter is also available in Spanish on page 31q.

Dear Family,

Ask your child to share what we'll be reviewing in the next few weeks: pairs of vowels that spell either a single sound (like ie in field) or a more complex vowel sound called a vowel diphthong (like ou in cloud). We'll also be learning that the number of syllables in a word is not determined by the number of vowels in the word, but by the number of vowel sounds that the word contains. (For example, the vowel pair oa contains two vowels but makes a single vowel sound.)

At-Home Activities

▶ Ask your child to show you the hidden pictures on the other side of this letter. Encourage him or her to write a story about the picture.

▶ Ask your child to find out the population of your city or town. If possible, have him or her also research three or four interesting facts about your city or town.

Book Corner

You and your child might enjoy reading these books together. Look for them at your local library.

Running Out of Time
by Margaret Peterson Haddix

A desperate child must leave the reconstructed 1840's village in which she lives and escape to the modern world in order to find medical help for her village.

Secret City, USA
by Felice Holman

Holman's moving novel depicts two friends who transform an abandoned building into a refuge for the inner city's homeless.

Sincerely,

_____

Carta para la casa

Estimada familia,

Pídanle a su hijo/a que comparta con ustedes lo que vamos a estar repasando en las próximas semanas: pares de vocales que tienen un sólo sonido, como la **ie** en **field** (**campo**) o un sonido de vocal más complejo llamado un diptongo de vocal, tal como **ou** en **cloud** (**nube**). También vamos a aprender que el número de sílabas en una palabra en inglés no se determina por el número de sonidos de vocal que contenga la palabra. (Por ejemplo, el par de vocales **oa** contiene dos vocales pero tiene el sonido de una vocal sencilla.)

Actividades para hacer en casa

▶ Pídanle a su hijo/a que les muestre las imágenes escondidas en la página 31 de su libro. Anímenle a que escriba un cuento sobre la ilustración.

▶ Pídanle a su hijo/a que averigüe la población de su ciudad o pueblo. Si es posible, pídanle que investigue tres o cuatro datos interesantes acerca de su pueblo o ciudad.

Rincón del libro

Su hijo/a y ustedes pueden disfrutar juntos de la lectura de estos libros. Búsquenlos en la biblioteca de su localidad.

Running Out of Time
por Margaret Peterson Maddix

Una niña desesperada se ve forzada a abandonar la aldea reconstruida de los años 1840 donde vive, para escapar al mundo moderno y hallar asistencia médica para su aldea.

Secret City, U.S.A.
por Felice Holman

Esta emotiva novela de Holman presenta dos amigos que transforman un edificio abandonado en un refugio para los desamparados de los barrios pobres de la ciudad.

Atentamente, _____

Unit 2

Pages 31–32

Words With ar, or, er, ir, ur;
Sounds of k, f, s; **Silent Letters; Syllables**

ASSESSING PRIOR KNOWLEDGE

To assess students' prior knowledge of words with ar, or, er, ir, ur; k, f, and s sounds; silent letters; and syllables, use the pretest on pages 31e–31f.

Unit Focus

USING THE PAGE

- Talk with students about the importance of being observant in everyday life. Then have them cover the questions at the bottom of page 31 and study the illustration carefully.

- Now have students cover the picture and recall what they saw. Read the questions at the bottom of the page for students to answer.

BUILDING A CONTEXT

- Write on the board had, hard; cod, cord; gem, germ; bid, bird; bun, burn. Ask students to say the pairs and notice the vowel sound changes when r follows the vowel.

- Write phone, laugh, face and chorus, unique. Say the words and ask what sound each set has in common. (/f/, /k/) Then have students compare the sound of qu in unique with the qu in quick. (/k/ and /kw/)

- Write seven, sure, and reason and ask students to compare the sound that s stands for in each word. (/s/, /sh/, /z/)

- Have students say the name of the sausage vendor in the picture. (Rhoda) Write Rhoda and ask if they hear the h when they say Rhoda.

- Write pointing on the board. Have students count the vowel letters (3) and vowel sounds (2). Explain that the number of vowel sounds is the number of syllables in a word.

31

UNIT 2 — Vowel Pairs, Digraphs, Diphthongs, Syllables

Which picture was the hardest to find? Which was the easiest to find? Why?

Circle the following items in the picture: an owl on a steeple, a toy sailboat, a woman wearing a shawl, a dog on a leash, a boy walking on tiptoe, a man wearing a sweater with an eagle design, a man pushing a wheelbarrow full of flowers, a fruit tree, a cloud in the shape of a sheep, a flowing fountain, a woman reading a newspaper, and a man with a bow tie playing the guitar.

Critical Thinking

Unit 2 Introduction   31

UNIT OPENER ACTIVITIES

TRACKING DETAILS

Begin a discussion again about the importance of memory and of keeping track of details. Ask some of the details students must remember each day, such as remembering to do household tasks, feed a pet, or do homework or practice a musical instrument.

EYEWITNESS ACCOUNT

Ask another teacher to dress in a silly disguise and burst unexpectedly into your room, shout something complicated, and erase something from the board before leaving the room. Have each student write down everything they saw and heard. Compare students' accounts and discuss witness reliability.

PICTURE DETAILS

Have students browse through discarded magazines to find a picture in which there is a lot going on. Ask them to make up four questions about details in their picture. Have students exchange pictures for two minutes and then ask their questions. What kind of details are the hardest to remember?

Home Letter

Dear Family,

Ask your child to share what we'll be reviewing in the next few weeks: pairs of vowels that spell either a single sound (like ie in field) or a more complex vowel sound called a vowel diphthong (like ou in cloud). We'll also be learning that the number of syllables in a word is not determined by the number of vowels in the word, but by the number of vowel sounds that the word contains. (For example, the vowel pair oa contains two vowels but makes a single vowel sound.)

At-Home Activities

▶ Ask your child to show you the hidden pictures on the other side of this letter. Encourage him or her to write a story about the picture.

▶ Ask your child to find out the population of your city or town. If possible, have him or her also research three or four interesting facts about your city or town.

You and your child might enjoy reading these books together. Look for them at your local library.

Running Out of Time
by Margaret Peterson Haddix

A desperate child must leave the reconstructed 1840's village in which she lives and escape to the modern world in order to find medical help for her village.

Secret City, USA
by Felice Holman

Holman's moving novel depicts two friends who transform an abandoned building into a refuge for the inner city's homeless.

Sincerely,

_____

Unit 2
Introduction

BULLETIN BOARD

Have students create a mural or bulletin-board collage of urban life entitled "Around Town." They can attach pictures and articles cut out from newspapers and magazines and downloaded from computer sources. Invite students to look for words that contain the word study elements of this unit.

● The Home Letter on page 32 is intended to acquaint family members with the word study skills students will be studying in the unit. Students can tear out the page and take it home. Suggest that they complete the activities with a family member and check out the library books pictured on page 32 to read together.

● The Home Letter can also be found on page 31q in Spanish.

CURRICULUM CONNECTIONS ✳

SCIENCE

Have students research where different wild animals make their homes and what they feed on in the city. An interesting example might be the peregrine falcon. Students might also learn about the hardships some animals, such as deer, face when wild areas are developed and urbanized. What are the challenges and the advantages that the animals face? (The article about eagles in Lesson 22 will be helpful for this activity.)

MATH

Population can be stated as the number of people who live within a city's limits or it can include the larger number of people who live in the suburbs around the city as well. The population of São Paulo, Brazil, is 8,490,763; while the population of the entire São Paulo area is about 16,832,285. Students can use state almanacs to find and list in order the largest cities in their state. Do the figures include city-only or entire-area populations? Does the ranking of the cities' sizes change if area figures are used as opposed to those for the cities only?

ART

Provide a variety of magazines, some that feature nature and animals and others that feature people and urban situations. Have students look for images in the magazines that they can cut out and add to the "Around Town" bulletin board or use to make their own "City Life/Country Life" collages.

Lesson 14

Pages 33–34

Vowel Pairs *ai*, *ay*

Lesson Focus

INTRODUCING THE SKILL

- Say the following sentence: *We watched a play today.* Ask which two words rhyme. (*play, today*)

- Repeat the exercise with the sentence: *We rode the train in the rain.* (*train, rain*)

- Ask students to identify the vowel sound in the rhyming words. (*long* a)

- Invite volunteers to write the two sentences from above on the board. Have a volunteer circle the letter pairs that represent the long *a* sound in the words. (*ay, ai*)

USING THE PAGES

- Have students read the long vowel rule in the box on page 33 and apply it to the vowel pairs *ai* and *ay* in *paint* and *may*. Explain that *y* is considered part of the vowel sound in *ay*.

- Ask students to read the four sets of directions on pages 33 and 34 and ask any questions they have. After they have completed the pages, encourage them to discuss what they have learned about the sound of the vowel pairs *ai* and *ay*.

Name _____

▶ Write a word from the word bank to correctly complete each sentence. Use each word only once.

1. More than 200 citizens gathered at the park last _____Saturday_____.

2. The _____mayor_____ was scheduled to make an important announcement.

3. She wanted to _____explain_____ the plans for building a new town library.

4. The crowd _____waited_____ patiently for the chief official to arrive.

5. Some people were feeling _____playful_____ and organized a ballgame.

6. Others were content to chat with old _____acquaintances_____.

7. Then the day turned cold and _____gray_____.

8. It began to _____rain_____ before the mayor arrived.

9. This _____delayed_____ the mayor's speech.

10. Many people did not _____stay_____ to hear her talk.

> **RULE**
> A **vowel pair** follows the long vowel rule: When a syllable contains two vowels, the first vowel usually has the long sound of its name and the second vowel is silent.
>
> The vowel pairs **ai** and **ay** follow the long vowel rule and can stand for the **a** sound.
>
> p**ai**nt   m**ay**

gray	waited
stay	playful
acquaintances	delayed
mayor	Saturday
explain	rain

▶ Underline each word in which **ai** stands for the **a** sound. Circle each word in which **ay** stands for the **a** sound.

waist   (crayon)   sailboat   scallops   faith   diagram   exclaim

magnify   train   (delay)   gain   daisy   fake   bait

taste   braid   painful   gnats   parcel   (bay)   (Tuesda...)

(playwright)   (may)   paid   (archway)   daily   (relay)   dainty

claim   aid

Lesson 14
Vowel pairs ai, ay   **33**

✦ FOCUS ON ALL LEARNERS ✦ ●◆■

ENGLISH LANGUAGE LEARNERS/ESL

Ask students to make the long *a* sound. Provide assistance as needed. Explain that different letter combinations can spell this sound in English and that this lesson covers two of them.

VISUAL LEARNERS

INDIVIDUAL Have students find ten words with each of the vowel pairs *ai* and *ay* in a textbook of their choice. Ask them to list the words and circle the ones whose meaning or pronunciation they are unsure of. Later have students write these words on the chalkboard and discuss them together.

KINESTHETIC LEARNERS

LARGE GROUP Invite students to select words with *ai* and *ay* and scramble the letters to write the words on the board. Students can call on classmates to unscramble and rewrite the words.

33

Read each numbered word below. Write the word from the word bank that has the opposite meaning.

gain	display	fail	plain	playful	rainy
decay	daytime	stay	afraid	delay	daily

1. fancy _plain_
2. brave _afraid_
3. conceal _display_
4. leave _stay_
5. serious _playful_
6. nightly _daily_
7. nighttime _daytime_
8. pass _fail_
9. sunny _rainy_
10. flourish _decay_
11. begin _delay_
12. lose _gain_

Each numbered word in the list below has something to do with transportation. Read each definition. Then write the letter of the correct definition by each word.

j 13. monorail
i 14. railway
h 15. driveway
a 16. sailboat
d 17. trail
e 18. alleyway
g 19. runway
c 20. subway
b 21. highway
f 22. trailer

a. a boat that is moved by one or more sails
b. a main road
c. an electric railroad running below the surface of city streets
d. a path hikers use
e. narrow back street in a city or town
f. a vehicle that is pulled behind a car
g. paved strip of land at an airport on which aircraft take off and land
h. path for cars that leads from a road to a garage or house
i. track made of rails
j. train that moves along on one rail

34   Lesson 14
Vowel pairs ai, ay

AUDITORY LEARNERS

SMALL GROUP

Invite students to use words from page 34 to create analogies that focus on opposites. As each analogy is said, suggest that students ask classmates to give the word to complete the analogy. For example: *dark is to nighttime as bright is to* ____ (daytime); *narrow is to alleyway as wide is to* ____(highway).

GIFTED LEARNERS

Invite students to use *ai* and *ay* words with rhyming elements to write couplets. Topics might include community gatherings, rainy weather, or different modes of transportation.

LEARNERS WHO NEED EXTRA SUPPORT

Review the sentences at the top of page 33 with students. Help them apply the long vowel rule to *ai* and *ay* words they are unsure of. **See Daily Word Study Practice, pages 183–186.**

SPELLING

You may use the following words and dictation sentences as a pretest for the first group of spelling words for Unit 2.

1. **acquaintance** Dad introduced his new **acquaintance**.
2. **delay** There was a **delay** when the parade reached Main Street.
3. **proceed** The passengers were told to **proceed** to the gate.
4. **ceiling** Jennifer glued stars to her bedroom **ceiling**.
5. **groan** The hiker let out a **groan** when he stumbled.
6. **tiptoe** The dancers ran on **tiptoe** across the stage.
7. **outgrow** I seem to **outgrow** my shoes as soon as I buy them.
8. **sweater** The red **sweater** was on sale for ten dollars.
9. **yield** Cars coming off the highway must **yield** to traffic.
10. **cried** The baby **cried** when her balloon floated away.

WRITING

Portfolio Have students write a brief speech for the mayor described on page 33. The speech should explain the plans for a new library and persuade the audience that the library is a good idea. Ask students to proofread their speeches, especially for correct use of *ai* and *ay* in words before presenting them to the group.

SOCIAL STUDIES

Engage students in creating a transportation timeline. Students can find information in social studies books, nonfiction library books or encyclopedias, and history magazines to show the development and decline of each type of transportation.

MATH

Have students call, write, or use published fares to obtain current rate, route, and schedule information for bus, plane, or train travel in the United States. Ask them to determine distances between pairs of destinations and use the schedules to learn how long the trips take.

Lesson 15

Pages 35–36

Vowel Pairs *ee, ei*

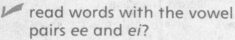

Lesson Focus

INTRODUCING THE SKILL

- Read aloud the sentence *Lee and Keith received three cards.* Ask students to identify the words that have the long *e* sound.

- Invite a student to write the sentence on the board. Ask a volunteer to circle the letter pairs that stand for the long *e* sound. *(ee, ei)*

- Write the words *weekly, marquee, protein, either,* and *leisure.* Have volunteers circle the long *e* vowel pairs and use each word in a sentence.

- Ask students to explain the rule that applies to the long vowel sound in these words. (See page 33.)

USING THE PAGES

Discuss the rule on page 35 and apply it to *bee* and *ceiling.* Be sure students understand the directions for pages 35 and 36 before beginning to work. Afterward, encourage them to discuss what they have learned about *ee* and *ei* in words.

Name _____

▶ Circle the letters that stand for the e sound.

> **RULE**
> The vowel pairs **ee** and **ei** can stand for the e sound.
> b**ee** c**ei**ling

1. thr**ee**
2. l**ei**sure
3. dungar**ee**s
4. proc**ee**d
5. s**ei**zure
6. w**ee**kly
7. pedigr**ee**
8. prot**ei**n
9. wh**ee**ls
10. c**ei**ling
11. marqu**ee**
12. n**ei**ther
13. st**ee**ple
14. br**ee**ze
15. agr**ee**

▶ Use a word from the list above to answer each riddle.

16. Found in such foods
As eggs, milk, and meat,
It helps build strong bones,
From our head to our feet.
What is it? **protein**

17. If you want to know
The name of the show,
Look on the sign
With its lights aglow.
What is it? **marquee**

18. Cars and buses have them.
Trucks and bikes do, too.
Some have four, some have sixteen,
and some have only two.
What are they? **wheels**

19. Best of the breed and winner of fame,
Sometimes a dog has papers that name
The ancestry from which it came.
What is it? **pedigree**

20. Time off from school,
From work, from chores—
It's time many people
Spend outdoors.
What is it?
leisure

21. Opposite the floor,
High above your head,
You may stare at this
When you're in bed.
What is it?
ceiling

22. One plus two,
Four minus one,
Solve either problem.
The riddle is done.
What is the answer?
three

FOCUS ON ALL LEARNERS

ENGLISH LANGUAGE LEARNERS/ESL

You may wish to have students work the puzzle on page 36 "backwards." Provide the lists of answer words, practice reading them with students, and then have students do the puzzle.

AUDITORY LEARNERS

INDIVIDUAL Challenge students to use as many words as possible with the long *e* sound in sentences to say aloud for the class. For example: *The three judges indeed agree that neither dog is a pedigree*

KINESTHETIC LEARNERS

PARTNER **Materials:** board-game letter tiles

Have partners give one another a set of letter tiles to arrange to form a word with *ee* or *ei*.

Find words in the puzzle that have the vowel pairs **ee** or **ei**. Some go across, and others go down. Circle each word you find. Then write the word in the correct column.

```
E I T H E R B C D A Z L M N G
B O E B F E E T L L F G D B C
D R I F G C P N M L F G D B C
T H T G R E E D N H A F R E E
L C H G L I Z M S U C C E E D
M C P C Z P H X E Y R F C A E
O U B C D T R E E T G M E Z X
A B Z Y X W Z N M K R A I Y E
D E C E I V E L S T Z B V W I
Z T G M C V O E R N W M E E T
```

ee words

feet	seems
free	succeed
greed	bee
meet	tree

ei words

either
deceive
receive
receipt

Write a word you found in the puzzle to complete each sentence.

1. I hope that I ____receive____ a good grade on my paper.
2. I should get ____either____ an A or a B.
3. It ____seems____ like I spent a month writing it!
4. I know it takes hard work to ____succeed____ .
5. This Saturday, however, I will enjoy some ____free____ time.
6. I plan to ____meet____ some friends.
7. At one o'clock they'll be in front of the oak ____tree____ in the park.

36   Lesson 15
Vowel pairs ee, ei

VISUAL LEARNERS

LARGE GROUP

Have volunteers compose riddles for any of the words on page 35 that were not used on the lower half of the page. Classmates can refer to the page to find, and then write on the board, the correct answers.

GIFTED LEARNERS

Have partners create hidden-word puzzles using *ee* and *ei* words, like the one on page 36. Encourage them to use words beyond those on the pages. Students can solve another pair's puzzle or you might duplicate puzzles for all students to share.

LEARNERS WHO NEED EXTRA SUPPORT

Review the words from the lesson by having each student choose the *ee* word and the *ei* word that are the most difficult for him or her, write them on a card, and use the words in speaking and writing at least once that day. **See Daily Word Study Practice, pages 183–186.**

SPELLING

On the board write the vowel pairs and vowel digraphs *ai, ay, oa, ee, ei, oe, ow, ea,* and *ie* as well as the spelling words with letters missing as shown:

proc__d, y__ld, acqu__ntance, outgr__ , gr__n, del__ , cr__d, c__ling, sw__ter, tipt__. Have students write in the correct vowels to complete the word that matches each definition you read aloud to them.

1. someone known slightly *(acquaintance)*
2. a pause *(delay)*
3. continue *(proceed)*
4. top part of a room *(ceiling)*
5. make a low, unhappy noise *(groan)*
6. on top of one's feet *(tiptoe)*
7. get too big for *(outgrow)*
8. a warm garment *(sweater)*
9. give in to *(yield)*
10. sobbed *(cried)*

WRITING

Reread the context sentences at the bottom of page 36. Then ask students to write their own ideas for "Ways to Succeed in School," using *ee* and *ei* words from pages 35 and 36 to convey some of their thoughts. List each different idea on a classroom chart. Invite students to note the spelling of *ee* and *ei* words that are included.

HEALTH

Portfolio Discuss what students know about protein and suggest that they read to find out more about it. Encourage students to obtain USDA dietary guidelines for protein. Have them check nutrition information on food labels and create low-fat daily menus that meet protein needs.

MATH

Invite students to conduct a poll among classmates to draw conclusions about favorite leisure activities. After asking what students like to do in their free time small groups can each display the results on a different type of graph, such as a bar graph, pictograph, circle graph, or a list of percentages.

Lesson 16

Pages 37–38

Vowel Pairs oa, oe, ow

INFORMAL ASSESSMENT OBJECTIVES

Can students

✔ associate the vowel pairs *oa*, *oe*, and *ow* with the long *o* sound?

✔ read words with the vowel pairs *oa*, *oe*, and *ow*?

Lesson Focus

INTRODUCING THE SKILL

- Ask students to identify the words with the long *o* sound in the following sentence: *Falling snow, heavy coats, and mistletoe remind me of winter.* (snow, coats, mistletoe)

- Invite a volunteer to write *snow*, *coats*, and *mistletoe* on the board. Have students contrast the spelling of the long *o* sound in the words and identify the letter pairs that represent the sound. *(ow, oa, oe)*

- Write *minnow*, *tiptoe*, and *toaster* on the board. Have volunteers tell which syllable in each word contains long *o* and circle the vowel pairs that stand for the sound.

USING THE PAGES

- Invite students to explain how the rule on page 37 fits the words *loan, toe,* and *flow.* Review the directions for both pages and identify the pictures on page 38 together.

- **Critical Thinking** Have students share their reactions to the context sentences on page 37 and the question that follows.

Name _____

▶ Fill in the circle beside the word that best completes each sentence. Write it on the line.

> **RULES**
> The vowel pairs **oa** and **oe** can stand for the **o** sound. The letters **ow** can also stand for the **o** sound.
> loan   toe   flow

1. Jack is an athletic boy who is always _____ boasting
   ○ floating   ● boasting   ○ outgrowing

2. He told everyone he got three strikes the last time he went _____ bowling .
   ○ floating   ○ glowing   ● bowling

3. He announced that he shot the _____ arrow into the center of the target.
   ○ mistletoe   ○ minnow   ● arrow

4. When he hit two home runs in a _____ row , Jack made sure everyone knew.
   ● row   ○ hoe   ○ mow

5. He notified the newspaper when he scored the most _____ goals in soccer.
   ● goals   ○ toes   ○ glows

6. Most of Jack's classmates _____ groan when he talks.
   ○ grow   ○ toe   ● groan

7. Some _____ tiptoe away so they won't have to listen.
   ○ outgrow   ○ throat   ● tiptoe

8. Others _____ throw up their hands in disgust.
   ○ tow   ○ toe   ● throw

9. Even the _____ coach is getting tired of Jack's attitude.
   ○ loaves   ○ bowstring   ● coach

10. He _____ slowly shakes his head when Jack brags.
    ● slowly   ○ showed   ○ stowaway

> **What do you think the other students could do to convince Jack to stop bragging?**
>
> Critical Thinking

Lesson 16
Vowel pairs oa, oe, ow   **37**

FOCUS ON ALL LEARNERS

ENGLISH LANGUAGE LEARNERS/ESL

Discuss words from students' first languages that have consecutive vowels. Do these vowels have separate sounds or do they combine to create one sound? Practice the lesson words, emphasizing the single sounds of the vowel pairs.

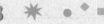

AUDITORY/VISUAL LEARNERS

LARGE GROUP

Have students brainstorm one-syllable and multisyllabic words with long *o*. Ask volunteers to write them on the board according to their vowel pairs. Create a column for long *o* words with other spellings if words such as *go, hope,* and *nose* are suggested.

KINESTHETIC LEARNERS

SMALL GROUP

Materials: magazines, newspapers, scissors

Invite students to cut out article titles and headlines that include *oa, oe,* and *ow* words. Suggest that they make a collage on a bulletin board.

Write the word from the word bank that names each picture. Then circle the letters that stand for the o sound.

boat	toaster	tiptoe	float	crow	coach
arrow	bowling	goat	elbow	goal	snow
wheelbarrow	loaves	soap	road		

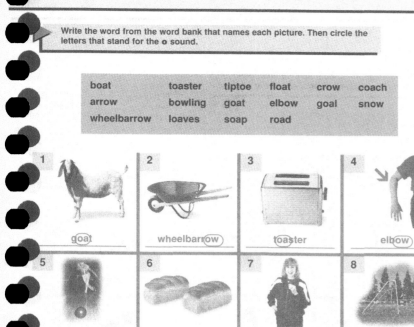

1. g**oa**t
2. wheelbarr**ow**
3. t**oa**ster
4. elb**ow**

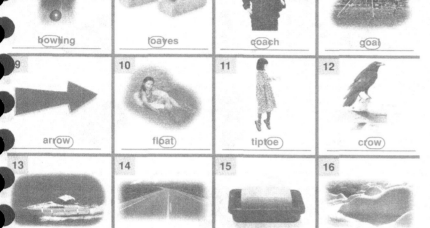

5. b**ow**ling
6. l**oa**ves
7. c**oa**ch
8. g**oa**l

9. arr**ow**
10. fl**oa**t
11. tipt**oe**
12. cr**ow**

13. b**oa**t
14. r**oa**d
15. s**oa**p
16. sn**ow**

AUDITORY/VISUAL LEARNERS

LARGE GROUP

Give clues to words from the lesson, or others, spelled with long *o* vowel pairs. Have volunteers spell each answer on the board and have others raise their hands if they agree with the answer and its spelling before the word is read.

GIFTED LEARNERS

Materials: audiocassette, cassette recorder

Invite students to see how many of the words from page 37 they can use in an original story that they record on an audiocassette.

LEARNERS WHO NEED EXTRA SUPPORT

Materials: index cards, stopwatch

Have students write all the words with *oa, oe,* and *ow* from pages 37 and 38 on separate cards. Have partners time one another as they read and sort the word cards according to vowel spelling. **See Daily Word Study Practice, pages 183–186.**

CURRICULUM CONNECTIONS ✳ ● ◆ ■ ◆ ●

SPELLING

Write the spelling words *acquaintance, delay, proceed, ceiling, groan, tiptoe, outgrow, sweater, yield,* and *cried* on the board. Divide students into teams of five and call two teams up to the front. Have students face one another. The first student on the team facing the board calls out a spelling word from the list and the student facing opposite must spell the word. Team members may encourage and help the speller. When the word has been spelled correctly, the two students exchange places by walking between the rows and taking a place at the end of the opposite team's row. Continue until all students have spelled a word.

WRITING

Portfolio Have students write brief pep talks they might give to athletes if they were coaches. Their talks should emphasize fair play and good sportsmanship. The context sentences on page 37 can serve as a basis for actions to avoid. Encourage students to word their advice as positive statements.

MATH

According to the American College of Sports Medicine, people need to exercise at their "training heart rate" to get the most out of aerobic exercise. Tell students to compute this rate for themselves by subtracting their age from 220, and then multiplying the answer by .6 and .8. The results indicate the range of their training heart rate—the range that their hearts should beat per minute when they are exercising.

ART

For thousands of years, artists have depicted people engaged in athletic activities, including ancient Greek statues showing athletes, Degas's paintings of ballet dancers, and photographs of contemporary sports heroes. Have students find examples of the athlete as art subject in books of art and art history.

Lesson 17
Pages 39–40

Vowel Digraph ea

INFORMAL ASSESSMENT OBJECTIVES

Can students

✔ associate the vowel digraph *ea* with the long *a*, long *e*, and short *e* sounds?

✔ read words with the vowel digraph *ea*?

Lesson Focus

INTRODUCING THE SKILL

- Say the words *stream, thread,* and *break*. Ask students to name the vowel sound they hear in each word. *(long e, short e, long a)*

- Invite volunteers to write *stream, thread,* and *break* on the board and name the vowel combination in each word. Lead students to conclude that *ea* stands for the long *e*, short *e*, and long *a* sounds.

- Explain that when *ea* stands for long *e*, it can be called a vowel pair. The long *e* sound is one of the vowel digraph sounds of *ea*. Read the rule on page 39 and ask how the meaning of a vowel digraph applies to the three sounds of *ea* in the words on the board. (The vowels *ea* together in each word make one long or short vowel sound.)

USING THE PAGES

- Have students apply the rule on page 39 to the words *steak, meat,* and *bread*. Identify the pictures on page 39 and explain the directions.

- Later, students can tell what they have learned about the vowel digraph *ea*.

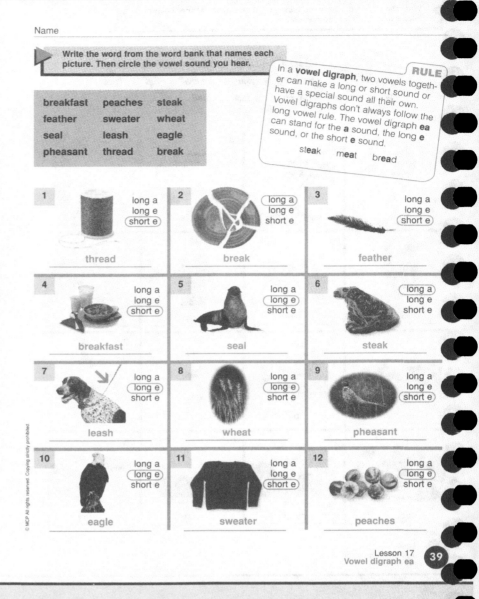

Name

Write the word from the word bank that names each picture. Then circle the vowel sound you hear.

breakfast	peaches	steak
feather	sweater	wheat
seal	leash	eagle
pheasant	thread	break

RULE

In a **vowel digraph**, two vowels together can make a long or short sound or have a special sound all their own. Vowel digraphs don't always follow the long vowel rule. The vowel digraph **ea** can stand for the **a** sound, the long **e** sound, or the short **e** sound.

steak   meat   bread

1. thread — long a / long e / (short e)
2. break — (long a) / long e / short e
3. feather — long a / long e / (short e)
4. breakfast — long a / long e / (short e)
5. seal — long a / (long e) / short e
6. steak — (long a) / long e / short e
7. leash — long a / (long e) / short e
8. wheat — long a / (long e) / short e
9. pheasant — long a / long e / (short e)
10. eagle — long a / (long e) / short e
11. sweater — long a / long e / (short e)
12. peaches — long a / (long e) / short e

FOCUS ON ALL LEARNERS

ENGLISH LANGUAGE LEARNERS/ESL

Remind learners that a vowel digraph represents a special vowel sound spelled with two vowels.

VISUAL LEARNERS

INDIVIDUAL **Materials:** newspapers

Ask students to circle words that contain the *ea* digraph in newspaper articles they have read. Later, compile and read the words. Note which words appear frequently in specific types of articles.

KINESTHETIC LEARNERS

PARTNER Have students write the *ea* words from page 39 on separate pieces of paper. Suggest that pairs of students create a word game using the word cards they have made. Pairs of students can teach one another how to play.

39

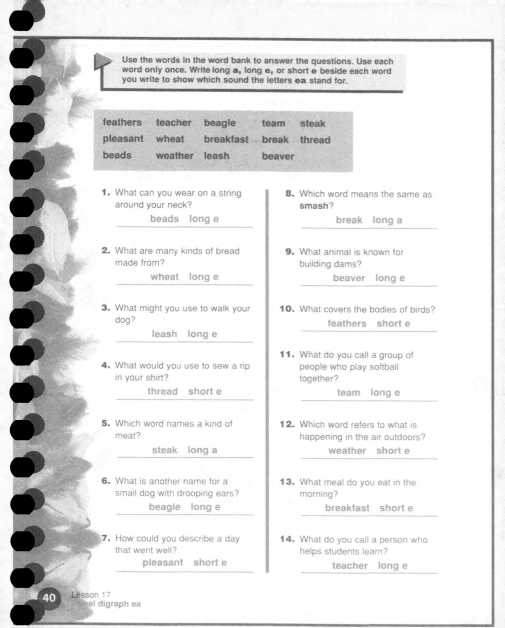

Use the words in the word bank to answer the questions. Use each word only once. Write long **a**, long **e**, or short **e** beside each word you write to show which sound the letters **ea** stand for.

feathers	teacher	beagle	team	steak
pleasant	wheat	breakfast	break	thread
beads	weather	leash	beaver	

1. What can you wear on a string around your neck?

    beads   long e

2. What are many kinds of bread made from?

    wheat   long e

3. What might you use to walk your dog?

    leash   long e

4. What would you use to sew a rip in your shirt?

    thread   short e

5. Which word names a kind of meat?

    steak   long a

6. What is another name for a small dog with drooping ears?

    beagle   long e

7. How could you describe a day that went well?

    pleasant   short e

8. Which word means the same as **smash**?

    break   long a

9. What animal is known for building dams?

    beaver   long e

10. What covers the bodies of birds?

    feathers   short e

11. What do you call a group of people who play softball together?

    team   long e

12. Which word refers to what is happening in the air outdoors?

    weather   short e

13. What meal do you eat in the morning?

    breakfast   short e

14. What do you call a person who helps students learn?

    teacher   long e

AUDITORY LEARNERS

LARGE GROUP

Challenge students to use as many *ea* words as possible in oral sentences, such as *I would rather eat wheat cereal with peaches for breakfast than eat steak and eggs.* Classmates can identify *ea* words that are used.

GIFTED LEARNERS

Have students sort the *ea* words on pages 39 and 40 into nouns, verbs, and other parts of speech. Then ask them to calculate what percentages of the words fall into each of the three categories.

LEARNERS WHO NEED EXTRA SUPPORT

Write *meat, bread,* and *steak* across the board. Tell students that they should write the *ea* words you say under the headings with the same digraph sound. Words might include *head, heat, feather, dream, great, peach, thread, beaver, sweater, teacher, break, leash,* and *wheat.* **See Daily Word Study Practice, pages 183–186.**

CURRICULUM CONNECTIONS ✳ ● ◆ ■ ◆ ●

SPELLING

Write these words on the board and ask students to choose one to complete each sentence that you read to them: *acquaintance, delay, proceed, ceiling, groan, tiptoe, outgrow, sweater, yield, cried.*

1. Is Will a friend of yours or just an ___? (*acquaintance*)
2. In a medical emergency, call for help without ___. (*delay*)
3. After you stop at the sign, you may ___ with caution. (*proceed*)
4. Lucy pointed at the spider on the ___. (*ceiling*)
5. Dad let out a ___ when he unwrapped his fourth tie. (*groan*)
6. Elizabeth walked down the stairs on ___ so that she wouldn't wake up her sleeping family. (*tiptoe*)
7. When you ___ this jacket, you can give it to your little brother. (*outgrow*)
8. I am knitting a ___ with three different colors of yarn. (*sweater*)
9. I want a television for my room, but my parents refuse to ___ to my request. (*yield*)
10. Clay ___ out in pain when the hornet stung him. (*cried*)

WRITING

Portfolio Tell students that words such as *squeak, bleat, creak,* and *squeal* are examples of *onomatopoeia*—words that name sounds and that sound like what they name. Have students write poems using these and other sound words.

SCIENCE

Challenge students to research interesting facts about animals with *ea* names from the lesson, such as *eagle, pheasant, seal, beagle,* and *beaver.*

MATH

As students do research on the eagle, pheasant, seal, beagle, and beaver, have them record body lengths. Then have students calculate the mean and median lengths of the animals.

Lesson 18

Pages 41–42

Vowel Digraph ie

Can students

✔ associate the vowel digraph *ie* with the long *e* sound and the long *i* sound?

✔ read words with the vowel digraph *ie*?

Lesson Focus

INTRODUCING THE SKILL

- On the board, write the sentence *The police chief was dissatisfied with the investigation.* Have a volunteer read the sentence.

- Underline *ie* in the words *chief* and *dissatisfied.* Ask whether the vowel sounds in the words match. (*no*) Ask what sounds the letters represent. (*long* e, *long* i)

- Guide students to conclude that the vowel digraph *ie* can stand for the long *e* sound or the long *i* sound.

- Write this sentence on the board and have a student read it aloud:

  I tried a piece of fried chicken.

- Ask volunteers to circle the word in which *ie* stands for the long *e* sound (*piece*) and to underline the words in which *ie* stands for the long *i* sound. (*tried, fried*)

USING THE PAGES

Have students read the rule on page 41 and apply it to *field* and *pie*. Be sure students understand the directions for pages 41 and 42.

41

Name _____

▶ Read the article. Circle each word in which the vowel digraph **ie** stands for the long **e** sound and underline each word in which **ie** stands for the long **i** sound.

> **RULE**
> The vowel digraph **ie** can stand for the long **e** sound or the long **i** sound.
> field   pie

Money! Money! Money!

Everyone knows what money is, but how did money come into being? Before people identified money, they bartered. Bartering is trading something that is no longer wanted or needed for something that is. Soon bartering became very difficult. People tried to make fair trades, but they grew more and more dissatisfied about retrieving equal value for the things they traded away. Don't forget, they also carried around with them everything they wanted to trade!

People began to believe that they needed to find a measure of exchange that everyone would agree to. Soon they identified a medium of exchange—that is, something against which the value of everything could be measured. In different parts of the world, different things were used as mediums of exchange. For centuries the medium of exchange in China was cowrie shells. Tea was the medium of exchange in Mongolia. In many countries people used salt. People tried everything from elephant's tails to fish hooks, dogs' teeth, feathers, and even petrified wood.

You may be wondering when things used as the medium of exchange yielded to money as we now know it. No one knows for certain, but it is commonly believed that about 5,000 years ago, people in Mesopotamia began using pieces of metal as money. Metal money made life much easier.

Metal money was used for thousands of years, but if traders had a lot of it, it could be heavy. Eventually a new species of money was born—paper money. It is not known for sure, but the earliest paper money is believed to have been made by the Chinese about A.D. 1300.

FOCUS ON ALL LEARNERS ☀ ● ◆ ■

ENGLISH LANGUAGE LEARNERS/ESL

Read the article about money together. Discuss the types of coins and paper money students may be familiar with from their native countries. Have students write the *ie* words from the article on cards and sort them according to vowel sound.

VISUAL LEARNERS

LARGE GROUP

Write base words ending in *y* on the board and have students add *-es* or *-ed,* causing the *y*'s to change to *i*'s and forming *ie* digraphs. Help students conclude that the digraph sounds match the *y* sounds in the base word. Base words might be *spy, try, fly, satisfy, carry, country, penny,* and *copy.*

AUDITORY/KINESTHETIC LEARNERS

SMALL GROUP

Have students write the *ie* words from page 41 on separate strips of paper. Have them take turns choosing a word to read and explain its connection to the history of money.

> Circle the vowel digraph in each **ie** word. Write long **i** if ie stands for the long i sound. Write long **e** if ie stands for the long e sound.

1. modified _____ long i
2. piece _____ long e
3. tie _____ long i
4. thief _____ long e
5. dissatisfied _____ long i
6. tried _____ long i

7. carries _____ long e
8. shield _____ long e
9. niece _____ long e
10. applied _____ long i
11. species _____ long e
12. horrified _____ long i

> Write a word from the word bank to complete each sentence.

Word Bank
identified
stories
bodies
species
flies
skies

13. In Brazil there are _____stories_____ of people attacked by tiny, winged alligators.
14. These creatures fly through the _____skies_____, terrifying all those who see them.
15. In reality there is no _____species_____ of alligator with wings!
16. However, scientists have _____identified_____ some strange-looking Brazilian insects.
17. These bugs are known either as lantern _____flies_____ or alligator bugs.
18. Attached to their small _____bodies_____ are large, alligator-shaped heads.

42 Lesson 18
Sounds of ie

VISUAL LEARNERS

PARTNER **Materials:** index cards

Have students select a sentence with at least one *ie* word from the article on page 41 and write each word on a separate card. Partners then reconstruct each other's sentence. Students can rotate to different partners and repeat the activity.

GIFTED LEARNERS

Have partners create word-search puzzles containing words with *ie*. Make copies of the puzzles for class use.

LEARNERS WHO NEED EXTRA HELP

Have students make lists of ten *ie* words from the lesson and underline the words with a long *i* sound in black and circle words with a long *e* sound in green. Have students read their lists by vowel sound. **See Daily Word Study Practice, pages 183–186.**

CURRICULUM CONNECTIONS

SPELLING

You may use the following words and dictation sentences as a posttest for the first set of spelling words for Unit 2.

1. **acquaintance** Mom saw a childhood **acquaintance**.
2. **delay** The flight **delay** was caused by weather.
3. **proceed** The wedding cannot **proceed** until the groom arrives.
4. **ceiling** The ball bounced so high it hit the **ceiling**.
5. **groan** I wanted to **groan** when I saw hot dogs for dinner again.
6. **tiptoe** Ballet dancers wear special shoes to dance on **tiptoe**.
7. **outgrow** If you **outgrow** that jacket, you can give it away.
8. **sweater** The **sweater** shrank when I washed it in hot water.
9. **yield** Mom will **yield** to our request to go to a movie.
10. **cried** Stephanie **cried** when her best friend moved away.

WRITING/SOCIAL STUDIES

Have students read to discover facts about the United States monetary system. Facts might include the meaning of the gold or silver standard, the history of U.S. money, how and where money is minted and printed, and changes taking place on some U.S. paper money. Students can record the facts on a chart.

MATH

If the rate of exchange between the English pound and the U.S. dollar is 1.56 dollars to 1 pound, what is the value in dollars of a British souvenir that costs 2 pounds? ($3.12) Have students write similar problems for solving.

SCIENCE

Portfolio After rereading the sentences about alligator bugs on page 42, find additional information about lantern flies or other interesting species found in the rainforests of South America. Students can choose an interesting way to share their findings.

42

Lesson 19
Pages 43–44

Vowel Digraphs ei, ey;
Vowel Digraphs au, aw

INFORMAL ASSESSMENT OBJECTIVES

Can students

✔ associate the vowel digraphs *ei* and *ey* with the long *a* sound?

✔ associate the vowel digraphs *au* and *aw* with the sound of *a* in *all*?

✔ read words with the vowel digraphs *ei*, *ey*, *au*, and *aw*?

Lesson Focus

INTRODUCING THE SKILLS

- Write *sleigh*, *weigh*, *they*, and *obey* on the board. Have volunteers read the words aloud and identify the two letters that stand for the long *a* sound in each word. *(ei* or *ey)*

- Write *August*, *laundry*, *fawn*, and *paw* on the board and have the class read them aloud. Ask volunteers to circle the two letters in each word that represent the sound of *a* heard in *all*. *(au* or *aw)*

- Help students conclude that the vowel digraphs *ei* and *ey* can stand for the long *a* sound. Guide students to note that the vowel digraphs *au* and *aw* both stand for the sound of *a* in *all*.

USING THE PAGES

- Read the directions and the rules on pages 43 and 44 before students begin.

- **Critical Thinking** Invite students to share their conclusions about the character of the celebrity on page 44.

Name _____

▶ Use the words from the word bank to work the crossword puzzle.

RULE
The vowel digraphs **ei** and **ey** can stand for the long **a** sound.
   rein   obey

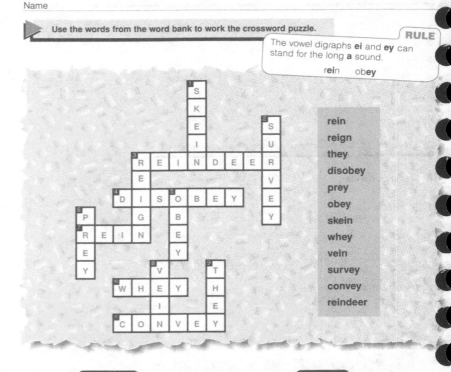

Word Bank:
rein
reign
they
disobey
prey
obey
skein
whey
vein
survey
convey
reindeer

Across

3. animal found in Greenland and some countries in northern Europe
4. to deliberately go against an order
7. a strap a horseback rider holds
10. thin, watery part of milk that appears when cheese is made
11. to take from one place to another

Down

1. a coil of yarn
2. to examine or inspect something
3. to rule over a country
5. to do what one is told
6. an animal that is hunted
8. a blood vessel that carries blood to the heart
9. a pronoun to describe persons, animals, or things

Lesson 19
Vowel digraphs ei, ey **43**

FOCUS ON ALL LEARNERS ✴ ● ◆ ■ ◆

ENGLISH LANGUAGE LEARNERS/ESL

As students work on these pages, explain that the vowel combinations in this lesson are examples of sounds that can be spelled in more than one way. Have students circle the spellings in digraph groups of words as they use the same sound to read them.

VISUAL LEARNERS

INDIVIDUAL Have students create written "equations" that link the vowel digraphs *ei*, *ey*, *au*, and *aw* with the sounds they make in certain words, for example, in *rein*, *ei* = long *a*.

VISUAL/KINESTHETIC LEARNERS

LARGE GROUP Have students take turns writing words on the board from pages 43 and 44, omitting the vowel digraph *ei*, *ey*, *au*, or *aw*. Students can then call on classmates to come to the board to write the missing vowel digraph and read the word.

Circle the correct word to complete each sentence. Then write the word on the line.

> **RULE**
> The vowel digraphs **au** and **aw** both stand for the same sound of **aw**.
> **au**to   cl**aw**s

1. The parade took place at the end of (autumn, author).   autumn
2. It was a blustery day and a (law, raw) wind was blowing.   raw
3. Cars and floats (caught, crawled) along the parade route.   crawled
4. They had an (awful, awesome) time getting through.   awful
5. A celebrity waved from a shiny white (authority, automobile).   automobile
6. Her sequined (shawl, straw) sparkled in the sunlight.   shawl
7. Her fans (audience, applauded) wildly.   applauded
8. Then they pushed through the crowd to get her (autograph, automatic).   autograph
9. The star (cautioned, scrawled) her name for her admirers.   scrawled
10. Later she had a conference with her (laundry, lawyer).   lawyer
11. He (cautioned, haunted) her to review her contract carefully.   cautioned
12. This rising young star often (fawns, flaunts) her success.   flaunts
13. Her critics describe her as being (haughty, awning).   haughty
14. She remains (precautioned, undaunted).   undaunted

> What conclusion can you draw about the star's character from this passage?

Critical Thinking

SPELLING

You may use these words and dictation sentences as a pretest for the second group of spelling words in Unit 2.

1. **vein** — The artist carefully drew each **vein** in the leaf.
2. **obey** — It is so important to **obey** traffic laws.
3. **autumn** — It is cheaper to travel in **autumn** than in summer.
4. **lawyer** — After the **lawyer** spoke to the jury, she sat down.
5. **juice** — This **juice** is a mixture of apple and grape.
6. **moist** — Use a **moist** cloth to wipe the table.
7. **enjoy** — Patrick pretended to **enjoy** the show.
8. **mountain** — From the top of that **mountain**, you can see three states.
9. **vowels** — You can't read a word without **vowels**.
10. **newspaper** — There was a picture of the fire in the **newspaper**.

WRITING

Portfolio Have students choose one sentence from page 44 as a topic sentence for a paragraph. Challenge students to write three or four sentences that give supporting details or evidence of the opening statements as well as a concluding statement.

SCIENCE

Challenge small groups of students to research information on reindeers, hawks, auks, or other animals whose names include the *ei, ey, au,* or *aw* digraphs. Have each group write a report or prepare a chart and oral presentation that tells about each animal's physical characteristics, behavior, food, and habitat.

LANGUAGE

Invite students to compose original dictionary entries for at least one of the words in the lesson that they were previously unfamiliar with. Entries should include respellings, definitions, sample sentences, and other forms of the entry word.

LARGE GROUP

AUDITORY LEARNERS

Invite students to give clues for the *ei, ey, au,* and *aw* words from the lesson and call on classmates to respond by naming and spelling the word. For example: *the writer of a book* (author).

GIFTED LEARNERS

Duplicate a list of words such as the following, omitting the letters in parentheses: *f(au)cet, d(aw)n, sk(ei)n, fl(aw), ob(ey), surv(ey), sl(ei)gh, gn(aw), v(au)lt, pr(ey).* Have students supply a vowel digraph from this lesson to correctly spell a word, checking dictionaries if necessary.

LEARNERS WHO NEED EXTRA SUPPORT

Materials: index cards cut into squares

Have small groups of students or partners write the letters for the page 43 crossword puzzle answers on square cards and then work the puzzle by laying the squares out on a flat surface. **See Daily Word Study Practice, pages 183–186.**

Lesson 20

Pages 45–46

Vowel Digraph oo

Lesson Focus

INTRODUCING THE SKILL

- On the board, write *I lost a boot for my foot in the flood.* Call on volunteers to read the sentence and underline the three words with *oo*. Invite students to say *boot*, *foot*, and *flood* slowly to hear the different sound of *oo* in each.

- Say the words *hook, blood, moon, woods,* and *gloomy*. Have volunteers write each under the word in the sentence with the matching sound.

- Introduce the three sound symbols for the vowel digraph *oo* that appear in the rule box on page 45. Write each symbol above its matching word in the sentence.

USING THE PAGES

Review directions for pages 45 and 46. Afterward, ask students to reveal the puzzle answer and review what they know about words with vowel digraph *oo*.

45

Name _____

▶ Show the sound that the vowel digraph **oo** stands for in each word. Write **o͞o, oo** or **u** on the line.

RULE
The vowel digraph **oo** can stand for the **o͞o** sound as in **goose**, the **oo** sound as in **look**, or the **u** sound as in **blood**.

1. swoop __o͞o__	2. snoop __o͞o__		
3. nook __oo__	4. brook __oo__		
5. moody __o͞o__	6. swoon __o͞o__		
7. tycoon __o͞o__	8. floodlight __u__	9. neighborhood __oo__	
10. moose __o͞o__	11. stood __oo__	12. loot __o͞o__	
13. bassoon __o͞o__	14. bloodless __u__	15. schooner __o͞o__	

▶ Read the list of make-believe mystery cases. Circle each word that has the digraph **oo**. Then write each circled word in the correct column.

16. The Clue of the Snowy (Footprints) in the (Woods)
17. The Case of the Missing (Driftwood) in (Gloomy)(Lagoon)
18. The Mystery of the (Crooked)(Footpath) at (Moonbeam) Hill
19. The Missing (Heirloom) of (Doom)
20. The (Bloodhound) That Discovered the Pirates of (Greenwood)
21. The Case of the Gold (Doubloons)
22. The Mystery of the (Flooded) House

oo as in look

Footprints	Driftwood	Footpath
Woods	Crooked	Greenwood

oo as in goose

Gloomy	Moonbeam	Doom
Lagoon	Heirloom	Doubloons

oo as in flood

Bloodhound	Flooded

Lesson 20
Vowel digraph oo   45

FOCUS ON ALL LEARNERS

ENGLISH LANGUAGE LEARNERS/ESL

Since the different pronunciations of *oo* words do not follow easy rules, have students first read aloud the words from the top of pages 45 and 46 as well as the list of titles on page 45 before beginning to work.

AUDITORY/VISUAL LEARNERS

SMALL GROUP Have each group list words with either the same vowel sound as *goose* or *look*. Each word with the correct sound and spelling earns as many team points as there are syllables in the word. Allow for use of compound words and suffix and prefix forms. Post the completed lists with scores.

VISUAL LEARNERS

INDIVIDUAL Refer students to the word lists generated in the previous activity. Tell them to write phrases using two or more words with the same sound of *oo*, such as *a good book, a loose tooth, a room in the school,* and *stood in the brook.*

Write the word from the word bank that matches each clue. Then read down to find the answer to the riddle.

uproot	rooster	raccoon	troop	loose	broom
brook	loon	coop	good	flood	hooves

1. small, furry animal with bushy, ringed tail
   r a c c o o n
2. small cage or pen for chickens
   c o o p
3. male chicken
   r o o s t e r
4. the opposite of bad
   g o o d
5. great flow of water over dry land
   f l o o d
6. the feet of a horse
   h o o v e s
7. a group of scouts
   t r o o p
8. small stream
   b r o o k
9. tear up by the roots
   u p r o o t
10. swimming bird similar to a duck
    l o o n
11. not tight
    l o o s e
12. tool to sweep with
    b r o o m

Riddle What do you get when you put a measuring stick in the freezer? _a cooler ruler_

46 Lesson 20
Vowel digraph oo

KINESTHETIC LEARNERS

SMALL GROUP

Materials: board-game letter tiles

Have students manipulate letter tiles or write letters on paper squares to form words with *oo*. Challenge them to change beginning and ending sounds and add other syllables to continue to form words.

GIFTED LEARNERS

Have pairs of students make their own lists of rhyming phrases in which at least one word contains *oo*, such as a *cooler ruler,* and create definitions for each phrase. For example: a *smooth,* straight board is *good wood.* Have them post the clues for classmates to guess and enjoy.

LEARNERS WHO NEED EXTRA SUPPORT

Practice reading the mystery titles on page 45 with students. Discuss the meanings of words as you talk about what might happen in a few of the mysteries. **See Daily Word Study Practice, pages 183–186.**

CURRICULUM CONNECTIONS

SPELLING

Write the spelling words on the chalkboard: *vein, obey, autumn, lawyer, juice, moist, enjoy, mountain, vowels, newspaper.* Read aloud each "hink pink" and have students complete it with a spelling word by saying the word aloud and writing it on the board.

1. A simple blood vessel is a "plain (*vein*)."
2. To follow orders from straw is to "(*obey*) hay."
3. If you got your new shoes last fall, you "bought 'em in (*autumn*)."
4. To make a picture of your attorney is to "draw yer (*lawyer*)."
5. A fruit drink for large animals with antlers is "moose (*juice*)."
6. A damp ski lift is a "(*moist*) hoist."
7. To have fun with a plaything is to "(*enjoy*) a toy."
8. A large hill that spouts water is a "(*mountain*) fountain."
9. Someone who cries out for letters of the alphabet, "howls for (*vowels*)."
10. A mystery involving a journalist is a "(*newspaper*) caper."

WRITING

Have students pick one of the titles on page 45 and write a mystery story. Tell them to focus on creating a vivid setting, introducing interesting characters, and creating suspense.

ART

Portfolio **Materials:** drawing paper

Invite students to fold the art paper in half to design covers to accompany their mystery stories from the writing activity above. Book covers can be displayed with the writing attached to the inside.

SCIENCE

Challenge students to learn all about various animals with names that include the *oo* digraph, such as raccoons, loons, baboons, and poodles. Assign or have groups of students identify an animal to research. Have students find out what the animal's physical characteristics are, where the animal lives, what it eats, and what its habitat is like.

46

Lesson 21

Pages 47–48

Vowel Digraph ui

INFORMAL ASSESSMENT OBJECTIVES

Can students

✓ associate the vowel digraph *ui* with the short *i* sound and the vowel sound in *boot*?

✓ read words with the vowel digraph *ui*?

Lesson Focus

INTRODUCING THE SKILL

- Ask students to identify the words with the matching vowel sounds in each of the following sentences you read.

  The juice from the fruit ran down my suit.

  I built this guitar myself.

- Write the two sentences from above on the board. Have a volunteer underline the words with the *ui* digraph.

- Ask students to identify the sound represented by the *ui* digraph in each word. Help them conclude that *ui* can stand for the short *i* sound, as in *built* and *guitar* or for /oo/, as in *juice*, *fruit* and *suit*.

USING THE PAGES

- Ask a volunteer to read the rule for vowel digraph *ui*. Have students read the directions for pages 47 and 48. You may wish to point out the exact opposite directions given for marking *ui* words on these pages.

- After completing the pages, encourage students to discuss what they learned about the vowel digraph *ui*.

Name _____

> Read each sentence. Underline the words in which **ui** sounds like the **ui** in bruise and circle the words in which **ui** sounds like the **ui** in guilty. Then write each word in the correct column.

RULE
The vowel digraph **ui** can stand for the **i** sound or the **oo** sound.

b**ui**ld   j**ui**ce

1. My father just (built) a new restaurant.
2. The unusual (building) attracts many customers.
3. Everyone is in pursuit of a reservation.
4. The restaurant was designed to look like a cruise ship.
5. In bad weather, however, it doesn't shake or (quiver.)
6. Customers must wear suitable clothing.
7. Bathing suits are not allowed.
8. The specialty is thick, juicy steaks.
9. The crisp, light (biscuits) are in demand.
10. The fresh fruit salad is also very popular.
11. The food is always served very (quickly.)
12. There is a pretty, quilted pattern on the tablecloths.
13. Customers enjoy listening to the (guitar) music.
14. No one ever causes a nuisance.

bruise	guilty
cruise	built
suitable	building
suits	quiver
juicy	biscuits
fruit	quickly
nuisance	guitar
pursuit	quilted

Lesson 21
Vowel digraph ui **47**

FOCUS ON ALL LEARNERS

ENGLISH LANGUAGE LEARNERS/ESL

Before beginning page 47, remind students that a vowel digraph is a pair of vowels that make one sound. Review vowel digraphs that students have learned in preceding lessons.

VISUAL LEARNERS

SMALL GROUP Have small groups of students work together to write the *ui* words on pages 47–48 in alphabetical order. Have them circle the words where *ui* spells short *i* and underline the words where *ui* spells /oo/.

KINESTHETIC/VISUAL LEARNERS

LARGE GROUP Using an overhead projector, flash words that contain *u*, *i*, and *ui*. Whenever students see a word with the vowel digraph *ui*, have them clap and quickly say the word aloud.

Use the words in the word bank to work the crossword puzzle.

| quilt | bruise | nuisance | suits | cruising |
| suitably | building | guilty | pursuit | build |

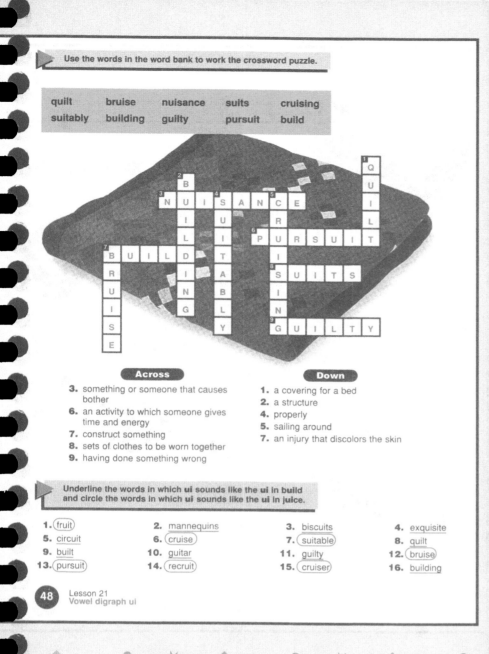

Across
3. something or someone that causes bother
6. an activity to which someone gives time and energy
7. construct something
8. sets of clothes to be worn together
9. having done something wrong

Down
1. a covering for a bed
2. a structure
4. properly
5. sailing around
7. an injury that discolors the skin

Underline the words in which **ui** sounds like the **ui** in **build** and circle the words in which **ui** sounds like the **ui** in **juice**.

1. fruit
2. mannequins
3. biscuits
4. exquisite
5. circuit
6. cruise
7. suitable
8. quilt
9. built
10. guitar
11. guilty
12. bruise
13. pursuit
14. recruit
15. cruiser
16. building

AUDITORY/VISUAL LEARNERS

INDIVIDUAL Have students work independently to write a paragraph using as many *ui* words as they can. Ask students to exchange paragraphs with a partner and read all the *ui* words aloud in each paragraph.

GIFTED LEARNERS

Challenge students to create their own crossword puzzles using words that contain the *ui* digraph.

LEARNERS WHO NEED EXTRA SUPPORT

Encourage students to memorize the simple phrase *fruit juice and quick biscuits,* and to use it to help themselves remember the two pronunciations of the vowel digraph *ui.* **See Daily Word Study Practice, pages 183–186.**

SPELLING

Write the incomplete spelling words as shown below on the chalkboard. Then write the following digraphs and diphthongs on separate slips of paper or index cards, and distribute them to students: *ey, au, aw, ui, oi, oy, ou, ei, ow, ew.* Point to a word and have the student holding the correct vowel pair come up and complete the word on the board. Invite the class to vote on whether the spelling is correct before moving on to another word.

1. ob____(*ey*)
2. ____tumn (*au*)
3. j____ce (*ui*)
4. enj____ (*oy*)
5. m____ntain (*ou*)
6. v____n (*ei*)
7. l____yer (*aw*)
8. v____els (*ow*)
9. n____spaper (*ew*)
10. m____st (*oi*)

WRITING

Portfolio Have students try their hands at writing lyrics for a song, using several of the words from pages 47–48. Advise students to try to rhyme some lines of the song.

SOCIAL STUDIES

Have small groups of students pretend that they are going to take a cruise from Miami, Florida, to the tip of South America. Have them use a map to see what countries they might pass and ask them to select five places where they might stop along the way. Have each group write a travel brochure describing the cruise, telling what can be seen at each port. Challenge them to use words containing the vowel digraph *ui* in their reports.

MUSIC

Many students may have the impression that guitarists play only rock or folk music. Explain that there is also classical music for the guitar. Share with students recordings of classical guitar music made by the great Spanish guitarist Andrés Segovia and others.

Lesson 22

Pages 49–50

Reading **Writing**

Reviewing Vowel Pairs and Vowel Digraphs

INFORMAL ASSESSMENT OBJECTIVES

Can students

✔ read an article that contains words with vowel pairs and vowel digraphs?

✔ write a description and a descriptive poem?

Lesson Focus

READING

● Write *eagle, flies, leisurely, keen, floating, prey,* and *because* on the board. Ask students to identify the vowel pair or vowel digraph in each (*ea, ie, ei, ee, oa, ey,* and *au*). Have them identify the sound each one makes in the word in which it appears.

● Tell students that they will read words containing these vowel pairs and digraphs in the article about eagles on page 49.

● After students have read the article, discuss some possible responses to the activity that follows. Then have students write their descriptive paragraphs, noting any vowel pair or digraph words used as they read it over.

WRITING

● Have students read the directions and use the guidelines listed as a help in writing their poems. Remind students to use words from the word bank as they write.

● A prewriting session for students to suggest descriptive phrases about eagles, using words from the list may be helpful.

49

Reading 🚩 Read the article. Then write your answer to the question at the end of the story.

Majesty in Motion

Floating leisurely overhead on an invisible breeze flies one of the most majestic of all creatures, the bald eagle. With a wingspan of six feet, gleaming white headfeathers, and powerful wings, the bald eagle is a chief among birds.

Eagles are large predatory birds that have long been a symbol of power, courage, and immortality. The eagle is a bird of prey, hunting from the sky, searching the fields and streams with keen eyes. Although the bald eagle is the national symbol of the United States, bald eagles have become rare in the wild. One reason is because much of the countryside that the eagle calls home has been covered with buildings and paved roads, leaving fewer wild places in which eagles can hunt. Poisons and pesticides have also played a role in killing off eagles, weakening the shells of the eagles' eggs. The bald eagle is now protected by law.

The eagle's nest, or aerie, is high in a tree or on a rocky ledge, where it cannot be reached by other animals. Because young eagles are helpless for a long period of time, this precaution is necessary. The same pair of eagles often returns to the nest year after year.

The female eagle usually lays from one to three brownish, spotted eggs. Either both parents or just the mother incubates the eggs. Baby eagles remain in the nest from 50 to 100 days, depending on the species.

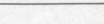

Imagine that you are on a trip to view bald eagles in the wild. What do you see on your travels? Write a description, characterizing the sights and sounds of your journey.

_____

FOCUS ON ALL LEARNERS

ENGLISH LANGUAGE LEARNERS/ESL

Before reading the article, discuss what students already know about eagles. Remind them to use context clues to help discover the meanings of unfamiliar words before looking them up in a dictionary.

VISUAL LEARNERS

INDIVIDUAL Have students skim through the article on page 49, looking for words containing vowel pairs or digraphs covered in lessons 14–21. Have them highlight or copy the words.

KINESTHETIC LEARNERS

PARTNER **Materials:** game-board letter tiles

Have pairs of students supply one another with the letter tiles needed to spell multisyllabic words from the article containing vowel pairs and digraphs. Students can check one another as the words are formed.

Writing

Suppose you are a poet. You have decided to write a descriptive poem about eagles. Use words from the word bank in your poem. Here are some guidelines to help you.

Decide whether or not your poem will rhyme.

Make a list of vivid words to describe the eagle.

Make a list of things to which you can compare the eagle.

Decide what overall mood or idea you want your poem to create.

Helpful Hints

stay	afraid	free	receive	arrow
break	thread	satisfied	cautioned	stood
prey	aerie	pair	year	creature
feature	say	slowly		

CURRICULUM CONNECTIONS

SPELLING

Write the following brief definitions on the board. Then call out the spelling words *vein*, *obey*, *autumn*, *lawyer*, *juice*, *moist*, *enjoy*, *mountain*, *vowels*, and *newspaper* and have volunteers write each word next to the correct definition.

1. carries blood (*vein*)
2. to follow orders (*obey*)
3. the time before winter (*autumn*)
4. person who works with court cases (*lawyer*)
5. drink made from fruit (*juice*)
6. damp (*moist*)
7. to have fun doing (*enjoy*)
8. a very tall pile of earth (*mountain*)
9. the letters *a*, *e*, *i*, *o*, and *u* (*vowels*)
10. a resource for daily information (*newspaper*)

FINE ARTS

Show students how to use a poetry index in the school or community library. Suggest that they look up eagles in the subject index and then practice and read aloud some of the lines from famous poems that refer to eagles.

SCIENCE/SOCIAL STUDIES

Have students identify locations in the United States where bald eagles or other types of eagles may be seen. Mark these locations on a map of the United States.

AUDITORY LEARNERS

LARGE GROUP

Read aloud pairs of words containing vowel digraphs that have different pronunciations (for example, *ea*, *ie*, and *ui*). Have students repeat the word pair if the digraph is pronounced the same in both words.

GIFTED LEARNERS

Have students pick several words from the article about eagles and look up the etymologies, or histories, of these words. Ask them to report their findings to the class.

LEARNERS WHO NEED EXTRA SUPPORT

Before students read the article on eagles, define and practice complex words such as *predatory*, *immortality*, *pesticides*, *incubate*, and *species*. **See Daily Word Study Practice, pages 183–186.**

Lesson 23

Pages 51–52

Diphthongs oi, oy

✳ ·•·'■·•·'✳·•·◆·■·•·◆·•

INFORMAL ASSESSMENT OBJECTIVES

Can students

✔ associate the diphthongs *oi* and *oy* with the vowel sound in *boy*?

✔ read words with the diphthongs *oi* and *oy*?

✔ identify the relationships of words in analogies?

Lesson Focus

INTRODUCING THE SKILL

- Say the words *toy* and *join* and ask what vowel sound students hear.

- Write *toy* and *join* on the board. Have volunteers circle the letters that stand for the vowel sound. *(oy, oi)* Explain that *oi* and *oy* are diphthongs. In a diphthong, two vowels are blended together to make one sound.

- Write these analogies on the board.

  Daisy is to flower as oak is to tree.

  Bear is to den as bee is to _____ .

- Tell students that an analogy shows a relationship between two things. The relationship in the first analogy is from something specific to something general. Ask students to explain how a bear and a den are related. What word will complete the analogy? *(hive)*

USING THE PAGES

Answer questions students may have about the directions on pages 51 and 52.

Name _____

▶ Read each word. Circle the diphthong **oi** or **oy**. Then write the word from the word bank that matches the definition.

> **DEFINITIONS**
> A **diphthong** consists of two vowels blended together as one vowel sound. The diphthongs **oi** and **oy** stand for the same vowel sound.
> c**oi**n   b**oy**

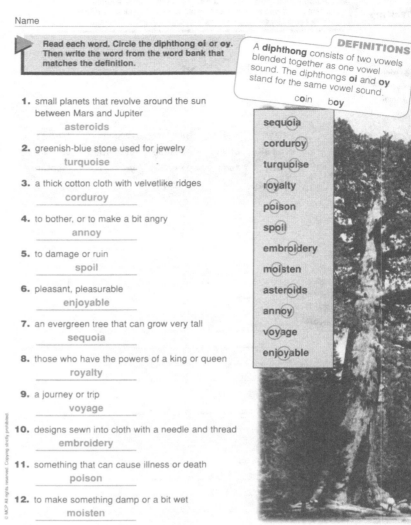

1. small planets that revolve around the sun between Mars and Jupiter
   asteroids

2. greenish-blue stone used for jewelry
   turquoise

3. a thick cotton cloth with velvetlike ridges
   corduroy

4. to bother, or to make a bit angry
   annoy

5. to damage or ruin
   spoil

6. pleasant, pleasurable
   enjoyable

7. an evergreen tree that can grow very tall
   sequoia

8. those who have the powers of a king or queen
   royalty

9. a journey or trip
   voyage

10. designs sewn into cloth with a needle and thread
    embroidery

11. something that can cause illness or death
    poison

12. to make something damp or a bit wet
    moisten

Word Bank: sequoia, corduroy, turquoise, royalty, poison, spoil, embroidery, moisten, asteroids, annoy, voyage, enjoyable

Lesson 23
Diphthongs oi, oy   **51**

FOCUS ON ALL LEARNERS ✳ ·•·◆·■·•·◆

ENGLISH LANGUAGE LEARNERS/ESL

Before beginning page 52, make sure that English language learners understand the meaning of all of the words used in the analogies.

VISUAL LEARNERS

INDIVIDUAL Have students make word-scramble puzzles. Ask students to list five words that contain the diphthong *oi* or *oy*. On the back of the paper, have students rewrite the letters for each word in scrambled form, such as *nyano* for *annoy*. Have students exchange their papers with a partner and unscramble the words.

KINESTHETIC LEARNERS

SMALL GROUP Challenge students to create "kinesthetic analogies," using movement and words to explore relationships. For example, students might demonstrate that *chair* is to *sit* as *pencil* is to _____. *(write)*

> **Circle the correct ending for each analogy and write it on the line.**

> **DEFINITION**
> An **analogy** compares different things. Analogies show how pairs of things are alike.
> **Puppy** is to **dog** as **kitten** is to **cat**.

1. **Fruit** is to **strawberry** as **tree** is to _____ sequoia _____.

  foil   spoil   (sequoia)

2. **Asteroid** is to the **sun** as **moon** is to the _____ earth _____

  loyal   (earth)   enjoy

3. **Corduroy** is to **pants** as **turquoise** is to _____ ring _____

  annoy   toil   (ring)

4. **Brush** is to **painting** as **needle** is to _____ embroidery _____.

  (embroidery)   ointment   moist

5. **Happy** is to **sad** as **satisfy** is to _____ disappoint _____

  appoint   (disappoint)   disappointment

6. **Queen** is to **royalty** as **dime** is to _____ coin _____

  (coin)   join   noisemaker

7. **Oyster** is to **ocean** as **earthworm** is to _____ soil _____.

  spoil   broil   (soil)

8. **Cat** is to **meow** as **pig** is to _____ oink _____

  squeal   (oink)   snort

9. **Adore** is to **enjoy** as **detest** is to _____ hate _____.

  envoy   point   (hate)

10. **Connect** is to **join** as **bake** is to _____ broil _____

  (broil)   toil   employ

11. **Build** is to **break** as **create** is to _____ destroy _____.

  annoy   (destroy)   appoint

> **Complete this analogy.**

12. **Boat** is to **water** as **car** is to _____ land _____.

CURRICULUM CONNECTIONS

SPELLING

Pick one of the following spelling words (*vein, obey, autumn, lawyer, juice, moist, enjoy, mountain, vowels, newspaper*) and write a blank for each letter on the board. Divide the class into two teams. Have the teams take turns guessing letters. Each time they guess a letter that is in the word, write it in the correct space. The team that first guesses and correctly spells the word, wins that round.

WRITING

Portfolio Have students either select one of the analogies on page 52 or create one of their own, and then use the analogy as the basis for a paragraph in which they explore the aspects of the relationship expressed in the analogy; for example, all the ways in which the relationship of an oyster to the ocean is like that of an earthworm to the soil.

MATH

Have students create "number analogies." For example: 3 is to 9 as 4 is to ___. (*12, because 3 is 1/3 of 9 as 4 is 1/3 of 12*) Their number analogies can be simple or complex, as long as the relationship between the two halves of the analogy are the same.

SCIENCE/CURRENT EVENTS

Have students research information about sequoias, such as their height, their age, where they grow, the environmental dangers they face, and efforts underway to save them.

AUDITORY LEARNERS

LARGE GROUP Read aloud the following beginnings of analogies. Encourage students to complete each analogy with a second pair of words: *Up is to down as ...; Collie is to dog as ...; Fish is to swim as ...; Page is to book as ...; Hat is to head as ....*

GIFTED LEARNERS

Challenge students to create analogies in which at least one of the four terms contains the diphthong *oi* or *oy*.

LEARNERS WHO NEED EXTRA SUPPORT

List some of the different kinds of relationships that analogies can express, such as whole to part, example to group, synonyms, antonyms, tool to activity, and feature to object. Help students construct one analogy for each type of relationship. **See Daily Word Study Practice, pages 183–186.**

Lesson 24

Pages 53–54

Diphthongs ou, ow

Lesson Focus

INTRODUCING THE SKILL

● Read the sentence *The proud cow frowned at the brown mouse.* Ask students which words in the sentence have the same vowel sound heard in *now.*

● Ask a volunteer to write the sentence on the board. Ask what letters stand for the vowel sound in the words *proud, cow, frowned, brown,* and *mouse.* (*ou* and *ow*)

● Guide students to understand that the diphthongs *ou* and *ow* can stand for the sound of *ow* in *now.*

● Allow time for students to suggest other words in which they hear the same vowel sound as in *now.*

USING THE PAGES

Review the rule in the box on page 53 and have students apply it to the words *out* and *scowl.* Identify the pictures on page 53 if needed and have students read the directions for both pages. After the pages are completed, encourage students to discuss what they learned about the diphthongs *ou* and *ow.*

Name _____

Read each word in the word bank. Circle the diphthong **ou** or **ow**. Then write the word from the box that names each picture.

RULE
The diphthongs **ou** and **ow** often stand for the vowel sound you hear in **ou**t and sc**ow**l.

cl**ou**ds	tr**ou**t	**ow**l	m**ou**ntains
sunfl**ow**er	v**ow**els	f**ou**ntain	pl**ow**

1 mountains
2 trout
3 vowels
4 plow
5 sunflower
6 fountain
7 owl
8 clouds

FOCUS ON ALL LEARNERS

ENGLISH LANGUAGE LEARNERS/ESL

Make sure that students understand the meanings of all the words in the first exercise on page 54 as well as being able to decode the diphthongs *ou* and *ow.*

VISUAL LEARNERS

LARGE GROUP

Invite students to play a synonym-antonym game. On the board, write a synonym or antonym for each of the following words: *town, mountain, shout, cloudy, crouch, out.* Write *S* next to synonym clues (for example, *village* for *town*) and *A* next to antonym clues (for example, *in* for *out*). Tell students that the answers all contain *ou* or *ow.* Have students take turns guessing the answers to the clues.

AUDITORY LEARNERS

SMALL GROUP

Have small groups of students play the synonym-antonym game described above, but have them give each other clues orally rather than in writing.

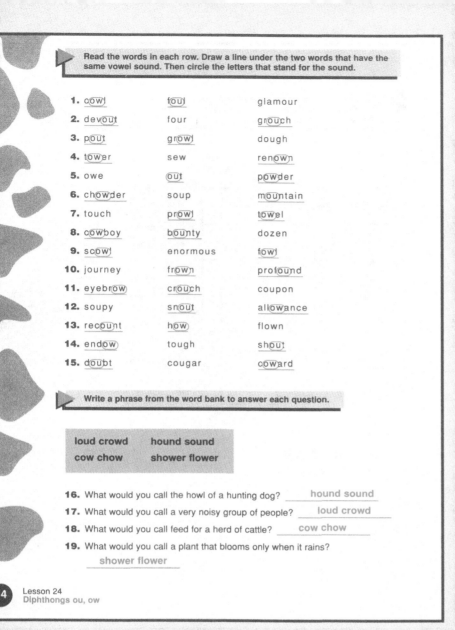

Read the words in each row. Draw a line under the two words that have the same vowel sound. Then circle the letters that stand for the sound.

1. cowl   foul   glamour
2. devout   four   grouch
3. pout   growl   dough
4. tower   sew   renown
5. owe   out   powder
6. chowder   soup   mountain
7. touch   prowl   towel
8. cowboy   bounty   dozen
9. scowl   enormous   fowl
10. journey   frown   profound
11. eyebrow   crouch   coupon
12. soupy   snout   allowance
13. recount   how   flown
14. endow   tough   shout
15. doubt   cougar   coward

Write a phrase from the word bank to answer each question.

loud crowd	hound sound
cow chow	shower flower

16. What would you call the howl of a hunting dog?   _hound sound_
17. What would you call a very noisy group of people?   _loud crowd_
18. What would you call feed for a herd of cattle?   _cow chow_
19. What would you call a plant that blooms only when it rains?   _shower flower_

54   Lesson 24
Diphthongs ou, ow

SPELLING

Have partners take turns saying a spelling word for the other to spell aloud: *moist, lawyer, obey, vowels, autumn, vein, newspaper, enjoy, juice, mountain.*

 WRITING

Portfolio Have students use words containing the sounds of diphthongs *ou* and *ow* to create their own rhyming word pairs like the ones at the bottom of page 54. Encourage students to write questions leading to the word pairs as shown in the exercise.

MATH

Tell students to pretend that they have $10.00 to spend. Ask them to think of things to buy whose names contain the diphthongs *ou* and *ow*. Then have students group similar expenditures, such as food, clothing, and entertainment. Ask them to total the amount of expenditures in each category and determine what percentage of their total allowance it represents. Have them represent this information in a pie chart.

ART/SOCIAL STUDIES

Have students prepare brief reports on the Leaning Tower of Pisa and other famous towers and skyscrapers, such as the Eiffel Tower, the Sears Tower, and the World Trade Center. Each report might include a picture of the tower, its location and use, the year it was built, and the materials from which it was constructed.

KINESTHETIC LEARNERS

PARTNER   **Materials:** posterboard, markers, dice

Invite pairs of students to create a game board using words with *ou* and *ow*. When finished partners can invite classmates to play.

GIFTED LEARNERS

Have small groups of learners prepare riddles that have as their answers words containing the diphthongs *ou* and *ow*. Then have the groups exchange their riddles with each other.

LEARNERS WHO NEED EXTRA SUPPORT

Review with students the exercise at the top of page 54. Remind students that not all words containing the letters *ou* and *ow* contain the sound of *ow* in *now*. **See Daily Word Study Practice, pages 183–186.**

Lesson 25
Pages 55–56

Diphthong ew; Syllables

Lesson Focus

INTRODUCING THE SKILL

● Say aloud the words *drew, chew, flew, new, crew*. Ask students what sound they hear at the end of each word. Tell them that the sound stands for the diphthong *ew*, two vowels blended into one sound.

● On the board, write *drew, chew, mildew, new, shrewd, view,* and *jewel*. Ask a volunteer to underline the diphthong *ew* in each word.

● On the board, write the words *clown, obey, counter, doubt, booster, neighbor, shower,* and *newspaper*.

● Call on students to identify the vowel digraph or diphthong in each word and tell how many syllables each word has.

USING THE PAGES

Have students read the rule on page 55. Review the directions for pages 55 and 56. After they have completed the work, encourage students to discuss what they learned about the diphthong *ew* and about syllables.

55

Name

Complete the crossword puzzle by finding the **ew** word in the word bank that fits each description. You will not need to use every word.

> **RULE**
> The diphthong **ew** stands for the vowel sound you hear in **few**. It is nearly the same vowel sound you hear in **moon**.

dew	chew
crew	blew
drew	few
flew	jeweler
mildew	nephew
new	newspaper
pewter	renewal
shrewd	steward
views	yew

Across

4. what you do to food before swallowing it
5. person who makes, sells, or repairs necklaces and watches
8. making something new or fresh again
9. clever or wise
11. kind of furry, white fungus that appears during damp weather
12. type of evergreen or shrub

Down

1. the news of the day is printed in this
2. a grayish metal made by mixing tin with lead, brass, or copper
3. opposite of **many**
4. group of sailors working on a ship
6. the son of a person's sister or brother
7. past tense of **fly**
10. past tense of **draw**

Lesson 25
Diphthong ew **55**

FOCUS ON ALL LEARNERS

ENGLISH LANGUAGE LEARNERS/ESL

Before beginning page 56, make sure that students can correctly pronounce the words in the list. Help them count the syllables of the first five to make sure they comprehend and can perform the task.

AUDITORY/VISUAL LEARNERS

INDIVIDUAL Encourage students to look through books for words of three, four, and five syllables. Tell them to read words aloud and list at least three words for each number of syllables.

KINESTHETIC LEARNERS

PARTNER **Materials:** dictionaries

After students have completed page 56, have partners randomly select words from the list for one another to find in a dictionary and check for number of syllables.

Write the number of syllables you hear in each word. Then write the vowel pair, vowel digraph, or diphthong that each word contains.

#	Word	Number of Syllables	Vowel Pair, Digraph, or Diphthong	#	Word	Number of Syllables	Vowel Pair, Digraph, or Diphthong
1.	juice	1	ui	2.	woodpecker	3	oo
3.	fellows	2	ow	4.	account	2	ou
5.	counter	2	ou	6.	treason	2	ea
7.	reign	1	ei	8.	pheasant	2	ea
9.	down	1	ow	10.	retrieve	2	ie
11.	portray	2	ay	12.	survey	2	ey
13.	treat	1	ea	14.	dauntless	2	au
15.	waterproof	3	oo	16.	withdrew	2	ew
17.	disobey	3	ey	18.	seamstress	2	ea
19.	treachery	3	ea	20.	reasonable	4	ea
21.	sluice	1	ui	22.	occupied	3	ie
23.	essay	2	ay	24.	board	1	oa
25.	thesaurus	3	au	26.	gingerbread	3	ea
27.	breaker	2	ea	28.	mayhem	2	ay
29.	withdraw	2	aw	30.	thundercloud	3	ou
31.	refugee	3	ee	32.	greedy	2	ee
33.	schoolmaster	3	oo	34.	growth	1	ow
35.	author	2	au	36.	however	3	ow
37.	soapy	2	oa	38.	tomorrow	3	ow
39.	oboe	2	oe	40.	upheaval	3	ea
41.	shower	2	ow	42.	feast	1	ea
43.	applause	2	au	44.	appoint	2	oi
45.	shook	1	oo	46.	hawthorn	2	aw
47.	renew	2	ew	48.	authentic	3	au

CURRICULUM CONNECTIONS

SPELLING

Call out each spelling word: *vein, obey, autumn, lawyer, juice, moist, enjoy, mountain, vowels, newspaper*. Have pairs of students write an original sentence using each word. Display the sets of sentences in the classroom.

WRITING

Portfolio Have the class generate a list of words that contain the diphthong *ew*. Write each word on the board as it is suggested. Then have students work in pairs to write an imaginary TV or radio news report, using as many of the listed words as possible.

SCIENCE

Encourage small groups of students to research a specific jewel, including where it is found, how it looks in its natural state, how it is made into jewelry, myths about the jewel, and other interesting facts. Ask each group to present an oral report to the class.

SOCIAL STUDIES

Have students research newspapers in America. Possible topics include the publication of newspapers in the colonial period, the role of newspapers in the muckraking movement at the turn of the century, and the life of publisher William Randolph Hearst.

AUDITORY/VISUAL LEARNERS

LARGE GROUP Have students compose a progressive, perhaps nonsensical, story using the *ew* words on page 55. Each student can add to the story, using one of the words. That word can then be written on the board and the story can continue.

GIFTED LEARNERS

Have students create "increasing sentences." The first word in the sentence should have one syllable, the second two syllables, and so on. Award one point for each word that fits the syllable requirements and an extra point for each word that contains the diphthong *ew*. The sentence with the most points wins.

LEARNERS WHO NEED EXTRA SUPPORT

Review with students the fact that if you say a word correctly out loud, you should be able to hear the number of syllables, just as you can hear the number of beats in a piece of music. **See Daily Word Study Practice, pages 183–186, 195.**

Lesson 26

Pages 57–58

Reading Writing

Reviewing Vowel Pairs, Vowel Digraphs, Diphthongs, Syllables

INFORMAL ASSESSMENT OBJECTIVES

Can students

✔ read an article that contains one-syllable and multisyllabic words with vowel pairs, vowel digraphs, and diphthongs?

✔ write an explanation and a magazine article?

Lesson Focus

READING

- Write the words *without, mayor, explain, retrieve, survey,* and *however* on the board. Ask students to identify the words with vowel pairs (*mayor, explain*), vowel digraphs (*retrieve, survey*) and diphthongs (*without, however*),

- Have students read the article on page 57. Then introduce the writing activity below it. Ask students what tips they should keep in mind as they write their explanations of video games.

WRITING

- Have students read the directions for page 58 along with possible words to include in their descriptions.

- As they begin to write, suggest that students focus on games with which they are most familiar. Have students proofread their articles, especially for correct use of vowel pairs, vowel digraphs, and diphthongs in words.

Name _____

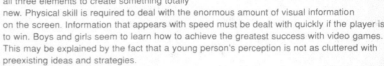
Reading ▶ Read the article. Then write your answer to the question at the end of the story.

★★★ ◄ ○○○○○○○○○ **START**

The Game's the Thing!

Solitaire is a game that is played by one individual. Without a doubt, one of the most extraordinary solitaire games of modern times is the video game. Video games are played in arcades, on home television screens, and on personal as well as hand-held computers.

The video game is not simply a game of physical skill, chance, or strategy, but combines all three elements to create something totally new. Physical skill is required to deal with the enormous amount of visual information on the screen. Information that appears with speed must be dealt with quickly if the player is to win. Boys and girls seem to learn how to achieve the greatest success with video games. This may be explained by the fact that a young person's perception is not as cluttered with preexisting ideas and strategies.

Many video games are programmed to allow apparently random events to occur, which makes them games of chance. In most video games, however, decisions must be made on the basis of perceived changes or a logical flow of events, so strategy is also involved.

Scientists are hoping that one day they can develop theories of how people can adapt to daily life based on some of the rules and strategies obeyed in video games. Perhaps such a theory may one day be developed.

★ ⇨ **GAME OVER**

○○○○○○○○○○○○○ ★

Imagine that scientists asked you to contribute your ideas about how the logic and strategies of video games work. Write a report, explaining how a video game that you are familiar with works.

_____
_____
_____
_____
_____
_____

Lesson 26 **57**
Review vowel pairs, vowel digraphs, diphthongs, syllables: Reading

---

FOCUS ON ALL LEARNERS ✳ • ◆ ■

ENGLISH LANGUAGE LEARNERS/ESL

Encourage English language learners to focus on their home culture in this writing activity by describing games popular in that culture.

VISUAL LEARNERS

SMALL GROUP Have groups of students create posters showing words related to games divided into syllables. Have them divide the posterboard into quadrants, and write one-syllable words in the first quadrant, two-syllable words in the second, and so on.

KINESTHETIC LEARNERS

SMALL GROUP Have each group decide on an active classroom or outside game that could be used to help classmates learn about diphthongs. Remind students to plan a logical sequence of instructions and strategies to help classmates understand and enjoy the game.

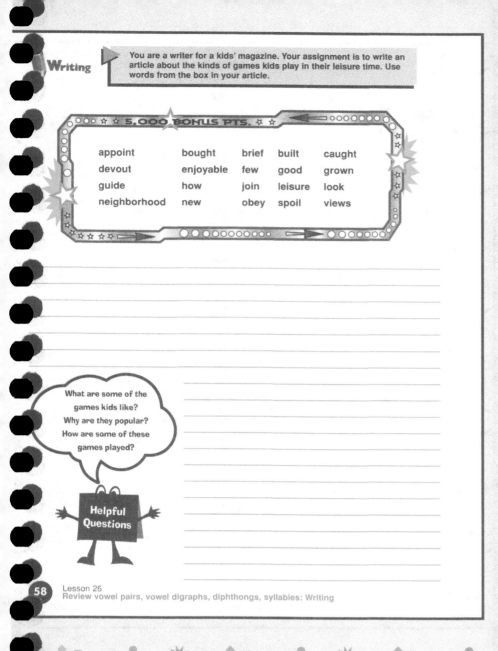

Writing ▶ You are a writer for a kids' magazine. Your assignment is to write an article about the kinds of games kids play in their leisure time. Use words from the box in your article.

★ ☆ 5,000 BONUS PTS. ☆ ★

appoint	bought	brief	built	caught
devout	enjoyable	few	good	grown
guide	how	join	leisure	look
neighborhood	new	obey	spoil	views

What are some of the games kids like?

Why are they popular?

How are some of these games played?

Helpful Questions

Lesson 26
Review vowel pairs, vowel digraphs, diphthongs, syllables: Writing

CURRICULUM CONNECTIONS ✹ ● ✦ ■ ✦ ●

SPELLING

You may use the following words and dictation sentences as a posttest for the second group of spelling words for Unit 2.

1. **vein** — The nurse drew blood from my **vein**.
2. **obey** — The little boy refused to **obey** the babysitter.
3. **autumn** — In **autumn** that tree turns bright gold.
4. **lawyer** — The **lawyer** drew up the will.
5. **juice** — The floor was sticky from spilled **juice**.
6. **moist** — It is important to keep the soil in the garden **moist**.
7. **enjoy** — If you **enjoy** exciting stories, you'll love this book.
8. **mountain** — Jane was panting by the time she had climbed to the top of the **mountain**.
9. **vowels** — Some speakers pronounce **vowels** very differently than others do.
10. **newspaper** — The kitten chewed up the **newspaper** before we read it.

MATH

Take a survey on the different video games students have played. Graph the results, showing the most and least popular games. Discuss differences in students' taste and how these differences effected the survey. If possible, share the survey with another sixth grade class and compare the graph that results with the original.

SOCIAL STUDIES

Have students select a few classic games, such as marbles, backgammon, checkers, hopscotch, and chess, and do research to discover how they developed. Encourage those who know how to play these games to give a demonstration and teach interested classmates the basics.

AUDITORY LEARNERS

PARTNER Have one partner read to the other his or her article on games. Have them emphasize each word containing a vowel pair diphthong or vowel digraph as it is read.

GIFTED LEARNERS

Have one student call out a word. The next student must quickly think of a new word beginning with the last letter of the first word, and so on. The catch is each word must contain a diphthong.

LEARNERS WHO NEED EXTRA SUPPORT

For students who have trouble understanding how diphthongs differ from vowel digraphs, pronounce words containing diphthongs very slowly and clearly so that students can hear the blended vowels.
See Daily Word Study Practice, pages 183–186, 195.

Lesson 27

pages 59–60

Unit Checkup

Reviewing Vowel Pairs, Vowel Digraphs, Diphthongs, and Syllables

Can students

✔ distinguish among the sounds made by vowel pairs, vowel digraphs, and diphthongs?

✔ identify vowel pairs, vowel digraphs, and diphthongs in words?

✔ identify the number of syllables in words?

Lesson Focus

PREPARING FOR THE CHECKUP

● Write the following sentences on the board.

A few boys offered to bake cookies to raise funds.

Others may mow lawns.

They need cash to build a clubhouse.

● Have volunteers circle each word that contains a pair of vowels and then indicate whether each is a vowel pair, vowel digraph, or a diphthong.

● Have students count the syllables in each word they have listed.

USING THE PAGES

● Be sure students understand the directions for the exercises on pages 59 and 60. After students finish the pages, have them take turns reading items 1–16 aloud and identifying the vowel sounds in all of the alternatives.

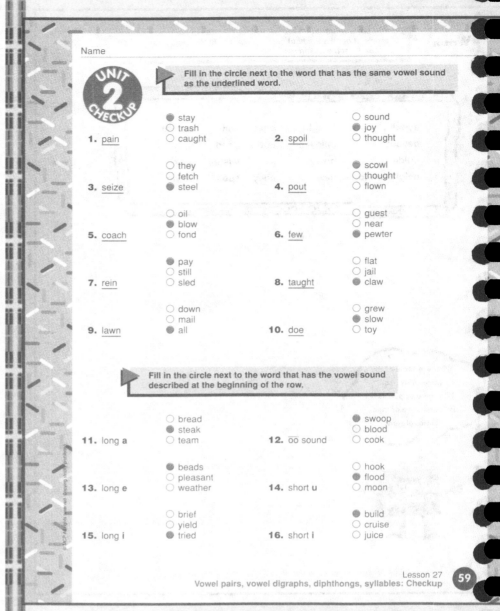

Name _____

UNIT 2 CHECKUP

▶ Fill in the circle next to the word that has the same vowel sound as the underlined word.

1. pain — ● stay / ○ trash / ○ caught
2. spoil — ○ sound / ● joy / ○ thought
3. seize — ○ they / ○ fetch / ● steel
4. pout — ● scowl / ○ thought / ○ flown
5. coach — ○ oil / ● blow / ○ fond
6. few — ○ guest / ○ near / ● pewter
7. rein — ● pay / ○ still / ○ sled
8. taught — ○ flat / ○ jail / ● claw
9. lawn — ○ down / ○ mail / ● all
10. doe — ○ grew / ● slow / ○ toy

▶ Fill in the circle next to the word that has the vowel sound described at the beginning of the row.

11. long a — ○ bread / ● steak / ○ team
12. oo sound — ● swoop / ○ blood / ○ cook
13. long e — ● beads / ○ pleasant / ○ weather
14. short u — ○ hook / ● flood / ○ moon
15. long i — ○ brief / ○ yield / ● tried
16. short i — ● build / ○ cruise / ○ juice

Lesson 27
Vowel pairs, vowel digraphs, diphthongs, syllables: Checkup **59**

FOCUS ON ALL LEARNERS

ENGLISH LANGUAGE LEARNERS/ESL

To build background for the story on page 60, ask students how they feel when, after a long spell of cold cloudy weather, a nice day arrives.

VISUAL LEARNERS

INDIVIDUAL Explain that *ow* can be either a digraph or a diphthong. Have students make lists of words with *ow*. Ask them to draw a picture of a bowl or an owl next to each word to indicate the sound *ow* makes in that word.

KINESTHETIC LEARNERS

SMALL GROUP Have students devise combinations of dance steps or sports moves to perform in synchronization with words they say aloud. For example, a push-up is a two-move sequence that would go with a two-syllable word.

UNIT 2 CHECKUP

▶ Read each sentence. Circle the word that contains a vowel pair, vowel digraph, or diphthong.

1. (Few) things are less (pleasant) than a (display) of bad manners.
2. One type of rudeness is (boasting)(about) one's (achievements.)
3. Acting (disappointed) with a gift is (unbelievably) rude!
4. Some folks (groan) and act (gloomy) when anything is wrong.
5. Others act as if they (doubt) that anyone (speaks) the truth.
6. Students who (annoy)(teachers) are (guilty) of rudeness.
7. Diners who (devour)(food) very quickly are not polite, (either.)
8. (Avoid) calling (acquaintances) at (mealtime.)
9. (Employing) words like (please) and thank you works wonders.
10. Give yourself a big (round) of applause for using (good) manners.

▶ Copy each word you circled and circle the vowel pair, vowel digraph, or diphthong it contains. Then write the number of syllables next to each word.

11. _____ (few) - 1, pl(ea)sant - 2, displ(ay) - 2
12. _____ b(oa)sting - 2, ab(ou)t - 2, achi(e)vements - 3
13. _____ disapp(oi)nted - 4, unbel(ie)vably - 5
14. _____ gr(oa)n - 1, gl(oo)my - 2
15. _____ d(ou)bt - 1, sp(ea)ks - 1
16. _____ ann(oy) - 2, t(ea)chers - 2, gu(i)lty - 2
17. _____ dev(ou)r - 2, f(oo)d - 1, (ei)ther - 2
18. _____ av(oi)d - 2, acqu(ai)ntances - 4, m(ea)ltime - 2
19. _____ empl(oy)ing - 3, pl(ea)se - 1
20. _____ r(ou)nd - 1, appl(au)se - 2, g(oo)d - 1

60
Lesson 27
Vowel pairs, vowel digraphs, diphthongs, syllables: Checkup

AUDITORY/VISUAL LEARNERS

LARGE GROUP Say aloud a word containing a diphthong. See how many words containing the same diphthong students can write in one minute.

GIFTED LEARNERS

Have students write analogies in which at least one of the four terms contains a diphthong or vowel digraph, for example, *owl: bird = ant: insect.*

LEARNERS WHO NEED EXTRA SUPPORT

Review the sentences on page 60. Have students look in each word for a sequence of two vowels. Say the word aloud. Listen to determine if the vowels form a digraph, a diphthong, or two separate syllables (as in *February*). **See Daily Word Study Practice, pages 183–186, 195.**

ASSESSING UNDERSTANDING OF UNIT SKILLS

Student Progress Assessment You may wish to review the observational notes you made as students worked through the activities in this unit. Your notes will help you evaluate the progress students made with vowel digraphs, diphthongs, and syllables.

Portfolio Assessment Review the materials students have collected in their portfolios. Talk with students individually to discuss their written work and the progress they have made since the beginning of this unit. As you review students' work, evaluate how well they use the unit word study skills.

Daily Word Study Practice For students who need additional practice with any of the topics in this unit, quick reviews are provided on pages 183–186, 195 in Daily Word Study Practice.

Word Study Posttest To assess students' mastery of skills covered in this unit, use the posttest on pages 31g–31h.

SPELLING

Use the following dictation sentences to review the spelling words in Unit 2.

1. **acquaintance** We waved at an old **acquaintance**.
2. **proceed** The passengers were told to **proceed** to the baggage claim.
3. **ceiling** Water dripped from the **ceiling**.
4. **outgrow** You will **outgrow** those boots.
5. **sweater** A button fell off my **sweater**.
6. **yield** A driver missed the **yield** sign.
7. **vein** A **vein** throbbed in his forehead.
8. **obey** The puppy is learning to **obey**.
9. **autumn** Classes start in late **autumn**.
10. **lawyer** Chris wants to be a **lawyer**.
11. **juice** The apple **juice** was icy and cold.
12. **moist** Her face felt **moist** and feverish.
13. **enjoy** Did you **enjoy** the video?
14. **mountain** The top of the **mountain** was hidden by clouds.
15. **vowels** How many **vowels** does this word contain?

Teacher Notes

INTRODUCING

Unit 3

Word Parts and Prefixes

Contents

Student Performance Objectives

In Unit 3, students will review the concept of word parts and meanings, and review and extend familiarity with prefixes and their meanings. As students apply concepts involving word parts, prefixes, and sentence combination, they will be able to

◆ Recognize and define *base word, root, prefix,* and *suffix* as parts of a whole word

◆ Associate the prefixes *ir-, im-, il-, in-, im-, em-, mis-,* and *mal-* with their common meanings

◆ Associate the prefixes *anti-, counter-, de-, fore-,* and *post-* with their common meanings

◆ Associate the prefixes *over-, ultra-, super-, trans-, semi-, sub-, mid-, uni-, mono-, bi-,* and *tri-* with their common meanings

UNIT 3 RESOURCES
Assessment Strategies	61c
Overview	61c
Unit 3 Pretest	61e–61f
Unit 3 Posttest	61g–61h
Unit 3 Student Progress Checklist	61i
Spelling Connections	61j–61k
Word Study Games, Activities, and Technology	61l–61o
Home Connection	61p–61q

TEACHING PLANS
Unit 3 Opener	61–62
Lesson 28: Units of Meaning in Words	63–64
Lesson 29: Prefixes *ir-, im-, il-, in-*	65–66
Lesson 30: Prefixes *im-, em-*	67–68
Lesson 31: Prefixes *mis-, mal-*	69–70
Lesson 32: Prefixes *anti-, counter-*	71–72
Lesson 33: Review Prefixes	73–74
Lesson 34: Prefix *de-*	75–76
Lesson 35: Prefixes *fore-, post-*	77–78
Lesson 36: Prefixes *over-, ultra-, super-*	79–80
Lesson 37: Prefixes *trans-, semi-*	81–82
Lesson 38: Prefixes *sub-, mid-*	83–84
Lesson 39: Prefixes *uni-, mono-, bi-, tri-*	85–86
Lesson 40: Review Prefixes	87–88
Lesson 41: Unit 3 Checkup	89–90

61b

Assessment Strategy Overview

In Unit 3, assess students' ability to recognize and define units of meaning, to recognize prefixes and their meanings, and combine sentences by using conjunctions There are various ways to assess students' progress. If desired, encourage students to evaluate their own work and participate in setting goals for their own learning.

FORMAL ASSESSMENT

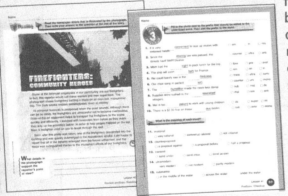

The Unit 3 Pretest on pages 61e–61f helps to assess a student's knowledge at the beginning of the unit and to plan instruction.

The Unit 3 Posttest on pages 61g–61h helps to assess mastery of unit objectives and to plan for reteaching, if necessary.

INFORMAL ASSESSMENT

The Reading & Writing pages and Unit Checkup in the student book are an effective means of evaluating students' performance.

Skill	Reading & Writing Pages	Unit Checkup
Recognizing Word Parts	73–74	89–90
Prefixes *ir-, im-, il-, in-*	73–74	89–90
Prefixes *im-, em-*	73–74	89–90
Prefixes *mis-, mal-*	73–74	89–90
Prefixes *anti-, counter-*	73–74	89–90
Prefix *de-*	87–88	89–90
Prefixes *fore-, post-*	87–88	89–90
Prefixes *over-, ultra-, super-*	87–88	89–90
Prefixes *trans-, semi-*	87–88	89–90
Prefixes *sub-, mid-*	87–88	89–90
Prefixes *uni-. mono-, bi-, tri-*	87–88	89–90

PORTFOLIO ASSESSMENT

Portfolio This logo appears throughout the teaching plans. It signals opportunities for collecting students' work for individual portfolios. You may also want to collect the following pages.

❖ Unit 3 Pretest and Posttest, pages 61e–61h

❖ Unit 3 Reading & Writing, pages 73–74, 87–88

❖ Unit 3 Checkup, pages 89–90

STUDENT PROGRESS CHECKLIST

Use the checklist on page 61i to record students' progress. You may want to cut the sections apart to place each student's checklist in his or her portfolio.

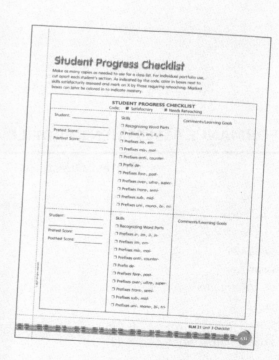

Administering and Evaluating the
Pretest and Posttest

DIRECTIONS

To help you assess students' progress in learning Unit 3 skills, tests are available on pages 61e–61h. Administer the Pretest before students begin the unit. The results of the Pretest will help you identify each student's strengths and needs in advance, allowing you to structure lesson plans to meet individual needs. Administer the Posttest to assess students' overall mastery of skills taught in the unit and to identify specific areas that will require reteaching.

PERFORMANCE ASSESSMENT PROFILE

The following chart will help you identify specific skills as they appear on the tests and enable you to identify and record specific information about an individual's or the class's performance on the tests.

Depending on the results of the tests, refer to the Reteaching column for lesson-plan pages where you can find activities that will be useful for meeting individual needs or for daily word study practice.

PERFORMANCE ASSESSMENT PROFILE

Skill	Pretest Questions	Posttest Questions	Reteaching Focus on All Learners	Daily Word Study Practice
Basic Word Parts	1–12	1–12	63–64	186–189
Prefixes ir-, im-, il-, in-	1, 2	2, 11, 12, 15	65–66, 73–74	186–189
Prefixes im-, em-	13, 14	1, 16	67–68, 73–74	186–189
Prefixes mis-, mal-	3, 15	3	69–70, 73–74	186–189
Prefixes anti-, counter-	4, 16	5, 18	71–74	186–189
Prefix de-	5	13	75–76, 87–88	186–189
Prefixes fore-, post-	6, 17	6, 17	77–78, 87–88	186–189
Prefixes over-, ultra-, super-	7, 18	4, 14, 24, 25	79–80, 87–88	186–189
Prefixes trans-, semi-	8, 19, 27	7, 19, 26	81–82, 87–88	186–189
Prefixes sub-, mid-	9, 20, 25	8, 20, 23, 27	83–84, 87–88	186–189
Prefixes uni-, mono-	10, 12, 22, 23, 24	9, 21	85–88	186–189
Prefixes bi-, tri-	11, 21, 26	10, 22	85–88	186–189

Name ______________________________

Fill in the circle under the answer that best completes each sentence.

1. In the word **irrational**, **ir** is the ____.	suffix ○	base word ○	prefix ○
2. In the word **improbable**, **able** is the ____.	suffix ○	base word ○	prefix ○
3. In the word **misread**, **read** is the ____.	suffix ○	base word ○	prefix ○
4. In the word **antifreeze**, **anti** is the ____.	suffix ○	base word ○	prefix ○
5. In the word **defroster**, **frost** is the ____.	suffix ○	base word ○	prefix ○
6. In the word **postscript**, **script** is the ____.	suffix ○	root ○	prefix ○
7. In the word **overtime**, **time** is the ____.	suffix ○	base word ○	prefix ○
8. In the word **transportation**, **ation** is the ____.	suffix ○	base word ○	prefix ○
9. In the word **midriff**, **mid** is the ____.	suffix ○	base word ○	prefix ○
10. In the word **monotonous**, **mono** is the ____.	suffix ○	base word ○	prefix ○
11. In the word **bicoastal**, **bi** is the ____.	suffix ○	base word ○	prefix ○
12. In the word **unisphere**, **sphere** is the ____.	suffix ○	base word ○	prefix ○

Go to the next page. →

> Fill in the circle beside the answer that best completes each sentence.

13. Jill did not want to miss the ____ meeting.   ○ irrelevant   ○ important   ○ insignificant

14. The travelers ____ for Europe at nine o'clock.   ○ emerged   ○ imported   ○ embarked

15. The doctor was certain he had not ____ the illness.   ○ misdiagnosed   ○ maladjusted   ○ misled

16. The nurse applied ____ to the wound.   ○ decay   ○ antiseptic   ○ counterpart

17. Rain forced the umpires to ____ the baseball game.   ○ forecast   ○ foretell   ○ postpone

18. He reacts badly to criticism because he is ____.   ○ ultramodern   ○ superhuman   ○ oversensitive

19. Special effects can make it look as though the magician is floating in ____.   ○ midday   ○ subsoil   ○ midair

20. Animals with two feet are classified as ____.   ○ tripods   ○ bipeds   ○ unicellular

21. Some modern roller coasters travel on one track, or a ____.   ○ biplane   ○ unicycle   ○ monorail

> Fill in the circle under the prefix that should be added to the word in parentheses.

	sub	ultra	mono
22. I embroidered my ____ on my new sweater. (gram)	○	○	○

	tri	uni	over
23. A ____ has only one wheel. (cycle)	○	○	○

	sub	tri	bi
24. We live in a ____ area outside New York. (urban)	○	○	○

	mid	bi	trans
25. Our visitors from France are ____. (lingual)	○	○	○

	tri	mono	trans
26. Let's ____ the tree to a shadier spot. (plant)	○	○	○

Possible score on Unit 3 Pretest is 26. Number correct _____

Name _____

> Fill in the circle under the answer that best completes each sentence.

1. In the word **immerse**, **im** is the _____.

suffix	base word	prefix
○	○	○

2. In the word **illiterate**, **il** is the _____.

suffix	base word	prefix
○	○	○

3. In the word **malodorous**, **ous** is the _____.

suffix	base word	prefix
○	○	○

4. In the word **supersonic**, **son** is the _____.

suffix	root	prefix
○	○	○

5. In the word **counteroffer**, **offer** is the _____.

suffix	base word	prefix
○	○	○

6. In the word **forehead**, **head** is the _____.

suffix	base word	prefix
○	○	○

7. In the word **semidarkness**, **semi** is the _____.

suffix	base word	prefix
○	○	○

8. In the word **submarine**, **sub** is the _____.

suffix	base word	prefix
○	○	○

9. In the word **uniform**, **uni** is the _____.

suffix	base word	prefix
○	○	○

10. In the word **tripod**, **pod** is the _____.

suffix	root	prefix
○	○	○

11. In the word **irregular**, **ir** is the _____.

suffix	base word	prefix
○	○	○

12. In the word **inaccurate**, **accurate** is the _____.

suffix	base word	prefix
○	○	○

Go to the next page. →

> Fill in the circle beside the answer that best completes each sentence.

13. Mother asked me to _____ the meat in the microwave oven.
○ maltreat   ○ defrost   ○ overcook

14. One hundred years ago, the automobile was considered _____.
○ ultralight   ○ superstitious   ○ ultramodern

15. The hurricane caused _____ suffering beyond the property damage.
○ inestimable   ○ inexpensive   ○ insufficient

16. My aunt _____ the intricate design on my dress.
○ improvised   ○ mislabeled   ○ embroidered

17. Karen had the _____ to take an umbrella in case of rain.
○ foreshadow   ○ foresight   ○ posterity

18. Carl turned the screwdriver _____ to loosen the screw.
○ antilock   ○ overhand   ○ counterclockwise

19. Diamonds are more valuable than _____ stones.
○ transparent   ○ semidark   ○ semiprecious

20. The class repeated the vowel sounds in _____.
○ monotone   ○ unison   ○ triplicate

21. Jason, who speaks English and German, is _____.
○ bilingual   ○ universal   ○ triennial

> Fill in the circle under the prefix that should be added to the word in parentheses.

22. The _____ traveled underwater for three weeks.
(marine)

ultra	over	sub
○	○	○

23. The library book was nearly two weeks _____.
(due)

semi	mono	over
○	○	○

24. _____ light is an invisible form of light.
(violet)

Super	Ultra	Sub
○	○	○

25. The gardener will _____ the tree in the spring.
(plant)

trans	uni	tri
○	○	○

26. Florida has a _____ climate.
(tropical)

bi	over	sub
○	○	○

Possible score on Unit 3 Posttest is 26. Number correct _____

BLM 20 Unit 3 Posttest: Prefixes

61h

Student Progress Checklist

Make as many copies as needed to use for a class list. For individual portfolio use, cut apart each student's section. As indicated by the code, color in boxes next to skills satisfactorily assessed and mark an X by those requiring reteaching. Marked boxes can later be colored in to indicate mastery.

STUDENT PROGRESS CHECKLIST
Code: ■ Satisfactory   ☒ Needs Reteaching

| Student: _____

_____

 Pretest Score: _____

 Posttest Score: _____ | **Skills**
 ❏ Recognizing Word Parts
 ❏ Prefixes *ir-, im-, il-, in-*
 ❏ Prefixes *im-, em-*
 ❏ Prefixes *mis-, mal-*
 ❏ Prefixes *anti-, counter-*
 ❏ Prefix *de-*
 ❏ Prefixes *fore-, post-*
 ❏ Prefixes *over-, ultra-, super-*
 ❏ Prefixes *trans-, semi-*
 ❏ Prefixes *sub-, mid-*
 ❏ Prefixes *uni-, mono-, bi-, tri-* | **Comments/Learning Goals** |
| Student: _____

_____

 Pretest Score: _____

 Posttest Score: _____ | **Skills**
 ❏ Recognizing Word Parts
 ❏ Prefixes *ir-, im-, il-, in-*
 ❏ Prefixes *im-, em-*
 ❏ Prefixes *mis-, mal-*
 ❏ Prefixes *anti-, counter-*
 ❏ Prefix *de-*
 ❏ Prefixes *fore-, post-*
 ❏ Prefixes *over-, ultra-, super-*
 ❏ Prefixes *trans-, semi-*
 ❏ Prefixes *sub-, mid-*
 ❏ Prefixes *uni-, mono-, bi-, tri-* | **Comments/Learning Goals** |

Spelling Connections

INTRODUCTION

The Unit Word List is a comprehensive list of spelling words drawn from this unit. The words are grouped according to prefixes. To incorporate spelling into your word study program, use the activity in the Curriculum Connections section of each teaching plan.

The spelling lessons utilize the following approach for each set of words.

1. Administer a pretest of the words that have not yet been introduced. Dictation sentences are provided.

2. Provide practice.

3. Reassess. Dictation sentences are provided.

A final test is provided in Lesson 41 on page 90.

DIRECTIONS

Make a copy of Blackline Master 22 for each student. After administering the pretest, give each student a copy of the appropriate word list.

Students can work with a partner to practice spelling the words orally and identifying the prefix and base word or root in each word. They can also make and use letter cards to form the words on the list. You may want to challenge students to identify other words that have the same prefixes, base words, or roots. Students can write words of their own on *My Own Word List* (see Blackline Master 22).

Have students store their list words in an envelope or plastic zipper bag in the back of their books or notebooks. Alternatively, you may want to suggest that students keep a spelling notebook, listing words with similar patterns. You could also invite students to build word-wall displays in the classroom. Each section of the wall can focus on words with a single word study element. The walls will become a good spelling resource when students are writing.

UNIT WORD LIST

Prefixes *ir-, im-, il-, in-; em-; mis-, mal-; anti-, counter-; de-*

irregular
imperfect
illegal
inexpensive
employment
misspelling
malpractice
antifreeze
counterpart
descend

Prefixes *fore-, post-; over-, ultra-, super-; trans-, semi-; sub-, mid-; uni-*

forenoon
postscript
overcrowded
ultrafine
supersonic
transfer
semicircle
submerge
midnight
unison

Name _____

 **S**pelling   UNIT 3 WORD LIST

Prefixes ir, im, il, in; em; mis, mal; anti, counter; de

irregular   misspelling

imperfect   malpractice

illegal   antifreeze

inexpensive   counterpart

employment   descend

My Own Word List

Prefixes fore, post; over, ultra, super; trans, semi; sub, mid; uni

forenoon   transfer

postscript   semicircle

overcrowded   submerge

ultrafine   midnight

supersonic   unison

Word Study Games, Activities, and Technology

The following collection of ideas offers a variety of opportunities to reinforce word study skills while actively engaging students. The games, activities, and technology suggestions can easily be adapted to meet the needs of your group of learners. They vary in approach so as to consider students' different learning styles.

● MISSION IMPOSSIBLE

Distribute a printed handout with the message as shown. Challenge students to substitute words that contain prefixes for the words and word parts in parentheses. (You could mention that the "fate of the world" depends on their success.) (Answer key: *ir-, mis-, il-, anti-, mid-, super-, post-, de-, dis-, mal-, fore-, counter-, semi-, im-, over-*)

Good Evening! Your mission, if you and your team choose to accept it, is to decode the following message by adding appropriate prefixes to the base words and roots in parentheses. If you succeed, you will save the earth's environment from a fiendish plot. Good luck!

An (rational) criminal has (behaved). He has put an (legal) lock on our (pollution) device that protects the environment. It is located on an island in (ocean), halfway between the United States and Asia. Use your (sonic) airplane to go there faster than the speed of sound. Do not (pone) your (parture). (able) the lock and correct the (function) that prevents the device from working. Be (warned). It will not be easy. Follow these directions exactly. Turn the lock backward, or (clockwise), halfway, or one (circle). (merse) the lock in cold water to prevent it from (heating).

▲ PREFIX THEME PARK

Tell the students that they have been hired to design and name the rides for an amusement park focusing on a theme of Fantastic Trips. Have students form small groups of three or four. Provide each group with colored pencils and a sheet of poster-board or mural paper on which to plan a layout for the park and write the names of rides. Write on the chalkboard a series of examples in two lists. Students can use the examples in List A to create names of rides, including prefixes if possible. They can add the suggested prefixes to the cues in List B to describe each ride on signs that will attract visitors to the theme park.

<u>List A</u>: a cross-country train ride featuring natural wonders, a voyage to the bottom of the sea, a trip on a plane that moves faster than the speed of sound, a roller coaster that travels on a single rail, a downhill race on a water vehicle with two wheels and handle bars, a balloon ride that ascends beyond the normal range of height.

<u>List B</u>: beyond belief (*in-*), beyond belief (*un-*), having an exalting effect (*in-*), cannot be foreseen (*un-*), far from what is usual (*ex-*), beyond description (*un-*).

◆ COMBINING SENTENCES

Explain that connecting words are like bridges that connect land on opposite sides of a river. To reach their destination, travelers must know which bridge to cross. To combine sentences, writers must choose the right connecting word. Invite partners to draw or trace five different bridges on index cards. (They might refer to a classroom encyclopedia or other reference book for illustrations.)

Tell them to write one of the following connecting words on each bridge: *but, so, and, since, because.* Have students write on strips of paper some sentences that could be combined by using each of the connecting words. Partners can exchange sentences and decide which "bridge" appropriately connects the other's sentences.

The Earl of Sandwich asked for a quick meal of meat between two slices of bread

The sandwich could be considered the first "fast food"

■ IS IT A ROOT OR A BASE?

Write the following words on the chalkboard: *predict, uncover, malform, distinct, important, subway.* Tell the students to copy the words and underline the root or base. Following each word, they should write *base* or *root* in parentheses, depending on which applies. You may allow students to consult a dictionary. Encourage them to add six more words to the list and continue the exercise.

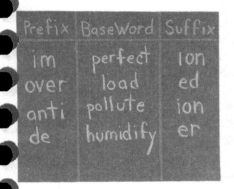

Prefix	Base Word	Suffix
im	perfect	ion
over	load	ed
anti	pollute	ion
de	humidify	er

✳ WORD BUILDERS

Tell students to write the column headings *Prefix, Base Word,* and *Suffix* on a sheet of notebook paper. Explain that each student should write ten base words in the appropriate column. You might model this activity for students on the chalkboard and allow students to refer to a dictionary, as necessary. When students have completed their lists, have them exchange papers with a partner. Partners should add a prefix and a suffix to each base word to form a new word. Have students point out any spelling changes in the base words.

● PREFIX PUZZLES

Invite pairs of students to make crossword puzzles using words with the prefixes *im-, de-, fore-, post-, sub-, mid-,* and *over-.* Challenge them to include at least one word for each prefix in their puzzles. Clues may contain the base word. After students have finished, encourage them to exchange papers with another set of partners and solve each other's puzzles.

Variation: Substitute other prefixes or allow students to choose six prefixes and create another puzzle.

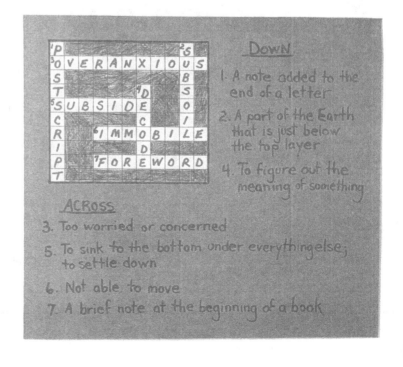

DOWN

1. A note added to the end of a letter
2. A part of the Earth that is just below the top layer
4. To figure out the meaning of something

ACROSS

3. Too worried or concerned
5. To sink to the bottom under everything else; to settle down
6. Not able to move
7. A brief note at the beginning of a book

▲ PREFIX DOWN THE LINE

Write the prefixes *ir-, in-, em-, mis-,* and *mal-* across the top of the chalkboard. Have the class divide into five teams and line up facing the chalkboard. Ask the first student in each line to walk up and write a word with the prefix *ir-*. That student should then walk back and hand the chalk to the next person in line, who will write a word with *in-*, and so on. The team that finishes first with the most correctly spelled words wins.

◆ PREFIX PICNIC

Tell students to imagine that they are attending a day-long picnic. There will be a parade featuring different kinds of decorated floats and wheeled vehicles. Various races and games are also scheduled. Several marching bands will perform. The picnic will conclude with a fireworks display. Invite students to write as many words as they can describing the sights they see and the sounds they hear. Challenge them to use words containing prefixes discussed in this unit.

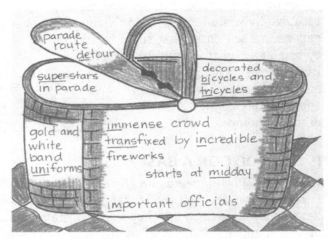

■ PREFIX CATEGORIES

Blackline Master 23 features a grid that resembles the game board on the game show *Jeopardy!*©. You might make a master copy by writing six prefixes of your choice as categories in the top row. Then make enough copies to distribute to teams of three students. As an alternative, you might allow team members to select six different prefixes discussed in this unit. Explain that each team should work together to write (on a separate sheet of paper) five words that fit each category and a short definition for each word. Pair teams. One team can play the three contestants. They should take turns picking a box in a category and trying to answer. The other team takes turns providing the definition and recording the number of correct responses for each contestant. The game continues until all the words have been identified. The player with the most correct responses wins. Teams then switch roles.

Technology

The following software products are designed to reinforce students' logical-thinking and language skills.

Word Hound   Chester Cheesewich, a hungry mouse, devises strategies to work his way through mazes. Students match pictures accompanied by speech, words, or pictures with words, to help Chester reach his goal—a hunk of cheese.
** Mindplay
   160 West Fort Lowell Street
   Tucson, AZ 85705
   (800) 221-7911

Top Secret Decoder   Practice in logical-thinking skills and language is provided through this program, which teaches students how to encode, print, and decode their own messages through the use of 16 coding tools.

** Houghton Mifflin Interactive
   120 Beacon Street
   Somerville, MA 02143
   (800) 829-7962

Reading Blaster   Through hundreds of word-skill games, students in grades 3–6 can practice skills such as alphabetical order, spelling, synonyms, antonyms, and following directions.
** Davidson & Associates, Inc.
   19840 Pioneer Avenue
   Torrance, CA 90503
   (800) 545-7677

Name _____

Prefix Categories

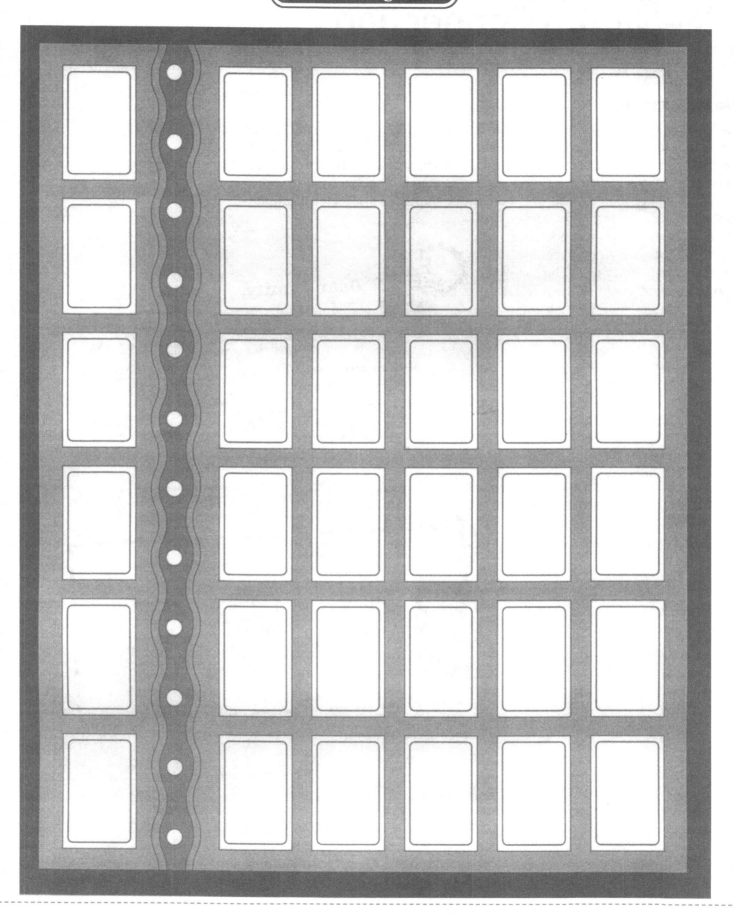

Home Connection

HOME LETTER

A letter is available to be sent home at the beginning of Unit 3. This letter informs family members that students will be learning to recognize and define word parts while focusing on prefixes and their meanings. The suggested home activity involves discovering words containing prefixes in newspapers, magazines, and homework papers. This activity promotes interaction between child and family members while supporting the student's learning of reading and writing words with the targeted word study skills. A letter is also available in Spanish on page 61q.

Home Letter

Dear Family,

During the next few weeks, your child will be learning more about prefixes, which are word parts that are added to the beginning of words. Words such as impossible, subdivide, and defrost contain prefixes. In this unit, we'll be focusing on prefixes and their meanings.

At-Home Activities

► Decode and read the message on the other side of this letter with your child. Ask your child to write out the decoded message. Then have him or her circle any words that contain the prefixes em, im, counter, de post, over, ultra, mid, uni, or bi. Discuss what these words mean. Encourage your child to look up any unfamiliar words in the dictionary.

► Encourage your child to make up his or her own coded message.

► Suggest that your child do research to learn about codes that are used by people today.

Book Corner

You and your child might enjoy reading these books together. Look for them in your local library.

Loads of Codes and Secret Ciphers

by Paul B. Janeczko

Would-be spies and detectives will enjoy learning how to break and build codes and transmit secret messages.

Windcatcher

by Avi

Eleven-year-old Tony embarks on his own mystery-adventure to uncover a sunken treasure while vacationing on the Connecticut coast.

Sincerely,

_____

Carta para la casa

Estimada familia,

Durante las próximas semanas, su hijo/a va a estar estudiando los prefijos, que son partes de palabras que se añaden al principio de las palabras. Palabras tales como **impossible** (**imposible**), **subdivide** (**subdividir**) y **defrost** (**descongelar**) contienen prefijos. En esta unidad, nos concentraremos en los prefijos en inglés y en sus significados.

Actividades para hacer en casa

▶Descifren y lean el mensaje en la página 61 del libro de su hijo/a. Pídanle a su hijo/a que escriba el mensaje descifrado. Luego pídanle que encierre en un círculo cualquier palabra que contenga los prefijos **em**, **im**, **counter**, **de**, **post**, **over**, **ultra**, **mid**, **uni** o **bi**. Comenten el significado de estas palabras. Animen a su hijo/a a buscar en el diccionario cualquier palabra desconocida.

▶Animen a su hijo/a a inventar su propio mensaje en clave.

Rincón del libro

Su hijo/a y ustedes pueden disfrutar juntos de la lectura de estos libros. Búsquenlos en la biblioteca de su localidad.

Loads of Codes and Secret Ciphers
por Paul B. Janeczko

Aspirantes a espías y a detectives gozarán de aprender a descifrar y a codificar claves para transmitir mensajes secretos.

Windcatcher
por Avi

Tony, un niño de once años de edad, se lanza en su propia aventura misteriosa para descubrir un tesoro sumergido mientras anda de vacaciones en la costa de Connecticut.

Atentamente,_____

Unit 3

Pages 61–62

Prefixes

ASSESSING PRIOR KNOWLEDGE

To assess students' prior knowledge of prefixes, use the pretest on pages 61e–61f.

Unit Focus

USING THE PAGE

- Explain that page 61 shows a letter written in a code made up of words, word parts, and pictures that stand for words or word parts.

- Help students identify the pictures in the first sentence (a *will*, some *bark*, a *ship*, and *night*) and decode it together. Write the sentence on the board.

- Have students decode the rest of the message. If a picture name does not create a meaningful word, suggest that they try other words for the rebus.

- The entire message reads: *You will embark on the ship at midnight. Important: Do not oversleep. Your counterpart will embrace you and say the code word* unicorn. *After you get off the ship, you will board a biplane or an ultralight. P.S. Your goal is to dethrone the illegal king.*

- **Critical Thinking** Read and discuss the question at the bottom of page 61. What other ways would students have encoded any parts of the message?

BUILDING A CONTEXT

- Discuss the likely meaning of *mid-* in *midnight*. (*middle*) Identify *mid-* as a prefix, a word part added to the beginning of a base word.

- Have students identify other message words with prefixes and suggest what the prefixes might mean. (Several of the prefix meanings are not obvious, and students may not recognize them at this point.)

This message uses rebuses, or combinations of pictures and letters, to stand for words. Which of the coded words did you have most trouble figuring out?

Critical Thinking

Decode and read the message. If you dare, share it with a friend.

Unit 3 Introduction 61

UNIT OPENER ACTIVITIES

RE-TURN 2 AND RE-READ THE MESSAGE

Ask students to decode the message aloud together. Discuss possible meanings of the instructions and where they might appear. (Possible responses: *a mystery novel, a movie, a cartoon*) Ask students to name places they have encountered coded messages.

MAGIC OF MYSTERIES

Many books, television shows, and movies are based on mystery and suspense. Discuss students' thoughts as to why confusion and tension, which are *not* pleasant emotions in real life, are enjoyable as elements of entertainment.

PUZZLING PREFIXES

Have students list the prefixes they recognize that appear in the message on page 61. Ask them to brainstorm other words they know that begin with these prefixes. Do the prefixes seem to mean the same thing in all the words? What do the prefixes mean in *encode* and *decode*? Invite students to create rebus symbols for some of the prefixes.

Home Letter

Dear Family,

During the next few weeks, your child will be learning more about prefixes, which are word parts that are added to the beginning of words. Words such as impossible, subdivide, and defrost contain prefixes. In this unit, we'll be focusing on prefixes and their meanings.

At-Home Activities

▶ Decode and read the message on the other side of this letter with your child. Ask your child to write out the decoded message. Then have him or her circle any words that contain the prefixes em, im, counter, de post, over, ultra, mid, uni, or bi. Discuss what these words mean. Encourage your child to look up any unfamiliar words in the dictionary.

▶ Encourage your child to make up his or her own coded message.

▶ Suggest that your child do research to learn about codes that are used by people today.

Book Corner

You and your child might enjoy reading these books together. Look for them in your local library.

Loads of Codes and Secret Ciphers
by Paul B. Janeczko
Would-be spies and detectives will enjoy learning how to break and build codes and transmit secret messages.

Windcatcher
by Avi
Eleven-year-old Tony embarks on his own mystery-adventure to uncover a sunken treasure while vacationing on the Connecticut coast.

Sincerely,

_____

BULLETIN BOARD

Prepare a bulletin board entitled "Prefixes We've Found." Have students suggest various locations in their school or home and illustrate a chart headed by the name of each location. Invite students to write lists of words containing prefixes that they might discover in each location.

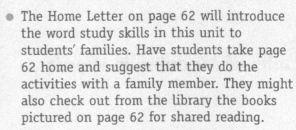

● The Home Letter on page 62 will introduce the word study skills in this unit to students' families. Have students take page 62 home and suggest that they do the activities with a family member. They might also check out from the library the books pictured on page 62 for shared reading.

● The Home Letter can also be found on page 61q in Spanish.

CURRICULUM CONNECTIONS ✳ • • ■ • •

WRITING

Have students create a short story about the spy who receives the message on page 61 and the adventure that results from it.

MATH

Many codes are number based. The simplest may be the substitution of numerals for alphabet letters in actual or reverse order. Provide books that students can use to investigate and experiment with various codes. *The Codebreaker Kids* and *The Codebreaker Kids Return*, by George Edward Stanley, are fiction books that have fascinating and challenging secret codes embedded in the plots.

SOCIAL STUDIES

Secret agents have played important roles in many world events, especially during wartime. Have students look up famous spies, such as Belle Boyd, and report on their escapades.

ART

Have pairs of students work together to create secret messages using the "word parts and pictures" technique shown on page 61. Rebus art can be cut from magazines or drawn. Suggest that students write their messages out longhand first and choose words to encode. They can trade completed messages with other students for decoding.

Lesson 28
Pages 63–64

Units of Meaning in Words

Lesson Focus

INTRODUCING THE SKILL

- Write *arrange* and *prearrangement* on the board. Ask a volunteer to read the words aloud and tell what has been added to the base word *arrange* to form *prearrangement*. (*the prefix* pre-, *the suffix* -ment)

- Write the word *predictable* on the board. Ask a volunteer to identify the prefix (*pre-*) and the suffix (*-able*). Explain that the word part *dict* is a root meaning "to speak."

- Use the outline on page 63 in the student text to write examples of each on the board. Include an explanation and give examples for base word, root, prefix, and suffix.

USING THE PAGES

Review the directions for pages 63 and 64, and provide assistance as needed. After students have completed the pages, have them share what they learned about units of meaning in words.

Name _____

▶ Study the outline. Then read each sentence and circle the answer that best completes it. Write the answer on the line.

Units of Meaning in Words

I. Basic parts of words
  A. A **base word** is a word to which word parts may be added.
    1. The base word of **uncover** is **cover**.
    2. The base word of **unlawful** is **law**.
  B. A **root** is a word part to which other word parts may be added.
    1. The root of **induction** is **duct**.
    2. The root of **important** is **port**.
II. Prefixes
  A. A **prefix** is a word part added to the beginning of a base word or root.
  B. A prefix may have one or more letters.
  C. A prefix changes the meaning of a base word or root.
    1. The prefix in **unwrap** is **un**.
    2. The prefix in **ablaze** is **a**.
III. Suffixes
  A. A **suffix** is a word part added to the end of a base word or root.
  B. A suffix may have one or more letters.
  C. A suffix changes the meaning of a base word or root.
    1. The suffix in **joyful** is **ful**.
    2. The suffix in **exports** is **s**.

1. The root of **transportation** is _____port_____.

    trans   (port)   ation

2. The root of **dictator** is _____dict_____.

    (dict)   ator   or

3. The prefix in **foresee** is _____fore_____.

    (fore)   see   foresee

4. The suffix in **unreadable** is _____able_____.

    un   read   (able)

5. The base word of **unspeakable** is _____speak_____.

    un   (speak)   able

Lesson 28
Units of meaning in words **63**

FOCUS ON ALL LEARNERS

ENGLISH LANGUAGE LEARNERS/ESL

Some students may be familiar with adding prefixes and suffixes to roots and base words. They may also speak languages that use many Latin bases, as English does. Some, however, may need extra help separating and labeling units of meaning in words.

LARGE GROUP

VISUAL LEARNERS

Write the following word parts on the board: prefix — *un-, in-, pre-*; basewords — *cook, play, read*; roots — *dict, scrib, ject*; suffixes — *-ed, -er, -ion, -ful*. Then have students form as many words as they can with the word parts. Encourage them to use a dictionary.

SMALL GROUP

KINESTHETIC LEARNERS

Materials: index cards

Adapt the exercise above by having students write the various word parts on index cards. Have them manipulate the cards to form as many words as possible and then write the words in a list.

Circle the answer that best completes each sentence. Then write it on the line.

1. **Pre** is the prefix in **precooks** and **predicted**. The base word of **precooks** is _____cook_____.

    pre   (cook)   s

2. The root of **predicted** is _____dict_____.

    pre   (dict)   ed

3. **Mis** is the prefix in **mistake**. The word **mistaken** has _____three_____ word part(s).

    one   two   (three)

4. A base word _____is_____ a word itself.

    (is)   is not

5. A root _____is not_____ always a word itself.

    is   (is not)

6. The word **prepackaged** has _____four_____ word parts.

    two   three   (four)

7. The word **unmistakable** has four word parts including _____two_____ prefixes.

    (two)   three   four

8. **En** is the prefix of **enlarge**. The word **enlargement** has _____three_____ word parts.

    two   (three)   four

Rewrite each word, putting vertical lines between word parts.

9. enforce   en/force
10. untrue   un/true
11. forceful   force/ful
12. misplace   mis/place
13. forcefully   force/ful/ly
14. renewable   re/new/able
15. reinforcing   re/in/forc/ing
16. entrust   en/trust
17. reinforcement   re/in/force/ment
18. singing   sing/ing
19. unbeatable   un/beat/able
20. rightful   right/ful
21. inscribe   in/scribe
22. player   play/er

Lesson 28
Units of meaning in words

64

AUDITORY LEARNERS

LARGE GROUP

Say aloud the following words: *distaste, enforcement, rejection, prediction, describable, precooked, misleading.* Tell students to identify the number of syllables and the units of meaning in each word. Repeat the words slowly as necessary.

GIFTED LEARNERS

Have students research the meanings and origins of the roots *scrib* and *ject*. Have them report their findings to classmates.

LEARNERS WHO NEED EXTRA SUPPORT

Have students use dictionaries to look up the definitions of several of the words they analyzed in the exercises on pages 63 and 64. Ask them to explain the meanings in their own words and use the words in sentences. **See Daily Word Study Practice, pages 186–189.**

CURRICULUM CONNECTIONS

SPELLING

You may use the following words and dictation sentences as a pretest for the first group of spelling words in Unit 3.

1. **irregular**	The shape is **irregular**.
2. **imperfect**	The photographer preferred people with **imperfect** features.
3. **illegal**	It is **illegal** to park on this side of the street.
4. **inexpensive**	I bought an **inexpensive** umbrella.
5. **employment**	Someone called seeking **employment** in the pet store.
6. **misspelling**	My computer highlights any **misspelling** I make.
7. **malpractice**	The doctor was accused of **malpractice**.
8. **counterpart**	Our principal met with her **counterpart** in the middle school.
9. **antifreeze**	The car ran out of **antifreeze**.
10. **descend**	You have to **descend** a long staircase to reach the subway.

WRITING

Portfolio Have students write short stories in which a wizard transforms things, people, and events by magically adding prefixes or suffixes to words. (For example: The wizard could change something tasty into something tast*less* and ruin a royal banquet).

SCIENCE

Remind students that much of our food today is precooked and prepackaged. Suggest that students research food preservation and processing. They might also look for information about such food "pioneers" as Gail Borden, Gustavus Swift, Philip Armour, and Clarence Birdseye.

 Technology

AstroWord, Suffixes; Prefixes; Multisyllabic Words. ©1998 Silver Burdett Ginn Inc. Division of Simon & Schuster.

Lesson 29

Pages 65–66

Prefixes ir-, im-, il-, in-

INFORMAL ASSESSMENT OBJECTIVES

Can students

✓ recognize the prefixes *ir-*, *im-*, *il-*, and *in-* in words?

✓ correctly use words containing the prefixes *ir-*, *im-*, *il-*, and *in-*?

Lesson Focus

INTRODUCING THE SKILL

- Write the following word pairs on the board: *relevant, irrelevant; possible, impossible; logical, illogical; sincere, insincere.* Read each first word aloud and have students respond with the second word.

- Call on volunteers to come to the board and circle the prefix in the second word in each pair. (*ir-, im-, il-, in-*)

- Have students use the word pairs in sentences. Ask what the words with the prefixes have in common. Help students conclude that the prefixes usually mean "not."

- Ask students for examples of other words with the prefixes *ir-, im-, il-,* and *in-.*

USING THE PAGES

- Ask students to read the rule and examples on page 65. Be sure that students understand the directions for pages 65 and 66. (Note: The number that appears in every answer word on page 66 is 7.)

- **Critical Thinking** Take time for students to respond to the question at the bottom of page 65 about Phil's dream.

Name _____

Complete each sentence by choosing a prefix from the box to add to the word below the line. Then write the word on the line.

ir   im   il   in

> **Ir, im, il,** and **in** are prefixes that usually mean **not.** RUL
>
> **ir**regular = not regular
> **im**perfect = not perfect
> **il**legal = not legal
> **in**expensive = not expensive

1. Phil thought that Saturday's airplane flight would be an ___**insignificant**___ event.

significant

2. Friday night, however, Phil found it ___**impossible**___ to avoid dreaming about airplanes.

possible

3. Phil's dream may have been ___**irrational**___, but it was exciting.

rational

4. Although Phil is an ___**inexperienced**___ pilot, he was flying a jet in his dream.

experienced

5. It is highly ___**irregular**___ for a young boy to be the pilot of a jet.

regular

6. Since Phil didn't have a license, it was ___**illegal**___ for him to fly the plane.

legal

7. All of a sudden, Phil was ___**incapable**___ of controlling the plane.

capable

8. Heavy fog had made the airport ___**invisible**___.

visible

9. Phil felt ___**ineffective**___ because he couldn't read the instruments very well.

effective

10. It was an ___**imperfect**___ landing, but the plane and passengers were safe.

perfect

How do you think Phil felt after he woke up from his dream?

Critical Thinking

Lesson 29
Prefixes ir-, im-, il-, in-   65

FOCUS ON ALL LEARNERS

ENGLISH LANGUAGE LEARNERS/ESL

Be sure students can read and understand the base words used in the exercises on pages 65 and 66 before they add prefixes to alter the meanings.

VISUAL LEARNERS

PARTNER Provide pairs of students with a newspaper or magazine and ask them to find words beginning with the prefixes *ir-, im-, il-,* or *in-.* Have students copy the words onto paper and divide them into prefix, suffix, and base or root.

KINESTHETIC LEARNERS

SMALL GROUP On the board, write phrases such as *not legible, not responsible, not efficient, not passable.* Invite students to erase each *not* but keep the original phrase's meaning by adding the prefix *ir-, im-, il-,* or *in-* to the base word. Read and check words for sense.

▶ **Fill in the blanks with a word from the word bank that fits the definition.**

illegible	illiterate	immobile
impolite	incapable	incomplete
inhospitable	irresistible	irresponsible

1. not showing a sense of duty
I R R E S P O N S I B L E
1 5 8 2 12 4 6 7 20 14 3 10 9

2. rude
I M P O L I T E
5 2 9 10 13 7 6 4

3. impossible to read
I L L E G I B L E
16 18 20 1 7 11 3 15 9

4. not kind to visitors
I N H O S P I T A B L E
14 11 7 2 16 20 8 18 4 5 15 3

5. too strong to fight against
I R R E S I S T I B L E
10 2 5 18 6 9 3 7 1 19 15 11

6. without motion
I M M O B I L E
4 10 7 16 14 11 13 2

7. without the ability needed
I N C A P A B L E
12 4 17 11 9 7 18 15 3

8. unable to read or write
I L L I T E R A T E
6 2 20 19 8 9 7 10 12 4

9. not whole or finished
I N C O M P L E T E
8 3 19 1 20 5 16 7 11 4

▶ **Look at the numbers below each blank. One number appears in every word. Write the letters above that number to spell the word that finishes the riddle.**

The number that appears in every word is 7.
What do you call a midnight horse? A __nightmare__.

What's the same about the spelling of all the answer words?
They begin with *i* and end with *e*

AUDITORY LEARNERS

LARGE GROUP Say words that contain the prefixes *ir-*, *im-*, *il-*, and *in-*. Words might include *irresponsible*, *illegible*, *inefficient*, and *impassable*. Ask students to spell the prefix in each word and give the word's meaning.

GIFTED LEARNERS

Present students with the following base words and root: *possible, ability, competent, literate, capable, pair*. Challenge them to add the correct prefixes *(ir-, im-, il-,* or *in-)* to give the bases and root a "not" meaning. Have students check their work with dictionaries.

LEARNERS WHO NEED EXTRA SUPPORT

Have pairs of students take turns giving each other the clues on page 66 orally and reciting the answers. Partners can practice spelling the words together. **See Daily Word Study Practice, pages 186–189.**

CURRICULUM CONNECTIONS ✳ ••• ◆

SPELLING

Create cards for the following prefixes and word parts: *ir-, im-, il-, in-, em-, mis-, mal-, counter-, anti-, de-, regular, perfect, legal, expensive, ployment, spelling, practice, part, freeze, -scend*. Have students match cards to create a spelling word for each definition below.

1. not regular *(irregular)*
2. not perfect *(imperfect)*
3. not lawful *(illegal)*
4. cheap *(inexpensive)*
5. work *(employment)*
6. spelling error *(misspelling)*
7. improper practice *(malpractice)*
8. similar person or thing *(counterpart)*
9. something that stops freezing *(antifreeze)*
10. go down *(descend)*

WRITING

 Ask students to select five base words from page 65 and use the words to write a paragraph on any subject they wish. Then have them rewrite their paragraphs, adding the prefix *ir-, im-, il-,* or *in-* to each base word. Discuss whether adding the prefixes gives each paragraph the opposite meaning. If not, ask what other changes are necessary for sense.

SOCIAL STUDIES

Discuss the meanings of *literacy* and *illiteracy*. Invite students to use dictionaries to learn the origin of the base word *literate*. Talk about the feelings and problems of people who are unable to read. Have students research what services and programs are available in your community to combat illiteracy.

SCIENCE

Does it seem *impossible* or *irrational* to students that humans have found a way to "fly?" Invite future aviators in your class to explore the worlds of *aeroplanes, aerodynamics, aerobatics,* or *aerospace*. Have students prepare a poster or 3D display to explain the scientific principles involved in these areas of *aeronautics*.

 AstroWord, Prefixes.©1998 Silver Burdett Ginn Inc. Division of Simon & Schuster.

Lesson 30

Pages 67–68

Prefixes im-, em-

Lesson Focus

INTRODUCING THE SKILL

- Write the following sentence on the board: *It was impossible to keep the immigrants from embracing the friends that greeted them.* Have volunteers underline the words with prefixes. *(impossible, immigrants, embracing)*

- Ask which word has a prefix meaning "not." *(impossible)* Explain that the prefix *im-*, as well as *em-*, can also mean "in," "into," or "on."

- Tell students that the base word *migrate* means to "move" and the root *brace* comes from a word meaning "arm." Invite them to apply those meanings and the prefix meanings to define *immigrants* and *embracing*.

USING THE PAGES

- Ask a volunteer to read the rule and examples on page 67. Have students read the directions for both pages and ask any questions they might have.

- You may wish to review the *im-* words in the word bank on page 68 in which *im-* means "not," and to discuss meanings for unfamiliar words.

Name

▶ Ten words with the prefix **im** or **em** are hidden in the puzzle. Some of the words go across and some go down. Circle each word as you find it in the puzzle. Then write the word beside its meaning.

RULE
The prefixes **im** and **em** usually mean **in**, **into**, or **on**. Remember, **im** can also mean **not**.

immigrants = people coming into a country

immeasurable = not measurable

embed = set something firmly into

```
E R V B S L O T U N I N L
M L X Z B T C I C D M N T
L E B I M M E R S E P O R
I K E M B R O I D E R Y C
M S R P A R B E M B O S S
I M P R O V I S E I P X A
A I M O M I M P U R E E R
J E I B E V I M P O R T B
T A N A N S F G H U Y I Z
L E M B R A C E M I S R W
H E W L I M P E R I L R T
T G X E C Z L N S B C Y G
```

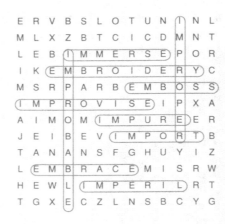

1. _____**emboss**_____ to put a decoration or raised design on an article

3. _____**immerse**_____ to sink into water

5. _____**impure**_____ not pure

7. _____**import**_____ to bring in something from another country

9. _____**imperil**_____ to put in danger

2. _____**embrace**_____ to hug

4. _____**embroidery**_____ needlework

6. _____**improper**_____ not correct or right

8. _____**improbable**_____ not likely to happen

10. _____**improvise**_____ to perform something with no preparation

FOCUS ON ALL LEARNERS

ENGLISH LANGUAGE LEARNERS/ESL

English language learners may have trouble finding the words embedded in the puzzle on page 67. Encourage them to work with a partner.

VISUAL LEARNERS

INDIVIDUAL Have students look through their dictionaries to find words beginning with the prefixes *im-* and *em-* that have not been covered in this lesson. Have students list up to ten of these new words with their meanings. Discuss how the meanings of the prefixes apply to the words.

AUDITORY LEARNERS

LARGE GROUP Invite volunteers to think of clues to give for the *im-* and *em-* prefix words from the pages. Have volunteers take turns speaking their clues as classmates respond, ask them to use the answer words in sentences.

Write a word from the word bank to complete each sentence.

embark	embedded	embraced	emerged	employing
empowered	imagined	immaturely	immediately	immerse
immigrated	impatience	important	improbable	improved

1. Miguel often ___imagined___ taking a great vacation with his family.

2. It was ___important___ to Miguel to spend time with his family.

3. Miguel thought the chances of a vacation this year were ___improbable___.

4. Miguel's father ___emerged___ from the den one night with a handful of maps.

5. "We are going to ___embark___ on a fantastic vacation," Miguel's father said.

6. "___Immediately___ after work tomorrow, we will leave."

7. Miguel was so happy he ___embraced___ his father.

8. Miguel waited for the next day with great ___impatience___.

9. He didn't want to act ___immaturely___, however, so he kept his thoughts to himself.

10. ___Embedded___ in Miguel's mind were his father's words "fantastic vacation."

Now write three sentences of your own. In each sentence, include at least one of the **em** or **im** words from the sentences above.

11. _____

_____

12. _____

_____

13. _____

_____

68   Lesson 30
     Prefixes im-, em-

SPELLING

Invite volunteers to write the spelling words on the board: *irregular, imperfect, illegal, inexpensive, employment, misspelling, malpractice, counterpart, antifreeze, descend.* Divide the class into two groups. Have the groups take turns asking one another to guess the word being described. They can call out clue words or phrases, such as synonyms, antonyms, or related concepts. For example, for *antifreeze,* players might call out *car, winter, ice,* and other words related to the concept.

WRITING

Portfolio Have students write a poem that contains numerous words with the prefixes *im-* and *em-.* Point out that poets often repeat sounds other than those at the end of lines. Repeating sounds at the beginning of words can also create a melodious effect.

ART

Embossing and *imprinting* are two techniques used by artists to add visual interest to an object. Encourage students to research these two topics. They can learn different ways the techniques are practiced and then find examples of embossed or imprinted designs to share with the class.

SOCIAL STUDIES

Have students research patterns of immigration in the United States. Students can work in small groups, concentrating on a certain era of U.S. history and the nationalities that were represented in immigration figures for that period. Or, student investigations might concentrate on the immigration patterns of one particular nationality throughout different eras.

Technology

AstroWord, Prefixes.©1998 Silver Burdett Ginn Inc. Division of Simon & Schuster.

KINESTHETIC LEARNERS

SMALL GROUP Have students draw two symbols on the board: one to represent *not* and one for *in* or *on.* Invite students to name *im-* and *em-* prefix words from the lesson or the dictionary. As they define each word, have students write the word under the appropriate symbol.

GIFTED LEARNERS

Have students look up the meanings or origins for the base words or roots of five of the *im-* or *em-* prefix words on the pages.

LEARNERS WHO NEED EXTRA SUPPORT

Talk about the meaning of the words on page 68. Have students read the words within the context of the sentences before writing them in the blanks. **See Daily Word Study Practice, pages 186–189.**

Lesson 31
Pages 69–70

Prefixes mis-, mal-

✦•✦•◆•✦•◆•✦•◆•◆•✦

INFORMAL ASSESSMENT OBJECTIVES

Can students

✔ recognize the prefixes *mis-* and *mal-* in words?

✔ correctly use words containing the prefixes *mis-* and *mal-*?

Lesson Focus

INTRODUCING THE SKILL

- Write the following words on the board: *mispronounce, misunderstand, malfunction, malnutrition.* Ask volunteers to read the words and explain their meanings.

- Ask the class to identify the prefixes in the words. (*mis-* and *mal-*)

- Explain that the prefixes *mis-* and *mal-* usually mean "bad" or "badly," or "wrong" or "wrongly." Ask students to define the words again using these meanings.

- Give students the opportunity to suggest other words that have the prefixes *mis-* and *mal-*. Write the words on the board and have students apply the prefix meanings to the words.

USING THE PAGES

Review the rule and sample words given on page 69. Have students read the directions for each section before beginning pages 69 and 70. Later, have students discuss what they have learned about the prefixes *mis-* and *mal-*.

Name _____

▶ **Circle each word in which mis or mal is used as a prefix.**

> **RULE**
> The prefixes **mis** and **mal** usually mean **bad** or **badly**, or **wrong** or **wrongly**.
> **mis**pronounce = pronounce wrongly
> **mal**adjustment = bad adjustment

1. (mispronounce)
2. male
3. (misunderstand)
4. Maltese
5. (malodorous)
6. (mislabel)
7. (malformation)
8. (misbehave)
9. (malnourished)
10. (misread)
11. (malpractice)
12. (maltreat)
13. missile
14. mallet
15. (maladjusted)
16. misery
17. (malnutrition)
18. (misspelling)
19. (malfunction)
20. (misquote)

▶ **Write the word from the above list that best completes each sentence.**

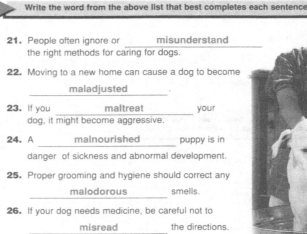

21. People often ignore or ___**misunderstand**___ the right methods for caring for dogs.

22. Moving to a new home can cause a dog to become ___**maladjusted**___ .

23. If you ___**maltreat**___ your dog. it might become aggressive.

24. A ___**malnourished**___ puppy is in danger of sickness and abnormal development.

25. Proper grooming and hygiene should correct any ___**malodorous**___ smells.

26. If your dog needs medicine, be careful not to ___**misread**___ the directions.

27. ___**Malnutrition**___ is often the cause of poor bone development.

28. Your dog will not ___**misbehave**___ if it has been properly trained.

Lesson 31
Prefixes mis-, mal-   **69**

FOCUS ON ALL LEARNERS ✦ •◆•◼

ENGLISH LANGUAGE LEARNERS/ESL

Materials: index cards

Put the answer words for the sentences on page 69 on cards. Lead a discussion about pet care, inviting students to use the words on the cards in their comments.

VISUAL LEARNERS

PARTNER Write these words on the board and discuss their meanings with the class: *maladjusted, misused, malfunction, misunderstood, misfortune, malnourished.* Challenge pairs of students to write three sentences, using two of the words in each.

KINESTHETIC LEARNERS

SMALL GROUP Invite students to take turns choosing a word from page 69 or 70 to demonstrate its meaning for the others to identify. Encourage students to use props or a partner, if needed.

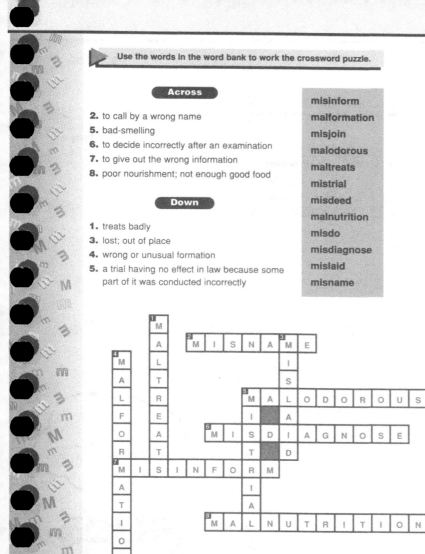

Use the words in the word bank to work the crossword puzzle.

Across

2. to call by a wrong name
5. bad-smelling
6. to decide incorrectly after an examination
7. to give out the wrong information
8. poor nourishment; not enough good food

Down

1. treats badly
3. lost; out of place
4. wrong or unusual formation
5. a trial having no effect in law because some part of it was conducted incorrectly

Word Bank:
misinform
malformation
misjoin
malodorous
maltreats
mistrial
misdeed
malnutrition
misdo
misdiagnose
mislaid
misname

Lesson 31
Prefixes mis-, mal-

70

SPELLING

Have students complete the sentences below by adding the spelling word that fits.

1. Chrissy chopped her bangs into an ___ shape. (*irregular*)
2. Museum officials recognized the ___ copy as a fake. (*imperfect*)
3. It is ___ to keep farm animals in a city neighborhood. (*illegal*)
4. The food in that restaurant is ___ but delicious. (*inexpensive*)
5. If you what to find summer ___, check the ads in the paper. (*employment*)
6. The editor corrected the writer's ___. (*misspelling*)
7. Deliberately ignoring a client's wishes would be an example of ___. (*malpractice*)
8. The spy passed the coded message to her ___. (*counterpart*)
9. We stopped at the gas station to get some ___. (*antifreeze*)
10. After you climb the hill, you will slowly ___ to the valley. (*descend*)

WRITING

Portfolio Have students write silly character sketches of imaginary people whose names are based on words containing the prefixes *mis-* and *mal-*, for example, Miss Diagnosis, a confused physician; or Mal Function, an inept mechanic. The characters' names should reflect their jobs or personalities.

SCIENCE

Malnutrition is a serious problem in many parts of the world. Have students research the causes, types, and symptoms of malnutrition and the treatments available for it.

SOCIAL STUDIES

Have students research information on how to prevent mistreatment and malnutrition of pets or other animals.

Technology

AstroWord, Prefixes.©1998 Silver Burdett Ginn Inc. Division of Simon & Schuster.

AUDITORY LEARNERS

LARGE GROUP Help the class orally brainstorm a list of words beginning with *mis-* and *mal-*. Have volunteers eliminate words in which *mis-* or *mal-* is not a prefix. Then ask students to use the prefix meanings to explain the meanings of the remaining words. Invite students to use dictionaries to check each other's oral answers.

GIFTED LEARNERS

Have small groups of students create their own crossword puzzles like the one on page 70. Each word in the puzzle must begin with or have a clue that begins with the prefix *mis-* or *mal-*.

LEARNERS WHO NEED EXTRA SUPPORT

It can be helpful for students to memorize one simple example for each prefix in this, or other, lessons. Have students pick a familiar word using *mis-*, such as *misspell*, and one for *mal-*, such as *malnutrition*. Students should mentally compare these words to harder ones they encounter with the same prefixes. **See Daily Word Study Practice, pages 186–189.**

Lesson 32

Pages 71–72

Prefixes anti-, counter-

* ◆ ● ■ ● ◆ ● ✦ ◆ ● ■ ● ◆

Lesson Focus

INTRODUCING THE SKILL

- Write the following words on the board: *antibiotic, antifreeze, antibody, counterclockwise, counterattack.* Have volunteers read the words and explain what they understand their meanings to be.

- Ask students to suggest what the prefixes *anti-* and *counter-* mean. Lead them to understand that they mean "against" or "the opposite of." Have students redefine each word by using one of the prefix meanings each time.

- Encourage students to supply additional words with the prefixes *anti-* and *counter-* and explain how their meanings fit the prefixes.

USING THE PAGES

- Read the rule and examples on page 71. Be sure that students understand the directions for pages 71 and 72. After completing the pages, encourage students to discuss what they learned about these prefixes.

- **Critical Thinking** Challenge students to suggest ways that the writer's brother is skilled with cars.

Name

 Write a word from the word bank to complete each sentence.

> **RULE**
> The prefixes **anti** and **counter** mean **against** or **opposite**.
> **anti**pollution = against pollution
> **counter**clockwise = in the opposite direction from the way a clock runs

Word bank:
counterbalance counterpart
antipollution counteroffers
counterclockwise antiknock antiseptic
countermeasure antifreeze antilock

1. My brother found a used car with _____antilock_____ brakes to keep the wheels from locking.

2. Its _____antipollution_____ devices limit dangerous exhaust fumes.

3. During the test drive he turned the wheel clockwise and _____counterclockwise_____ to check the steering.

4. He checked the weights on the tire rims which _____counterbalance_____ the wheels to keep them from wobbling.

5. After several offers and _____counteroffers_____ , my brother bought the car.

6. As a _____countermeasure_____ against tire problems my brother bought a spare.

7. On the way home he bought gas with _____antiknock_____ ingredients to keep the engine from knocking.

8. At home I helped my brother put _____antifreeze_____ in the car to protect the engine in cold weather.

9. We installed one headlight, but we broke its _____counterpart_____ .

10. My brother cut his hand on the glass and had to put an _____antiseptic_____ on it.

> What evidence do you have that the writer's brother knows about cars?

 **Critical Thinking**

Lesson 32
Prefixes anti-, counter- **71**

FOCUS ON ALL LEARNERS ✦ ● ◆ ■ ◆

ENGLISH LANGUAGE LEARNERS/ESL

Before beginning page 71, direct students' attention to the vocabulary words in the word bank at the top of the page. Talk about the meanings of the base words and the words with prefixes.

VISUAL LEARNERS

PARTNER Instruct pairs of students to use a dictionary to create a list of words that combine the prefix *anti-* or *counter-* with a root rather than a base word. (Possible answers are: *antibiotic, antidote, antipathy, antipodes, countermand,* and *counterfeit.*)

KINESTHETIC LEARNERS

SMALL GROUP **Materials:** one index card per student

Have students write *anti* on one side of their cards and *counter* on the other. On the board, list base words or roots that can be combined with one of the prefixes. Let students take turns placing the correct side of their cards, by trial and error if necessary, in front of the base words or roots and using the new words in sentences.

> **Write a word from the word bank to finish each rhyme.**

> antifreeze   countermove   antibiotic

1. John knew his chess playing had to improve

when Jill captured his king in a _____countermove_____.

2. The car engine is cold from the wintry breeze.

What that engine needs is some _____antifreeze_____.

3. Poor Sue is sick. What can she do?

The doctor may prescribe an _____antibiotic_____ or two.

> **Write the letter of the sentence that answers the question.**

_b_ **4.** Which sentence gives a **counterproposal**?
  a. I think our kitchen cabinets need to be replaced.
  b. I disagree that we should buy a new car, but
  perhaps we might buy a used car.
  c. I think we should buy a new radio.

_a_ **5.** Which sentence expresses **antipathy**?
  a. I hate spiders!
  b. My new rollerskates are gone.
  c. Greg prefers hiking off the trails.

_b_ **6.** Which sentence expresses **antisocial** feelings?
  a. Come to my party.
  b. Leave me alone.
  c. Do your homework.

_c_ **7.** Which sentence contains a **countersign**?
  a. Saturday will be warm and sunny.
  b. We have five more months of school.
  c. The password is "cheeseburger."

_b_ **8.** Which sentence supports **antilittering** laws?
  a. Litter is a part of life.
  b. Our city fines people who throw trash into the streets.
  c. Empty soda cans and newspapers are scattered
  all over the park.

72 Lesson 32
Prefixes anti-, counter-

AUDITORY LEARNERS

LARGE GROUP
Give as a clue the meaning of one of the prefix words
from pages 71 or 72. When a student responds with the
correct word, he or she gives the next clue. Have students continue
the activity.

GIFTED LEARNERS

Have students create their own multiple-choice questions like the ones
at the bottom of page 72. Have them exchange "tests" with a partner.

LEARNERS WHO NEED EXTRA SUPPORT

Have students take turns reading the sentences with answers on
page 71. Ask them to explain what each sentence means, using the
prefix word to help. For confusing sentences, look up the answer
words together in dictionaries. **See Daily Word Study Practice,
pages 186–189.**

CURRICULUM CONNECTIONS

SPELLING

Write the prefixes *ir-, im-, il-, in-, em-, mis-,
mal-, counter-, anti-,* and *de-,* in a column on
one side of the board, and the word parts
*regular, perfect, legal, expensive, ployment,
spelling, practice, part, freeze,* and *-scend* in
another. Column in random order. Invite
volunteers to go to the board to draw a line
between a prefix and word part to create a
spelling word. Have them say and spell the
entire word aloud. Continue until all the
words have been discovered.

WRITING

Portfolio Have students write and present
humorously grumpy speeches in
which they list and describe all the things
they are against. Encourage them to think of
ways to include words containing *anti-* and
counter- in their speeches. Suggest that they
use the dictionary to find words that might
be appropriate.

SCIENCE

Tell students that antibiotics are an important
weapon in the battle against disease. Look up
and discuss together the meaning of *antibiotic*
and its root. Have students research when and
how antibiotics were discovered, how they
work, and how some bacteria are becoming
resistant to antibiotics.

HEALTH

Talk about the meanings of the word units in
antiseptic. Invite a physician, nurse, or health
department worker to speak to students about
what *antiseptics* are and when and why they
are used. Students should be encouraged to
research information on their own. Have
students list the names of some common
antiseptics and tell why they are important.

Technology

AstroWord, Prefixes.©1998 Silver
Burdett Ginn Inc. Division of
Simon & Schuster.

Lesson 33

Pages 73–74

 **Reading** **Writing**

Reviewing Prefixes

INFORMAL ASSESSMENT OBJECTIVES

Can students

✔ read a diary entry that contains words with prefixes?

✔ write a persuasive paragraph and an advice column?

Lesson Focus

READING

- Write *insignificant, illiterate,* and *impatient* on the board. Ask students to identify the prefix in each word and to tell what the prefix means. (*in-, il-, im-,* "not")

- Display *embraced* and *imperil.* Have students identify the prefixes (*em-, im-*) and their meanings ("in" or "into").

- Write *misunderstood* and *maladjusted* on the board. Ask what the prefixes *mis-* and *mal-* mean. ("badly" or "wrongly")

- Tell students that they will read these and other words with prefixes in the diary entry on page 73. Ask them to put themselves in Jean's place as they read the passage. Then ask students to imagine that they are friends of Jean's and to write a response.

WRITING

- Have students read the directions and topic hints on page 74. Remind them to use words from the word bank.

- Some students may wish to write their advice columns, using a typical question-and-answer format.

Name

 Reading ▶ Read the diary entry. Then write your answer to the question at the end of the story.

Dear Diary,   *September 14*

Since transferring to my new school, I feel insignificant and illiterate. Let me explain why.

When I get on the bus in the morning, everyone usually acts as if I'm invisible. This morning, however, Mom embraced me as I walked out the door. I had warned her never to imperil my reputation by hugging me in public, but she can be very irrational. Was I ever embarrassed!

When I got on the bus, everyone was snickering—especially Monica Morris, the most important girl in sixth grade, and her immature sidekick, Shelly Raines. The morning just got worse. In my new school, I have to take Spanish class. Everyone else has been immersed in Spanish since fourth grade. At one point the teacher asked me a question. I stared at her in silence as she grew more and more impatient. Finally I muttered an answer. Once more, everyone began to giggle. I had completely misunderstood the question and mispronounced the answer!

I felt so shy sitting by myself in the cafeteria that I ate only half my lunch. By the middle of the afternoon, I felt completely malnourished! Then, feeling weak and dizzy from lack of food, I bumped into Monica in the hall and she looked at me as if I was malodorous and maladjusted. The rest of my life is clearly going to be impossible!

Miserably yours,
Jean

You are a friend trying to make Jean feel better. How will you convince her that her life will improve?

_____
_____
_____
_____
_____

Lesson 33
Review prefixes: Reading   **73**

FOCUS ON ALL LEARNERS ✳ • ◆ ▪ ◆

ENGLISH LANGUAGE LEARNERS/ESL

Have students compare any experiences they have had of moving to a new home or going to a new school to Jean's experiences. Ask what advice they would give each other about problems similar to Jean's.

 VISUAL/KINESTHETIC
INDIVIDUAL **LEARNERS**

Have students copy words from the diary entry that contain the prefixes taught in Lessons 29–32. Students can highlight the prefixes with colored pens or markers, using a separate color for each prefix group if possible. Ask them to divide each word into units of meaning.

LARGE GROUP **VISUAL LEARNERS**

Copy the words from the word bank on page 74 onto the board. As you point to each word, have students who used the word in their advice columns read the sentences that contain it. Ask other students what the words mean in the context of the sentences.

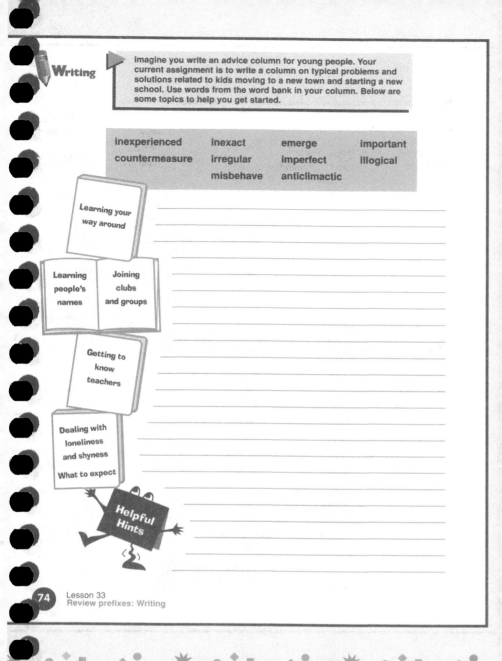

Writing

Imagine you write an advice column for young people. Your current assignment is to write a column on typical problems and solutions related to kids moving to a new town and starting a new school. Use words from the word bank in your column. Below are some topics to help you get started.

inexperienced	inexact	emerge	important
countermeasure	irregular	imperfect	illogical
	misbehave	anticlimactic	

Learning your way around

Learning people's names

Joining clubs and groups

Getting to know teachers

Dealing with loneliness and shyness

What to expect

Helpful Hints

AUDITORY/KINESTHETIC LEARNERS

LARGE GROUP

Assign each of three groups one of the following prefix groups: *ir-, im-, il-, in-; im-, em-; mis-, mal-*. Read the diary passage on page 73 aloud. Challenge students to raise their hands each time they hear a word with one of their group's prefixes. Caution students to distinguish between *im-* meaning "not" and "in" or "on".

GIFTED LEARNERS

Have students write dictionary definitions for several words from Lessons 28–32 that they find difficult. Entries should include division of each word into units of meaning, meaning of each prefix and root or base word, meaning of the whole word, and a sample sentence.

LEARNERS WHO NEED EXTRA SUPPORT

Read and discuss phrases containing words with prefixes from the diary entry on page 73, for example, *imperil my reputation, completely malnourished, more and more impatient*. **See Daily Word Study Practice, pages 186–189.**

CURRICULUM CONNECTIONS

SPELLING

Give students cards on which you have written the spelling words *irregular, imperfect, illegal, inexpensive, employment, misspelling, malpractice, counterpart, antifreeze,* and *descend*. Have each cardholder try to communicate his or her word in the style of charades by acting out words that sound like various syllables of the target word. For example, for antifreeze, a student might act out First Syllable—an ant, Second Syllable—an eye, Third Syllable-freezing cold. When a classmate guesses the target word correctly, he or she must then spell it orally.

SOCIAL STUDIES

Prompt students to discuss what Jean might write in her diary three months after the entry on page 73, once she has begun to make friends in her new school. Talk about how it feels to be the new person in school, at a club, or in the neighborhood. Brainstorm some tips for making new people feel comfortable and for making friends when you are the new person.

READING

Much literature is made up of first-person accounts of people's lives—from diaries, to collected letters, to autobiographies. Have each student locate and read one such work. Then have students do presentations of the material they have learned, by talking as if they were the subject of the accounts.

Technology

AstroWord, Prefixes.©1998 Silver Burdett Ginn Inc. Division of Simon & Schuster.

Lesson 34

Pages 75–76

Prefix de-

INFORMAL ASSESSMENT OBJECTIVES

Can students

✓ recognize the prefix *de-* in words?

✓ correctly use words containing the prefix *de-*?

Lesson Focus

INTRODUCING THE SKILL

- Write the following sentences on the board.

  Depress this key to turn on the computer.

  Your fever will decrease when you take this medicine.

- Have volunteers read the sentences and underline each word with the prefix *de-*.

- Explain that the prefix *de-* can mean "down" or "away." Ask what is going down or away in the sentences with the words *depress* and *decrease*.

- Note that *de-* is not a prefix in every word where it appears at the beginning. Write *decode, depth, deflate, detouring, dear, detached,* and *dentist.* Have students cross out words without a prefix (*depth, dear, dentist*).

- Invite students to define the *de-* words, using the meanings "down" or "away."

USING THE PAGES

Read the rule and examples on page 75 with students. Be sure that students understand the directions for pages 75 and 76.

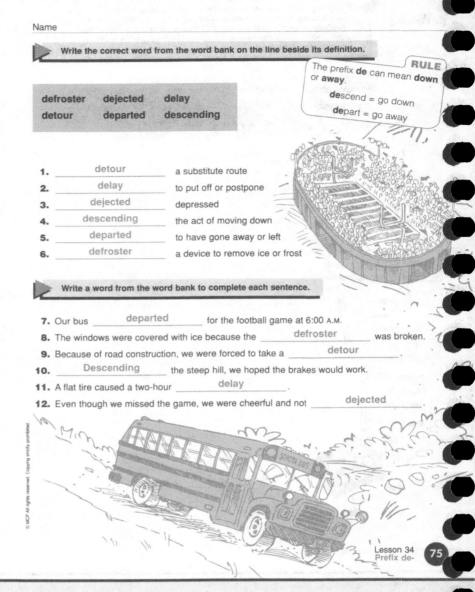

Name _____

▶ Write the correct word from the word bank on the line beside its definition.

| defroster | dejected | delay |
| detour | departed | descending |

> **RULE**
> The prefix **de** can mean **down** or **away**.
> de**scend** = go down
> de**part** = go away

1. ____detour____   a substitute route
2. ____delay____   to put off or postpone
3. ____dejected____   depressed
4. ____descending____   the act of moving down
5. ____departed____   to have gone away or left
6. ____defroster____   a device to remove ice or frost

▶ Write a word from the word bank to complete each sentence.

7. Our bus ____departed____ for the football game at 6:00 A.M.
8. The windows were covered with ice because the ____defroster____ was broken.
9. Because of road construction, we were forced to take a ____detour____.
10. ____Descending____ the steep hill, we hoped the brakes would work.
11. A flat tire caused a two-hour ____delay____.
12. Even though we missed the game, we were cheerful and not ____dejected____.

Lesson 34
Prefix de-   75

FOCUS ON ALL LEARNERS

ENGLISH LANGUAGE LEARNERS/ESL

Remind students that when they are uncertain about the meaning of a word with a prefix, they should check a dictionary. Model for students how to locate a sample base word, check its meaning, then check the meaning of the base plus the prefix.

VISUAL LEARNERS

INDIVIDUAL Have students use the dictionary to locate words new to them that begin with the prefix *de-*. Have them study the definitions and use five of the words correctly in sentences. Remind students that *de-* at the beginning of a word is not always a prefix.

KINESTHETIC LEARNERS

SMALL GROUP Have volunteers act out verbs that contain the prefix *de-*. Verbs might include *depart, detach, descend, detour,* and *deplane.* Have the rest of the students try to guess the verbs being mimed.

> Circle each word that contains the prefix de.

dean (deodorize) dealt decimal (deflate) dear
(decamp) (denounce) dentist (debrief) (derailed) (decrease)
ecade (decry) (defrost) (decode) depth (dehumidifier)
(departure) denim (deplane) (detach) (dethrone) (detract)

> Use words from the first activity to complete the crossword puzzle.

Across

. to figure out the meaning of something that is written in secret writing
. a machine that takes moisture out of the air
6. to get off an airplane
. to unfasten or disconnect
. to let air out

Down

1. to take away or cover up the smell of something
3. taken away or made less
4. to remove frost or ice
5. a going away or leaving

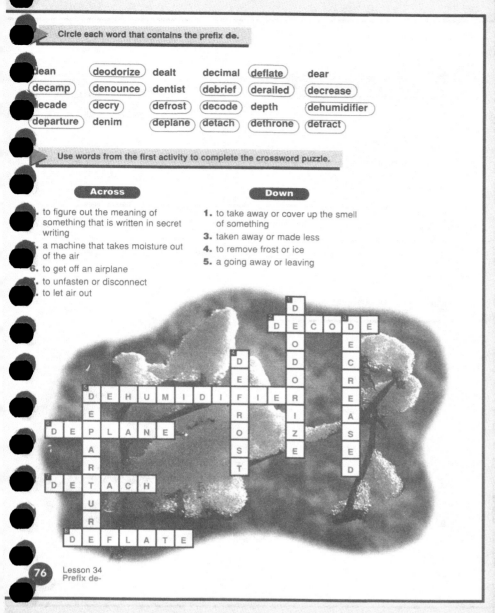

76
Lesson 34
Prefix de-

AUDITORY LEARNERS

SMALL GROUP

Read aloud each sentence at the bottom of page 75 two times. The first time say *blank* for the missing word; the second time, pause for students to say a *de-* word that makes sense.

GIFTED LEARNERS

Have students investigate *de-* words built on roots, such as *detour, depart, deduct, descend, dejected, detach,* and *deflate*. Encourage them to find out the meanings and origins of the roots and list other words constructed from the same roots.

LEARNERS WHO NEED EXTRA SUPPORT

Review with students all of the *de-* words covered in this lesson. Help them determine the meaning of *de-* in each word. **See Daily Word Study Practice, pages 186–189.**

CURRICULUM CONNECTIONS

SPELLING

You may use the following words and dictation sentences as a posttest for the first group of spelling words for Unit 3.

1. **irregular** — The dentist said Ike's teeth were very **irregular**.
2. **imperfect** — The match between the two colors was **imperfect**.
3. **illegal** — It is **illegal** to sell stolen goods.
4. **inexpensive** — I am looking for an **inexpensive** gift.
5. **employment** — My mother is seeking **employment** as a detective.
6. **misspelling** — There was a **misspelling** on the sign.
7. **malpractice** — The lawyer was accused of **malpractice**.
8. **counterpart** — Dad liked the actor in the stage play, but Mom preferred his **counterpart** in the movie.
9. **antifreeze** — Check the **antifreeze** in your car before a long trip.
10. **descend** — Be careful as you **descend** that tall ladder.

WRITING

Portfolio Have each student write about an imaginary or real experience that could be titled "Delayed Departure," using words with *de-* as a prefix.

MATHEMATICS

Explain if a ball is dropped and bounces multiple times, the height of each bounce will decrease. The height of the first bounce is 0.6 multiplied by the initial height of the drop. The second bounce will be 0.6 times the height of the first bounce, and so on. If a ball is dropped from 100 meters, how high will it bounce on the fourth bounce? (*12.96 meters*)

AstroWord, Prefixes.©1998 Silver Burdett Ginn Inc. Division of Simon & Schuster.

Lesson 35

Pages 77–78

Prefixes fore-, post-

INFORMAL ASSESSMENT OBJECTIVES

Can students

✔ recognize the prefixes *fore-* and *post-* in words?

✔ correctly use words containing the prefixes *fore-* and *post-*?

Lesson Focus

INTRODUCING THE SKILL

- Write *foreleg, foreground, postgraduate,* and *postnasal* on the board. Then write the sentences below, omitting the words in parentheses.

  The horse's right (foreleg) was hurt.

  Bob did (postgraduate) work at the university.

  A (postnasal) drip is making Becky cough.

  Rhonda is in the (foreground) of the photo.

- Ask volunteers to come to the board and complete each sentence with the word that makes the most sense.

- Ask what the prefixes *fore-* and *post-* seem to mean. Guide students to conclude that *fore-* means "in front of" or "before" and *post-* means "after." Have students define the words in the context of the sentences.

USING THE PAGES

Have students read the rule and examples on page 77. Review the definition of *analogy* and the sample given. Be sure that students understand the directions for pages 77 and 78.

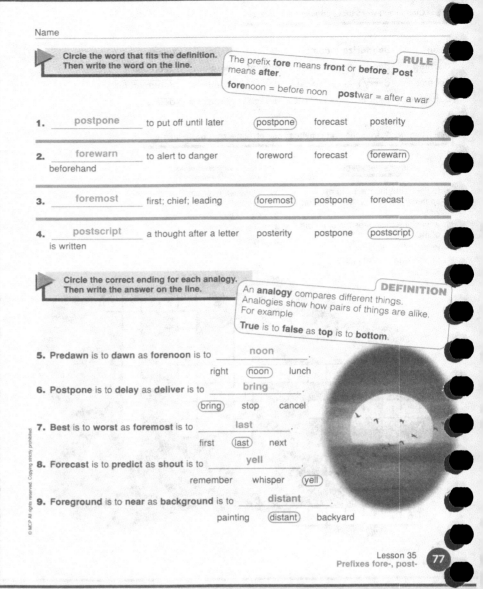

Name _____

▶ Circle the word that fits the definition. Then write the word on the line.

RULE
The prefix **fore** means **front** or **before**. Post means **after**.
forenoon = before noon   **post**war = after a war

1. _____postpone_____ to put off until later   (postpone) forecast posterity

2. _____forewarn_____ to alert to danger beforehand   foreword forecast (forewarn)

3. _____foremost_____ first; chief; leading   (foremost) postpone forecast

4. _____postscript_____ a thought after a letter is written   posterity postpone (postscript)

▶ Circle the correct ending for each analogy. Then write the answer on the line.

DEFINITION
An **analogy** compares different things. Analogies show how pairs of things are alike. For example
True is to **false** as **top** is to **bottom**.

5. **Predawn** is to **dawn** as **forenoon** is to _____noon_____
   right (noon) lunch

6. **Postpone** is to **delay** as **deliver** is to _____bring_____
   (bring) stop cancel

7. **Best** is to **worst** as **foremost** is to _____last_____
   first (last) next

8. **Forecast** is to **predict** as **shout** is to _____yell_____
   remember whisper (yell)

9. **Foreground** is to **near** as **background** is to _____distant_____
   painting (distant) backyard

Lesson 35
Prefixes fore-, post-   **77**

FOCUS ON ALL LEARNERS ✳ ●◆■

ENGLISH LANGUAGE LEARNERS/ESL

Explain the difference between the prefix *post-* and the noun *post* (The noun means "mail" or "an upright piece of wood or metal").

VISUAL LEARNERS

LARGE GROUP

Write the following words on the board: *paw, war, paid, arm, script, see.* Ask students to add the prefix *fore-* or *post-* to each word. Have them check their dictionaries to see whether their words are correct.

VISUAL/KINESTHETIC LEARNERS

LARGE GROUP

Divide the class in half, assigning the prefix *fore-* to one group and *post-* to the other group. Write the following word bases on the board, one at a time: *cast, war, pone, head, graduate, word, warn, script, noon.* As you write each base, the group that can form a word with its prefix announces the word.

Choose the word from the word bank that completes each sentence.
Write the letters of the words on the lines.

forefinger	forehead
foremost	foreshadow
foresight	foretell
forewarned	posterity
postgraduate	postpone

1. We hoped the rain on Friday did not f o r e s (h) a d o w a terrible weekend.

2. Not even the meteorologist could f o r e t e (l) l the weekend weather.

3. We made a group decision not to p o s (t) p o n e our camping trip.

4. Frank had the f o r e s i (g) h t to suggest that we pack our rain gear.

5. Lucas wanted to film our trip for p o s t (e) r i t y.

6. He filmed a ranger with a bandanna across her f o r e (h) e a d.

7. The ranger f (o) r e w a r n e d us that swimming in the river was dangerous.

8. She told us about the park's f o r e m o (s) t hiking trails.

9. She pointed to the best trail with her f o r e f (i) n g e r.

10. She explained that she had learned about becoming a ranger when she was a p o s t g r a d (u) a t e student.

Answer the riddle by writing each circled letter above the number of its sentence.

What house weighs the least?

A l i g h t h o u s e !
2 9 4 6 3 1 7 10 8 5

Lesson 35
Prefixes fore-, post-

SPELLING

You may use the following words and dictation sentences as a pretest for the second group of spelling words for Unit 3.

1. **forenoon** — The baby takes one nap in the **forenoon**.
2. **postscript** — Amanda wrote a **postscript** to her letter.
3. **overcrowded** — The bus station was **overcrowded** and hot.
4. **ultrafine** — The recipe called for **ultrafine** sugar.
5. **supersonic** — The **supersonic** jet boomed overhead.
6. **transfer** — We land in Chicago and then **transfer** to another flight.
7. **semicircle** — The snowman's mouth is a **semicircle** of raisins.
8. **submerge** — On a hot day, **submerge** your feet in cold water.
9. **midnight** — At **midnight**, an owl began to hoot.
10. **unison** — The chorus members sang in perfect **unison**.

WRITING

Portfolio Have small groups of students work to create analogies similar to those on page 77, using words with the prefix *fore-* or *post-*.

SCIENCE

Have students research animals' behaviors used to forewarn enemies. For example, a cat arches its back and hisses; the hair on its back and tail may stand erect.

ART

In many paintings, there is a distinct foreground and a distinct background. Have students analyze famous works of art to identify these elements.

Technology

AstroWord, Prefixes.©1998 Silver Burdett Ginn Inc. Division of Simon & Schuster.

AUDITORY LEARNERS

LARGE GROUP Point to a student and say either *fore-* or *post-*. Challenge the student to say a word beginning with the prefix. The student then points to another student and says one of the two prefixes. The second student must say a matching word, and so on.

GIFTED LEARNERS

Invite students to work in pairs to create nonexistent but plausible new words using the prefixes *fore-* and *post-*. Have students write definitions for their new words, then trade the new words with their partners. Each student then writes sentences using the partner's words.

LEARNERS WHO NEED EXTRA SUPPORT

Have students copy the rule at the top of page 77. Then work with them to write similar word equations for several of the words in the lesson. **See Daily Word Study Practice, pages 186–189.**

Lesson 36

Pages 79–80

✳ ◆ ● ◆ ● ◆ ● ✳ ◆ ● ◆ ■ ◆ ■ ● ◆

Prefixes over-, ultra-, super-

INFORMAL ASSESSMENT OBJECTIVES

Can students

✔ recognize the prefixes *over-*, *ultra-*, and *super-* in words?

✔ correctly use words containing the prefixes *over-*, *ultra-*, and *super-*?

Lesson Focus

INTRODUCING THE SKILL

- Write these words on the board: *overburden, supernatural, ultraviolet, overwhelm, superpower, ultrasonic.* Call on volunteers to read the words and underline the prefixes. Discuss the possible meanings of the words.

- Guide the class to conclude that the prefix *over-* means "too" or "too much" and that *ultra-* and *super-* usually mean "very."

- Allow time for students to suggest additional words that contain the prefixes *over-*, *ultra-*, and *super-*. Encourage students to define the words and use them in sentences.

USING THE PAGES

Have students read the rule and word examples on page 79. Review with students the directions on pages 79 and 80. After students have completed the pages, encourage them to discuss what they learned about the prefixes *over-*, *ultra-*, and *super-*.

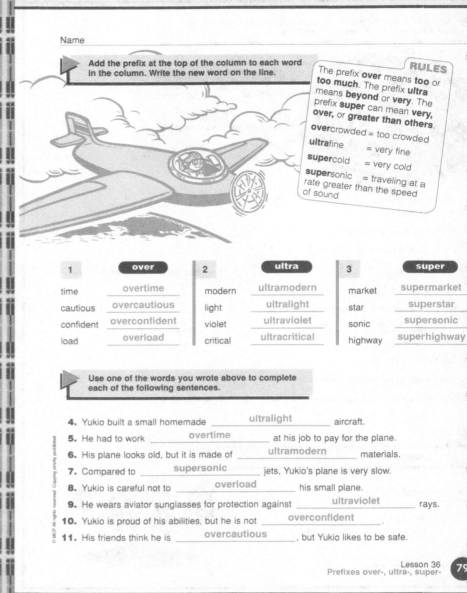

Name _____

▶ Add the prefix at the top of the column to each word in the column. Write the new word on the line.

RULES

The prefix **over** means **too** or **too much**. The prefix **ultra** means **beyond** or **very**. The prefix **super** can mean **very, over,** or **greater than others.**

overcrowded = too crowded
ultrafine = very fine
supercold = very cold
supersonic = traveling at a rate greater than the speed of sound

1	**over**	**2**	**ultra**	**3**	**super**
time	overtime	modern	ultramodern	market	supermarket
cautious	overcautious	light	ultralight	star	superstar
confident	overconfident	violet	ultraviolet	sonic	supersonic
load	overload	critical	ultracritical	highway	superhighway

▶ Use one of the words you wrote above to complete each of the following sentences.

4. Yukio built a small homemade _____ultralight_____ aircraft.
5. He had to work _____overtime_____ at his job to pay for the plane.
6. His plane looks old, but it is made of _____ultramodern_____ materials.
7. Compared to _____supersonic_____ jets, Yukio's plane is very slow.
8. Yukio is careful not to _____overload_____ his small plane.
9. He wears aviator sunglasses for protection against _____ultraviolet_____ rays.
10. Yukio is proud of his abilities, but he is not _____overconfident_____.
11. His friends think he is _____overcautious_____, but Yukio likes to be safe.

Lesson 36
Prefixes over-, ultra-, super- **79**

FOCUS ON ALL LEARNERS ✳ ● ◆ ■ ◆

ENGLISH LANGUAGE LEARNERS/ESL

Mix and match the prefixes in *overactive, superhero,* and *ultramodern* to show students that although the prefixes *over-, super-,* and *ultra-* have almost the same meaning, there are slight differences and these prefixes are generally not interchangeable.

VISUAL/KINESTHETIC LEARNERS

INDIVIDUAL

Materials: newspapers, magazines, art paper, scissors, glue

Have students look through news article headlines or advertisements for words with *over-, ultra-,* and *super-*. Invite students to cut out and glue the words to create an original ad for a real or imaginary product. Allow students to cut out or draw pictures and hand-letter other text as desired.

VISUAL LEARNERS

SMALL GROUP

Have volunteers read aloud the sentences from page 79 and give the meanings of the words they chose to complete the sentences.

Fifteen words containing the prefixes **over-**, **ultra-**, and **super-** are hidden in the puzzle. Some of the words go across, and some go down. Circle each word and write it next to its definition.

1.	ultramodern	very up-to-date
2.	overanxious	too worried
3.	superstar	very big star
4.	ultrafine	very fine
5.	overact	act to excess
6.	overdue	past due
7.	overslept	slept too long
8.	overpay	pay too much
9.	overeat	eat too much
10.	superhuman	greater than that of a normal person
11.	overripe	too ripe
12.	ultraviolet	beyond the violet end of visible light
13.	supersonic	greater than the speed of sound
14.	ultralight	extremely light
15.	overtime	extra time beyond regular number of hours of work

```
s u p e r h u m a n h o
u l t r a m o d e r n v
p t o e g o v e r d u e
e r v e o v e r p a y r
r a e o v e r s l e p t
s v r t s r e i t a t i
o i a t h a a e s u p m
n o i r e r c t m a r k e
i l p u l t r a f i n e
c e e s u p e r s t a r
e t u l t r a l i g h t
o v e r a n x i o u s t
```

Take the uncircled letters out of the puzzle and write them on the line. Then answer the question.

Where does Superman get the kind of food he needs to keep him strong?

Riddle

He gets it at the supermarket.

80 Lesson 36
Prefixes over-, ultra-, super-

AUDITORY/LEARNERS

LARGE GROUP

As you read the base words *clean, natural, cast, throw, conservative,* and *human* and other words from the lesson, have students add the appropriate prefix and use each word in a sentence to tell about themselves.

GIFTED LEARNERS

Have students review the words in this lesson by indicating which words seem to have a positive meaning (such as *ultramodern*) and which a negative meaning (such as *overconfident*). Discuss the reasons for their judgments.

LEARNERS WHO NEED EXTRA SUPPORT

Have students copy the three columns of words at the top of page 79 and add other words covered in this lesson on page 80 to the appropriate columns. **See Daily Word Study Practice, pages 186–189.**

SPELLING

Divide the class into two teams and hold a spelling bee. Have the members of each team stand in a line. Each time you say a spelling word, the first person in line should call out the first letter, the second member the second letter, and so on. The spelling words are *forenoon, postscript, overcrowded, ultrafine, supersonic, transfer, semicircle, submerge, midnight,* and *unison.*

WRITING

Portfolio Have students work with partners to create a three- or four-panel cartoon strip featuring an original superhero. Encourage students to write dialogue for their comics that includes words with the prefixes *over-, ultra-,* and *super-.*

ART

Explain to students that older more traditional homes are often made of wood or brick and contain design elements, such as carved woodwork. Ultramodern homes may have more streamlined styles and may contain materials such as steel and plastic. Have pairs of students look through design magazines for home exteriors and interiors they would consider ultramodern. Have students compare their findings.

SCIENCE

Have students research ultralight aircraft— how they are designed, what they are made of, and how they work. Encourage students to create a diagram or model of one of these aircraft.

Technology

AstroWord, Prefixes.©1998 Silver Burdett Ginn Inc. Division of Simon & Schuster.

Lesson 37

Pages 81–82

Prefixes trans-, semi-

INFORMAL ASSESSMENT OBJECTIVES

Can students

- recognize the prefixes *trans-* and *semi-* in words?
- correctly use words containing the prefixes *trans-* and *semi-*?

Lesson Focus

INTRODUCING THE SKILL

- Write the following sentence on the board: *The gardener transplanted the seedlings into a semicircle in front of the tree.*
- Ask students to identify the sentence words with prefixes. *(transplanted, semicircle)* Have volunteers underline the prefixes and circle the base words.
- Explain that *trans-* means "across" or "over" and *semi-* means "half" or "partly." Have students use these meanings to define *transplanted* and *semicircle*.
- Write the prefixes *trans-* and *semi-* on the board. Invite students to suggest other words that begin with these prefixes. List each under the appropriate prefix. Ask students to use the prefix meanings to explain the words.

USING THE PAGES

- Focus attention on the prefix rule and examples on page 81. Review directions for pages 81 and 82.
- **Critical Thinking** Take time for students to offer their opinions in response to the question on page 82.

Name

Add the prefix trans or semi to each base word or root below. The word you make should fit the definition.

RULE

The prefix **trans** means **across, over,** or **beyond**. The prefix **semi** means **half** or **partly**.

transfer = to move from one place to another
transmit = to send across or pass along
semicircle = half a circle
semidark = partly dark

1. trans **parent**: able to be seen through
2. trans **actions**: business deals
3. semi **skilled**: partly skilled
4. trans **fer**: move from one person or place to another
5. trans **form**: change the appearance of
6. semi **precious**: somewhat precious
7. trans **ported**: carried over long distances

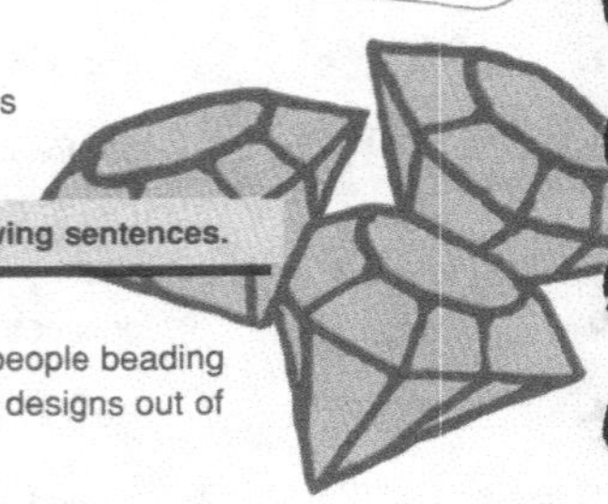

Use the words you wrote above to complete the following sentences.

8. Jewelry makers range from semiskilled craftspeople beading simple necklaces to master artisans creating elaborate designs out of silver and gold.
9. Some jewelers will work only with the most valuable gems, while others prefer semiprecious stones such as turquoise.
10. In order to transform a diamond from a rough stone into a sparkling gem, one must make numerous tiny cuts in the stone.
11. The process of making cuts to reflect light is used with other transparent stones, such as sapphires and rubies.
12. Many sapphires and rubies are mined in Asia and transported to markets throughout the world.
13. Business transactions involving millions of dollars' worth of gems take place in trading centers such as New York and Amsterdam.
14. To avoid the attention of thieves, it is common to transfer diamonds from one jeweler to another in uninsured packages through the ordinary mail!

FOCUS ON ALL LEARNERS

ENGLISH LANGUAGE LEARNERS/ESL

Give students an opportunity to talk about favorite relatives in their families and what makes them interesting or special.

VISUAL/KINESTHETIC LEARNERS

SMALL GROUP

Have students draw a circle and a semicircle. Discuss the difference between the two shapes and ask students to list places or objects that have these shapes.

KINESTHETIC LEARNERS

LARGE GROUP

Bring to class a hard cheese (such as ungrated parmesan), a soft cheese (such as cream cheese), and a semisoft cheese (such as Edam). Let students press on each type with a knife and sample each one to note the differences.

Write the word from the box that correctly completes the sentence.

1. The cousins sat in a _____semicircle_____ in front of the rocking chair.

2. It was the night of the _____semiyearly_____ family reunion, and Uncle Kevin was about to begin one of his famous stories.

3. "Tell us the one about the _____transcontinental_____ trip you took after college graduation," begged Ashley.

4. "Yes, when you had to _____translate_____ the instructions from Chinese before you could put the unicycle together," added Chad.

5. "Tell about the time you shaved your head and your eyebrows for the swimming _____semifinals_____ in college," urged Melissa.

6. "I'd rather hear the one about the time you wore baggy shorts and a tee-shirt to the _____semiformal_____ dance and got kicked out," grinned Chris.

7. Uncle Kevin smiled at his nieces and nephews in the _____semidarkness_____ of the candlelit room.

8. "Did I ever tell you about the time I got a job playing _____semiprofessional_____ baseball, and all the players had to dress like clowns?"

9. "I think the one about the business _____transaction_____ involving 12 dozen rotten eggs is funnier," commented Drew.

10. "I know," said Uncle Kevin. "There's one about how I _____transformed_____ a mangy mutt into a prize-winning Dalmatian with a few blobs of black paint!"

semicircle
semidarkness
semifinals
semiformal
semiprofessional
semiyearly
transaction
transcontinental
transformed
translate

What do you think it would be like to have Uncle Kevin in your family?

Critical Thinking

AUDITORY LEARNERS

LARGE GROUP

One by one call out the base words *form, dark, annual, port, precious, Atlantic*. Ask students to add the prefix *trans-* or *semi-* to each word. Discuss the meanings of the new words with the class.

GIFTED LEARNERS

Have students create word puzzles for which all the answers are *trans-* words or *semi-* words. Suggest that students use dictionaries to find ideas for new words and meanings.

STUDENTS WHO NEED EXTRA SUPPORT

Reread the context sentences on page 82 together, filling in the answer words. Decide on definitions for the prefix words and discuss how the prefixes help determine the meanings. **See Daily Word Study Practice, pages 186–189.**

SPELLING

Write the following prefixes on the board: *fore-, post-, over-, ultra-, super-, trans-, semi-, sub-, mid-, uni-.* Then call out the spelling words *forenoon, postscript, overcrowded, ultrafine, supersonic, transfer, semicircle, submerge, midnight,* and *unison*—one at a time. Each time you call out a word, have a volunteer step up to the board, point out the prefix which that word contains, and add the rest of the word to the prefix.

WRITING

Portfolio Have students write news or sports stories, as if for a news broadcast. Ask them to use at least three of the words from the following list: *semifinal, semiprofessional, semiskilled, semiannual, semidarkness, transmission, transfer, transport, transform.* Remind news writers to include information that tells the *who, what, when, where, why* and *how* of their stories.

ART

Have students research the subject of precious and semiprecious gems and jewelry-making. Some students may want to research the techniques of specific cultures, such as the ancient Maya of Mexico, or the Ashanti people of Ghana. Others may prefer to investigate books showing the work of contemporary designers.

HEALTH

According to many experts, relaxed periods of time spent visiting and talking with family and friends—including (or especially!) family pets—help people stay healthy. Discuss with students what family or group activities make them feel the most content and relaxed. Ask students what the benefits are of family time like that described in the context sentences on page 82.

Technology

AstroWord, Prefixes.©1998 Silver Burdett Ginn Inc. Division of Simon & Schuster.

Lesson 38

Pages 83–84

Prefixes sub-, mid-

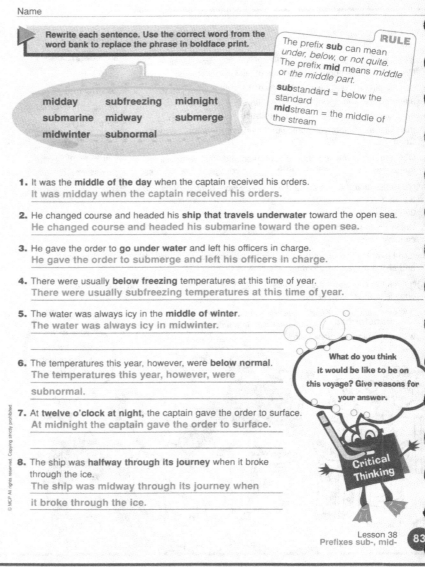

Name _____

Rewrite each sentence. Use the correct word from the word bank to replace the phrase in boldface print.

RULE

The prefix **sub** can mean *under, below,* or *not quite.* The prefix **mid** means *middle* or *the middle part.*

substandard = below the standard
midstream = the middle of the stream

midday	subfreezing	midnight
submarine	midway	submerge
midwinter	subnormal	

1. It was the **middle of the day** when the captain received his orders.
   It was midday when the captain received his orders.

2. He changed course and headed his **ship that travels underwater** toward the open sea.
   He changed course and headed his submarine toward the open sea.

3. He gave the order to **go under water** and left his officers in charge.
   He gave the order to submerge and left his officers in charge.

4. There were usually **below freezing** temperatures at this time of year.
   There were usually subfreezing temperatures at this time of year.

5. The water was always icy in the **middle of winter**.
   The water was always icy in midwinter.

6. The temperatures this year, however, were **below normal**.
   The temperatures this year, however, were subnormal.

7. At **twelve o'clock at night**, the captain gave the order to surface.
   At midnight the captain gave the order to surface.

8. The ship was **halfway through its journey** when it broke through the ice.
   The ship was midway through its journey when it broke through the ice.

What do you think it would be like to be on this voyage? Give reasons for your answer.

Critical Thinking

© MCP All rights reserved. Copying strictly prohibited

Lesson 38
Prefixes sub-, mid-

83

INFORMAL ASSESSMENT OBJECTIVES

Can students

✔ recognize the prefixes *sub-* and *mid-* in words?

✔ correctly use words containing the prefixes *sub-* and *mid-*?

Lesson Focus

INTRODUCING THE SKILL

- Write these following sentences on the board.

  The boat submerged in the heavy waves.

  I like to stay indoors when temperatures are subfreezing.

  The dog caught the ball in midair.

  I tripped and fell midstream.

- Have volunteers read the sentences and identify the words that begin with the prefixes *sub-* and *mid-*. (*submerged, subfreezing, midair, midstream*) Discuss the meanings of the words.

- Help students understand that, in general, *mid-* means "the middle part" and *sub-* can mean "under," "below," or "not quite."

USING THE PAGES

- Have students read the rule on page 83 and the sample words and definitions. Be sure that students understand the directions for pages 83 and 84.

- **Critical Thinking** Take time for students to share their responses to the question on page 83.

FOCUS ON ALL LEARNERS

ENGLISH LANGUAGE LEARNERS/ESL

Discuss the meanings of the words *submarine* and *midnight*. Help students relate their knowledge of these words to other *sub-* and *mid-* prefix words in the lesson.

VISUAL LEARNERS

INDIVIDUAL Have students draw silly scenes that incorporate items related to at least one *sub-* word and one *mid-* word. Ask them to use the words with prefixes to write humorous captions for the pictures.

KINESTHETIC LEARNERS

SMALL GROUP Materials: index cards

Have students write several words that begin with *sub-* and *mid-* on separate cards. Then have them create a game using the word cards. Groups can teach one another how to play the games they created.

83

Read each sentence and fill in the circle under the word that best completes it. Write the answer on the line.

1. __Midsummer__ vacations are the best.
   ● Midsummer ○ Midriff ○ Midship

2. My cousin lives on a farm in the __Midwest__.
   ○ midair ● Midwest ○ midstream

3. I left my home in the __suburbs__ for one month to visit him.
   ○ subside ○ submarine ● suburbs

4. First I rode on the __subway__ to get to the airport.
   ○ midway ● subway ○ subscribe

5. I was on a plane in __midair__ before I knew it.
   ● midair ○ midtown ○ suburbs

6. I tightened the seat belt against my __midriff__.
   ○ subway ● midriff ○ midyear

7. Then I read a book with an interesting __subplot__.
   ○ midstream ○ sublet ● subplot

8. I fell asleep __midway__ through the flight.
   ● midway ○ sublet ○ midland

9. A terrible storm had just __subsided__ when I got to the farm.
   ○ subdued ○ substantial ● subsided

10. Everyone stopped chattering and became very __subdued__.
    ○ subsurface ● subdued ○ midpoint

11. A flooded creek had eroded the topsoil, exposing the __subsoil__.
    ○ midair ○ midriff ● subsoil

12. At __midstream__ the creek was six feet deep.
    ○ midlevel ○ subfloor ● midstream

13. My cousin's hideout had become a __submarine__ cave.
    ● submarine ○ midland ○ subsoil

14. At __midnight__, after the clouds were gone, we went outside to look at the stars.
    ○ midday ● midnight ○ midriff

CURRICULUM CONNECTIONS

SPELLING

Have pairs of students create two-word phrases consisting of one spelling word plus another word beginning with the same letter. The phrases can be silly, but must have some meaning. For example, *turtle transfer, midnight meeting, unique unison.* Call out the spelling words (*forenoon, postscript, overcrowded, ultrafine, supersonic, transfer, semicircle, submerge, midnight, unison*) one at a time, and have partners write their phrases on a piece of paper. Invite volunteers to share their phrases with the class.

WRITING

Portfolio Have students write fantasy travelogues about a *midsummer* trip on a *submarine.* Details of the trip might include reasons they were able to make the voyage, their route and destinations, any stops along the way, life on board, the purpose of the trip, and sights seen through the submarine's periscope. Encourage students to find the meaning of the base word *marine* if they do not already know it.

SOCIAL STUDIES

Have students create a simple outline of facts about the Midwest. Major topics might include the states of the Midwest, geographical features, agricultural products, and major industries. Have students note their sources and cross-check each other's facts.

PHYSICAL EDUCATION

Have students interview a physical education teacher to learn exercises to strengthen their midriffs. They can also look in books and magazines for recommended exercises. Have them share their findings with demonstrations.

AstroWord, Prefixes.©1998 Silver Burdett Ginn Inc. Division of Simon & Schuster.

LARGE GROUP

AUDITORY LEARNERS

Have students take turns giving clues for any of the answer choices on page 84 as classmates skim the page to find the words. The student responding must use the word correctly in a sentence in order to give the next clue.

GIFTED LEARNERS

Divide the class into several groups. Call out either *mid-* or *sub-* and see how many words the group can write down for that prefix in a limited period of time.

LEARNERS WHO NEED EXTRA SUPPORT

Discuss the answers for the sentences on page 84 by having students decide how the meanings of the prefixes apply to the words. **See Daily Word Study Practice, pages 186–189.**

Lesson 39

Pages 85–86

Prefixes uni-, mono-, bi-, tri-

INFORMAL ASSESSMENT OBJECTIVES

Can students

✔ recognize the prefixes *uni-*, *mono-*, *bi-*, and *tri-* in words?

✔ correctly use words containing the prefixes *uni-*, *mono-*, *bi-*, and *tri-*?

Lesson Focus

INTRODUCING THE SKILL

- Ask volunteers to draw a unicycle, a bicycle, and a tricycle on the board. Label the pictures and have students circle the part of each word that is the same. *(cycle)*

- Have students identify the prefixes in the words and define them. *(uni-* means "one"; *bi-* means "two"; *tri-* means "three")* Ask which of the vehicles could have been named a *monocycle*. (The unicycle; *mono-* also means "one.")

- Write the words *monologue, monocle, unison, bimonthly, bilingual, trio,* and *tripod.* Invite students to look up any unfamiliar words in the dictionary.

- Ask students to suggest other words with these prefixes. Discuss their meanings with the class.

USING THE PAGES

Review the information in the rule box on page 85 and the directions for both pages. When finished, ask students to list some new words with the prefixes *uni-*, *mono-*, *bi-*, and *tri-* that they learned.

Name _____

▶ Use the words in the word bank to answer the questions. Use each word only once.

RULE
Uni, mono, bi, and tri are prefixes that show number. Uni and mono mean one. Bi means two. Tri means three.

bilingual	biped
biplane	monolingual
monotone	monotonous
tricycle	triplets
unicorn	unicycle

1. Which vehicle has three wheels?
   tricycle

2. Which word describes people who can speak two languages?
   bilingual

3. What is the name of an imaginary animal that resembles a horse with one long horn in the center of its forehead?
   unicorn

4. How could you describe a boring job in which you do one thing over and over again?
   monotonous

5. What is another name for a two-footed animal?
   biped

6. What are three babies born at the same time to one mother called?
   triplets

7. What do you call a flat speaking voice that uses just one dull tone?
   monotone

8. Which word describes someone who speaks only one language?
   monolingual

9. What kind of plane has two sets of wings, one above the other?
   biplane

10. What is a one-wheeled vehicle that a circus clown might ride?
    unicycle

Lesson 39
Prefixes uni-, mono-, bi-, tri- **85**

FOCUS ON ALL LEARNERS

ENGLISH LANGUAGE LEARNERS/ESL

Cover a game cube with masking tape and print the numerals 1, 2, and 3 twice on the taped surface. As students roll a number, they must find, read, and define a word with the matching number prefix on page 85 or 86.

VISUAL LEARNERS

INDIVIDUAL Give students five to ten minutes to write as many words as they can that contain the prefixes *uni-*, *mono-*, *bi-*, and *tri-*. Permit them to use dictionaries if they wish. Compile students' words into a class list and note whether any students were the only ones to include any one word.

KINESTHETIC LEARNERS

SMALL GROUP Have students take turns choosing a word with the prefix *uni-*, *mono-*, *bi-*, or *tri-* to illustrate on the board. Volunteers can be called upon to identify the word and label the drawing.

You are reporting on a town's 200-year anniversary celebration for your school newspaper. Study the scene below, then answer the questions about it.

| bicycle | tripod | biplane | bicentennial | monocle | triangle |
| triplets | binoculars | unicorn | unicycle | uniforms | |

1. What is a 200-year anniversary called?
   a bicentennial

2. What are the three women who look alike called?
   triplets

3. What kind of plane is flying overhead?
   a biplane

4. What are the band members wearing?
   uniforms

5. What is pictured on the plane's banner?
   a unicorn

6. What is the woman with a feather in her hat playing?
   a triangle

7. What kinds of bikes are shown in the picture?
   a unicycle, a bicycle, and a tricycle

8. What is holding up the photographer's camera?
   a tripod

9. What is the man in the grandstand wearing on his eye?
   monocle

10. What is the child looking through?
    binoculars

86
Lesson 39
Prefixes uni-, mono-, bi-, tri-

AUDITORY LEARNERS

LARGE GROUP
Do page 85 in reverse. Call out each of the words in the word bank and have volunteers give a definition in their own words.

GIFTED LEARNERS

Have students create puzzles in which each answer begins with the prefix *uni-, mono-, bi-,* or *tri-* and each clue contains the word *one, two,* or *three*. Students might draw bicycle wheels as answer sheets, having classmates write their responses on the wheel spokes.

LEARNERS WHO NEED EXTRA SUPPORT

Have students read each question on page 85 and circle the number clue before choosing a word from the box to write in the blank. **See Daily Word Study Practice, pages 186–189.**

CURRICULUM CONNECTIONS

SPELLING

Call out the spelling words *forenoon, postscript, overcrowded, ultrafine, supersonic, transfer, semicircle, submerge, midnight,* and *unison.* Have student pairs write down the words and then work together to create a short dictionary using these words. Each word should have a brief definition and the entries should be arranged in alphabetical order. Display the dictionaries in the classroom.

WRITING

Portfolio Have students write a poem about a unicorn. Before beginning to write, encourage students to look up the subject and become familiar with the mythology about unicorns. Encourage them to use at least two words besides *unicorn* that begin with one of the prefixes covered in this lesson.

ART

Write the word *monogram* on the board and discuss its meaning. Elicit that a person's initials are often combined in a single design and printed on stationery or sewn on clothing, luggage, or towels. Draw or show an example of your own monogram. Then encourage students to create their own monograms.

SOCIAL STUDIES

The year 1976 marked the bicentennial of the United States. Have students research the units of meaning in the word *bicentennial* and then gather information about events that celebrated the anniversary.

PHYSICAL EDUCATION

The Hawaii Ironman is perhaps the most famous triathlon. Have students research and report on the specific sports activities that are part of a triathlon and what triathletes do to train for this event. Encourage students to include the definitions of the prefix tri and the words triathlon and triathlete in their reports.

Technology AstroWord, Prefixes.©1998 Silver Burdett Ginn Inc. Division of Simon & Schuster.

Lesson 40

Pages 87–88

 Reading Writing

Reviewing Prefixes

INFORMAL ASSESSMENT OBJECTIVES

Can students

✔ read a newspaper article which contains words with prefixes?

✔ write a newspaper editorial and explain what an editorial is.

Lesson Focus

READING

- Write the following words on the board: *foremost, superstars, overcast, semidarkness, midday, postponed, ultracareful, overzealous, transport, binoculars, submerged, descended.*

- Have students identify the prefix in each word, discuss the meaning of the prefix, and define the word.

- Point out that these words and others containing prefixes are found in the news story about firefighters on page 87.

- After students read the article, have them write about details in the photograph that correspond to the reporter's version of the fire.

WRITING

- Explain that on page 88 students will write an editorial based on another photograph. Describe an editorial as a statement of a writer's opinions and beliefs on a subject. An editorial states a strong, clear position and then uses facts and logic to back it up.

- Tell students to read the directions and the writing tips. Remind them to use the word bank list as they write.

 Reading ▶ Read the newspaper article that is illustrated by the photograph. Then write your answer to the question at the end of the story.

FIREFIGHTERS: COMMUNITY HEROES

Some of the foremost employees in our community are our firefighters. In fact, this reporter would call these women and men superstars. The photograph shows firefighters battling a blaze on an overcast, midsummer day. The thick smoke creates semidarkness, even at midday.

All personal business is postponed when the siren sounds. Although there can be no delay, the firefighters are ultracareful not to become overzealous. State-of-the-art equipment helps to transport the firefighters to the scene quickly and efficiently. I watched with binoculars from below as they made their way up the extension ladder. In order to help people trapped on the top floor, a firefighter used an axe to break through the roof.

Soon after this photo was taken, one of the firefighters descended into the building and was quickly submerged in the malodorous smoke. I am happy to report that all of the tenants emerged from the house unharmed, and the blaze was extinguished thanks to the triumphant efforts of our firefighters.

What details in the photograph support the reporter's point of view?

_____
_____
_____
_____

FOCUS ON ALL LEARNERS ✳ ∙◆∙ ■ ◆

ENGLISH LANGUAGE LEARNERS/ESL

To familiarize students with vocabulary, invite them to talk about fires and firefighters before they read page 87. Point out that the article is written in the first person, from the point of view of the reporter.

VISUAL LEARNERS

INDIVIDUAL **Materials:** magazines and newspapers

Have students hunt for magazine or newspaper photographs or drawings of items with names that begin with the prefixes *de-, fore-, post-, over-, sub-, mid-, uni-, tri-,* and others from the unit. Examples might include *subways, bicycles, overcoats,* and *foreheads.*

AUDITORY/KINESTHETIC LEARNERS

LARGE GROUP Have students create hand and/or body movements to demonstrate the meanings of the words with suffixes in the article. Read the passage aloud slowly, inviting students to demonstrate word meanings.

Writing

Imagine that you work for a newspaper as a reporter. You have been assigned to write an editorial based on the photograph. Use words from the word bank in your editorial. Here are some tips to help you.

decrease	delay	foreground	foremost	midnight
overemotional	suburbs	transform	transparent	ultraquiet

Describe :
• what is happening.
• how you feel about it.
• the mood or emotion.
• any interesting details.

Helpful Hints

AUDITORY LEARNERS

PARTNER Have pairs of students play a game in which one calls out a prefix and the other must quickly name one word that begins with that prefix. In the second round the player must call out two words, and in the third round, three words.

GIFTED LEARNERS

Challenge students to name subjects in which they would be likely to read words containing the prefixes in Lessons 34–39. Have them look up these subjects on the Internet or on a CD-ROM and find words with these prefixes.

LEARNERS WHO NEED EXTRA SUPPORT

Have students use their dictionaries to find words beginning with the prefixes in this unit. Have them read the definitions and use the words in sentences. **See Daily Word Study Practice, pages 186–189.**

CURRICULUM CONNECTIONS

SPELLING

You may use the following words and dictation sentences as a posttest for the second group of spelling words in Unit 3.

1. **forenoon** — My aunt always has a fruit snack in the **forenoon**.
2. **postscript** — In the **postscript** to her letter, Lisa promised to write again soon.
3. **overcrowded** — There was nowhere to sit in the **overcrowded** waiting room.
4. **ultrafine** — Melissa needs a special brush for her **ultrafine** hair.
5. **supersonic** — The **supersonic** airplane reaches Europe in about two hours.
6. **transfer** — Cory plans to **transfer** to another school next year.
7. **semicircle** — The ancient stones were arranged in a **semicircle**.
8. **submerge** — Because of an ear problem, Dinah can't **submerge** her head in the pool.
9. **midnight** — The phone rang at **midnight** and woke everybody.
10. **unison** — Sometimes the twins speak in **unison**.

SOCIAL STUDIES

Have students research some of the major fires in history, such as the Great Fire of London, the Chicago Fire, or the fires caused by the 1906 San Francisco earthquake.

HEALTH

Have students obtain from their local fire department information on home safety plans in case of fires. Have students develop evacuation plans, including alternative routes and outside meeting sites, with their families.

Technology

AstroWord, Prefixes.©1998 Silver Burdett Ginn Inc. Division of Simon & Schuster.

Lesson 41

Pages 89–90

Unit Checkup

Reviewing Prefixes

INFORMAL ASSESSMENT OBJECTIVES

Can students

✔ choose the correct prefix for the context of a given sentence?

✔ determine the meanings of words containing prefixes?

✔ identify prefixes and bases in words?

Lesson Focus

PREPARING FOR THE CHECKUP

- Write on the board the prefixes *anti-, counter-, de-, em-, fore-, il-, im-, in-, mal-, mid-, mis-, mono-, over-, pre-, semi-, sub-, super-, trans-, ultra-,* and *uni-.*

- Ask volunteers to identify words that have each of these prefixes. Invite other volunteers to use each prefix word in a sentence.

USING THE PAGES

Read the directions for each section of pages 89 and 90. Answer any questions students may have before they begin the Checkup. Later, encourage students to discuss which prefixes or words they still find difficult.

Name _____

Fill in the circle next to the prefix that should be added to the underlined word. Then add the prefix to the word.

1. It is very _____ <u>convenient</u> to lace up skates with mittened hands. ○ em ● in ○ mis

2. Since the _____ <u>littering</u> law was passed, the streets have been cleaner. ○ counter ○ ultra ● anti

3. Mom had the _____ <u>sight</u> to pack lunch for the trip. ● fore ○ pre ○ over

4. The ship will soon _____ <u>bark</u> for France. ● em ○ im ○ in

5. We could barely see in the _____ <u>darkness</u>. ○ trans ○ ultra ● semi

6. Our choir sang in perfect _____ <u>son</u>. ○ counter ● uni ○ mon

7. The _____ <u>humidifier</u> made the room less damp. ○ sub ○ mid ● de

8. Supplies were rushed to the _____ <u>nourished</u> villagers. ● mal ○ em ○ anti

9. Mel is too _____ <u>patient</u> to work with young children. ○ de ○ super ● im

10. There is a $2.00 fine on those _____ <u>due</u> books. ○ sub ● over ○ mono

What is the meaning of each word?

11. irrational
○ very rational ○ somewhat rational ● not rational

12. counterproposal
● a proposal against ○ a proposal before ○ half a proposal

13. transmit
○ send under ○ send once ● send across

14. ultramodern
● very modern ○ not modern ○ partly modern

15. submarine
○ in the middle of the water ○ across the water ● under the water

---

FOCUS ON ALL LEARNERS

ENGLISH LANGUAGE LEARNERS/ESL

Remind students to ask questions if they are confused by the instructions for any part of the Checkup. Some students may benefit from working on the test orally with you first before going back and completing the answers on their own.

VISUAL LEARNERS

INDIVIDUAL Write the categories *Negative Prefixes* and *Numerical Prefixes* on the board. Then write the prefixes *mono-, ir-, im-, bi-, tri-, il-, ir-,* and *uni-.* Have students copy the headings and write the correct set of prefixes under each. List the prefixes for each category. Have students self-check and then write at least one word and sentence for each prefix.

AUDITORY/KINESTHETIC LEARNERS

LARGE GROUP Give directions that volunteers can do at the board or that all students can do at their seats. Some examples are *Write your name legibly and illegibly; Trace a perfect circle and then draw an imperfect circle; Label a picture and then mislabel it; Move your hand in a clockwise and then counterclockwise direction.*

UNIT 3 CHECKUP

▶ Read each sentence. Circle each word that contains a prefix.

1. We were watching the (bimonthly) softball game.

2. The game was beginning to seem (monotonous).

3. All of a sudden, one of the home team's (superstars) hit a home run to tie the game.

4. With the score tied, the opposing team needed a hit or they could be (defeated).

5. They didn't score, causing (postgame) extra innings.

6. As (illogical) as it seems, something amazing happened next.

7. One home team player (transported) the ball out of the park and won the game.

8. Everyone was (overexcited).

9. The opponents felt as though they were (misguided) ever to have come to play.

10. The home team had 7 wins and no losses, and it was only (midseason).

▶ Write each word you circled and then write its base word.

11.	bimonthly	month
12.	monotonous	tone
13.	superstar	star
14.	defeated	feat
15.	postgame	game
16.	illogical	logical
17.	transported	port
18.	overexcited	excite
19.	misguided	guide
20.	midseason	season

90 Lesson 41
Prefixes: Checkup

Lesson 41 teacher notes

AUDITORY LEARNERS

SMALL GROUP

Read aloud sentences at random from the various lessons in the unit. Have students raise their hands whenever they hear a word with a prefix. Ask a volunteer to explain its meaning and use the word in another sentence.

GIFTED LEARNERS

Challenge students to write additional test questions in the same formats as the questions provided, but using different example prefixes and sentences.

LEARNERS WHO NEED EXTRA SUPPORT

Write on the board the following pairs of words: *subway, midway; bicycle, tricycle; inconvenient, ultraconvenient.* Ask students how the prefixes change the meanings of the base words. **See Daily Word Study Practice, pages 186–189.**

ASSESSING UNDERSTANDING OF UNIT SKILLS

Student Progress Assessment You may wish to review the observational notes you made as students worked through the activities in this unit. Your notes will help you evaluate the progress students made with prefixes.

Portfolio Assessment Review the materials students have collected in their portfolios. Talk with students individually to discuss their written work and the progress they have made since the beginning of the unit. As you review students' work, evaluate how well they use the unit word study skills.

Daily Word Study Practice For students who need additional practice with any of the topics in this unit, quick reviews are provided on pages 186–189 in Daily Word Study Practice.

Word Study Posttest To assess students' mastery of skills covered in this unit, use the posttest on pages 61g–61h.

SPELLING

Use the following dictation sentences to review the spelling words in Unit 3.

1. **irregular** The artist drew an **irregular** line to represent the river.
2. **imperfect** Daniel was upset because his performance was **imperfect.**
3. **illegal** It is **illegal** to mistreat a pet.
4. **inexpensive** The ring was **inexpensive.**
5. **malpractice** Doctors must pay for **malpractice** insurance.
6. **antifreeze** Keep **antifreeze** away from pets.
7. **forenoon** The **forenoon** is my favorite time of day.
8. **postscript** Add a **postscript** to your letter.
9. **ultrafine** The dress is a **ultrafine** fabric.
10. **semicircle** The dancers formed a **semicircle.**
11. **submerge** The submarine will **submerge.**
12. **unison** Answer the question in **unison.**
13. **supersonic** My uncle is a pilot on a **supersonic** jet.
14. **transfer** The company plans to **transfer** its operations to a new location.
15. **midnight** The show ran until **midnight.**

Teacher Notes

Unit 4

Roots, Compounds, Possessives, Contractions, and Syllables

Student Performance Objectives

In Unit 4, students will review and extend their understanding of roots and their meanings, review the use of the apostrophe in forming possessives and contractions, and review rules of syllabication. As students learn to apply concepts involving roots, compounds, possessives, contractions, and syllables, they will be able to

◆ Associate the roots *pos, pel, pul, port,* and *ject* with their meanings

◆ Associate the roots *aud, dict, cap, cept,* and *ceipt* with their meanings

◆ Associate the roots *spec, spect, mit, miss,* and *man* with their meanings

◆ Recognize compound words

◆ Recognize the use of the apostrophe in possessives and contractions

◆ Recognize the number of syllables in a word

Contents

UNIT 4 RESOURCES

Assessment Strategies 91c
   Overview 91c
   Unit 4 Pretest 91e–91f
   Unit 4 Posttest 91g–91h
   Unit 4 Student Progress Checklist 91i
Spelling Connections 91j–91k
Word Study Games, Activities, and Technology 91l–91o
Home Connection 91p–91q

TEACHING PLANS

   Unit 4 Opener 91–92
   Lesson 42: Roots *pos, pel, pul, port,* and *ject* 93–94
   Lesson 43: Roots *aud, dict, cap, cept,* and *ceipt* 95–96
   Lesson 44: Roots *spec, spect, mit, miss,* and *man* 97–98
   Lesson 45: Compound Words 99–100
   Lesson 46: Possessives 101–102
   Lesson 47: Contractions 103–104
   Lesson 48: Syllables 105–106
   Lesson 49: Review Roots, Compound Words, Possessives, Contractions, Syllables 107–108
   Lesson 50: Unit 4 Checkup 109–110

Assessment Strategy Overview

In Unit 4, assess students' ability to recognize and understand roots and their meanings, compound words, the use of the apostrophe in forming possessives and contractions, and the number of syllables in a word. There are various ways to assess students' progress. Encourage students to evaluate their own work and participate in setting goals for their own learning.

FORMAL ASSESSMENT

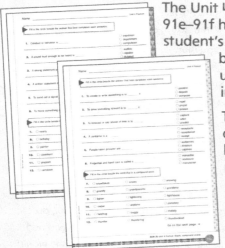

The Unit 4 Pretest on pages 91e–91f helps to assess a student's knowledge at the beginning of the unit and to plan instruction.

The Unit 4 Posttest on pages 91g–91h helps to assess mastery of unit objectives and to plan for reteaching, if necessary.

INFORMAL ASSESSMENT

The Reading & Writing pages and Unit Checkup in the student book are an effective means of evaluating students' performance.

Skill	Reading & Writing Pages	Unit Checkup
Roots *pos, pel, pul*	107–108	109–110
Roots *port, ject*	107–108	109–110
Roots *aud, dict*	107–108	109–110
Roots *cap, cept, ceipt*	107–108	109–110
Roots *spec, spect, mit, miss*	107–108	109–110
Root *man*	107–108	109–110
Compound Words	107–108	109–110
Possessives	107–108	109–110
Contractions	107–108	109–110
Syllables	107–108	109–110

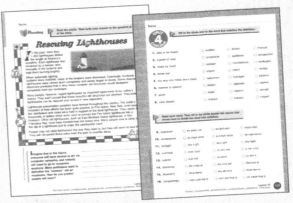

PORTFOLIO ASSESSMENT

This logo appears throughout the teaching plans. It signals opportunities for collecting students' work for individual portfolios. You may also want to collect the following pages.

❖ Unit 4 Pretest and Posttest, pages 91e–91h

❖ Unit 4 Reading & Writing, pages 107–108

❖ Unit 4 Checkup, pages 109–110

STUDENT PROGRESS CHECKLIST

Use the checklist on page 91i to record students' progress. You may want to cut the sections apart to place each student's checklist in his or her portfolio.

Administering and Evaluating the
Pretest and Posttest

DIRECTIONS

To help you assess students' progress in learning Unit 4 skills, tests are available on pages 91e–91h. Administer the Pretest before students begin the unit. The results of the Pretest will help you identify each student's strengths and needs in advance, allowing you to structure lesson plans to meet individual needs. Administer the Posttest to assess students' overall mastery of skills taught in the unit and to identify specific areas that will require reteaching.

PERFORMANCE ASSESSMENT PROFILE

The following chart will help you identify specific skills as they appear on the tests and enable you to identify and record specific information about an individual's or the class's performance on the tests.

Depending on the results of the tests, refer to the Reteaching column for lesson-plan pages where you can find activities that will be useful for meeting individual needs or for daily word study practice.

PERFORMANCE ASSESSMENT PROFILE

Skill	Pretest Questions	Posttest Questions	Reteaching Focus on All Learners	Reteaching Daily Word Study Practice
Roots *pos, pel, pul*	1, 2, 21		93–94, 107–108	189–190
Roots *port, ject*	22	1	93–94, 107–108	189–190
Roots *aud, dict*	3	2, 3	95–96, 107–108	189–190
Roots *cap, cept, ceipt*	4, 5	4, 22	95–96, 107–108	189–190
Roots *spec, spect, mit, miss*		5	97–98, 107–108	189–190
Root *man*	6	6, 25	97–98, 107–108	189–190
Compound Words	7–12, 23, 24, 26	7–12, 23, 24, 26	99–100, 107–108	189–190
Possessives	13–16	13–16	101–102, 107–108	189–190
Contractions	17–20	17–20	103–104, 107–108	189–190
Syllables	21–26	21–26	105–108	195

> Fill in the circle beside the answer that best completes each sentence.

1. To create or write something is to _____ it.
   - ○ position
   - ○ deposit
   - ○ compose

2. To drive something forward is to _____ it.
   - ○ repel
   - ○ propel
   - ○ protect

3. To forecast or say ahead of time is to _____.
   - ○ capture
   - ○ edict
   - ○ predict

4. A container is a _____.
   - ○ receptacle
   - ○ receptionist
   - ○ receipt

5. People taken prisoner are _____.
   - ○ audiences
   - ○ dictators
   - ○ captives

6. Fingernail and hand care is called a _____.
   - ○ manacles
   - ○ manicure
   - ○ manuscript

> Fill in the circle beside the word that is a compound word.

7. ○ snowflakes   ○ snowy   ○ snowing

8. ○ grandly   ○ grandparents   ○ grandiose

9. ○ lighter   ○ lightening   ○ lighthouse

10. ○ midair   ○ airplane   ○ planetary

11. ○ ladybug   ○ buggy   ○ malady

12. ○ thunder   ○ thundering   ○ thundercloud

Go to the next page. →

> Fill in the circle under the possessive that matches each clue.

13. the dog belonging to Jerry   Jerrys' dog   Jerrys dog   Jerry's dog
                                        ○   ○   ○

14. work of the committee   committees work   committee's work   committees' work
                                        ○   ○   ○

15. the flowers of the shrub   shrub's flowers   shrubs' flowers   shrubs flowers
                                        ○   ○   ○

16. clothes of the children   childrens clothes   children's clothes   childrens' clothes
                                        ○   ○   ○

> Fill in the circle beside the two words that make up each contraction.

17. didn't   ○ did have   ○ did not   ○ will have

18. you're   ○ you have   ○ they are   ○ you are

19. I'll   ○ I will   ○ I am   ○ I have

20. we've   ○ we will   ○ we have   ○ we had

> Read the words below. Then divide them into syllables, using slash marks.

21. propulsion   **23.** thunderclap   **25.** oppose

22. reject   **24.** yearbook   **26.** wallpaper

Possible score on Unit 4 Pretest is 26. Number correct _____

> Fill in the circle beside the answer that best completes each sentence.

1. Conduct or behavior is _____.
   - ○ expulsion
   - ○ deportment
   - ○ compulsion

2. A sound loud enough to be heard is _____.
   - ○ audible
   - ○ capable
   - ○ dictated

3. A strong statement or command is an _____.
   - ○ audition
   - ○ edict
   - ○ admission

4. A written statement of something received is a _____.
   - ○ reject
   - ○ deceive
   - ○ receipt

5. To send out a signal is to _____.
   - ○ transmit
   - ○ omit
   - ○ manacle

6. To move something around skillfully is to _____ it.
   - ○ dismiss
   - ○ manipulate
   - ○ manual

> Fill in the circle beside the word that is a compound word.

7. ○ nearly   ○ nearby   ○ bicycle

8. ○ birthday   ○ rebirth   ○ Thursday

9. ○ painter   ○ painting   ○ paintbrush

10. ○ casement   ○ bookcase   ○ telephone

11. ○ pinpoint   ○ pinch   ○ pointed

12. ○ rainstorm   ○ raining   ○ rained

Go to the next page. →

▶ Fill in the circle under the possessive that matches each clue.

13. home of my grandparents   grandparents home   grandparent's home   grandparents' home
○   ○   ○

14. the desk of my teacher   teachers' desk   teachers desk   teacher's desk
○   ○   ○

15. the branches of a tree   tree's branches   tree branches'   trees' branches
○   ○   ○

16. the car belonging to Jack   Jacks car   Jack's car   Jacks' car
○   ○   ○

▶ Fill in the circle beside the two words that make up each contraction.

17. we're   ○ we have   ○ we did   ○ we are

18. you'd   ○ you will   ○ you had   ○ you are

19. she'd   ○ he would   ○ she would   ○ she is

20. wouldn't   ○ would have   ○ could not   ○ would not

▶ Read the words below. Then divide them into syllables, using slash marks.

21. inducement   **23.** rainbow   **25.** manacle

22. capture   **24.** butterfly   **26.** steamship

Possible score on Unit 4 Posttest is 26. Number correct _____

Student Progress Checklist

Make as many copies as needed to use for a class list. For individual portfolio use, cut apart each student's section. As indicated by the code, color in boxes next to skills satisfactorily assessed and mark an X by those requiring reteaching. Marked boxes can later be colored in to indicate mastery.

STUDENT PROGRESS CHECKLIST

Code: ■ Satisfactory   ☒ Needs Reteaching

Student: _____ _____ Pretest Score: _____ Posttest Score: _____	**Skills** ❏ Roots ❏ Compound Words ❏ Possessives ❏ Contractions ❏ Syllables	**Comments / Learning Goals**
Student: _____ _____ Pretest Score: _____ Posttest Score: _____	**Skills** ❏ Roots ❏ Compound Words ❏ Possessives ❏ Contractions ❏ Syllables	**Comments / Learning Goals**
Student: _____ _____ Pretest Score: _____ Posttest Score: _____	**Skills** ❏ Roots ❏ Compound Words ❏ Possessives ❏ Contractions ❏ Syllables	**Comments / Learning Goals**
Student: _____ _____ Pretest Score: _____ Posttest Score: _____	**Skills** ❏ Roots ❏ Compound Words ❏ Possessives ❏ Contractions ❏ Syllables	**Comments / Learning Goals**

Spelling Connections

INTRODUCTION

The Unit Word List is a comprehensive list of spelling words drawn from this unit. The words are grouped by roots, compounds, possessives, contractions, and syllables. To incorporate spelling into your word study program, use the activity in the Curriculum Connections section of each teaching plan.

The spelling lessons utilize the following approach for each set of words.

1. Administer a pretest of six words that have not yet been introduced. Dictation sentences are provided.

2. Provide practice.

3. Reassess. Dictation sentences are provided.

A final test is provided in Lesson 50 on page 110.

DIRECTIONS

Make a copy of Blackline Master 30 for each student. After administering the pretest, give each student a copy of the appropriate word list.

Students can work with a partner to practice spelling the words orally and identifying the word study element in each word. They can also make and use letter cards to form the words on the list. You may want to challenge students to identify other words that have the same root, or that are compounds, contractions, or possessives. Students can write words of their own on *My Own Word List* (see Blackline Master 30).

Have students store their list words in an envelope or plastic zipper bag in the back of their books or notebooks. Alternatively, suggest that students keep a spelling notebook, listing words with similar patterns. You could also invite students to build word-wall displays in the classroom. Each section of the wall can focus on words with a single word study element. The walls will become a good spelling resource when students are writing.

Name _____

**S**pelling

UNIT 4 WORD LIST

pos, pel, pul, port, ject; aud, dict, cap, cept, ceipt

deposit   audience
repel   dictate
expulsion   capture
portable   acceptance
eject   receipt

My Own Word List

spec, spect; miss, mit; man; Compounds, Contractions, Syllables

specimen   sweatshirt
spectator   they'll
dismiss   should've
submit   you're
manual   thunderstorm

Word Study Games, Activities, and Technology

The following collection of ideas offers a variety of opportunities to reinforce word study skills while actively engaging students. The games, activities, and technology suggestions can easily be adapted to meet the needs of your group of learners. They vary in approach so as to consider students' different learning styles.

● WHAT IN THE WORLD IS IT?

Tell students to imagine that they are twenty-third century archaeologists—scientists who study ancient civilizations. They host a television show on which they display objects from the remote past, such as American civilization in the 1990s. Allow time for each student to think of a compound word that names an object people 400 years from now might think mysterious (for example, a wristwatch, a flashlight, a horseshoe, a rowboat). Have them draw a picture of the object on posterboard or make a clay model. Then tell them to write a sentence or two describing its use. Place a large black box on your desk. Then have each student take a turn placing his or her object or drawing on the box and covering it with a piece of black felt. After you say, *What in the world is it?* the student removes the felt, holds up the object for the audience to see, and names it. He or she then describes its use.

▲ LIGHTS, CAMERA, ACTION!

Tell students to imagine that they are trying out for a part in an upcoming movie. Invite them to write a paragraph describing the experience. Challenge them to include as many of the following words as they can: *positive, compelling, portable, projector, audition, diction, captivate, reception, spectators, admit.* You might extend the activity by asking them to expand the paragraph by adding compound words such as *masterpiece, stagehand, sweatshirt,* and *sunrise.*

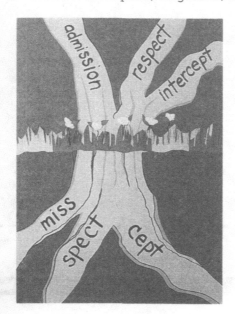

◆ WORD HUNTS

Tell students to look through any reading materials in the classroom to find words containing the roots discussed in this unit. Have them copy the words on a sheet of paper, circle the roots, and define the words, using a dictionary if necessary. Encourage students to compare lists and add new words to each of their lists. You might also combine lists to create a class word wall in the form of a tree with the roots written on thick lines extending down from the trunk and the words extending up and out from the trunk like branches. Encourage students to add "new growth" in the form of other words as you progress through the unit.

■ PRACTICING POSSESSIVES

Write these phrases on the board, omitting the answers.

1. the house owned by Terry (*Terry's house*)
2. the toys that the children had (*the children's toys*)
3. the uniforms of the players (*the players' uniforms*)

Ask volunteers to write the correct possessive form for each phrase on the board. Have students write their own phrases based on the models. Partners can exchange phrases and rephrase one another's work.

✳ TRANSPORTATION INNOVATIONS IN SEQUENCE

Write the word *transportation* on the board and have students identify the root *port*. Ask a volunteer to define the word. Then write the following definitions on the board and ask volunteers to identify the compound word to which each refers.

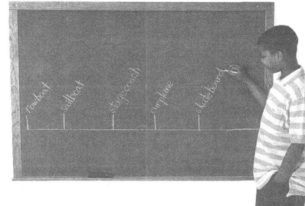

a flying machine powered by an engine (*airplane*)

a horse-drawn carriage (*stagecoach*)

a narrow piece of wood or plastic mounted on wheels (*skateboard*)

a boat propelled by wind currents (*sailboat*)

a small boat propelled by oars (*rowboat*)

After the words have been identified, challenge the students to place each in its appropriate location on a horizontal time line. They do not need to know the exact date when each innovation first appeared, but they must arrange them in proper sequence from left (earliest) to right (most recent).

● ROOTS IN OPPOSITION

Have partners work together to list pairs of words containing roots discussed in this unit that have opposite or nearly opposite meanings. The paired words may have the same root but a different prefix or they may have different roots but the same prefix. Examples include *compose, dispose; import, export; inject, eject; subject, object; accept, reject; admit, dismiss.* Tell partners to create a "railroad track" by drawing 12-inch parallel lines on either side of a ruler. At 2-inch intervals, they should draw perpendicular lines to represent stations. On each of these lines, have them write one pair of words. Partners can exchange papers with other pairs and take turns trying to ride from station to station on one another's "root systems." If a team defines both words in a pair, they move to the next station; if not, they lose a turn. The first pair to complete the ride wins.

▲ SILLY COMPOUNDS

Write the following sentences on the chalkboard: *I've never seen a hat box in a ring or heard a hat band play music. I've never seen butter fly.*

Challenge students to create their own examples of compound words that can be separated for humorous effect in a sentence. You might have students draw cartoons illustrating the examples above and their own creations. Combine the individual works into a class humor anthology.

I've never seen a star fish.

◆ THANK-YOU NOTES

Have students write thank-you notes to people who have done something nice for them. Ask them to include contractions in their notes so that they will sound natural and informal. To reinforce the difference between formal and informal language, you might show the class an example of an invitation to a wedding or graduation exercise and discuss the differences. Encourage students to deliver their thank-you notes to the people for whom they were intended.

■ DINING AT THE WORD COMPOUND

Have pairs of students work together to design a menu for a new restaurant that specializes in foods whose names are compound words. For example, breakfast may feature oatmeal and grapefruit, the luncheon special might be peanut butter sandwiches, the chef's choice for dinner could be swordfish. Desserts could include cupcakes and watermelon. Encourage students to make up catchy names for their restaurants and to decorate their menus. They could also write "rave reviews" that include compound words (*outstanding food, each dish is a masterpiece*, and so on).

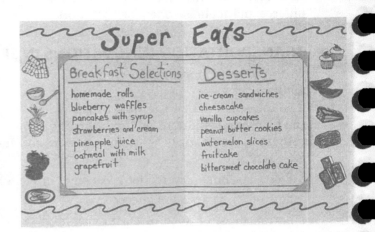

✳ THE ROOT DERBY

Use Blackline Master 31 to make a game board featuring roots explored in this unit. You might make a master copy by writing each of the 15 roots in one of the spaces on the game board. Begin at the Start position and move clockwise around the track. At the halfway point, repeat so that each root appears twice on the board. Make enough copies of the game board to distribute one each to teams of three or four students. Have team members make simple cardboard tokens, numbered 1 through 4, to represent their horses. Players take turns rolling a number cube or die and moving the number of spaces indicated. As a player lands on a space, he or she must say and define a word containing that root. More than one player can occupy the same space during any round. Players who cannot answer correctly must return their tokens to the previous position. Play continues until one player reaches Finish.

Technology

The following software products are designed to develop students' vocabulary.

Word Smart   This vocabulary-drill software is set in a movie studio. Older students learn the meanings of new words as they encounter them in movie scripts. 1,600 words and 8 levels of difficulty are offered.
**Princeton Review Software
   50 Mall Road
   Burlington, MA 01803
   (800) 566-7737

Word Attack 3   A "vocabulary builder" for students ages 10 to adult, this product encourages students to engage in crossword puzzles and arcade games to master definitions, spellings, and pronunciations of thousands of words.

**Davidson & Associates, Inc.
   19840 Pioneer Avenue
   Torrance, CA 90503
   (800) 545-7677

Merriam-Webster's Dictionary for Kids   Children can use this online dictionary to find the meanings of 20,000 words and play a variety of word games.
**Mindscape
   88 Roland Way
   Novato, CA 94945
   (800) 234-3088

Name _____

The Root Derby

Home Connection

HOME LETTER

A letter is available to be sent home at the beginning of Unit 4. This letter informs family members that students will be learning more about word roots, reviewing how the apostrophe is used when forming contractions and possessives, and learning more about compound words and the rules of syllabication. The suggested home activity revolves around the elements of a play or film. This activity promotes interaction between child and family members while supporting the student's learning of reading and writing words with the targeted word study skills. A letter is also available in Spanish on page 91q.

Home Letter

Dear Family,

In the upcoming weeks your child will learn more about certain word parts called roots and will review how the apostrophe is used when forming contractions and possessives. He or she will also learn more about compound words and the rules of syllabication.

At-Home Activities

▶ Discuss with your child which elements of a play or filmed performance they pay closest attention to (for example, the actors, sets, costumes, plot, special effects, or clever dialogue).

▶ Encourage your child to research various jobs and occupations related to the theater.

▶ Encourage your child to write a description of a performance he or she participated in or attended and what her or his impressions were.

Book Corner

You and your child might enjoy reading these books together. Look for them at your local library.

Stage Fright—A Sebastian Barth Mystery

by James Howe

Sebastian is on the scene to investigate a series of strange theater accidents and occurrences that involve the play's leading lady.

The Watchers—A Mystery at Alton Towers

by Helen Cresswell

Two runaways, Kathy and Josh, find mystery and intrigue at an amusement park where a homeless woman becomes something quite different after dark.

Sincerely,

Carta para la casa

Estimada familia,

En las próximas semanas, su hijo/a aprenderá más acerca de ciertas partes de las palabras en inglés llamadas raíces, y repasaremos cómo el apóstrofo se usa para formar contracciones y posesivos. También aprenderá más sobre palabras compuestas y las reglas del silabeo en inglés, o separación de las palabras en sílabas.

Actividades para hacer en casa

He aquí algunas actividades que su hijo/a y ustedes pueden realizar juntos.

▶ Comenten con su hijo/a a cuáles elementos de una obra teatral o de una película le prestan más atención (por ejemplo, a los actores, al escenario, a los disfraces, al argumento, a los efectos especiales o al diálogo inteligente).

▶ Animen a su hijo/a a investigar varios trabajos y ocupaciones relacionados con el teatro.

▶ Animen a su hijo/a a escribir una descripción de un acto que vio o en el cual participó, y cuáles fueron sus impresiones al respecto.

Rincón del libro

Su hijo/a y ustedes pueden disfrutar juntos de la lectura de estos libros. Búsquenlos en la biblioteca de su localidad.

Stage Fright—A Sebastian Barth Mystery
por James Howe

Sebastian está presente para investigar una serie de extraños accidentes de teatro que tienen que ver con la protagonista de la obra.

The Watchers—A Mystery at Alton Towers
por Helen Cresswell

Dos fugitivos, Katy y Josh, hallan misterio e intriga en el parque de diversiones donde una vagabunda se convierte en algo muy diferente al anochecer.

Atentamente, _____

Unit 4

Pages 91–92

Roots, Compound Words, Possessives, Contractions, and Syllables

ASSESSING PRIOR KNOWLEDGE

To assess students' prior knowledge of roots, compound words, possessives, contractions, and syllables, use the pretest on pages 91e–91f.

Unit Focus

USING THE PAGE

- Read aloud "Who's Watching?" in a voice that gradually reveals surprise.
- Discuss the title of the poem. Then have volunteers read the five stanzas aloud.
- **Critical Thinking** Read the questions at the bottom of page 91. Invite students to share their experiences attending live performances.

BUILDING A CONTEXT

- Ask students to find words in the poem that contain the following roots: *aud, spect, pel, ject. (audience, inspecting, compel, project)* Explain that roots are not words themselves, but words can "grow" from them.
- Ask students to identify contractions in the poem. *(Who's, you're, didn't, isn't)* What two words make up each one?
- Point out that the apostrophe in *director's* signifies a possessive noun. Ask whether the word indicates one or more than one director. *(one)*
- Write the compound word *backstage* on the board. Ask students to find other words made of two smaller words. *(onstage, inside, yourself)*
- Have students identify words in the poem with two or more syllables.

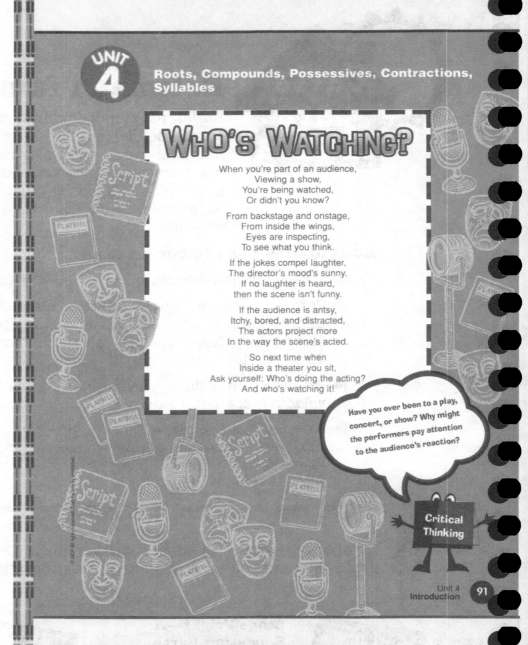

UNIT 4 — Roots, Compounds, Possessives, Contractions, Syllables

WHO'S WATCHING?

When you're part of an audience,
Viewing a show,
You're being watched,
Or didn't you know?

From backstage and onstage,
From inside the wings,
Eyes are inspecting,
To see what you think.

If the jokes compel laughter,
The director's mood's sunny.
If no laughter is heard,
then the scene isn't funny.

If the audience is antsy,
Itchy, bored, and distracted,
The actors project more
In the way the scene's acted.

So next time when
Inside a theater you sit,
Ask yourself: Who's doing the acting?
And who's watching it!

Have you ever been to a play, concert, or show? Why might the performers pay attention to the audience's reaction?

Critical Thinking

Unit 4 Introduction 91

UNIT OPENER ACTIVITIES

"WHO'S WATCHING?" AGAIN

Invite the class to do a choral reading of the poem. Ask students if they have ever acted in a play or performed for an audience in another way, such as dancing or playing an instrument. Does the poem remind them of their experiences, and if so, how?

KINDS OF PERFORMERS

Have students make a list of different kinds of performers, such as magicians, circus performers, and musicians. Have students discuss how different professional performers might adapt their performances to the reactions of their audiences.

IN THEIR OWN WORDS

Encourage students to find magazine articles or autobiographies in which well-known actors or performers discuss their feelings about live audiences. Have students compare and contrast different people's reactions.

Home Letter

Dear Family,

In the upcoming weeks your child will learn more about certain word parts called roots and will review how the apostrophe is used when forming contractions and possessives. He or she will also learn more about compound words and the rules of syllabication.

At-Home Activities

▶ Discuss with your child which elements of a play or filmed performance they pay closest attention to (for example, the actors, sets, costumes, plot, special effects, or clever dialogue).

▶ Encourage your child to research various jobs and occupations related to the theater.

▶ Encourage your child to write a description of a performance he or she participated in or attended and what her or his impressions were.

Book Corner

You and your child might enjoy reading these books together. Look for them at your local library.

Stage Fright—A Sebastian Barth Mystery

by James Howe
Sebastian is on the scene to investigate a series of strange theater accidents and occurrences that involve the play's leading lady.

The Watchers—A Mystery at Alton Towers

by Helen Cresswell
Two runaways, Kathy and Josh, find mystery and intrigue at an amusement park where a homeless woman becomes something quite different after dark.

Sincerely,

_____

BULLETIN BOARD

For an "All the World's a Stage" bulletin board, have students work together to draw a floor plan or elevation of a theater stage and label it with terms that name different areas. Students can research the project by looking under "Theater" in library resources.

● The Home Letter on page 92 is intended to acquaint family members with the word study skills students will be studying in the unit. Students can tear out page 92 and take it home. Suggest they complete the activities with a family member and look for the books pictured on page 92 in the library to read together.

● The Home Letter can also be found on page 91q in Spanish.

CURRICULUM CONNECTIONS ✳

WRITING

Have students fill out "job applications" for various performance and behind-the-scenes jobs in live entertainment. They can write about what they think they have a talent for or would just like to try. Some people enjoy being the center of attention, while others think it is fun to work in support jobs, such as being a director, playwright, pit musician, costume designer, or set builder. Job applicants should tell why they want a certain position, what experience they have had, and why they would do a good job.

SOCIAL STUDIES

Have students study a form of traditional theater from some part of the world, such as Balinese puppet theater or Japanese No theater. Encourage them to use electronic resources (the Internet or a CD-ROM encyclopedia) as well as reference and nonfiction books for their research. Have students report on what they learned or prepare a short presentation in the style of the theater they studied.

MUSIC

Ask the music teacher to help you gather samples of recordings and librettos of operas, operettas, and musicals. Have students listen to the recordings and read the librettos or any accompanying descriptions of the plots for each.

Lesson 42
Pages 93–94

Roots pos, pel, pul, port, ject

INFORMAL ASSESSMENT OBJECTIVES

Can students

✔ recognize the roots *pos, pel, pul, port,* and *ject* in words?

✔ associate the roots *pos, pel, pul, port,* and *ject* with their meanings?

Lesson Focus

INTRODUCING THE SKILL

- Review *root* as "a word part to which prefixes and suffixes can be added to make words." A root's meaning often comes from the language in which the root originated.

- Write these sentences on the board, omitting the underlines.

  She wanted a position on the team.

  The light helped dispel Mike's fear.

  The truck will transport the food.

  The aircraft flew by jet propulsion.

  The movie projector is new.

- Begin a wall chart with the following roots and their meanings.

pos	put or place
pel, pul	push, drive, thrust
port	carry
ject	throw or force

- Have students underline each root in the sentences and use its meaning to define the words.

USING THE PAGES

Have students read the definition and the rules. Review the directions with students.

93

Name _____

▶ Write the word from the word bank that matches each clue. Then copy the letters in the boxes into the caption beneath the picture.

position	positive	compose
posture	opposite	expel
propel	deposit	compulsion
expose	impelled	composition
repulsion		

DEFINITION

A **root** is a word part to which prefixes and suffixes can be added to make words. If you know the meanings of word parts, you can often figure out the meaning of a new word.

RULES

The root **pos** usually means **put** or **place**. The roots **pel** and **pul** usually mean **push** or **drive**.

posture = the way one usually holds one's body

re**pel** = to drive back

1. strong need to do something — **c o m p u l s i o n**
2. way of holding one's body — **p o s t u r e**
3. forced — **i m p e l l e d**
4. absolutely certain — **p o s i t i v e**
5. totally different — **o p p o s i t e**
6. location — **p o s i t i o n**
7. push out — **e x p e l**
8. drive forward — **p r o p e l**
9. essay — **c o m p o s i t i o n**
10. disgust — **r e p u l s i o n**
11. uncover — **e x p o s e**
12. money placed in — **d e p o s i t**
13. write music — **c o m p o s e**

c o m p o s e r of **m u s i c**

© MCP All rights reserved. Copying strictly prohibited.

FOCUS ON ALL LEARNERS

ENGLISH LANGUAGE LEARNERS/ESL

Before students do the exercise, read the words in the word banks on pages 93 and 94 with students and discuss the words' meanings together.

VISUAL LEARNERS

SMALL GROUP Write the following clues and roots on the board, omitting the answers: *1. A fluid shot into the body—ject (injection); 2. A person who carries luggage—port (porter); 3. to get rid of—pos (dispose)* Have students use the clues to identify and write the answers. Continue with other clues and roots.

KINESTHETIC LEARNERS

PARTNER Have pairs of students act out verbs containing the roots covered in this lesson. For example, have one *reject* the other, or *propel* an imaginary ball toward the other, or *deposit* a pencil on the other's desk.

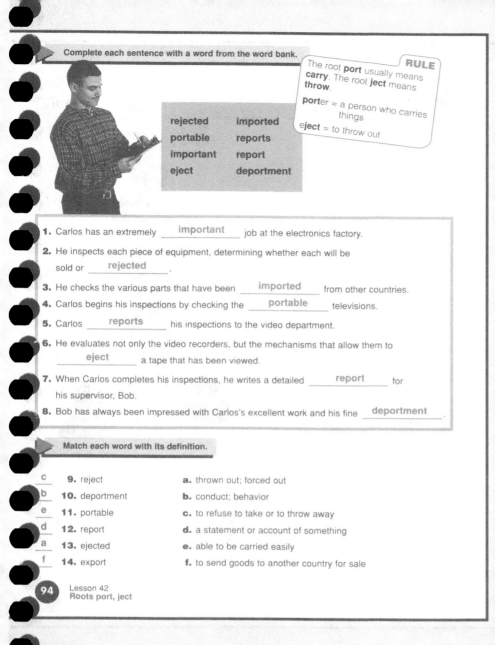

Complete each sentence with a word from the word bank.

RULE

The root **port** usually means **carry**. The root **ject** means **throw**.

porter = a person who carries things

e**ject** = to throw out

rejected	imported
portable	reports
important	report
eject	deportment

1. Carlos has an extremely _____important_____ job at the electronics factory.

2. He inspects each piece of equipment, determining whether each will be sold or _____rejected_____ .

3. He checks the various parts that have been _____imported_____ from other countries.

4. Carlos begins his inspections by checking the _____portable_____ televisions.

5. Carlos _____reports_____ his inspections to the video department.

6. He evaluates not only the video recorders, but the mechanisms that allow them to _____eject_____ a tape that has been viewed.

7. When Carlos completes his inspections, he writes a detailed _____report_____ for his supervisor, Bob.

8. Bob has always been impressed with Carlos's excellent work and his fine _____deportment_____

Match each word with its definition.

c	**9.** reject	**a.**	thrown out; forced out
b	**10.** deportment	**b.**	conduct; behavior
e	**11.** portable	**c.**	to refuse to take or to throw away
d	**12.** report	**d.**	a statement or account of something
a	**13.** ejected	**e.**	able to be carried easily
f	**14.** export	**f.**	to send goods to another country for sale

94 Lesson 42
Roots port, ject

CURRICULUM CONNECTIONS

SPELLING

You may use the following words and dictation sentences as a pretest for the first group of spelling words in Unit 4.

1. **deposit** — **Deposit** the money in the bank.
2. **repel** — This spray will **repel** insects.
3. **expulsion** — The misbehaving student was threatened with **expulsion**.
4. **portable** — Andrew asked for a **portable** radio.
5. **eject** — The club voted to **eject** the noisy member.
6. **audience** — The actors chose a member of the **audience** to join them on the stage.
7. **dictate** — The students listened to the teacher **dictate** sentences.
8. **capture** — The dog officer must **capture** all dogs without collars.
9. **acceptance** — The actor made a funny **acceptance** speech.
10. **receipt** — The salesclerk handed me the **receipt**.

WRITING

Portfolio Have students read about the life of a famous composer or contemporary songwriter and write a one-page imaginary interview with that person. Invite students to choose partners to assist them in presenting their interviews.

FINE ARTS

Play a recording of a Beethoven composition. Encourage students to relate their initial reaction to the music. Then play another piece by Beethoven and have students compare the mood, tempo, and intensity of both selections.

SCIENCE

Explain that a piano creates sound when the player presses a key, which makes a small felt-covered wooden hammer hit a string, causing the string to vibrate. Have students each choose an instrument and find out how it makes music.

 Technology

AstroWord, Base Words. ©1998 Silver Burdett Ginn Inc. Division of Simon & Schuster.

LARGE GROUP ### AUDITORY LEARNERS

Read words from the pages or say other words built on the roots in the lesson. As students hear them, have them identify the root and meaning of each, using the wall chart from the Lesson Focus.

GIFTED LEARNERS

Have students explain the meanings of words with prefixes in this lesson, using the prefix meanings studied earlier and the roots introduced here. Encourage students to find additional words with prefixes that are based on the same roots.

LEARNERS WHO NEED EXTRA SUPPORT

Materials: index cards

Have students create word equation cards in which a prefix or a suffix is added to a root and makes a new word, such as re + ject = reject. Discuss with students the meaning of each element of the equation. **See Daily Word Study Practice, pages 189–190.**

Lesson 43

Pages 95-96

Roots aud, dict, cap, cept, eipt

Lesson Focus

INTRODUCING THE SKILL

- Write the following words on the board and underline the roots: <u>aud</u>ible, pre<u>dict</u>, <u>cap</u>able, re<u>cept</u>acle, and re<u>ceipt</u>.

- Introduce the meaning of *aud* as "to hear." Ask what *audible* would mean. *(able to be heard)*

- Ask students what *predict* means. *(to tell what is going to happen)* Explain that the root *dict* means "to say" or "tell." Invite volunteers to use the words *audible* and *predict* in sentences.

- Explain that *cap, cept,* and *ceipt are* forms of the same root and mean "take or seize." Discuss the meanings of *capable, receptacle,* and *receipt* and have volunteers use the words in sentences.

USING THE PAGES

Have students review the rules and examples on pages 95 and 96. Add the root meanings to the wall chart introduced in the previous lesson. Be sure that students understand the directions to the exercises on the pages.

Name _____

▶ Read the sentences and underline each word that contains the root **aud** or **dict**.

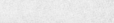

RULE
The root **dict** usually means **tell** or **say**. The root **aud** means **hear**.
dictate = to say with authority
audible = loud enough to be heard

1. The crew is working to create the <u>audio</u> portion of a commercial.

2. Abby, who will perform the voice-over, speaks with crisp <u>diction</u>.

3. At the <u>audition</u> the commercial's director was impressed with her.

4. He knew Abby's pleasant voice would appeal to an <u>audience</u>.

5. Abby looked in her pocket <u>dictionary</u> for a word's pronunciation.

6. The director issued an <u>edict</u> to Abby and the crew: "Begin recording!"

7. When he played back the recording, it was barely <u>audible</u>.

8. "I <u>predict</u> we will find that something is wrong with our equipment," he said.

▶ Match each word with its definition.

c	9. audio	a. a strong statement or command
e	10. dictator	b. a group of people who listen or watch
a	11. edict	c. involving sound or hearing
g	12. audiotape	d. a book containing definitions for words
h	13. contradict	e. a person whose commands must be obeyed
d	14. dictionary	f. to forecast; to say ahead of time
f	15. predict	g. a tape used to record sound
b	16. audience	h. to deny; to say the opposite of

Lesson 43
Roots aud, dict **95**

FOCUS ON ALL LEARNERS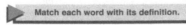

ENGLISH LANGUAGE LEARNERS/ESL

Romance language speakers may be familiar with the roots covered in this lesson from their own native languages. Help students as they practice pronouncing English words built on these roots.

LARGE GROUP

VISUAL LEARNERS

Write the paragraph on the board. Invite students to use context clues and root meanings to define the underlined words.

The pirates were a <u>captive</u> <u>audience</u> as their leader issued an <u>edict</u>. The captain demanded that they <u>intercept</u> the next ship and <u>capture</u> the crew. No one dared to <u>contradict</u>. They had to <u>accept</u> the orders.

SMALL GROUP

AUDITORY/ KINESTHETIC LEARNERS

Have students play charades, trying to guess each other's clues as they act out words from the lesson that contain the roots *aud, dict, cap, cept,* and *ceipt.*

Complete each sentence with a word from the word bank.

capable	reception		
accept	capacity	captured	receiving
acceptance	receipts	receptacle	captivating

1. Last night we attended an elegant ___reception___ .

2. The huge room was filled to ___capacity___ .

3. Carol Parks gave a speech to ___accept___ the nomination for governor.

4. Everyone knows she is ___capable___ of being a great governor.

5. An excellent speaker, Ms. Parks ___captured___ the crowd's attention.

6. It was an especially ___captivating___ speech.

7. She asked that written suggestions be placed in a ___receptacle___ .

8. She offered ___receipts___ to those who made contributions.

9. Today the newspapers praised her ___acceptance___ speech.

10. She has been ___receiving___ phone calls all day from people wishing her success.

CAROL PARKS FOR GOVERNOR

Match each word with its definition.

c 11. captives   a. to take something offered

a 12. receive   b. a person in an office who greets people

d 13. intercept   c. people taken prisoner

e 14. receptacle   d. to seize something that is on its way from one place to another

b 15. receptionist   e. a container

96   Lesson 43
Roots cap, cept, ceipt

AUDITORY LEARNERS

PARTNER Have pairs of students write and present two-speaker radio infomercials announcing the availability and benefits of a new CD-ROM audio dictionary for computers. Ask students to build their infomercials around the words in the lesson.

GIFTED LEARNERS

Have students find more words that contain the roots *aud*, *dict*, *cap*, *cept*, and *ceipt*, using dictionaries as a tool. Ask them to write new words in sentences that reveal their meanings.

LEARNERS WHO NEED EXTRA SUPPORT

Help students relate the meanings of the roots *aud*, *dict*, *cap*, *cept*, and *ceipt* to the words with those roots in the lesson. Have them compose new sentences for those words. **See Daily Word Study Practice, pages 189–190.**

CURRICULUM CONNECTIONS

SPELLING

You may use the following words and dictation sentences as a posttest for the first group of spelling words in Unit 4.

1. **deposit** — You have to fill out a **deposit** slip for the exact amount.

2. **repel** — Old castles were designed to **repel** invaders.

3. **expulsion** — The principal discussed **expulsion** with students.

4. **portable** — Grandma won a **portable** television at the party.

5. **eject** — Push the top button to **eject** the cassette.

6. **audience** — The **audience** roared with laughter.

7. **dictate** — Should parents **dictate** what their children wear?

8. **capture** — The reporter announced the **capture** of the thief.

9. **acceptance** — The President nodded to show his **acceptance** of the proposal.

10. **receipt** — Did you remember to keep the **receipt**?

WRITING

Portfolio Have students write speeches in which they accept a nomination for a political office, such as student council president, state governor, or county judge. In their speeches have students thank those who nominated them and outline plans for what they hope to achieve if elected.

SOCIAL STUDIES

In past centuries, flags were frequently used to identify the owners or residents of forts, settlements, and sailing ships. When a flag was taken down and a different flag hoisted aloft, it was sometimes due to a captured by enemy forces. Challenge students to research locations and events in history where flags played unforgettable roles.

AstroWord, Base Words. ©1998 Silver Burdett Ginn Inc. Division of Simon & Schuster.

Lesson 44
Lesson 97–98

Roots spec, spect, mit, miss, man

Lesson Focus

INTRODUCING THE SKILL

- Write these sentences on the board.

  The artist moved to get a new perspective on the scene.

  This ticket will admit me to all exhibits.

  We had an early dismissal because of the blizzard.

  The driver shifted the gears manually.

- Ask students to underline one word in each sentence that means:

  "different look" (*perspective*), "let go in" (*admit*), "letting go" (*dismissal*), "in a manner done by hand" (*manually*)

- Explain the root meanings: *spec* and *spect* mean "see," "look," or "examine"; *mit* and *miss* mean "send" or "let go"; *man* means "hand." Add the root meanings to the wall chart begun in Lesson 42.

USING THE PAGES

Read the rule boxes and the directions on pages 97 and 98 with students. After the pages are finished, discuss with students what they have learned.

Name _____

Ten words containing the roots **spec, spect, mit, miss,** are hidden in the puzzle. Some of the words go across and some go down. Circle each word and write it on the line.

RULE

The roots **spec** and **spect** mean **see, look,** or **examine**. The roots **mit** and **miss** mean **send** or **let go**.

spectator = an onlooker

dis**miss** = to send away

```
S T Q A D M I T I R S P
U P E B N K N I U P F E
B P H S I N S P E C T R
M A S R C H P B D Q G S
I K X E M V E W O J T P
T R M S P E C I M E N E
F E B P H J T E V C X C
U M O E G Z O M I T V T
Z I G C O A R W D I L I
G T Y T A W R V F J D V
D I S M I S S A L M Z E
```

1.	admit	6.	inspector
2.	submit	7.	specimen
3.	inspect	8.	omit
4.	perspective	9.	remit
5.	respect	10.	dismissal

Complete each sentence with a word from the puzzle.

11. I ____admit____ I was squeamish at first.

12. From my ____perspective____, it wasn't really fun.

13. I certainly ____respect____ the nurse who drew the blood.

14. She said she would ____submit____ the sample to the lab.

15. There, the ____specimen____ will be evaluated.

Lesson 44
Roots spec, spect, mit, miss

97

FOCUS ON ALL LEARNERS

ENGLISH LANGUAGE LEARNERS/ESL

Explain that some of the groups of words in the exercise on page 98 contain synonyms, or words that have the same or nearly the same meaning. Other groups of words are related because of a specific subject; for example, *manacles, jails,* and *locks* are related to the subject of prison or captivity.

VISUAL LEARNERS

INDIVIDUAL Have students write on paper as a column head each of the five roots in this lesson. Then list as many words containing the roots as they can. Students can refer to the lesson, a dictionary or thesaurus, or their prior knowledge.

AUDITORY/KINESTHETIC LEARNERS

LARGE GROUP Read words at random from the lesson that have the root *man*. Invite them to define each word in which *man* means "hand." Students can demonstrate word meaning, if appropriate.

> Look up each word in boldface print and then cross out the word or words that do not belong in the same category.

> **RULE**
> The root **man** means **hand**.
> **man**ual = made or done by hand

1. manager	supervisor	director	boss	~~customer~~
2. manipulate	handle	control	~~purchase~~	~~view~~
3. manners	~~rude~~	respectable	proper	decent
4. manicure	file	~~break~~	trim	polish
5. demand	ask	require	~~agree~~	~~beg~~
6. manacles	jails	locks	~~jewelry~~	~~animals~~
7. manuscript	~~video~~	essay	composition	article
8. manual	guide	~~interview~~	instructions	~~advertisement~~
9. manufacture	~~grow~~	make	build	construct
10. maneuver	move	~~listen~~	direct	~~notice~~
11. command	~~plead~~	force	rule	order
12. reprimand	~~praise~~	scold	blame	~~encourage~~

> Write sentences for six of the boldface words.

13. _____
_____

14. _____
_____

15. _____
_____

16. _____
_____

17. _____
_____

18. _____
_____

98
Lesson 44
Root: man

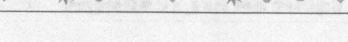

AUDITORY LEARNERS

LARGE GROUP Invite students to take turns calling out words containing the roots *spec, spect, mit, miss,* and *man,* and having classmates identify and spell the root in each word.

GIFTED LEARNERS

Ask students to create book titles, and perhaps one-sentence story summaries, of mysteries that might be written using the following words: *manacles, mission, prospector, spectacles, spectator, specimen,* and other words containing the roots *spec, spect, mit, miss,* and *man.*

LEARNERS WHO NEED EXTRA SUPPORT

To enhance understanding of word meaning, invite students to choose words from the lesson to use in sentences that tell about personal experiences. **See Daily Word Study Practice, pages 189–190.**

CURRICULUM CONNECTIONS

SPELLING

The following words and dictation sentences may be used as a pretest for the second group of spelling words in Unit 4.

1. **spectator** — The **spectator** at the game wore dark glasses.
2. **submit** — It is wrong to **submit** to a bully.
3. **dismiss** — It was time to **dismiss** the class.
4. **specimen** — We examined the **specimen** under the microscope.
5. **manual** — The **manual** explained how to operate the oven.
6. **sweatshirt** — Ben bought a hooded **sweatshirt**.
7. **they'll** — **They'll** call us when they get to Boston.
8. **should've** — You **should've** told me you felt sick.
9. **you're** — If **you're** sure you want the book, order it right away.
10. **thunderstorm** — The cat can tell whenever a **thunderstorm** is coming.

WRITING

Portfolio Have students write mysteries, using the titles developed for the Gifted Learners activity or other titles they invent. Remind them that each mystery must have a problem or puzzle to be solved, must provide clues, and should reveal the culprit or explain the mystery at the end. Encourage students to use words containing the roots *spec, spect, mit, miss,* and *man.*

HEALTH

Challenge students to use reference materials or interview professionals to discover the kinds of health problems that can be detected by a blood test.

FINE ARTS

Provide materials and guidelines for students to do simple perspective drawings.

Technology AstroWord, Base Words. ©1998 Silver Burdett Ginn Inc. Division of Simon & Schuster.

Lesson 45

Compound Words

INFORMAL ASSESSMENT OBJECTIVES

Can students

✔ recognize compound words?

✔ form compound words?

Lesson Focus

INTRODUCING THE SKILL

- On the board, write the following sentence.

  We'll need to buy a flashlight, a screwdriver, and some thumbtacks.

- Ask students to identify the words in the sentence that are made up of two other words. *(flashlight, screwdriver, thumbtacks)* Have volunteers circle the two words in each of these compound words.

- Invite students to suggest other compound words they know. List them on the chalkboard or a chart.

USING THE PAGES

Have students read the definition on page 99 and apply it to the words from the previous activity, *matchbox,* and *rattlesnake.* Ask students to follow each set of directions to complete pages 99 and 100. Later, discuss with students what they learned about compound words.

Name _____

1. My <u>grandparents</u> live next to a famous <u>lighthouse</u> on the ocean.
2. Each year, for my <u>birthday</u>, we have a celebration at their house.
3. Since my <u>birthday</u> occurs in the <u>summertime</u>, we play <u>outdoor</u> games.
4. My sisters like to play <u>baseball</u>, but I prefer <u>volleyball</u>.
5. My <u>grandfather</u> and my mother, who is in a <u>wheelchair</u>, play chess <u>outside</u>.
6. They lean over the <u>chessboard</u> with great concentration.
7. Dad usually plays <u>horseshoes</u> with my <u>grandmother</u>.
8. <u>Sometimes</u> my dad, my sisters, and I go <u>horseback</u> riding at a <u>nearby</u> stable.
9. After <u>sunset</u> we use a <u>flashlight</u> to try to signal the <u>lighthouse</u>.
10. Then, dressed in warm <u>sweatshirts</u>, we eat <u>cupcakes</u> and drink milk.

> Choose the correct compound word from those you underlined and write it on the line beside its definition.

11.	the parents of someone's father or mother	grandparents
12.	a portable electric light	flashlight
13.	small cakes	cupcakes
14.	a chair mounted on wheels	wheelchair
15.	heavy cotton shirts	sweatshirts

Lesson 45
Compound words **99**

FOCUS ON ALL LEARNERS

ENGLISH LANGUAGE LEARNERS/ESL

Use compound words from the lesson to emphasize how the meanings of two words can change when they are joined to form a compound word.

VISUAL LEARNERS

 PARTNER Have pairs of students list the compound words found in the context sentences on page 99, think of categories that at least some of the words would fit in, and then brainstorm other compound words to add to the same categories.

KINESTHETIC LEARNERS

 SMALL GROUP **Materials:** posterboard, dice, game markers, index cards

Provide materials for groups of students to create gameboards featuring compound words. Each group can teach classmates how to play.

Choose a word from the word bank and write it on the line in front of the correct word to make a compound word.

1.	row	boat	2.	box	car
3.	beef	steak	4.	snow	flakes
5.	hot	cakes	6.	thunder	clap
7.	pine	apple	8.	hail	stones
9.	water	melon	10.	rain	drops
11.	air	plane	12.	steam	ship

water	thunder
row	hot
snow	air
pine	rain
box	hail
beef	steam

Write each compound word you made under the correct heading.

Food		Vehicles		Weather	
13.	beefsteak	17.	rowboat	21.	snowflakes
14.	hotcakes	18.	boxcar	22.	thunderclap
15.	pineapple	19.	airplane	23.	hailstones
16.	watermelon	20.	steamship	24.	raindrops

Choose words from the word bank. Use them to make compound words of your own and write the words on the lines.

25. _____   26. _____

(100) Lesson 45
Compound words

AUDITORY LEARNERS

LARGE GROUP

Have students form two teams. Appoint a leader who will say aloud words to which another word can be added to form a compound word. The first team to respond scores a point. If more than one compound word can be formed, award a point for each correct response. Use words from the lesson to play.

GIFTED LEARNERS

Give students the following word groups: *wrist, watch, dog; quick, sand, paper; ware, house, boat.* Tell students to find the word in each group that can be added to the end of one word and the beginning of another to make two compound words.

LEARNERS WHO NEED EXTRA SUPPORT

Have students read aloud the sentences on page 99. Tell them how many compound words to look for in each sentence. **See Daily Word Study Practice, pages 189–190.**

CURRICULUM CONNECTIONS

SPELLING

On the chalkboard, write a series of blanks for each spelling word (one space for each letter or apostrophe). Fill in the first and last letter of each word. Then call out the spelling words (*spectator, submit, dismiss, specimen, manual, sweatshirt, they'll, should've, you're, thunderstorm*) and have volunteers identify the correct set of blanks and fill in the missing letters and apostrophes.

WRITING

Portfolio Have students write a letter to friends from an imaginary seaside location where they have been vacationing. Have students use correct personal letter format, and include vivid details about what they have seen and done on vacation. Encourage them to use at least four compound words in their letters.

SCIENCE

The names for many plants are compound words, such as *dogwood, snapdragon, goldenrod,* and *primrose.* Have each student pick one of these words, or find another, and compile a short list of information about the plant it names, adding illustrations of the plant if possible.

PHYSICAL EDUCATION

Have students choose a sport with a name that is a compound word, such as volleyball, football, basketball, or baseball, and research its development, teams, and current popularity in the United States and elsewhere. How do the two components of each of these sport names describe important elements of the sport?

Technology

AstroWord, Compound Words.
©1998 Silver Burdett Ginn Inc.
Division of Simon & Schuster.

Lesson 46

Pages 101–102

Possessives

INFORMAL ASSESSMENT OBJECTIVES

Can students

✔ recognize singular and plural possessives?

✔ form singular and plural possessives?

Lesson Focus

INTRODUCING THE SKILL

- Write these phrases on the board: *the secretary's word processor, the boss's telephone, the women's briefcases, the managers' desks.*

- Ask students to tell how many people have the word processor (*one secretary*), the telephone (*one boss*), briefcases (*more than one woman*) and desks (*more than one manager*).

- Have volunteers explain how each possessive is formed. Lead students to conclude:
  possessives of singular nouns are formed by adding -'s. (*secretary's, boss's*)
  possessives of plural nouns that do not end in -s are formed by adding -'s. (*women's*)
  possessives of plural nouns that end in -s are formed by adding -s'. (*managers'*)

USING THE PAGES

- Review the rules and examples on pages 101 and 102. Have volunteers read the directions aloud.

- **Critical Thinking** Encourage students to share their responses to the question on page 102.

Name _____

▶ Read each group of words. If the words show that only one person or animal has something, write **one** on the first line. If the words show that more than one person or animal has something, write **more than one**. Then on the second line write the possessive form that can stand for each phrase.

> **RULE**
> The possessive form is used to show that a person or an animal owns, has, or possesses something. To make a singular word show possession, usually add an apostrophe and an **s** (**'s**). If a word is plural and ends in **s**, just add an apostrophe.
>
> Ellen**'s** skateboard = a skateboard belonging to Ellen
>
> the dog**'s** feet = the feet belonging to the dog
>
> girls**'** uniforms = the uniforms belonging to the girls

1. the coat of Blair	one	Blair's
2. the snout of the seal	one	seal's
3. the market of the farmers	more than one	farmers'
4. the owners of the dogs	more than one	dogs'
5. the nest of the owls	more than one	owls'
6. the locker room of the boys	more than one	boys'
7. the scores of the bowlers	more than one	bowlers'
8. the skin of the snake	one	snake's
9. the boat of Mike	one	Mike's
10. the home of the zebras	more than one	zebras'
11. the kitchen of Mom	one	Mom's
12. the home of the muskrat	one	muskrat's

FOCUS ON ALL LEARNERS ✴ • • ■ ♦

ENGLISH LANGUAGE LEARNERS/ESL

This lesson may confuse English language learners in whose primary languages the formation of possessives may be simpler. Work with students as they examine whether possessive words in the lesson are singular or plural, and whether or not a plural ends in -s.

VISUAL LEARNERS

INDIVIDUAL Have students scan a text, library book, or reading selection looking for possessive nouns. Ask students to list each possessive noun with the noun that follows it and label the possessives as either *singular* or *plural*.

KINESTHETIC LEARNERS

PARTNER Have pairs of students write sentences using possessive forms but omitting apostrophes as they write. The partners can then exchange papers and fill in apostrophes where needed. When finished, partners can check one another's work.

Read each sentence. Write the correct possessive form of the word at the right.

1. The highlight of my __family's__ summer was the neighborhood talent show. (family)

2. The show was held in Ms. __Morris's__ enormous backyard. (Morris)

3. The __children's__ events were held first. (children)

4. Leslie and Nathan Schwab announced that they would demonstrate their two __terriers'__ new tricks. (terriers)

5. When the dogs failed to perform, the __twins'__ frustration was comical. (twins)

6. My __sister's__ dancing exhibition was next. (sister)

7. Unfortunately, __Jess's__ shoes fell off in mid-dance. (Jess)

8. Nevertheless, the __audience's__ applause was sincere. (audience)

9. __Matt's__ magic trick with mice was very effective. (Matt)

10. When the __mice's__ tails disappeared, everyone gasped. (mice)

11. The __men's__ diving events were quite impressive. (men)

12. Mr. __Chang's__ splash drenched everyone near the pool. (Chang)

13. Everyone joined in with the __wives'__ laughter. (wives)

14. The husbands announced that they were looking forward to the __women's__ events. (women)

> **RULE**
>
> To make a word show possession: **1.** add **'s** to a singular word, **2.** add **'s** to a plural word not ending in **s**, **3.** add an apostrophe (**'**) to a plural word ending in **s**.
>
> Bill**'s** house = a house belonging to Bill
>
> the children**'s** books = the books belonging to the children
>
> the bear**s'** home = the home belonging to the bears

Critical Thinking

If you lived in this neighborhood, would you enjoy being part of this talent show? Why or why not? If you participated, what might you do?

Lesson 46
Possessives

102

SPELLING

Write the following definitions on the board for students to copy on paper. Then call out the spelling words, and ask students to write each word next to its definition. The spelling words are *spectator, submit, dismiss, specimen, manual, sweatshirt, they'll, should've, you're, thunderstorm.* Have students exchange papers to check their work.

1. contraction containing *will* (*they'll*)
2. someone who watches (*spectator*)
3. to make go away (*dismiss*)
4. contraction containing *are* (*you're*)
5. by hand (*manual*)
6. a piece of clothing (*sweatshirt*)
7. contraction containing *have* (*should've*)
8. to give in (*submit*)
9. weather event involving loud noises (*thunderstorm*)
10. an example (*specimen*)

WRITING

Portfolio Invite students to write a paragraph comparing the ways they celebrate different holidays of the year. The paragraph should include several possessive holiday names, such as *New Year's Day, Father's Day, President's Day,* and *April Fool's Day.* You may wish to generate a list of possibilities before students write. Encourage students to see how many different holidays they can mention as they write.

MATH

Give students the following information: The world high-diving record is 176 feet 10 inches, by Olivier Favre of Switzerland. A meter equals 39.37 inches. Have students calculate the height of Favre's record-winning dive in meters.

HEALTH/PHYSICAL EDUCATION

Certain safety precautions must be observed when diving. Have students explore *American Red Cross Swimming and Diving* or other safety guidelines for diving. Ask students to explain a few basic guidelines or create a list of tips for divers.

AUDITORY LEARNERS

LARGE GROUP Instruct students to write the possessive form as you read each of the following phrases: *the brooms of the janitors (janitors' brooms), the number of the bus (the bus's number), the workbooks the children have (the children's workbooks), the office of the principal (the principal's office).*

GIFTED LEARNERS

Have students write additional sentences that go with the theme of the sentences on page 102. Challenge students to include at least one possessive form of a plural word that does not end in *s.*

LEARNERS WHO NEED EXTRA SUPPORT

Remind students that the reason it is important to form possessives correctly is to distinguish between singular and plural nouns. Answer students' questions as they work. **See Daily Word Study Practice, pages 189–190**

Lesson 47

Lesson 103–104

Contractions

Lesson Focus

INTRODUCING THE SKILL

- Read aloud this definition: *A contraction is a word formed when two words are written together with one or more letters left out. An apostrophe takes the place of the missing letter or letters.*

- Write these contractions on the board: *aren't, she'll, he's, I'm, you're, we've.*

- Ask students to say two words that can replace *aren't* in the sentence *We aren't finished playing the game. (are not)* Write *are not* and have students name the letter left out of the contraction. *(o in not)*

- Have volunteers write the two words that are represented by each remaining contraction. Ask them to name the letter or letters that are replaced by each apostrophe.

USING THE PAGES

Invite students to read the definition and examples on page 103. Review the directions for pages 103 and 104. When finished, encourage students to discuss what they learned about contractions.

103

Name _____

Choose one of the contractions below the line to complete each sentence. Then, on the line at the right, write the two words that form the contraction.

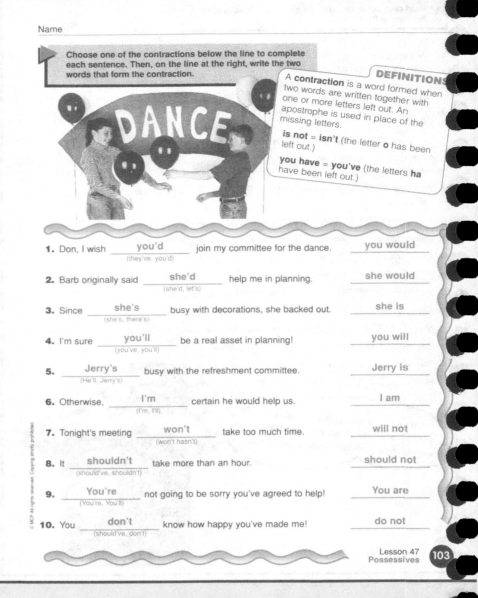

DEFINITIONS

A **contraction** is a word formed when two words are written together with one or more letters left out. An apostrophe is used in place of the missing letters.

is not = isn't (the letter **o** has been left out.)

you have = you've (the letters **ha** have been left out.)

1. Don, I wish __**you'd**__ join my committee for the dance.   **you would**
   (they've, you'd)

2. Barb originally said __**she'd**__ help me in planning.   **she would**
   (she'd, let's)

3. Since __**she's**__ busy with decorations, she backed out.   **she is**
   (she's, there's)

4. I'm sure __**you'll**__ be a real asset in planning!   **you will**
   (you've, you'll)

5. __**Jerry's**__ busy with the refreshment committee.   **Jerry is**
   (He'll, Jerry's)

6. Otherwise, __**I'm**__ certain he would help us.   **I am**
   (I'm, I'll)

7. Tonight's meeting __**won't**__ take too much time.   **will not**
   (won't, hasn't)

8. It __**shouldn't**__ take more than an hour.   **should not**
   (should've, shouldn't)

9. __**You're**__ not going to be sorry you've agreed to help!   **You are**
   (You're, You'll)

10. You __**don't**__ know how happy you've made me!   **do not**
    (should've, don't)

Lesson 47
Possessives   103

FOCUS ON ALL LEARNERS

ENGLISH LANGUAGE LEARNERS/ESL

Work with examples of possessives and contractions in context to help students understand the different use of apostrophes in these two word forms.

✋ VISUAL LEARNERS

INDIVIDUAL   Have students rewrite the following sentences, replacing the underlined words with contractions: *I will miss you when you move. You are the best friend I have ever had. Let us promise that we will always keep in touch.*

✋ KINESTHETIC LEARNERS

INDIVIDUAL   **Materials:** note paper, art paper, scissors, glue

Ask students to write the words *I, you, he, she, we, where, it, that, is, are, will, have,* and *not* on slips of paper. Have students create contractions by cutting letters out of the appropriate words, gluing combined words onto art paper and writing in apostrophes where needed.

Put the two words on the puzzle pieces together by writing the contraction that is formed from the two words.

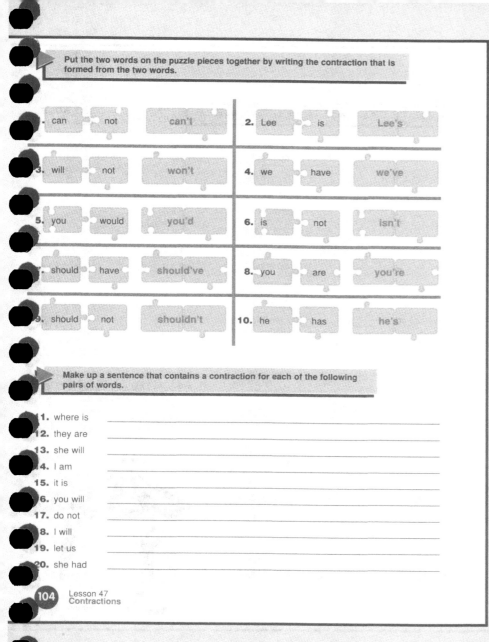

1. can + not = can't
2. Lee + is = Lee's
3. will + not = won't
4. we + have = we've
5. you + would = you'd
6. is + not = isn't
7. should + have = should've
8. you + are = you're
9. should + not = shouldn't
10. he + has = he's

Make up a sentence that contains a contraction for each of the following pairs of words.

11. where is _____
12. they are _____
13. she will _____
14. I am _____
15. it is _____
16. you will _____
17. do not _____
18. I will _____
19. let us _____
20. she had _____

SPELLING

Write the following words on the board: *spectator, submit, dismiss, specimen, manual, sweatshirt, they'll, should've, you're, thunderstorm.* Call out each set of words below, pausing for students to tell you which spelling word completes the set.

1. T-shirt, undershirt, (*sweatshirt*)
2. rain, lightning, (*thunderstorm*)
3. submarine, subject, (*submit*)
4. laboratory, microscope, (*specimen*)
5. directions, workbook, (*manual*)
6. would've, could've, (*should've*)
7. audience, bleachers, (*spectator*)
8. we're, they're, (*you're*)
9. dislike, disconnect, (*dismiss*)
10. I'll, he'll, (*they'll*)

WRITING

Portfolio Have students write the text of an advertisement to be read as a school announcement. The ad should describe a social activity, such as an after-school dance or a student-faculty basketball game. Encourage students to use contractions and persuasive language to highlight the details in their ads.

PHYSICAL EDUCATION

Have students ask older relatives and friends what sorts of dances were popular at their school dances. Encourage students to learn a few steps of these dances and then demonstrate or describe them to their classmates.

FINE ARTS

Share recordings of dance music representative of different ethnic groups, such as Viennese waltzes, Irish step dancing, Brazilian sambas and Slavic polkas. Have students compare and contrast elements of the music in terms of mood (major or minor key), tempo (speed), rhythm (tap out the pattern), and the instruments used. Encourage students to demonstrate steps they may know or to invent movements for the dances.

AUDITORY LEARNERS

LARGE GROUP Read aloud the following proverbs: *Don't cry over spilt milk; All that glitters isn't gold; Don't count your chickens before they're hatched.* Have students identify the contractions and their component parts. Talk about the meaning of each proverb.

GIFTED LEARNERS

Challenge small groups of students to identify homonyms for contractions. Model the following example: *we'd, weed.* (Possible answers include *I'll, aisle; they're, there, their; we've, weave; he'd, heed; he'll, heel, heal; you'll, yule; we'll, wheel, wheal.*)

LEARNERS WHO NEED EXTRA SUPPORT

Have students look through books and articles for contractions. Ask students to copy each contraction and write out the words it combines. If necessary, explain the difference between contractions and possessive nouns. **See Daily Word Study Practice, pages 189–190.**

Lesson 48

Pages 105–106

Syllables

INFORMAL ASSESSMENT OBJECTIVE

Can students

✔ identify the number of syllables in words?

✔ divide words with prefixes into syllables?

✔ divide words with suffixes into syllables?

✔ divide compound words into syllables?

Lesson Focus

INTRODUCING THE SKILL

- As a volunteer reads each of the syllabication rules on page 105, have another student come to the board and divide the following words into syllables.

Compound words: *flash-light, bas-ket-ball*
Words with prefixes: *mis-lead, in-ter-state, coun-ter-clock-wise*
Words with suffixes: *care-ful, ring-mas-ter*
Words with both a prefix and a suffix: *re-paint-ed, im-press-ing*

USING THE PAGES

- Review with students the directions to complete pages 105 and 106. When the pages are completed, discuss what students learned about dividing words into syllables.

- **Critical Thinking** Invite students to respond to the question on page 106.

Name _____

▶ Write the number of vowel sounds you hear in each word. Write each word, then divide it into syllables using slash marks.

1.	compel	2	com/pel
2.	wallpaper	3	wall/pa/per
3.	propose	2	pro/pose
4.	rejected	3	re/ject/ed
5.	icebreaker	3	ice/break/er
6.	yearbook	2	year/book
7.	captivate	3	cap/ti/vate
8.	accept	2	ac/cept
9.	submit	2	sub/mit
10.	inspect	2	in/spect
11.	predictable	4	pre/dict/ab/le
12.	posture	2	pos/ture
13.	barefoot	2	bare/foot
14.	admit	2	ad/mit
15.	propulsion	3	pro/pul/sion
16.	battleship	3	bat/tle/ship
17.	deceiving	3	de/ceiv/ing
18.	dismissal	3	dis/miss/al
19.	imported	3	im/port/ed
20.	ringmaster	3	ring/mas/ter
21.	collarbone	3	col/lar/bone
22.	oppose	2	op/pose
23.	contradict	3	con/tra/dict
24.	intercept	3	in/ter/cept

RULE

Remember these rules for dividing words into syllables.

1. When a word has a prefix, divide the word between the prefix and the base word or the root. Some prefixes have more than one syllable.

2. When a word has a suffix, divide the word between the suffix and the base word or the root. Some suffixes have more than one syllable.

3. Sometimes a word has a prefix and a suffix with the base word or the root. If each word part has a vowel sound, then each part is a syllable.

4. Divide a compound word between the words that make up the compound word. Then divide the smaller words into syllables if necessary.

Lesson 48
Syllables **105**

FOCUS ON ALL LEARNERS

ENGLISH LANGUAGE LEARNERS/ESL

Since syllabication is dependent on pronunciation, it is important for students to practice pronouncing words correctly. For example, *-ed* in *walked* is not a syllable, while *-ed* in *painted* is.

VISUAL LEARNERS

INDIVIDUAL Write the following words on the board, omitting the hyphens: *mid-sum-mer, sand-pa-per, un-hap-pi-ness, mi-cro-phone, drag-on-fly, dis-con-tin-u-ing*. Have students divide the words into syllables and discuss which rules each word follows.

AUDITORY/KINESTHETIC LEARNERS

PARTNER

Materials: dice

Challenge partners to take turns rolling a die and saying a word with the number of syllables indicated on the die. No words may be repeated. If students question a response, a dictionary can be used to verify.

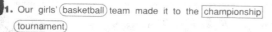

Read each sentence. Underline each two-syllable word. Circle each three-syllable word. Draw a box around each four-syllable word. Then write each word in the correct column, and use vertical lines to divide the words into syllables.

1. Our girls' (basketball) team made it to the [championship] (tournament).

2. The team has played [excellently] during the winter season.

3. Playing forward, Beth has achieved an (impressive) record.

4. Beth is tall and [dedicated,] and she shoots [accurately.]

5. The team's (cocaptains,) (Susanna) and Jo, have been (outstanding) this year.

6. Each game has (attracted) (numerous) cheering fans.

7. Last night's game was [incredibly] (exciting.)

8. Beth [executed] some [complicated] moves.

9. The outcome of the game was not [predictable.]

10. The score was [surprisingly] close.

What qualities do you think an outstanding cocaptain might have?

Critical Thinking

Two Syllables	Three Syllables	Four Syllables
dur/ing	bas/ket/ball	cham/pi/on/ship
win/ter	tour/na/ment	ex/cel/lent/ly
sea/son	im/pres/sive	ded/i/cat/ed
play/ing	co/cap/tains	ac/cu/rate/ly
for/ward	Su/san/na	in/cred/i/bly
a/chieved	out/stand/ing	ex/e/cut/ed
rec/ord	at/tract/ed	com/pli/cat/ed
cheer/ing	nu/mer/ous	pre/dict/a/ble
out/come	ex/cit/ing	sur/pris/ing/ly

CURRICULUM CONNECTIONS ✱ • • ■ • ◆

SPELLING

Read aloud the following spelling words: *spectator, submit, dismiss, specimen, manual, sweatshirt, they'll, should've, you're,* and *thunderstorm.* Have students call out how many syllables each word contains and then spell the word.

WRITING

Portfolio Explain to students that haiku is a form of traditional Japanese poetry form, which often describes a scene in nature. It contains 17 syllables in three lines. (Lines 1 and 3 have five syllables, and line 2 has seven syllables.) Read examples of haiku to students, then invite them to try their hand at writing their own.

MATH

Have students find sports statistics in books, newspapers, and magazines, and discuss with them how the various statistics are calculated and what they mean. For example, the method for finding baseball batting averages is an exercise in decimals and percentages that students can learn to compute.

Technology

AstroWord, Multisyllabic Words. ©1998 Silver Burdett Ginn Inc. Division of Simon & Schuster.

AUDITORY LEARNERS

LARGE GROUP Read aloud words from pages 105 and 106 to students, pausing distinctly at the end of each syllable. Have students repeat the words, using the same pauses. Then ask how many vowel sounds (syllables) are heard in each word.

GIFTED LEARNERS

Invite students to work in small groups to analyze the number of syllables per line in various poems. Provide an assortment of poems to examine, including some traditional poems with a regular number of syllables per line and some free verse with an irregular number of syllables. Give examples of haiku if possible.

LEARNERS WHO NEED EXTRA SUPPORT

Pair students who need practice with syllabication with students who are more comfortable with it. Have partners work together to divide words from the lesson into syllables. **See Daily Word Study Practice, page 195.**

Lesson 49

Lesson 107–108

 **Reading**  **Writing**

Reviewing Roots, Compound Words, Possessives, Contractions, Syllables

INFORMAL ASSESSMENT OBJECTIVES

Can students

✔ read an article which contains word roots, compound words, and possessives?

✔ write a prediction and a journal entry?

Lesson Focus

READING

- Have students scan page 107 to find compound words (*lighthouse, fundraisers, clambakes*), possessive forms (*nation's, public's*), and a contraction (*won't*).

- Write *manually, dismissed, dejected, important, specimens, capacities, reception, positive, spectacular,* and *permit* on the board. Ask students to identify the root and its meaning for each word. Have students use each word in a sentence.

- Invite students to read the article about lighthouses. At the end of page 107, have students write their predictions of the public's reaction.

WRITING

- Ask students to write an imaginary journal entry for a lighthouse keeper.

- Have a volunteer read the premise at the top of page 108. Discuss ideas students might include in their journal entries. Remind students to include words from the word bank.

 Reading ▶ Read the article. Then write your answer to the question at the end of the story.

Rescuing Lighthouses

In the past, more than 1,400 lighthouses dotted the length of America's coastline. Each lighthouse was inhabited by a keeper, who manually lit the lanterns and kept them burning brightly.

When automatic lighting systems were installed, many of the keepers were dismissed. Eventually, hundreds of lighthouses were closed down completely and slowly began to decay. Some dejected observers predicted that in time these romantic old structures would disappear completely from our landscape.

Many people, however, regard lighthouses as important specimens of our nation's history. They won't accept that these beautiful old structures are doomed. They believe lighthouses can be rescued and reused in new capacities.

Lighthouse preservation societies have formed throughout the country. The public's reception of their efforts has been quite positive. In Fire Island, New York, fund-raisers such as clambakes and races were held in support of the local lighthouse. They raised many thousands of dollars which were used to convert the Fire Island lighthouse into a museum. Other old lighthouses, such as East Brothers Island lighthouse, in San Francisco Bay, have been transformed into luxury inns. Many people love to climb to the top of a lighthouse just to enjoy the spectacular view!

People may not need lighthouses the way they used to, but they still seem to love them. They will not permit these relics from the past to crumble away.

Imagine that in the future, everyone will have access to art via computer networks, and nobody will need to go to museums anymore. Many politicians want to demolish the "useless" old art museums. How do you predict people will react? _____

Lesson 49
Review roots, compounds, possessives, contractions, syllables: Reading **107**

FOCUS ON ALL LEARNERS

ENGLISH LANGUAGE LEARNERS/ESL

Ask students if they have ever seen a lighthouse or pictures of lighthouses. Encourage them to share their knowledge about the functions and characteristics of lighthouses and their experiences with them.

🖐 VISUAL LEARNERS

INDIVIDUAL Have students copy each word from page 107 that contains one of the roots covered in this unit. Have them use colored markers to highlight the roots.

🖐 VISUAL/KINESTHETIC LEARNERS

INDIVIDUAL

Materials: art paper, markers, posterboard

Engage students in creating posters with messages to make the public aware of the importance of preserving buildings and objects of historical significance. Ask students to pay attention to words they use that focus on word study skills in Unit 4.

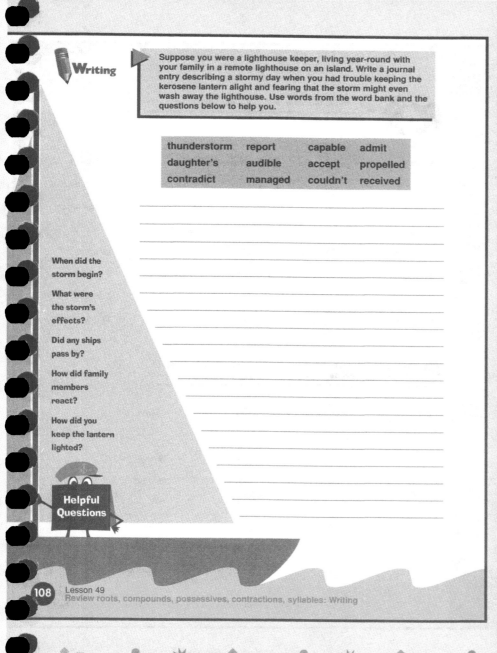

Writing

Suppose you were a lighthouse keeper, living year-round with your family in a remote lighthouse on an island. Write a journal entry describing a stormy day when you had trouble keeping the kerosene lantern alight and fearing that the storm might even wash away the lighthouse. Use words from the word bank and the questions below to help you.

thunderstorm	report	capable	admit
daughter's	audible	accept	propelled
contradict	managed	couldn't	received

When did the storm begin?

What were the storm's effects?

Did any ships pass by?

How did family members react?

How did you keep the lantern lighted?

Helpful Questions

Review roots, compounds, possessives, contractions, syllables: Writing

---

AUDITORY LEARNERS

PARTNER Have partners take turns reading aloud each other's paragraphs from the article on page 107 and identifying words that contain the roots they have learned in the unit. Students can then use each word in a new sentence that helps explain its meaning.

GIFTED LEARNERS

Invite students to look up information on lighthouses in the United States. Which states have the most? Which are the most famous and why are they famous? Students may enjoy making a map showing the names and locations of lighthouses they have learned about.

LEARNERS WHO NEED EXTRA SUPPORT

Reread the passage on page 107, with students, paragraph by paragraph. Help them identify and practice words that are still difficult for them to read or understand. **See Daily Word Study Practice, pages 189–190, 195.**

CURRICULUM CONNECTIONS ✳ ● ◆ ■ ◆

SPELLING

You may use the following words and dictation sentences as a posttest for the second group of spelling words in Unit 4.

1. **spectator** Rachel would rather be a performer than a **spectator**.
2. **submit** Jim will not be able to **submit** his work on time.
3. **dismiss** The ballet teacher decided to **dismiss** the class early.
4. **specimen** The scientist studied a **specimen.**
5. **manual** George lost the **manual** for his computer.
6. **sweatshirt** I left my **sweatshirt** in the cafeteria.
7. **they'll** Our neighbors promise that **they'll** trim the hedge.
8. **should've** Everybody **should've** finished the race by now.
9. **you're** **You're** stepping on my foot.
10. **thunderstorm** Come inside if there is a **thunderstorm**.

SOCIAL STUDIES

Discuss the places or things students would like to see saved or protected for future generations. Students should give reasons why the buildings or locations have value for them and society.

MATH

Ask students to list the following lighthouses in order from shortest to tallest, based on the following information, which you can read or display on a chart or the board: *The Old Red Lighthouse is taller than Big Bell Lighthouse; the Old Red Lighthouse is shorter than South Cove Lighthouse, but taller than North Cove Lighthouse; Big Bell Lighthouse is shorter than North Cove Lighthouse.* (Big Bell, North Cove, Old Red, South Cove)

Technology

AstroWord, Compound Words. ©1998 Silver Burdett Ginn Inc. Division of Simon & Schuster.

Lesson 50

Pages 109–110

Unit Checkup

Reviewing Roots, Compound Words, Possessives, Contractions, Syllables

INFORMAL ASSESSMENT OBJECTIVES

Can students

- ✔ match words containing roots to their definitions?
- ✔ divide words into syllables?
- ✔ identify compound words?
- ✔ write contractions and possessive forms?

Lesson Focus

PREPARING FOR THE CHECKUP

- On the board, write *roots*. Ask volunteers to define the term and to list examples of word roots under the heading.

- Ask volunteers to create words by adding suffixes and prefixes to the roots. Then have them divide the words into syllables.

- Write *compound words* and have volunteers list examples and divide the words into syllables.

- Write the words *boss, carpenter, children,* and *immigrants* on the board. Ask volunteers to create the possessive form of each word and add a noun for each.

- Write the words *should* and *have* on the board. Ask students to form a contraction from the words.

USING THE PAGES

Have students read the directions for each section on pages 109 and 110 before beginning the assessment. Circulate through the class to be sure students understand what they are to do. Later, review each item together.

109

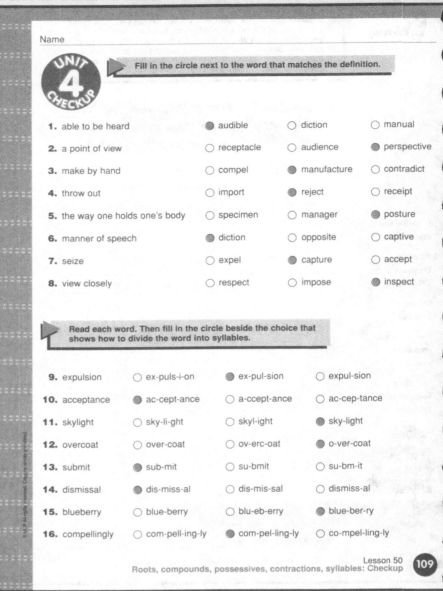

Name _____

UNIT 4 CHECKUP

▶ Fill in the circle next to the word that matches the definition.

1.	able to be heard	● audible	○ diction	○ manual
2.	a point of view	○ receptacle	○ audience	● perspective
3.	make by hand	○ compel	● manufacture	○ contradict
4.	throw out	○ import	● reject	○ receipt
5.	the way one holds one's body	○ specimen	○ manager	● posture
6.	manner of speech	● diction	○ opposite	○ captive
7.	seize	○ expel	● capture	○ accept
8.	view closely	○ respect	○ impose	● inspect

▶ Read each word. Then fill in the circle beside the choice that shows how to divide the word into syllables.

9.	expulsion	○ ex-puls-i-on	● ex-pul-sion	○ expul-sion
10.	acceptance	● ac-cept-ance	○ a-ccept-ance	○ ac-cep-tance
11.	skylight	○ sky-li-ght	○ skyl-ight	● sky-light
12.	overcoat	○ over-coat	○ ov-erc-oat	● o-ver-coat
13.	submit	● sub-mit	○ su-bmit	○ su-bm-it
14.	dismissal	● dis-miss-al	○ dis-mis-sal	○ dismiss-al
15.	blueberry	○ blue-berry	○ blu-eb-erry	● blue-ber-ry
16.	compellingly	○ com-pell-ing-ly	● com-pel-ling-ly	○ co-mpel-ling-ly

Roots, compounds, possessives, contractions, syllables: Checkup **109**

FOCUS ON ALL LEARNERS ✹ • ◆ ■

ENGLISH LANGUAGE LEARNERS/ESL

To build background for the connected sentences on page 110, discuss thunder, hail, and other characteristics of storms with students. Encourage the use of body language to illustrate word meanings.

VISUAL LEARNERS

INDIVIDUAL Remind students that an apostrophe signals a contraction or a possessive noun. Have them scan several pages in a book, looking for apostrophes. Ask them to identify each word containing an apostrophe as a contraction or a possessive.

KINESTHETIC LEARNERS

PARTNER **Materials:** note paper, envelopes

Have each member of a pair of students write ten compound words and then cut each word into its base words and put the resulting 20 words into an envelope. Have the partners switch bags and put the compounds back together.

UNIT 4 CHECKUP

▶ Read each sentence. Circle each compound word.

1. I got off the (schoolbus) wearing my light fall jacket.
2. There was a sudden (cloudburst).
3. (Raindrops) spattered around me, rapidly soaking my clothes.
4. I found myself in the middle of a fierce (thunderstorm).
5. I scurried along the (sidewalk), eager to get home.
6. Then I heard a loud "ping" as a (streetlight) shattered.
7. (Hailstones) the size of large marbles were bouncing around me.
8. I was just starting down our long (driveway) when a deafening roll of thunder made me jump.
9. "Move over, Mandy!" I yelled as I ducked into the (doghouse).

▶ Read each sentence. Write a contraction or possessive form of a word in the word bank, adding an apostrophe to each word you write.

storm	mother	You are	Everything is
hound	I will	cloud	tree

10. Inside the doghouse, my ____hound's____ eyes regarded me mournfully.
11. "____You're____ scared, too," I said to Mandy.
12. The ____storm's____ fierceness gradually decreased.
13. All of the ____trees'____ leaves stopped blowing.
14. "____I'll____ get out of here and give you some room," I told the dog.
15. On the driveway stood puddles full of the many ____clouds'____ reflections.
16. Then I heard my ____mother's____ voice nervously calling my name.
17. "____Everything's____ OK," I called back to reassure her.

(110) Lesson 50
Roots, compounds, possessives, contractions, syllables: Checkup

AUDITORY LEARNERS

PARTNER Have students make a list of words containing the roots covered in this unit. Have them take turns reading aloud definitions or synonyms for each word to their partner and identifying and spelling the words.

GIFTED LEARNERS

Have students create a word-search puzzle, using words that exemplify word study elements taught in this unit. Students can trade puzzles with each other or they can make copies for other students to use.

LEARNERS WHO NEED EXTRA SUPPORT

Help learners create their own simple test of the skills covered in this unit. Writing test items can provide a different path toward understanding and mastering the content. **See Daily Word Study Practice, pages 189–190, 195.**

ASSESSING UNDERSTANDING OF UNIT SKILLS ✳

Student Progress Assessment You may wish to review the observational notes you made as students worked through the activities in this unit. Your notes will help you evaluate the progress students made with roots, compound words, possessives, contractions, and rules for dividing syllables.

Portfolio Assessment Review the materials students have collected in their portfolios. Talk with students individually to discuss their written work and the progress they have made since the beginning of the unit. As you review students' work, evaluate how well they use the unit word study skills.

Daily Word Study Practice For students who need additional practice with any of the topics in this unit, quick reviews are provided on pages 189–190, 195 in Daily Word Study Practice.

Word Study Posttest To assess students' mastery of skills covered in this unit, use the posttest on pages 91g–91h.

SPELLING

Use the following dictation sentences to review the spelling words in Unit 4.

1. **deposit**   **Deposit** the money in the bank.
2. **repel**   That smell will **repel** deer from the garden.
3. **expulsion**   **Expulsion** is a harsh punishment.
4. **audience**   Most of the **audience** left early.
5. **capture**   **Capture** the sunset on film.
6. **receipt**   Keep the **receipt** from your purchase.
7. **spectator**   One **spectator** kept calling out.
8. **submit**   Taxpayers must **submit** their forms by April 15.
9. **specimen**   The animal is a poor **specimen**.
10. **manual**   The **manual** is written in Chinese.
11. **sweatshirt** The sale of each **sweatshirt** goes to save the rain forest.
12. **should've**   They **should've** taken that route.
13. **you're**   When **you're** sick, rest a lot and drink fluids.
14. **thunderstorm** The **thunderstorm** knocked out power to three towns.

Teacher Notes

INTRODUCING

Unit 5   Suffixes

Contents

UNIT 5 RESOURCES

Assessment Strategies 111c
   Overview 111c
   Unit 5 Pretest 111e–111f
   Unit 5 Posttest 111g–111h
   Unit 5 Student Progress Checklist 111i
Spelling Connections 111j–111k
Word Study Games, Activities, and Technology ... 111l–111o
Home Connection 111p–111q

TEACHING PLANS

   Unit 5 Opener 111–112
   Lesson 51: Suffixes -er, -or, -ist 113–114
   Lesson 52: Suffixes -er, -est 115–116
   Lesson 53: Suffixes -ous, -al 117–118
   Lesson 54: Suffixes -ward, -en, -ize 119–120
   Lesson 55: Suffixes -ful, -ness 121–122
   Lesson 56: Suffixes -hood, -ship, -ment 123–124
   Lesson 57: Suffixes -able, -ible 125–126
   Lesson 58: Suffixes -ion, -ation, -ition 127–128
   Lesson 59: Suffixes -ance, -ence, -ive, -ity . 129–130
   Lesson 60: Review Suffixes 131–132
   Lesson 61: Unit 5 Checkup 133–134

Student Performance Objectives

In Unit 5, students will extend their understanding of suffixes and review the ways that suffixes change the meanings of base words. As students learn to apply concepts involving suffixes, they will be able to

◆ Associate the suffixes -er, -or, -ist, -er, -est, -ous, -al, -ward, -en, -ize, -ful, and -ness with their common meanings

◆ Associate the suffixes -hood, -ship, -ment, -able, -ible, -ion, -ation, -ition, -ance, -ence, -ive, and -ity with their common meanings

◆ Decode words by looking at the word parts to determine the meaning of the word

Assessment Strategy Overview

Throughout Unit 5, assess students' ability to recognize suffixes and understand how suffixes change the meanings of base words. There are various ways to assess students' progress. You may also want to encourage students to evaluate their own work and participate in setting goals for their own learning.

FORMAL ASSESSMENT

The Unit 5 Pretest on pages 111e–111f helps to assess a student's knowledge at the beginning of the unit and to plan instruction.

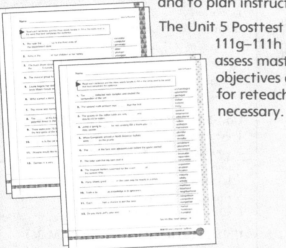

The Unit 5 Posttest on pages 111g–111h helps to assess mastery of unit objectives and to plan for reteaching, if necessary.

INFORMAL ASSESSMENT

The Reading & Writing pages and Unit Checkup in the student book are an effective means of evaluating students' performance.

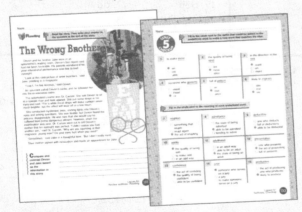

PORTFOLIO ASSESSMENT

Portfolio This logo appears throughout the teaching plans. It signals opportunities for collecting students' work for individual portfolios. You may also want to collect the following pages.

❖ Unit 5 Pretest and Posttest, pages 111e–111h

❖ Unit 5 Reading & Writing, pages 131–132

❖ Unit 5 Checkup, pages 133–134

STUDENT PROGRESS CHECKLIST

Use the checklist on page 111i to record students' progress. You may want to cut the sections apart to place each student's checklist in his or her portfolio.

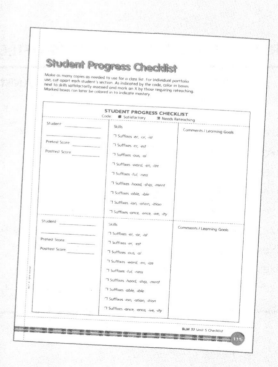

Skill	Reading & Writing Pages	Unit Checkup
Suffixes -er, -or, -ist	131–132	133–134
Suffixes -er, -est	131–132	133–134
Suffixes -ous, -al	131–132	133–134
Suffixes -ward, -en, -ize	131–132	133–134
Suffixes -ful, -ness	131–132	133–134
Suffixes -hood, -ship, -ment	131–132	133–134
Suffixes -able, -ible	131–132	133–134
Suffixes -ion, -ation, -ition	131–132	133–134
Suffixes -ance, -ence, -ive, -ity	131–132	133–134

Administering and Evaluating the
Pretest and Posttest

DIRECTIONS

To help you assess students' progress in learning Unit 5 skills, tests are available on pages 111e–111h. Administer the Pretest before students begin the unit. The results of the Pretest will help you identify each student's strengths and needs in advance, allowing you to structure lesson plans to meet individual needs. Administer the Posttest to assess students' overall mastery of skills taught in the unit and to identify specific areas that will require reteaching.

PERFORMANCE ASSESSMENT PROFILE

The following chart will help you identify specific skills as they appear on the tests and enable you to identify and record specific information about an individual's or the class's performance on the tests.

Depending on the results of the tests, refer to the Reteaching column for lesson-plan pages where you can find activities that will be useful for meeting individual needs or for daily word study practice.

ANSWER KEYS

Unit 5 Pretest, page 111e (BLM 33)

1. geologist	7. repairable
2. trickier	8. location
3. ornamental	9. maturity
4. apologize	10. falsehood
5. plentiful	11. competitor
6. excitement	12. humorous

Unit 5 Pretest, page 111f (BLM 34)

13. photograph	21. bright
14. author	22. down
15. nation	23. mountain
16. thick	24. organ
17. modern	25. thank
18. combine	26. favor
19. depend	27. state
20. prevent	28. enroll

Unit 5 Posttest, page 111g (BLM 35)

1. escalator	7. enjoyable
2. youngest	8. destruction
3. dangerous	9. attendance
4. harmonize	10. Automotive
5. fitness	11. novelist
6. scholarship	12. dependable

Unit 5 Posttest, page 111h (BLM 36)

13. optometry	21. busy
14. scholar	22. on
15. mischief	23. education
16. prompt	24. profess
17. standard	25. faith
18. connect	26. deduct
19. clear	27. adult
20. objective	28. pave

PERFORMANCE ASSESSMENT PROFILE

Skill	Pretest Questions	Posttest Questions	Reteaching Focus on All Learners	Reteaching Daily Word Study Practice
Suffixes -er, -or, -ist	1, 11, 13, 24	1, 11, 13, 24	113–114, 131–132	191–192
Suffixes -er, -est	2, 21	2, 21	115–116, 131–132	191–192
Suffixes -ous, -al	3, 12, 15, 23	3, 15, 23	117–118, 131–132	191–192
Suffixes -ward, -en, -ize	4, 17, 22	4, 17, 22	119–120, 131–132	191–192
Suffixes -ful, -ness	5, 16, 25	5, 16, 25	121–122, 131–132	191–192
Suffixes -hood, -ship, -ment	6, 10, 14, 27, 28	6, 14, 27, 28	123–124, 131–132	191–192
Suffixes -able, -ible	7, 26	7, 12, 26	125–126, 131–132	191–192
Suffixes -ion, -ation, -ition	8, 18	8, 18	127–128, 131–132	191–192
Suffixes -ance, -ence, -ive, -ity	9, 19, 20	9, 10, 19, 20	129–132	191–192

> ▶ Read each sentence and the three words beside it. Fill in the circle next to the word that best completes the sentence.

1. The _____ collected rock samples and studied the composition of the soil.
   - ○ archaeologist
   - ○ optometrist
   - ○ geologist

2. The second math problem was _____ than the first.
   - ○ trickier
   - ○ trickiest
   - ○ tricky

3. The grapes on the coffee table are only _____ and should not be eaten.
   - ○ comical
   - ○ ornamental
   - ○ educational

4. Janet is going to _____ for not sending Bill a thank-you note sooner.
   - ○ realize
   - ○ apologize
   - ○ harmonize

5. When Europeans arrived in North America, buffalo were _____ on the prairie.
   - ○ plentiful
   - ○ careful
   - ○ dreadful

6. The _____ of the fans was apparent even before the game started.
   - ○ enrollment
   - ○ placement
   - ○ excitement

7. The tailor said that my torn coat is _____.
   - ○ breakable
   - ○ repairable
   - ○ convertible

8. The treasure hunters searched for the exact _____ of the sunken ship.
   - ○ population
   - ○ eruption
   - ○ location

9. Harry shows great _____ in the calm way he reacts in a crisis.
   - ○ maturity
   - ○ oddity
   - ○ activity

10. Truth is to _____ as knowledge is to ignorance.
    - ○ livelihood
    - ○ falsehood
    - ○ neighborhood

11. Each _____ had a chance to win the race.
    - ○ competition
    - ○ competitive
    - ○ competitor

12. Do you think Jeff's joke was _____?
    - ○ humor
    - ○ humorous
    - ○ humorist

Go to the next page. →

▶ Fill in the circle beside the correct base word for each word with a suffix.

13. photographer

- ○ photo
- ○ photograph
- ○ graph

14. authorship

- ○ authority
- ○ shipment
- ○ author

15. national

- ○ nation
- ○ nationality
- ○ international

16. thickness

- ○ thickest
- ○ thick
- ○ thicker

17. modernize

- ○ model
- ○ moderate
- ○ modern

18. combination

- ○ comb
- ○ combine
- ○ combining

19. dependence

- ○ depend
- ○ pending
- ○ dependent

20. preventive

- ○ prevention
- ○ preventing
- ○ prevent

▶ Read the suffix at the top of each box. Fill in the circle beside the word to which the suffix can best be added.

21. est

- ○ fun
- ○ bright
- ○ danger

22. ward

- ○ skill
- ○ short
- ○ down

23. ous

- ○ hill
- ○ mountain
- ○ plain

24. ist

- ○ organ
- ○ trumpet
- ○ drum

25. ful

- ○ dark
- ○ inspect
- ○ thank

26. able

- ○ father
- ○ favor
- ○ member

27. hood

- ○ city
- ○ county
- ○ state

28. ment

- ○ enroll
- ○ admit
- ○ expel

Possible score on Unit 5 Pretest is 28. Number correct _____

> Read each sentence and the three words beside it. Fill in the circle next to the word that best completes the sentence.

1. We rode the _____ up to the third level of the department store.
   - ○ escalator
   - ○ computer
   - ○ generator

2. Anna is the _____ of four children in her family.
   - ○ older
   - ○ younger
   - ○ youngest

3. The truck driver steered carefully through the _____ S-curves.
   - ○ humorous
   - ○ dangerous
   - ○ mischievous

4. The musical group learned to _____ as high school friends.
   - ○ modernize
   - ○ standardize
   - ○ harmonize

5. Laurie begins her daily _____ program with a brisk fifteen-minute walk.
   - ○ fitness
   - ○ strictness
   - ○ promptness

6. Willie earned a merit _____ based on his academic record.
   - ○ membership
   - ○ scholarship
   - ○ championship

7. The movie was humorous and _____.
   - ○ readable
   - ○ disagreeable
   - ○ enjoyable

8. The _____ of the Amazon rain forest is a potential threat to the environment.
   - ○ destruction
   - ○ construction
   - ○ connection

9. There were over 70,000 people in _____ at the first game of the World Series.
   - ○ admittance
   - ○ attendance
   - ○ alliance

10. _____ is to the car as aeronautical is to the airplane.
    - ○ Creative
    - ○ Productive
    - ○ Automotive

11. Roxane would like to become a famous _____.
    - ○ novella
    - ○ novel
    - ○ novelist

12. Damien is a very _____ person who is always on time.
    - ○ depending
    - ○ dependable
    - ○ depended

Go to the next page. →

Name _____

Fill in the circle beside the correct base word for each word with a suffix.

13. optometrist
- ○ optimist
- ○ optician
- ○ optometry

14. scholarship
- ○ scholarly
- ○ scholar
- ○ school

15. mischievous
- ○ mischief
- ○ chief
- ○ achieve

16. promptness
- ○ prom
- ○ promote
- ○ prompt

17. standardize
- ○ stand
- ○ standard
- ○ stander

18. connection
- ○ connect
- ○ conduct
- ○ connector

19. clearance
- ○ clearly
- ○ clarity
- ○ clear

20. objectivity
- ○ object
- ○ objective
- ○ subject

Read the suffix at the top of each box. Fill in the circle beside the word to which the suffix can best be added.

21. est
- ○ bus
- ○ busy
- ○ business

22. ward
- ○ on
- ○ under
- ○ an

23. al
- ○ correct
- ○ humor
- ○ education

24. or
- ○ profit
- ○ profess
- ○ profession

25. ful
- ○ faith
- ○ false
- ○ charity

26. ible
- ○ manage
- ○ thought
- ○ deduct

27. hood
- ○ youth
- ○ adult
- ○ ail

28. ment
- ○ pave
- ○ road
- ○ street

Possible score on Unit 5 Posttest is 28. Number correct _____

Student Progress Checklist

Make as many copies as needed to use for a class list. For individual portfolio use, cut apart each student's section. As indicated by the code, color in boxes next to skills satisfactorily assessed and mark an X by those requiring reteaching. Marked boxes can later be colored in to indicate mastery.

STUDENT PROGRESS CHECKLIST
Code: ■ Satisfactory   ☒ Needs Reteaching

| Student: _____

 _____

 Pretest Score: _____

 Posttest Score: _____ | **Skills**

 ❑ Suffixes *-er, -or, -ist*

 ❑ Suffixes *-er, -est*

 ❑ Suffixes *-ous, -al*

 ❑ Suffixes *-ward, -en, -ize*

 ❑ Suffixes *-ful, -ness*

 ❑ Suffixes *-hood, -ship, -ment*

 ❑ Suffixes *-able, -ible*

 ❑ Suffixes *-ion, -ation, -ition*

 ❑ Suffixes *-ance, -ence, -ive, -ity* | **Comments / Learning Goals** |
| Student: _____

 _____

 Pretest Score: _____

 Posttest Score: _____ | **Skills**

 ❑ Suffixes *-er, -or, -ist*

 ❑ Suffixes *-er, -est*

 ❑ Suffixes *-ous, -al*

 ❑ Suffixes *-ward, -en, -ize*

 ❑ Suffixes *-ful, -ness*

 ❑ Suffixes *-hood, -ship, -ment*

 ❑ Suffixes *-able, -ible*

 ❑ Suffixes *-ion, -ation, -ition*

 ❑ Suffixes *-ance, -ence, -ive, -ity* | **Comments / Learning Goals** |

Spelling Connections

INTRODUCTION

The Unit Word List is a comprehensive list of spelling words drawn from this unit. The words are grouped by suffixes. To incorporate spelling into your word study program, use the activity in the Curriculum Connections section of each teaching plan.

The spelling lessons utilize the following approach for each set of words.

1. Administer a pretest of the words that have not yet been introduced. Dictation sentences are provided.

2. Provide practice.

3. Reassess. Dictation sentences are provided.

A final test is provided in Lesson 61 on page 134.

DIRECTIONS

Make a copy of Blackline Master 38 for each student. After administering the pretest for each set of suffixes, give each student a copy of the appropriate word list.

Students can work with a partner to practice spelling the words orally and identifying the suffix in each word. They can also make and use letter cards to form the words on the list. You may want to challenge students to identify other words that have the same suffixes. Students can write words of their own on *My Own Word List* (see Blackline Master 38).

Have students store their list words in an envelope or plastic zipper bag in the back of their books or notebooks. Alternatively, you may want to suggest that students keep a spelling notebook, listing words with similar patterns. You could also invite students to build word-wall displays in the classroom. Each section of the wall can focus on words with a single word study element. The walls will become a good spelling resource when students are writing.

UNIT WORD LIST

Suffixes -er, -or, -ist; -er, -est; -ous, -al; -ward, -en, -ize

mixer
editor
soloist
wearier
busiest
courageous
comical
homeward
wooden
legalize

Suffixes -hood, -ship, -ment; -able, -ible; -ion, -ation, -ition; -ance, -ence; -ive, -ity

neighborhood
friendship
improvement
breakable
digestible
connection
presentation
addition
clearance
dependence
impressive
sincerity

Name _____

 **S**pelling

UNIT 5 WORD LIST

Suffixes er, or, ist; er, est; ous, al; ward, en, ize

mixer	courageous
editor	comical
soloist	homeward
wearier	wooden
busiest	legalize

My Own Word List

Suffixes hood, ship, ment; able, ible; ion, ation, ition; ance, ence; ive, ity

neighborhood	presentation
friendship	addition
improvement	clearance
breakable	dependence
digestible	impressive
connection	sincerity

Word Study Games, Activities, and Technology

The following collection of ideas offers a variety of opportunities to reinforce word study skills while actively engaging students. The games, activities, and technology suggestions can easily be adapted to meet the needs of your group of learners. They vary in approach so as to consider students' different learning styles.

● PICTURING SUFFIXES

Students can make lists of words that contain the suffixes -er, -or, -ist, -ment, -ion, -ation, and -ition. Have students define the words. Then suggest that they search for magazine photographs that illustrate their definitions. Encourage students to combine their words, definitions, and photographs to make books.

▲ MAGICAL MISTER MISTOFFELEES

Provide students with a printed copy of the poem "Mr. Mistoffelees" (from *Old Possum's Book of Practical Cats* by T. S. Eliot). Have them underline words with suffixes. Discuss the poem and the use of suffixes. Encourage students to write sentences describing Mr. Mistoffelees, using words with suffixes discussed in this unit. You might extend the activity by challenging students to write four rhymed lines describing another phenomenal trick that Mr. Mistoffelees might have performed. Some students might enjoy using prose or rhyme to describe a mysterious or magical cat they know or have seen.

◆ SENTENCES WITH SUFFIXES

Invite pairs of students to write sentences containing at least two words with different suffixes discussed in this unit. Encourage volunteers to write their sentences on the board, underlining the suffixes. Discuss why each suffix was added.

■ COMPARING AND CONTRASTING WORDS

Write the following pairs of words on the chalkboard: *geologist, archaeologist; logical, fallacious; likelihood, probability; factual, fictitious; modernity, newness; funnier, sillier; lengthen, shorten.* Have partners work together to create a Comparison-Contrast chart and list each pair of words on the appropriate side. Those words that are linked by similarities should appear in the Comparison column of the chart; those that are linked by opposition should appear in the Contrast column. Encourage partners to find and add to each column their own pairs of words with suffixes discussed in the unit. Challenge students to find synonyms with different suffixes and antonyms with the same suffix. You might extend the activity by asking partners to demonstrate the link between several pairs of words by writing sentences or constructing analogies.

✳ SUFFIX CHALLENGE

Write the following suffixes on the chalkboard: *-ness, -hood, -ship, -ment, -ance, -ity*. Have the class divide into teams of six and take turns lining up ten feet from the board. Ask the first student in line to walk to the board and write a word with the suffix *-ness*. The student should walk back and hand the chalk to the next team member in line, who will write a word with *-hood*, and so on. The winner is the team that writes the most correctly spelled words in the shortest time.

● COMPARING NATIONAL PARKS

With the class, brainstorm a list of national parks in the United States. You might display a map or list from an encyclopedia or other reference work to help generate ideas. When you have finished, tell individual students to select a park, draw on their own knowledge or consult an encyclopedia, and write a brief description of attractions found there. Challenge students to use as many words with suffixes discussed in this unit as they can. Tell them to underline the suffixes. Extend the activity by having partners combine descriptions of different parks into a written work that emphasizes comparison and contrast. Encourage students to illustrate their work. Combine the projects to make a booklet and display it in the classroom for all to read.

▲ SUFFIX CONCENTRATION

Partners can play "suffix concentration." Give each pair of students 16 index cards. They can write each of the following suffixes on two different cards: *-ous, -al, -ward, -en, -ize, -ful, -able, -ible*. Have students shuffle the cards and place them face down in rows of four to form a grid. Students then take turns turning over any two cards. If a player turns over a match (two cards with the same suffix), he or she can keep those cards by saying and spelling a word with that suffix. If the player can't think of a word with that suffix or if the cards turned do not match, the cards are replaced in the same positions and the other player takes a turn. Play continues until no cards are left. Players receive one point for each card in their hands at the end of play.

Variation: Award a bonus point if the player saying a word uses it correctly in a sentence.

◆ SUFFIX ART

Invite partners to illustrate through art how suffixes change the meanings of words. On one sheet of paper, the first partner draws a picture illustrating a base word and writes a label for the drawing. On another sheet of paper, the second partner writes a word containing that base and a suffix and draws a picture illustrating the new word. Partners then reverse roles. You might ask partners to explain their illustrated word pairs to the rest of the class.

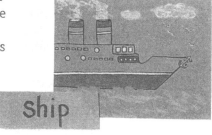

■ WRITING ABOUT OCCUPATIONS

Have students write a paragraph about an occupation that interests them. Suggest that they use words containing suffixes discussed in this unit. After they have finished, invite students to share their paragraphs with one another in small groups. Encourage them to compare and contrast different occupations.

✳ CRITICS' CORNER

Invite partners to role-play movie critics discussing a film on television. They can select a movie both have seen. First tell them to organize their thoughts on paper by listing comments under various headings such as Act<u>ors</u>, Writ<u>er</u>(s), Comic<u>al</u> Moments, Seri<u>ous</u> Moments, Skill<u>ful</u> Special Effects. Next they should revise their comments to include words containing suffixes from this unit. Then allow each pair to discuss the movie in front of the class, stressing what each partner liked and disliked about it.

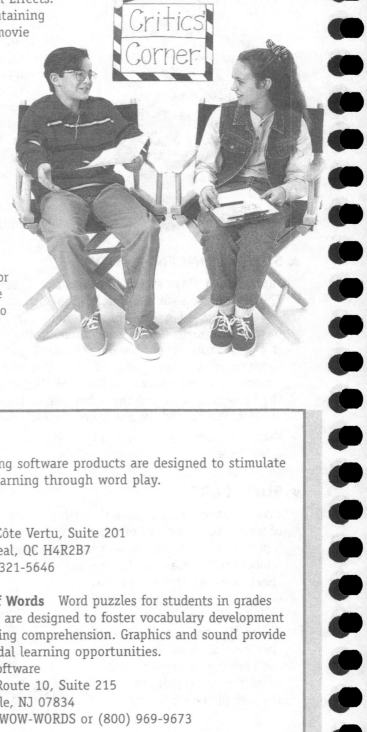

● SUFFIX HOME IMPROVEMENTS

Blackline Master 39 features a house to which an extension has been added. Make enough copies to distribute to individual students or partners. Explain that students should think of base words and then write them in the space inside the main part of the house. They should then add suffixes to the base words and write the new words in the space inside the extension. Encourage them to use base words to which they can add more than one suffix and to create as many new words as possible. Suggest that they consider words they associate with different rooms, objects, or descriptive words in or about a house. They might also include base words that form part of the names of various people who live in or visit the house. Each student should write at least 20 new words in the space inside the addition.

Extension: Challenge students to write sentences on the back of the paper, using their new words.

Technology

The following software products are designed to stimulate language learning through word play.

Smart Games Challenge 1   A variety of visual and verbal logic puzzles are featured in this software program for advanced readers. Each is designed to tap into students' thinking and reasoning skills.
**Random Soft
  201 East 50th Street
  New York, NY 10022
  (800) 788-8815

MicroWorlds Language Art   Students in grades 4-8 develop language skills by combining words, text, and images to write rhymes, haiku, advertisements, and visual poetry.

**LCSI
  3300 Côte Vertu, Suite 201
  Montreal, QC H4R2B7
  (800) 321-5646

World of Words   Word puzzles for students in grades 6 and up are designed to foster vocabulary development and reading comprehension. Graphics and sound provide multimodal learning opportunities.
**RES Software
  3155 Route 10, Suite 215
  Denville, NJ 07834
  (800) WOW-WORDS or (800) 969-9673

Name _____

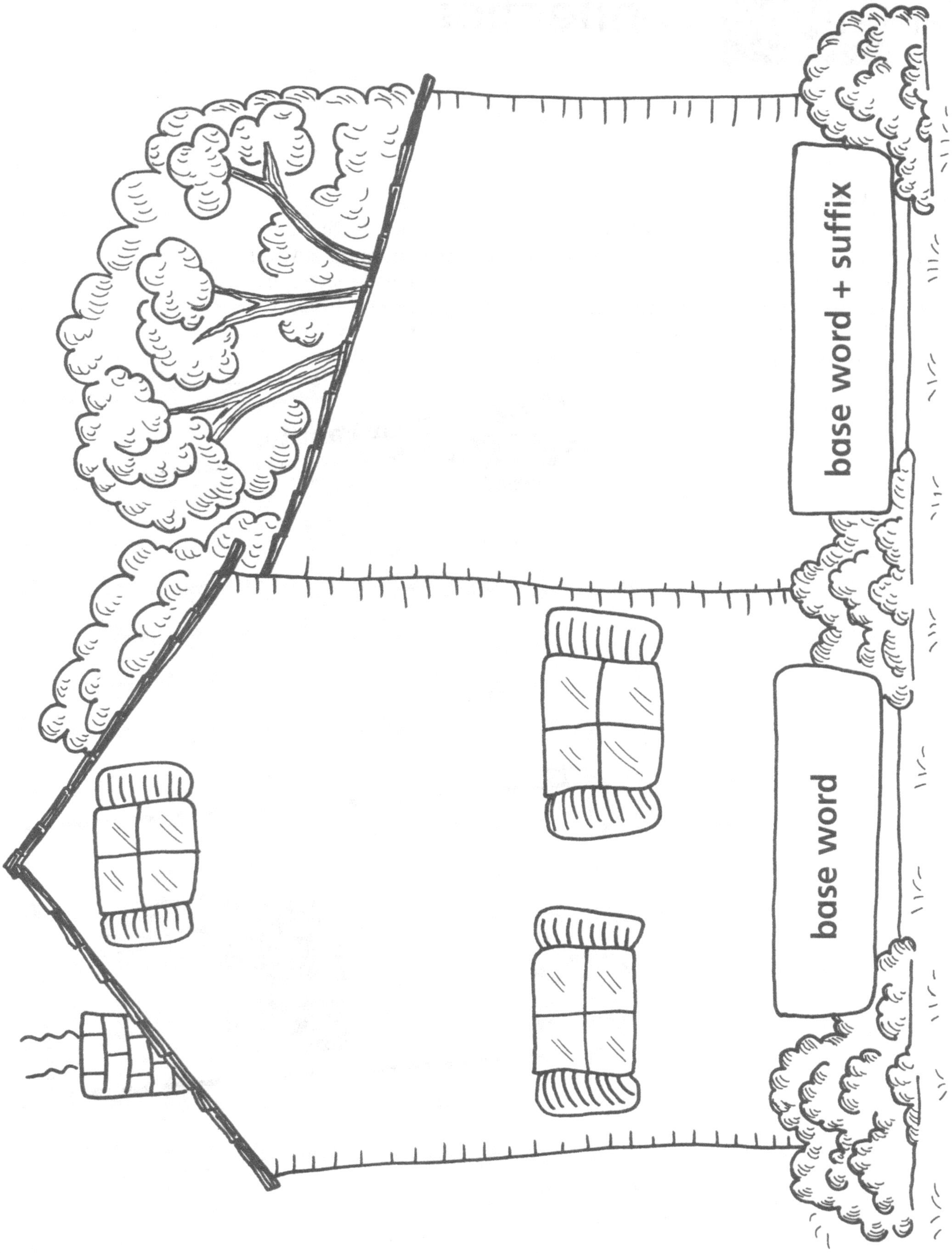

base word + suffix

base word

Home Connection

HOME LETTER

A letter is available to be sent home at the beginning of Unit 5. This letter informs family members that students will be learning how different suffixes change the meanings of base words. The suggested home activity revolves around locating words with suffixes in a given song. This activity promotes interaction between child and family members while supporting the student's learning of reading and writing words with the targeted word study skills. A letter is also available in Spanish on page 111q.

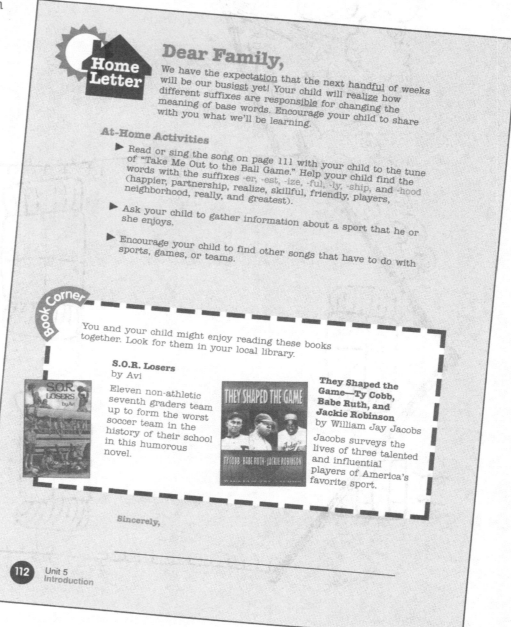

Home Letter

Dear Family,

We have the expectation that the next handful of weeks will be our busiest yet! Your child will realize how different suffixes are responsible for changing the meaning of base words. Encourage your child to share with you what we'll be learning.

At-Home Activities

▶ Read or sing the song on page 111 with your child to the tune of "Take Me Out to the Ball Game." Help your child find the words with the suffixes -er, -est, -ize, -ful, -ly, -ship, and -hood (happier, partnership, realize, skillful, friendly, players, neighborhood, really, and greatest).

▶ Ask your child to gather information about a sport that he or she enjoys.

▶ Encourage your child to find other songs that have to do with sports, games, or teams.

Book Corner

You and your child might enjoy reading these books together. Look for them in your local library.

S.O.R. Losers
by Avi

Eleven non-athletic seventh graders team up to form the worst soccer team in the history of their school in this humorous novel.

They Shaped the Game—Ty Cobb, Babe Ruth, and Jackie Robinson
by William Jay Jacobs

Jacobs surveys the lives of three talented and influential players of America's favorite sport.

Sincerely,

_____

Carta para la casa

Estimada familia,

¡Tenemos la expectativa (**expectation**) de que las próximas pocas (**handful**) semanas serán las más atareadas (**busiest**)! Su hijo/a se dará cuenta (**realize**) de cómo los diversos sufijos son responsables (**responsible**) de cambiarle el significado a las palabras base en inglés. Animen a su hijo/a a compartir con ustedes lo que vamos a aprender.

Actividades para hacer en casa

► Lean o canten la canción en la página 111 con su hijo/a a la melodía de "**Take Me Out to the Ball Game**". Ayuden a su hijo/a a hallar las palabras con los sufijos **er**, **est**, **ize**, **ful**, **ly**, **ship** y **hood** (**happier**, **partnership**, **realize**, **skillful**, **friendly**, **players**, **neighborhood**, **really** y **greatest**).

► Pídanle a su hijo/a que reúna información acerca de un deporte que a él o a ella le gusta.

► Animen a su hijo/ a a buscar otras canciones que tengan que ver con los deportes, los juegos o los equipos.

Rincón del libro

Su hijo/a y ustedes pueden disfrutar juntos de la lectura de estos libros. Búsquenlos en la biblioteca de su localidad.

S.O.R. Losers
por Avi

Once alumnos no atléticos de séptimo grado se unen para formar el peor equipo de fútbol soccer en la historia de su colegio en esta cómica novela.

They Shaped the Game—Ty Cobb, Babe Ruth, and Jackie Robinson
por Jay Jacobs

Jacobs repasa las vidas de tres talentosos e importantes jugadores del deporte favorito de Estados Unidos.

Atentamente, _____

Unit 5

Pages 111–112

Suffixes

Unit Focus

USING THE PAGE

- Recite or sing the verses on page 111 to the tune of "Take Me Out to the Ball Game." Encourage students to read and sing along with you.

- Have students discuss how the narrator of the song feels about soccer and whether they share similar feelings about soccer or any other sport.

- **Critical Thinking** Invite students to suggest answers to the question following the song, based on the lyrics in it.

BUILDING A CONTEXT

- Ask students to find a word with the suffix -*er* in the third line. *(happier)* How does -*er* change the meaning of the base word *happy*?

- Write the word *partnership* on the board and ask what the suffix -*ship* might mean.

- Invite students to find words with endings added to base words in the third verse. Have them write the words on the board and circle the suffixes. (Accept any words with endings for this exercise, including plurals and inflected verbs.)

- Explain that identifying suffixes and knowing their meanings can help students decode unfamiliar words.

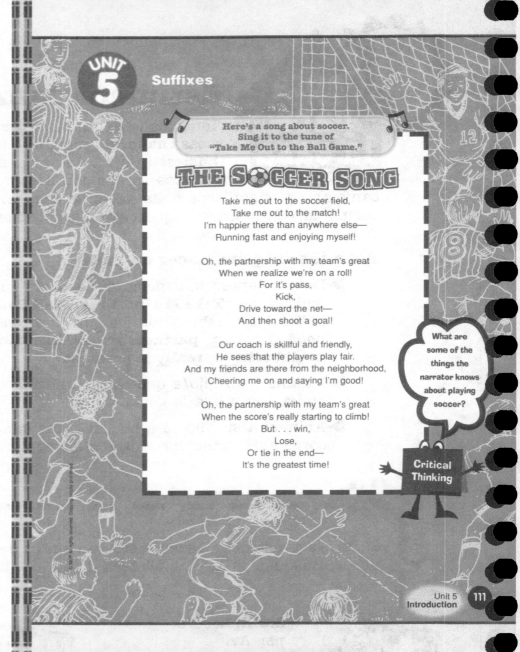

UNIT OPENER ACTIVITIES

"TAKE ME OUT TO THE SOCCER FIELD"

Ask a group of volunteers to perform the song by acting out words or to sing it as a rap. Discuss the basic elements of soccer. Encourage students who are knowledgeable about soccer to share strategies for playing.

IT ISN'T WHETHER YOU WIN OR LOSE . . .

Introduce the saying, "It isn't whether you win or lose, but how you play the game." Ask students to share their reactions. Invite students to think of the benefits of playing games besides winning. What benefits might come from losing a game?

FAIR PLAY

The concept of fair play applies to many everyday aspects of life. Propose a few examples (such as friendship, schoolwork, family or community relationships, politics) and ask students to describe situations in which people do or do not play fair.

Dear Family,

We have the expectation that the next handful of weeks will be our busiest yet! Your child will realize how different suffixes are responsible for changing the meaning of base words. Encourage your child to share with you what we'll be learning.

At-Home Activities

▶ Read or sing the song on page 111 with your child to the tune of "Take Me Out to the Ball Game." Help your child find the words with the suffixes -er, -est, -ize, -ful, -ly, -ship, and -hood (happier, partnership, realize, skillful, friendly, players, neighborhood, really, and greatest).

▶ Ask your child to gather information about a sport that he or she enjoys.

▶ Encourage your child to find other songs that have to do with sports, games, or teams.

You and your child might enjoy reading these books together. Look for them in your local library.

S.O.R. Losers
by Avi
Eleven non-athletic seventh graders team up to form the worst soccer team in the history of their school in this humorous novel.

They Shaped the Game—Ty Cobb, Babe Ruth, and Jackie Robinson
by William Jay Jacobs
Jacobs surveys the lives of three talented and influential players of America's favorite sport.

Sincerely,

_____

BULLETIN BOARD

The narrator of the song is happiest on the soccer field. Ask your students where *they* are happiest. Have students design a "Where I'm Happiest" bulletin board using captioned drawings of themselves engaged in favorite activities. Look for words with suffixes in the captions.

- The Home Letter on page 112 includes words with suffixes in a message that communicates the skills students will be practicing in this unit. Have students take home the page and suggest that they look it over with a family member. The letter includes a few activities to share and titles of books that can be found at the library.

- The Home Letter can also be found on page 111q in Spanish.

CURRICULUM CONNECTIONS ✳

WRITING

As students progress through the unit lessons, deposit word cards for the different suffixes in a box in the writing center. Students in the center can select words to include in sentences that describe their favorite activities at different points in their lives.

MATH

Display a word problem, such as this one, in the math center for students to solve: *At last week's soccer match, the Red Team's score was a square number between 1 and 5, and the Yellow Team's score was both a factor of 12 and a factor of 15. What was the score? (4 to 3)* Ask students to find the answer and then compose other sports-related math problems to leave in the center for class "teammates" to solve. Problems can center around such things as scores, jersey numbers, and length of games.

SCIENCE

What happens when a human foot meets a soccer ball? Why does a kick propel the ball forward? Have students use reference sources to learn about different types of energy and properties of motion.

Lesson 51

Pages 113–114

Suffixes
-er, -or, -ist

✦ ● ■ ● ◆ ● ✦ ◆ ● ■ ● ◆ ●

INFORMAL ASSESSMENT OBJECTIVE

Can students

✔ read and recognize the meanings of words containing the suffixes *-er, -or,* and *-ist*?

Lesson Focus

INTRODUCING THE SKILL

● Read these riddles.

I am someone who sings. Who am I? I am someone who invents. Who am I? I am someone who studies geology. Who am I? Ask students to write the answers on the board. *(singer, inventor, geologist)* and identify the suffix in each word. *(-er, -or, -ist)*

● Help students conclude that the suffixes *-er, -or,* and *-ist* mean *"someone who does something."*

● Read the rule on page 113. Ask students to apply the meaning *"something that does something"* to the words *computer, mixer,* and *escalator.*

● Have volunteers identify the verb bases in *swimmer* and *actor* to show how suffixes change verbs into nouns. *(swim, act)* Then ask what nouns are base words for *biologist* and *organist* *(biology, organ)* to show how suffixes can change one noun into another.

USING THE PAGES

Read the directions for pages 113 and 114. Later discuss what students learned about suffixes *-er, -or,* and *-ist*.

113

Name _____

▶ Write the word from the word bank that goes with each meaning.

photographer	farmer
optometrist	customer
geologist	generator
stretcher	organist
juror	collector
machinist	creator
computer	

RULE

The suffixes **er** and **or** mean *something or someone that does something*. They can change a verb into a noun. The suffix **ist** also means *someone who does something.* But it changes one kind of noun into another kind of noun.

edit**or** = someone who edits

mix**er** = something that mixes

archaeolog**ist** = someone who knows the science of archaeology

1. one who grows crops — **farmer**

2. one who studies rocks — **geologist**

3. one who takes pictures — **photographer**

4. something that produces electricity — **generator**

5. something that works quickly with numbers and facts — **computer**

6. one who serves on a jury — **juror**

7. one who plays a musical instrument — **organist**

8. one who shops for goods — **customer**

9. one who works with machines — **machinist**

10. one who makes something — **creator**

11. something that can be used to carry a person — **stretcher**

12. one who gathers large numbers of similar items — **collector**

13. one who tests vision and prescribes glasses — **optometrist**

Lesson 51
Suffixes -er, -or, -ist **113**

FOCUS ON ALL LEARNERS ✦ ● ◆ ■ ●

ENGLISH LANGUAGE LEARNERS/ESL

Review the words on pages 113 and 114. Discuss the occupations that many of them name. Explain any that are not familiar to students.

VISUAL LEARNERS

PARTNER Write the suffixes *-er, -or,* and *-ist* and the following base words on the board: *consume, tour, senate, motor, prospect, develop, generate, supervise, therapy.* Ask partners to make new words by adding a suffix to each base word. Direct students to check their spelling in a dictionary.

KINESTHETIC LEARNERS

INDIVIDUAL Have students incorporate words with suffixes *-er, -or,* and *-ist* in word-search puzzles like that on page 114. Students can trade puzzles to solve.

There are 18 words hidden in the puzzle that have the suffixes **er**, **or**, or **ist**. Some of the words go across, and some go down. Circle each word as you find it, and write it in the correct column.

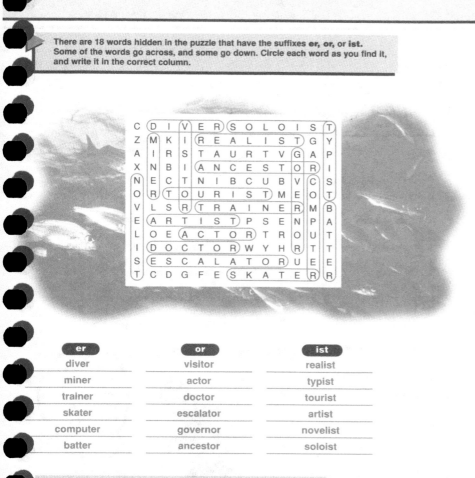

 **er**	**or**	 **ist**
diver	visitor	realist
miner	actor	typist
trainer	doctor	tourist
skater	escalator	artist
computer	governor	novelist
batter	ancestor	soloist

Now write the correct word from the puzzle beside its definition.

1. a moving stairway that carries people up or down	escalator
2. one who travels	tourist
3. one who teaches animals to do tricks	trainer

 114   Lesson 51
Suffixes -er, -or, -ist

SPELLING

Use the following words and sentences as a pretest for the first group of spelling words in Unit 5.

1. **mixer** — Dad bought an electric **mixer**.
2. **editor** — The **editor** works for the newspaper.
3. **soloist** — The **soloist** sang the national anthem.
4. **wearier** — Jake felt **wearier** after his nap.
5. **busiest** — Some people are happiest when they are **busiest**.
6. **courageous** — The movie was about a **courageous** leader.
7. **comical** — Derek read a **comical** poem.
8. **homeward** — After the picnic we headed **homeward**.
9. **wooden** — The **wooden** steps need repair.
10. **legalize** — Is it right to **legalize** child labor?

WRITING

Portfolio Have students conduct an interview with an individual whose occupation name ends with *-er, -or,* or *-ist,* such as *lawyer, dentist, computer operator,* or *pianist.* Students can write profiles of the individuals based on the interviews.

SCIENCE

Discuss and list different areas of science and medicine such as biology, botany, zoology, geology, meteorology, gemology, astronomy, optometry, internal medicine, and dermatology. Then have students list the words for people who practice those fields.

PHYSICAL EDUCATION

Have students research the skills required for and training involved in becoming either a scuba diver, a figure skater, or hockey player.

 Technology

AstroWord, Suffixes. ©1998 Silver Burdett Ginn Inc. Division of Simon & Schuster.

AUDITORY LEARNERS

LARGE GROUP Read aloud the words *writer, visitor, skier, zoologist, word processor,* and *cartoonist.* Call on volunteers to identify the base word and suffix in each. Ask volunteers to explain how the meaning of the base word was changed by the suffix.

GIFTED LEARNERS

Remind students that many words ending with *-er, -or,* or *-ist* describe occupations (for example, *typist*). Have students list and define as many occupations ending with these suffixes as they know or can find.

LEARNERS WHO NEED EXTRA SUPPORT

Have students identify the base word and suffix for each word in the word hunt on page 114. Discuss how the suffixes alter the meanings of the base words. **See Daily Word Study Practice, pages 191–192.**

Lesson 52

Pages 115–116

Suffixes
-er, -est

Lesson Focus

INTRODUCING THE SKILL

- Write *long, longer,* and *longest* on the board and have students circle the suffixes -*er* and -*est.* Help them recognize that -*er* is used to compare two persons, places, or things, while -*est* is used to compare more than two. Invite students to use the words in sentences to demonstrate meaning.

- Ask students to spell the base words for *wiser* and *happiest.* (*wise, happy*) Discuss the spelling rules in the directions on page 115.

- Have students explain the difference between the meanings of *er* in *camper* and *younger.* Which is a noun? (*camper*) an adjective? (*younger*) Invite students to give other word examples.

USING THE PAGES

- Offer help as needed with the directions for both pages. After students have completed and checked their work, invite them to discuss the skill.

- **Critical Thinking** Read and discuss the question on page 115.

Name _____

Add **er** or **est** to the base word you see below the line. Remember that when the base word ends in **e**, drop the **e** before adding **er** or **est**. If the base word ends in **y**, change the **y** to **i** before adding **er** or **est**.

> **RULE**
> The suffix **er** is used to compare two objects or people. The suffix **est** is used to compare more than two objects or people.
>
> Kim is tall**er** than Jo, but Peg is the tall**est** of the three.

1. Jesse is the _____youngest_____ person in the babysitting course.
(young)

2. He plans to start babysitting when he is one year _____older_____ than he is now.
(old)

3. Sitters who take the course are _____wiser_____ than those who don't.
(wise)

4. The teacher of the course tells the _____funniest_____ stories about babysitting!
(funny)

5. She says it is _____harder_____ to babysit for a toddler than for a baby.
(hard)

6. Toddlers move _____faster_____ than babies and get into more trouble.
(fast)

7. According to her, the _____naughtiest_____ children of all are the 3-year-olds.
(naughty)

8. The _____easiest_____ children to care for are infants.
(easy)

9. The teacher says infants are _____easier_____ than older babies or toddlers because they stay put.
(easy)

10. Jesse thought the _____neatest_____ part of the course was the section on safety.
(neat)

11. It is very important for parents to buy the _____safest_____ products on the market.
(safe)

12. The day he graduated from babysitting school was the _____proudest_____ day of Jesse's life!
(proud)

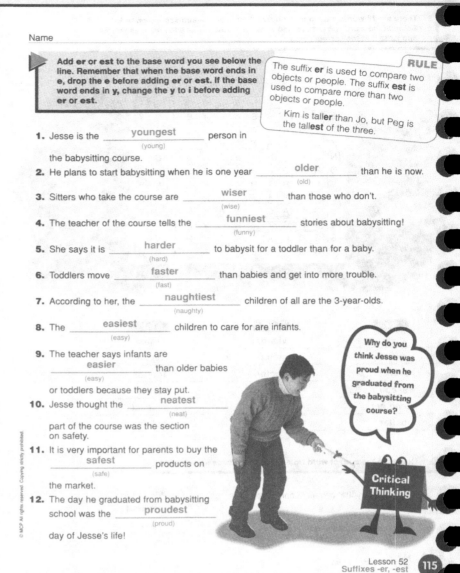

> Why do you think Jesse was proud when he graduated from the babysitting course?
> Critical Thinking

Lesson 52
Suffixes -er, -est **115**

FOCUS ON ALL LEARNERS ✳ ● ◆ ■ ◆

ENGLISH LANGUAGE LEARNERS/ESL

To review comparing two or more things (nouns) using adjectives ending in -*er* and -*est,* have students make up sentences comparing different-size classroom objects using *longer* and *longest* or *shorter* and *shortest;* for example, *This pencil is longer than that one; that pencil is the longest of all.*

VISUAL LEARNERS
LARGE GROUP

Write sentences on the board, using adjectives that contain the suffixes -*er* and -*est.* Have volunteers underline the adjective in each sentence and tell whether two or more than two items are being compared.

KINESTHETIC LEARNERS
SMALL GROUP

Provide objects for students to handle and compare. Have students identify an adjective to use when comparing the two objects, and determine whether to use -*er* or -*est.*

Look at the base word in boldface print. Then read each short paragraph. Use the base word or the base word plus the suffix er or est to complete each unfinished sentence. You may use a word twice.

1. busy

The _____ busy _____ highway was the scene of many traffic jams. The _____ busiest _____ corner was Randle and Foote Streets. Even on Sundays this corner is _____ busier _____ than any other.

2. long

The new trail to the top of the mountain was _____ long _____ . Maybe it seemed _____ longer _____ than the old one because we were so hungry. It really seemed like the _____ longest _____ trail we had ever hiked.

3. wet

George gets _____ wetter _____ in a rainstorm than anyone I know. He doesn't carry an umbrella. He says he's afraid it will get _____ wet _____ .

4. happy

Hannah always seems to be _____ happy _____ . She is _____ happier _____ than her brother Hal. I wonder what she's so _____ happy _____ about.

5. high

Connie can jump _____ higher _____ than Alice. She can jump the _____ highest _____ of anyone on the track team. Everyone on the team can jump _____ higher _____ than I can.

6. bright

That star is the _____ brightest _____ one in the sky. It is _____ brighter _____ than the one close to it, which is also a very _____ bright _____ star.

116   Lesson 52
Suffixes -er, -est

AUDITORY LEARNERS

LARGE GROUP

Say sentences such as the following: *He bought the newer bike; you picked up the heaviest package.* Ask students how many bikes are being compared (two), and how many packages (*more than two*). Have students spell the *-er and -est* words and offer sentences of their own.

GIFTED LEARNERS

Encourage students to monitor their daily speech, being aware of each time they use an adjective ending in *est*. Do they ever catch themselves using *est* incorrectly to compare only two things? Over a few-day period, have them record examples in a daily log.

LEARNERS WHO NEED EXTRA SUPPORT

Have students practice adding the suffixes *-er* or *-est* to words, such as *happy, empty, tricky, silly, wide, wise, red,* and *wet.* **See Daily Word Study Practice, pages 191–192.**

CURRICULUM CONNECTIONS

SPELLING

Write the following words on the board: *mixer, editor, soloist, wearier, busiest, courageous, comical, homeward, wooden, legalize.* Say or write the following sentences and have students fit the correct word in each blank.

1. Use the electric (*mixer*) to make the cake.
2. The workers trudged (*homeward*) at the end of the day.
3. The clown gave a (*comical*) smile.
4. The firefighter was given a medal for her (*courageous*) action.
5. The (*editor*) works for a newspaper.
6. Jenny bought an old (*wooden*) chair.
7. Of all the restaurants, the Mexican one was the (*busiest*).
8. Can they (*legalize*) requiring teachers to give no homework on weekends?
9. A (*soloist*) played the melody on the violin.
10. I don't think I could be any (*wearier*) than I was last night.

WRITING

Portfolio Have students write a comparison of different babysitters they have had and/or experiences they have had taking care of children. Encourage them to use adjectives ending in *-er* and *-est.*

SCIENCE

Have students use reference sources on child development and talk to family members to create a time line of major developmental milestones in infancy and toddlerhood (for example: laughing, turning over, sitting up, crawling, first tooth, first words).

LITERATURE

Have students review literature for young children with the help of a school or community librarian and create mini-collections of books they could read to children of various ages if they were babysitting.

Technology AstroWord, Suffixes. ©1998 Silver Burdett Ginn Inc. Division of Simon & Schuster.

Lesson 53

Pages 117–118

Suffixes
-ous, -al

Lesson Focus

INTRODUCING THE SKILL

- Write these sentences on the board.
  The clown is a <u>comic</u>.
  The clown is <u>comical</u>.
  The team went on to <u>victory</u>.
  The team is <u>victorious</u>.

- Ask volunteers to read the sentences and identify the meanings and parts of speech of the underlined words.

- Point out that -*ous* and -*al* change noun bases into adjectives. Also, if a base word ends in *y*, such as *victory*, the *y* changes to *i* before the suffix is added.

- Write *mischief and mischievous*. Note the change of *f* to *v* before the suffix is added.

USING THE PAGES

Ask students to read the rule on page 117 and apply the suffix meanings to *courageous, comical, victorious,* and *mischievous*. After students complete the pages, review what they learned about suffixes.

117

Name _____

Form an adjective by adding the suffix **ous** or **al** to each word below. If the base word ends in **y**, change the **y** to **i** before adding the suffix. If it ends in **f**, usually change the **f** to **v** before adding the suffix.

> **RULE**
> The suffix **ous** means **like, full of,** or **having**. The suffix **al** means **like** or **having to do with**. Both suffixes can change a noun into an adjective.
> courage**ous** = full of courage
> comic**al** = having to do with comedy

1. historic + al = __historical__
2. glory + ous = __glorious__
3. education + al = __educational__
4. ornament + al = __ornamental__
5. mischief + ous = __mischievous__
6. tradition + al = __traditional__
7. colony + al = __colonial__
8. humor + ous = __humorous__

9. danger + ous = __dangerous__
10. comic + al = __comical__
11. fallacy + ous = __fallacious__
12. nerve + ous = __nervous__

Use some of the words you have made to create a word-search puzzle. Words can be written across, down, or diagonally. Exchange puzzles with a partner and find the hidden words.

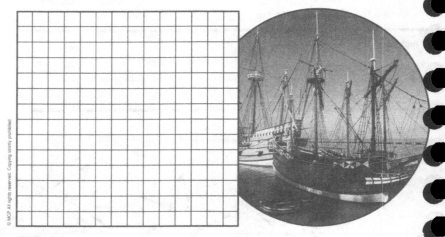

FOCUS ON ALL LEARNERS

ENGLISH LANGUAGE LEARNERS/ESL

Remind students that a noun is a word that names a person, place, or thing and that an adjective is a word that describes a noun. Encourage volunteers to list two or three phrases with examples of each, using words from the pages; for example, *humorous story* or *national heroes*.

VISUAL LEARNERS

 INDIVIDUAL Tell students to copy the suffixes -*al* and -*ous* and the following base words from the board onto paper: *logic, humor, danger, critic, nation,* and *poison*. Instruct students to create new words by adding one of the suffixes to each word.

KINESTHETIC LEARNERS

PARTNER Suggest that partners create scrambled word games using words with -*ous* and -*al* to challenge classmates to solve.

| sentimental | poisonous | nervous | national | mysterious |
| ornamental | natural | famous | fallacious | mountainous |

Across

1. having to do with a country
6. full of mystery
7. having a reputation; being well-known
8. full of feeling
9. mistaken

Down

1. being tense
2. having to do with nature
3. full of harmful substances
4. having many mountains
5. for decoration

 AUDITORY LEARNERS

LARGE GROUP

Read words with -ous and -al in similes for students to finish; for example, as humorous as . . . , as comical as . . . , as marvelous as . . . ornamental like a . . . .

GIFTED LEARNERS

Have pairs of students play a game in which they take turns naming a synonym for a word that contains the suffix -ous or -al. The other student must guess the word; for example, A synonym for *wrong* is *fallacious*.

LEARNERS WHO NEED EXTRA SUPPORT

Have students write sentences that use words containing the suffixes -ous and -al. Have students evaluate each other's correct word usage and spelling. **See Daily Word Study Practice, pages 191–192.**

SPELLING

Write the suffixes *-er, -or, -ist, -est, -ous, -al, -ward, -en, -ize, -ful,* and *-ness* on the board. Then say the spelling words *soloist, busiest,* and *legalize,* one by one. Call on volunteers to come to the board, point out the suffix they hear in each word, and then spell the entire word. Continue with the spelling words *mixer, editor, wearier, courageous, comical, homeward,* and *wooden.*

WRITING

Portfolio Have students work in small groups to write greeting cards that convey the same basic message in a variety of different styles, such as sentimental, traditional, and humorous versions of a birthday card.

SCIENCE

Copy the labels of several common cleaners, paints, and other household products that contain harmful or poisonous substances. Have students analyze the various issues associated with using these substances, such as carefully reading any warnings, dealing with accidents during usage, storing the products safely, and disposing of them properly. Students may create informative posters and display them in the school.

SOCIAL STUDIES

Have the students identify mountainous regions of the United States. Have them identify the tallest mountains in various regions and compare the relative altitudes and ages of mountainous areas near the east and west coasts with those of the Rocky Mountains.

 Technology

AstroWord, Suffixes. ©1998 Silver Burdett Ginn Inc. Division of Simon & Schuster.

Lesson 54

Pages 119–120

Suffixes
-ward, -en, -ize

INFORMAL ASSESSMENT OBJECTIVES

Can students

✔ correctly add the suffixes -*ward*, -*en*, and -*ize* to base words?

✔ read and recognize the meanings of words containing the suffixes -*ward*, -*en*, and -*ize*?

Lesson Focus

INTRODUCING THE SKILL

- Write these suffixes and their meanings on the board: -*ward*=*toward*, -*en*=*made of*, -*ize*=*to make*.

- As you read the following clues, have students write a word on the board that ends with one of the suffixes: toward the north (*northward*), made of wood (*wooden*), to make modern (*modernize*), to make an apology (*apologize*), toward the sky (*skyward*), made of gold (*golden*).

- Invite students to compare the parts of speech of the words before and after each suffix was added.

USING THE PAGES

- Ask if students have any questions regarding the directions for the pages. Have students check their work when finished.

- **Critical Thinking** Provide an opportunity for students to respond to the question on page 120.

Name _____

▶ Read the sentences and underline each word with the suffix **ward, en,** or **ize.** Then write each word you underlined in the correct column.

RULES

The suffix **ward** means **toward** or **in the direction of**. It can change a noun into an adjective or adverb. The suffix **en** means **to make, to become,** or **made of**. It can change a noun into a verb or an adjective. The suffix **ize** means **to make** or **to become**. It can change a noun into a verb.

home**ward** = toward home
wood**en** = made of wood
legal**ize** = to make legal

1. I did not <u>realize</u> that going out in the boat would <u>frighten</u> you.
2. I <u>apologize</u> for assuming that you would want to go <u>seaward</u> with us.
3. You can watch from the shore as we <u>loosen</u> the ropes and go <u>forward</u>.
4. Before we get into the boat, we always make sure to <u>fasten</u> our life jackets.
5. Gregory kicks off from the shore with a <u>backward</u> push.
6. I look <u>skyward</u> to make sure the weather is good.
7. When we are on the boat, we all like to sing and <u>harmonize</u> loudly.
8. We like to <u>modernize</u> old songs.
9. When the days begin to <u>shorten</u>, we don't stay in the boat very long.

en	ward	ize
frighten	seaward	realize
loosen	forward	apologize
fasten	backward	harmonize
shorten	skyward	modernize

FOCUS ON ALL LEARNERS ✳ ● ◆ ▮

ENGLISH LANGUAGE LEARNERS/ESL

Be certain that these learners understand the contexts of the exercises on pages 119 (boating) and 120 (airplane travel).

VISUAL/KINESTHETIC LEARNERS

SMALL GROUP Invite small groups to write "word equations" on the board. Write *base word + suffix = new word*. Have students use the formula or a variation of it to write words with the suffixes -*ward*, -*en*, and -*ize*; for example, *apology - y - + ize = apologize*.

KINESTHETIC LEARNERS

LARGE GROUP As you read a series of words ending in -*ward*, such as *downward, northward,* and *skyward*, have students demonstrate their meaning.

Complete each sentence by adding **ward**, **en**, or **ize** to each base word below the line.

1. This delay on the ground will certainly _____**lengthen**_____ our travel time.
   length

2. I had hoped that the clear skies and strong wind would _____**shorten**_____ it.
   short

3. Does it _____**sadden**_____ you to wait motionless on the ground for so long?
   sad

4. It was nice of the pilot to _____**apologize**_____ for the long delay.
   apology

5. The flight attendant asks us to look _____**forward**_____ as he demonstrates safety procedures.
   for

6. Make sure Danny is not looking _____**backward**_____ during the demonstration.
   back

7. The flight attendants _____**standardize**_____ the information they present.
   standard

8. The airplane finally finishes taxiing down the runway and moves _____**skyward**_____
   sky

9. Its gleaming silver nose points _____**upward**_____ .
   up

10. As we soar into the sky, my spirits begin to _____**lighten**_____ .
    light

11. Now I can _____**realize**_____ my dream of a vacation.
    real

12. Danny and I look _____**downward**_____ at the landscape.
    down

13. Hardly a word is _____**spoken**_____ as we gaze at the scenery below.
    spoke

Why do you think the flight attendants standardize the information they present?

Critical Thinking

120

Lesson 54
Suffixes -ward, -en, -ize

CURRICULUM CONNECTIONS

SPELLING

Write the spelling words *mixer, editor, soloist, wearier, busiest, courageous, comical, homeward, wooden* and *legalize* on the board. Ask students to choose a word to fit each clue.

1. humorous *(comical)*
2. made from a tree *(wooden)*
3. works with words *(editor)*
4. brave *(courageous)*
5. in the direction of home *(homeward)*
6. used in cooking *(mixer)*
7. suffix means "more" *(wearier)*
8. suffix means "most" *(busiest)*
9. plays alone *(soloist)*
10. done by changing a law *(legalize)*

WRITING

Portfolio Ask students to write detailed accounts of trips they have made by air, sea, train, bus, car, on horseback, or on foot. Encourage them to vividly describe the sights, sounds, smells, and other sensations of the trip. Have them arrange the details in a logical order, such as chronologically.

MATH

Determine how far each student in class lives from the school. Parents may be able to supply this information. Tell students the exact number of school days in the year. Have each student calculate how many miles he or she travels to and from school annually.

SCIENCE

Ask students which scientists look skyward to learn more about their subject. Discuss what students know about an astronomer's work. List this information on an idea web. Have students look for additional information about astronomy in science books and encyclopedias. Ask students to add new words or phrases to the web.

Technology

AstroWord, Suffixes. ©1998 Silver Burdett Ginn Inc. Division of Simon & Schuster.

Lesson 55

Pages 121–122

Suffixes
-ful, -ness

INFORMAL ASSESSMENT OBJECTIVES

Can students

✔ correctly add the suffixes *-ful* and *-ness* to base words?

✔ read and recognize the meanings of words containing the suffixes *-ful* and *-ness*?

Lesson Focus

INTRODUCING THE SKILL

- Display the chart below on the board. Use it as a reference to discuss the meanings of *careful*, *armful*, and *gladness*.

Suffix	Definition	Example
-ful	full of or tending to be	careful
-ful	a certain amount	armful
-ness	quality or condition	gladness

- Ask students to think of other words that contain the suffixes *-ful* and *-ness* and to add them to the appropriate row on the chart.

- Have students refer to the suffix definitions to define their words and then use the words in sentences.

USING THE PAGES

- Study the rules and the sample words on page 121 together. Then ask students to read directions for pages 121 and 122. Have students work in pairs to check their work.

- **Critical Thinking** Encourage students to respond to the question on page 121.

Name _____

▶ Complete each sentence by adding **ful** or **ness** to each base word below the line.

1. Jill felt rather _____ **fearful** _____ as she approached the hot air balloon.
   <small>fear</small>

2. She had been so _____ **joyful** _____ when her father had promised her a ride in one for her birthday!
   <small>joy</small>

3. She regretted her _____ **foolishness** _____ in accepting the gift.
   <small>foolish</small>

4. She carried an _____ **armful** _____ of treats for the trip.
   <small>arm</small>

5. She was chewing a _____ **mouthful** _____ of apple, but was too nervous to enjoy it.
   <small>mouth</small>

6. Her father followed behind with a _____ **bagful** _____ of gaily wrapped presents.
   <small>bag</small>

7. It was too late to back out now, Jill realized with _____ **hopelessness** _____.
   <small>hopeless</small>

8. She couldn't repay her father's generosity and _____ **kindness** _____ by refusing to go up.
   <small>kind</small>

9. With _____ **eagerness** _____, Jill's father climbed into the balloon's large basket.
   <small>eager</small>

10. The _____ **helpful** _____ owner of the balloon reached out to assist Jill.
    <small>help</small>

11. As the balloon slowly started to rise, poor Jill felt _____ **weakness** _____ in her legs.
    <small>weak</small>

12. The _____ **slowness** _____ of the climb made her feel better.
    <small>slow</small>

13. As the balloon rose above the treetops, the quiet _____ **emptiness** _____ of the sky seemed beautiful.
    <small>empty</small>

14. Jill gazed down at the fields below with _____ **happiness** _____.
    <small>happy</small>

15. Suddenly she was _____ **thankful** _____ for her gift.
    <small>thank</small>

How do you think Jill will feel when her balloon ride is over?

Critical Thinking

Lesson 55
Suffixes -ful, -ness **121**

FOCUS ON ALL LEARNERS ✳ • ◆ ▪

ENGLISH LANGUAGE LEARNERS/ESL

Point out that because the suffix *-ful* sounds like the word *full* and can mean "full of," they should note and remember that this suffix is spelled with only one *l*.

AUDITORY LEARNERS

LARGE GROUP

Say the words *careful*, *darkness*, and *truthful*. Then have students call out the answer to each riddle as you say it: *I do not tell lies. What am I?* (truthful) *I surround you when the lights are off. What am I?* (darkness) *I always look before crossing the street. What am I?* (careful) Announce three more words and have students compose the trio of riddles.

VISUAL/KINESTHETIC LEARNERS

LARGE GROUP

Invite students to create a crossword puzzle of words with *-ful* and *-ness* by writing words vertically and horizontally on the board.

There are 12 words containing the suffixes **ful** or **ness** hidden in the puzzle. Some of the words go across and some go down. Circle each word as you find it, and write it in the correct column.

ful

careful
harmful
bagful
skillful
pailful
healthful

ness

blackness
strictness
dampness
newness
fitness
darkness

```
B C F G H J B L D R S D
H A R M F U L A X Y T A
S R B N G C A F Y Z R M
Z E A S N D C D P Q I P
P F G T M X K L M R C N
W U F N E W N E S S T E
G L U D F G E H K M N S
T D L P H T S N I T E S
F I T N E S S O L V S T
T F O C R Z P R L W S L
Q J B F P A I L F U L B
B H E A L T H F U L D C
D A R K N E S S L M N P
```

Write a word from the puzzle to complete each sentence.

1. Jack is very _____careful_____ about maintaining his good health.

2. He exercises every day to improve his physical _____fitness_____ .

3. Jack always eats _____healthful_____ foods so his body will be strong.

4. He would never do anything that would be _____harmful_____ to his body.

122 Lesson 55
Suffixes -ful, -ness

VISUAL LEARNERS

INDIVIDUAL   Have students write common-sense slogans using words with the suffixes -*ful* and -*ness*.

GIFTED LEARNERS

Have students combine research of good nutrition information with interviews of classmates to create a guide to healthful snacks that kids will actually eat. Have students "publish" and distribute their guide throughout the school.

LEARNERS WHO NEED EXTRA SUPPORT

For students having difficulty with the puzzle on page 122, suggest this strategy: First look for the letter a suffix starts with (such as *f*) and then look in each direction for the letters *ul*. When they find the suffix, they can look for the rest of the word. **See Daily Word Study Practice, pages 191–192.**

SPELLING

Use the following words and sentences as a posttest for the first group of spelling words in Unit 5.

1. **mixer** — James used the electric **mixer** to combine the eggs and flour.

2. **editor** — The **editor** proofread the article.

3. **soloist** — Everyone praised the beautiful singing of the **soloist**.

4. **wearier** — Kelly feels **wearier** after playing basketball than soccer.

5. **busiest** — The day after Thanksgiving is the year's **busiest** shopping day.

6. **courageous** — It was **courageous** of Sam to defend his beliefs.

7. **comical** — Mel has a **comical** way of wrinkling up her nose.

8. **homeward** — Everyone fell asleep during the **homeward** journey.

9. **wooden** — Pinocchio was a **wooden** puppet.

10. **legalize** — Many people debated whether or not to **legalize** gambling.

WRITING

Portfolio Have students write travelogues of hot-air balloon rides, describing what they think the world would look like from the balloon.

SCIENCE

Have students use reference sources to determine when and how the hot-air balloon was invented and how these balloons work.

PHYSICAL FITNESS

Ask a physical education teacher or other expert to talk with the class about activities to develop muscular strength, cardiovascular fitness, and flexibility.

Technology   **AstroWord**, Suffixes. ©1998 Silver Burdett Ginn Inc. Division of Simon & Schuster.

Lesson 56

Pages 123–124

Suffixes
-hood, -ship, -ment

Can students

✔ read and recognize the meanings of words containing the suffixes *-hood, -ship,* and *-ment*?

Lesson Focus

INTRODUCING THE SKILL

- Write these sentences on the board.
  Grandmother talked about her childhood.
  A membership to a health club is a good gift.
  The negotiators reached an agreement.

- Ask volunteers to underline the words that contain the suffixes *-hood, -ship,* and *-ment.* Have them identify the base words and define words.

- Have students check their conclusions against the suffix rule in the box on page 123.

- Invite students to write and define other words with the suffixes *-hood, -ship,* and *-ment.*

USING THE PAGES

- Review the directions for pages 123 and 124 together. After students have finished, discuss the riddle answer and where it was found.

- **Critical Thinking** Encourage students to share experiences in response to the question on page 123.

Name _____

▶ Fill in the circle under the word that correctly completes each sentence.

RULE

The suffix **hood** means **state or condition of being.** The suffix **ship** means **state of, rank of,** or **art of something.** The suffix **ment** means **act of** or **state of something.**

mother**hood** = the condition of being a mother

governor**ship** = the rank of governor

improve**ment** = the act of improving

1. Sara and Joan share a special ____ .	● friendship	○ courtship	○ falsehood
2. They grew up in the same ____ .	○ motherhood	○ authorship	● neighborhood
3. They tell stories about their ____ .	○ enrollment	● childhood	○ likelihood
4. They recall one story with great ____ .	○ authorship	● enjoyment	○ adulthood
5. The girls had a shared ____ —measles.	○ friendship	● ailment	○ kinship
6. Suffering through it was a ____ .	○ falsehood	○ placement	● hardship
7. The experience created a special ____ .	○ governorship	● kinship	○ statement
8. Sara has never had an ____ with Joan.	● argument	○ authorship	○ amendment
9. Joan has never told Sara a ____ .	○ brotherhood	● falsehood	○ astonishment
10. Many people view the girls with ____ .	○ amendment	○ childhood	● astonishment
11. They marvel at this incredible ____ .	○ livelihood	● partnership	○ craftsmanship
12. They have a ____ to each other.	● commitment	○ womanhood	○ championship

What experiences do Sara and Joan share that are similar to— or different from—those you've shared with a friend?

Critical Thinking

Lesson 56
Suffixes -hood, -ship, -ment
123

FOCUS ON ALL LEARNERS

ENGLISH LANGUAGE LEARNERS/ESL

Encourage students to work with an English-speaking partner to complete the puzzle and riddle on page 124.

VISUAL/KINESTHETIC LEARNERS

SMALL GROUP

On the board, write the following in two columns: *Base Word, knight, craftsman, friend, resent, neighbor, accompany; Suffix, -hood, -ship, -ment.* Have volunteers draw a line from each base word to the suffix that can be added to it to create a new word, then say and define each new word.

VISUAL LEARNERS

PARTNER

Invite partners to write analogies using words with the suffixes *-hood, -ship,* and *-ment;* for example, *Boredom is to excitement as truth is to falsehood; Baseball is to game as World Series is to championship.*

Choose a word from the word bank that is either a synonym, an antonym, or related to the clue word. Write the word on the lines next to the clue word. Then read down to find the answer to the riddle.

championship	neighborhood	statement	kinship
pavement	payment	scholarship	falsehood
ailment	statehood	agreement	likelihood
adjustment	childhood	excitement	friendship
sisterhood			

1. fee — p a y m e n t
2. nationhood — s t a t e h o o d
3. understanding — a g r e e m e n t
4. education — s c h o l a r s h i p
5. truth — f a l s e h o o d
6. World Series — c h a m p i o n s h i p
7. brotherhood — s i s t e r h o o d
8. adulthood — c h i l d h o o d
9. report — s t a t e m e n t
10. community — n e i g h b o r h o o d
11. cement — p a v e m e n t
12. probability — l i k e l i h o o d
13. illness — a i l m e n t
14. hatred — f r i e n d s h i p
15. boredom — e x c i t e m e n t
16. change — a d j u s t m e n t
17. relationship — k i n s h i p

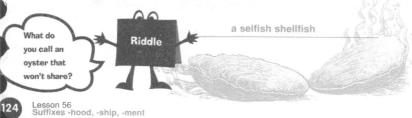

What do you call an oyster that won't share?

Riddle — a selfish shellfish

124 Lesson 56
Suffixes -hood, -ship, -ment

CURRICULUM CONNECTIONS

SPELLING

Use the following words and sentences as a test for the second group of spelling words in Unit 5.

1. **neighborhood** We live in a friendly **neighborhood.**
2. **friendship** Your **friendship** is important to me.
3. **improvement** Jan sees an **improvement** in her math skills.
4. **breakable** Don't give the baby a **breakable** cup.
5. **digestible** Applesauce is an easily **digestible** food.
6. **connection** The radio has a bad **connection.**
7. **presentation** Matt made a **presentation** on space travel to the class.
8. **addition** The family built a small **addition** to their house.
9. **clearance** The store held a **clearance** sale.
10. **dependence** Kate's **dependence** on her big sister grows less.
11. **sincerity** Our mayor spoke with **sincerity.**
12. **impressive** There was an **impressive** display of fireworks.

WRITING

Portfolio Have students write a brief memoir of their very first friend, using words with suffixes when possible.

SCIENCE

Encourage students to research the subject of shellfish. Have students list different varieties and record interesting facts.

PHYSICAL EDUCATION

Assign athletic championships for students to research, including World Series (baseball), Superbowl (football), Stanley Cup (hockey), World Cup (soccer), and America's Cup (sailing).

AstroWord, Suffixes. ©1998 Silver Burdett Ginn Inc. Division of Simon & Schuster.

AUDITORY LEARNERS

LARGE GROUP After students have completed the puzzle on page 124, call out the clues in random order and have students say the *-hood, -ship,* and *-ment* answer words and spell them orally.

GIFTED LEARNERS

Have students work in small groups to brainstorm other words containing the suffixes *-hood, -ship,* and *-ment* and then write a story incorporating any ten of the words.

LEARNERS WHO NEED EXTRA SUPPORT

Material: index cards

Put separate groups of students in charge of making word cards for the *-hood, -ship,* and *-ment* words in the lesson and others they know. Invite students to quiz each other reading and giving the meaning of the words. **See Daily Word Study Practice, pages 191–192.**

Lesson 57
Pages 125–126

Suffixes
-able, -ible

✶ • • ◆ • ■ ◆ • ✶ • • ■ • ◆ • ●

INFORMAL ASSESSMENT OBJECTIVES

Can students

✔ correctly add the suffixes *-able* and *-ible* to base words?

✔ read and recognize the meanings of words containing the suffixes *-able* and *-ible*?

Lesson Focus

INTRODUCING THE SKILL

- Write the suffixes *-able* and *-ible* on the board. Invite students to read the rule on page 125 to learn the meanings of suffixes. (*able to be, full of*)

- Then write the words *perish, enjoy, imagine, read, like, collapse, reduce, sense,* and *convert.* Have volunteers choose a word to write with the suffix *-able* or *-ible*. Remind students to drop the final e in base words before adding the suffix.

- Point out that *-able* and *-ible* can change a noun or verb into an adjective. Ask students to use the words on the board in sentences.

USING THE PAGES

- Be sure students understand how to complete the exercises on both pages. After they have finished, discuss what they learned about the suffixes *-ible* and *-able*.

- **Critical Thinking** Students can read and answer the question that follows the sentences on page 126.

125

Name _____

> Circle the base word in each word in boldface print. Then use the base word and the suffix in parentheses to form the word that will complete each sentence.

> **RULE**
> The suffixes **able** and **ible** mean **able to be**. The suffix **able** can also mean **full of**. These suffixes can change a noun or a verb into an adjective.
>
> break**able** = able to be broken
> digest**ible** = able to be digested
> charit**able** = full of charity

1. Something that can be (repair)ed is _____ repairable . (able)

2. Something that can be (reverse)d is _____ reversible . (ible)

3. Something that you (like)d was _____ likable . (able)

4. Something that can be (reproduce)d is _____ reproducible _____ . (ible)

5. Something that can be (insure)d is _____ insurable _____ . (able)

6. Something that can be (convert)ed is _____ convertible _____ . (ible)

7. Something that can be (deduct)ed is _____ deductible _____ . (ible)

8. Something that can be (enjoy)ed is _____ enjoyable _____ . (able)

9. Something that can be (fix)ed is _____ fixable _____ . (able)

10. Something that can be (notice)d is _____ noticeable _____ . (able)

> Now use one of the words you wrote to complete each sentence.

11. My brother Joe bought a car with a soft, _____ convertible _____ top.

12. The car needs some work, but Joe believes it is _____ repairable _____

13. When Joe drives with the top down, he wears his _____ reversible _____ jacket.

14. He always has an _____ enjoyable _____ time in his car!

Lesson 57
Suffixes -able, -ible **125**

FOCUS ON ALL LEARNERS ✶ • ◆ ■ ◆

ENGLISH LANGUAGE LEARNERS/ESL

Explain that the word *able* has almost the same meaning as the suffix *-able*. Have students define words with the suffix *-able*, using the word *able* when it makes sense for the words.

VISUAL LEARNERS

INDIVIDUAL On the board, write the suffixes *-ible* and *-able* and the base words *break, read, avoid, change, digest,* and *flex*. Instruct students to write sentences using words created by combining the base words with the suffixes given.

KINESTHETIC LEARNERS

SMALL GROUP Encourage students to demonstrate how items can be *flexible, readable, reversible, wearable, reproducible, breakable, convertible,* and *inflatable*.

Read the base words in the word bank. Use each base word and suffix to form a new word that will complete one of the sentences. If the base word ends in e, drop the e before adding a suffix beginning with a vowel.

break (able)	flex (ible)	read (able)
enjoy (able)	disagree (able)	wear (able)
favor (able)	response (ible)	play (able)
excite (able)	inflate (able)	convert (ible)

1. Tammy is happy that her baby-sitting job is quite _____ enjoyable _____

2. She works for the Manns, who find her extremely trustworthy and _____ responsible _____

3. Tammy works each weekend, but her hours are _____ flexible _____

4. The two children enjoy Tammy's company because she is never _____ disagreeable _____

5. The children are _____ excitable _____, but Tammy can calm them down.

6. Tammy never allows them to play with anything _____ breakable _____.

7. She helps them practice their printing so that it will be _____ readable _____.

8. She helps them take care of their clothes so that they will be _____ wearable _____

9. They listen to tapes so old that they are barely _____ playable _____.

10. Tammy takes the children outside when weather conditions are _____ favorable _____.

11. When the children play in the pool, Tammy floats on an _____ inflatable _____ raft.

12. The Manns drive Tammy home in their _____ convertible _____.

How is Tammy doing more than just baby-sitting?

Critical Thinking

126   Lesson 57
Suffixes -able, -ible

AUDITORY LEARNERS

LARGE GROUP Have volunteers think of items that can be described with each *-ible* and *-able* word from page 125.

GIFTED LEARNERS

Have student partners use a variety of dictionaries to look up entries for the suffixes *-ible* and *-able*. Have them write down the examples of words using the suffixes that are listed in the entries and then use the words in sentences.

LEARNERS WHO NEED EXTRA SUPPORT

Have each student write a meaningful, memorable sentence that contains one word with *-able* and one with *-ible* on the bulletin board. **See Daily Word Study Practice, pages 191–192.**

CURRICULUM CONNECTIONS

SPELLING

Divide the class into small groups. Hold a spelling bee, calling out spelling words *neighborhood, friendship, improvement, breakable, digestible, connection, presentation, addition, clearance, dependence, sincerity,* and *impressive* one at a time. Have the members of each group consult with each other on how to spell the word before choosing a spokesperson to call out the answer.

WRITING

Portfolio Have students create flyers listing their qualifications as baby sitters. The wording should be concise, catchy, and persuasive. Encourage students to use words ending in *-ible* or *-able*, such as *dependable* and *responsible*.

SCIENCE

Many things that were once made of highly breakable glass are now made of plastic. Have students research when plastic was invented, how it is made, and some of its many uses. Invite them to make short oral reports to the class.

SOCIAL STUDIES

Many materials are now recyclable. Have students find information on recycling in their community. What materials are recycled? What are the recyclables used for? Are there recyclable materials, such as certain types of plastics, that are not currently being recycled and why not?

Technology **AstroWord**, Suffixes. ©1998 Silver Burdett Ginn Inc. Division of Simon & Schuster.

Lesson 58

Pages 127–128

Suffixes
-ion, -ation, -ition

INFORMAL ASSESSMENT OBJECTIVES

Can students

✔ correctly add the suffixes -*ion*, -*ation*, and -*ition* to base words?

✔ read and recognize the meanings of words containing the suffixes -*ion*, -*ation*, and -*ition*?

Lesson Focus

INTRODUCING THE SKILL

- Ask volunteers to write the following words on the board: *connection*, *presentation*, *addition*, *composition* and *location*.

- Guide students in identifying the base and suffix in each word. Ask what each word means.

- Have students check the spelling and meanings of the words on the board using the information in the Rule box on page 127. Point out that the final *e* was dropped from the base words *admire*, *compose*, and *locate* before adding -*ation*, -*ition*, and -*ion*.

USING THE PAGES

- Have students read the directions for pages 127 and 128. After students have completed the pages, discuss what they learned about the suffixes -*ion*, -*ation*, and -*ition*.

- **Critical Thinking** Invite students to mention information from the sentences as they answer the question on page 128.

Name _____

> Read the words in the word bank. Notice that there is a noun and a verb in each pair. Choose the word that best completes each definition.

> **RULE**
> The suffixes **ion**, **ation**, and **ition** usually mean **the act of** or **a condition of being**. Each of these suffixes can change a verb into a noun.
>
> connec**tion** = the condition of being connected
>
> present**ation** = the act of presenting
>
> add**ition** = the condition of being added

erupt, eruption	admire, admiration	reject, rejection
celebrate, celebration	obstruct, obstruction	compose, composition
relate, relation	tax, taxation	direct, direction
locate, location	select, selection	combine, combination

1. to create or write something — **compose**
2. the act of adding to the price of something by the government — **taxation**
3. a sudden burst of lava and rock from a volcano — **eruption**
4. a place — **location**
5. a large barrier or thing that blocks — **obstruction**
6. to think well of, respect — **admire**
7. the choosing of something — **selection**
8. to refuse or not accept — **reject**
9. any family member — **relation**
10. one in a series of steps to follow — **direction**
11. to enjoy oneself as at a party — **celebrate**
12. to put together — **combine**

Lesson 58
Suffixes -ion, -ation, -ition
127

FOCUS ON ALL LEARNERS

ENGLISH LANGUAGE LEARNERS/ESL

Remind students that, while -*ion*, -*ation*, and -*ition* can change the meaning of a word in different ways, these suffixes always create a word that is a noun.

VISUAL LEARNERS

LARGE GROUP

Write the suffixes -*ion*, -*ation*, and -*ition* and the following base words on the board: *demote*, *demonstrate*, *present*, *tax*, *propose*, and *add*. Have volunteers change each base word into a correctly spelled noun. (*demotion*, *demonstration*, *presentation*, *taxation*, *proposition*, *addition*)

KINESTHETIC/VISUAL LEARNERS

PARTNER

Have pairs of students play hangman with words ending with the suffixes -*ion*, -*ation*, and -*ition*. The first student thinks of a word and writes a series of blanks corresponding to the number of letters in the word. The second student must guess enough letters to be able to identify the word correctly.

Add a word from the word bank to the suffix below the line to complete each sentence. If the base word ends in e, drop the e before adding it to the suffix.

1. Our Midwestern _____location_____ makes us a prime target for tornadoes.
   ion

2. Yesterday we waited in nervous _____expectation_____ of a fierce tornado's arrival.
   ation

3. Its _____combination_____ of speed and whirling air made it a menace.
   ation

4. It had struck a nearby town, creating widespread _____destruction_____ .
   ion

5. Thankfully, none of the town's _____population_____ was injured.
   ion

6. In the basement we could feel the _____vibration_____ of the winds.
   ion

7. We kept the radio on, listening attentively for further _____information_____ .
   ation

8. News broadcasts included the _____addition_____ of safety procedure stories.
   ition

9. We felt too anxious to engage in any _____conversation_____ .
   ation

10. We cheered as a news _____presentation_____ finally stated that the tornado had bypassed us.
   ation

> Using details from these sentences, how would you describe a tornado to someone who had never seen one?

Critical Thinking

expect   vibrate
destruct   converse
present   add
combine   locate
inform   populate

128 Lesson 58
Suffixes -ion, -ation, -ition

AUDITORY LEARNERS

INDIVIDUAL   Have students write poems that contain rhyming words ending with -tion. Encourage them to illustrate their poems and share them with classmates.

GIFTED LEARNERS

Challenge students to use as many -ion, -ation, and -ition words as possible in one sentence.

LEARNERS WHO NEED EXTRA SUPPORT

Create and read aloud sentences using the answer words on page 128. Ask students to identify each word that contains -ion, -ation, or -ition, identify the base word, and tell which of the three suffixes it contains. **See Daily Word Study Practice, pages 191–192.**

CURRICULUM CONNECTIONS

SPELLING

Write the spelling words on the board in random order: *breakable, neighborhood, digestible, connection, presentation, clearance, dependence, improvement, sincerity, addition, impressive,* and *friendship.* Then write the following words in a vertical column. Next to each of these words have students write the spelling word that shares the same suffix. Use the words *partnership, creative, clarity, childhood, believable, flexible, admittance, location, excitement, rejection, composition,* and *confidence.*

WRITING

Portfolio   Write these words on the board: *location, population, information,* and *vacation.* Invite students to write letters to a visitor's center or the chamber of commerce in a real or imaginary vacation site or town, asking for information about a place or places they would like to visit. Have students include the four words in their letters and use additional words with the suffixes *-ion, -ation,* and *-ition* if they can.

SCIENCE

Talk about tornadoes, including the safety precautions needed during these storms. Discuss other weather phenomena that occur in your area, perhaps hurricanes or frequent blizzards. Have students read to learn the scientific explanations for these occurrences. Local television meteorologists may have information available for the asking.

SOCIAL STUDIES

Have students research the sites of famous volcanic eruptions, such as Vesuvius, Krakatoa, Mount Tambora, Mount St. Helen's, and Mauna Loa. Have them determine the location of each volcano and the history of its eruptions.

Technology

AstroWord, Suffixes. ©1998 Silver Burdett Ginn Inc. Division of Simon & Schuster.

Lesson 59

Pages 129–130

Suffixes

**-ance, -ence,
-ive, -ity**

* ◆ • ● ◆ ● ◆ ● ✳ ◆ ● ◆ ■ ● ◆ ●

INFORMAL ASSESSMENT OBJECTIVES

Can students

✔ read and recognize the meanings of words containing the suffixes *-ance* and *-ence*?

✔ read and recognize the meanings of words containing the suffixes *-ive* and *-ity*?

Lesson Focus

INTRODUCING THE SKILL

● On the board, write these base words and suffixes.

clear + ance, depend + ence, sincere + ity, and *impress + ive.*

● Have volunteers combine each base word and suffix and write the new word on the board, explaining any spelling changes made in the base word.

● Ask students to use the rules on pages 129 and 130 and to explain what the words mean.

USING THE PAGES

● Review the directions for both pages. After students have completed the pages, discuss what they have learned about suffixes.

● **Critical Thinking** Invite students to respond to the questions related to the context of the sentences on pages 129 and 130.

129

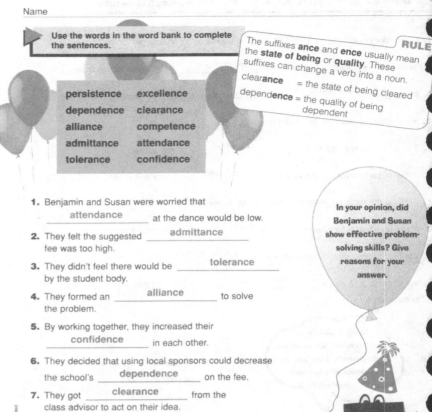

Name _____

 Use the words in the word bank to complete the sentences.

> **RULE**
> The suffixes **ance** and **ence** usually mean the **state of being** or **quality**. These suffixes can change a verb into a noun.
> clear**ance** = the state of being cleared
> depend**ence** = the quality of being dependent

persistence	excellence
dependence	clearance
alliance	competence
admittance	attendance
tolerance	confidence

1. Benjamin and Susan were worried that _____**attendance**_____ at the dance would be low.

2. They felt the suggested _____**admittance**_____ fee was too high.

3. They didn't feel there would be _____**tolerance**_____ by the student body.

4. They formed an _____**alliance**_____ to solve the problem.

5. By working together, they increased their _____**confidence**_____ in each other.

6. They decided that using local sponsors could decrease the school's _____**dependence**_____ on the fee.

7. They got _____**clearance**_____ from the class advisor to act on their idea.

8. They sought sponsors with a great deal of business _____**competence**_____.

9. They were proud of the _____**persistence**_____ they had shown in solving the problem.

10. The class advisor commended them for _____**excellence**_____ in working through a problem.

In your opinion, did Benjamin and Susan show effective problem-solving skills? Give reasons for your answer.

 Critical Thinking

Lesson 59
Suffixes -ance, -ence **129**

FOCUS ON ALL LEARNERS ✳ ● ◆ ■

ENGLISH LANGUAGE LEARNERS/ESL

Review the definitions of nouns and adjectives as you point out that the suffixes *-ance*, *-ence*, and *-ity* are used to form nouns, while the suffix *-ive* is used to form adjectives.

VISUAL LEARNERS

LARGE GROUP

Write additional word equations on the board involving subtraction rather than addition; for example, *competence - ence = compete.* Include examples for each suffix in this lesson for students to complete. Then have them write equations of their own.

VISUAL LEARNERS

SMALL GROUP

Have some groups of students create crossword puzzles with words containing *-ance, -ence, -ive,* and *-ity.* Then the other groups can write the clues for the puzzle words.

© MCP All rights reserved. Copying strictly prohibited.

Use the words in the box to complete the sentences.

RULE

The suffix **ity** can mean the **quality, condition,** or **fact of being.** This suffix can change an adjective into a noun. The suffix **ive** means **likely to** or **having to do with.** It can change a verb into an adjective.

sincer**ity** = the quality of being sincere

impress**ive** = likely to impress

impressive	passive
destructive	active
creativity	aggressive
sincerity	ability
probability	possibility

1. My little sister Sarah is very _____**active**_____—always running and climbing.

2. Unfortunately, since she drew all over my math book, I learned she can also be _____**destructive**_____ as well.

3. Mom is investigating the _____**possibility**_____ of enrolling her in a preschool.

4. They have an art program that would be a good outlet for Sarah's _____**creativity**_____

5. They also have swings and climbers where she could show off her _____**impressive**_____ gymnastic skills.

6. Mom warned the staff that Sarah can sometimes be _____**aggressive**_____ with younger children, especially if she wants their toys.

7. The teachers said with deep _____**sincerity**_____ that Sarah was an adorable and lively child!

8. They said that in all _____**probability**_____ it would take Sarah a day or two to adjust.

9. As mom talked with the staff, Sarah was quite _____**passive**_____, sitting quietly in a chair, coloring.

10. I just wish she had the _____**ability**_____ to sit still all of the time!

How do you think Sarah will react to preschool? What makes you think so?

Critical Thinking

130 Lesson 59
Suffixes -ive, -ity

SPELLING

Read these clues and have students identify and spell the words from the Unit List that match.

1. able to be digested (*digestible*)
2. the state of being sincere (*sincerity*)
3. something that connects other things (*connection*)
4. able to be broken (*breakable*)
5. a residential area (*neighborhood*)
6. something that is presented (*presentation*)
7. likely to impress (*impressive*)
8. the process of adding (*addition*)
9. a relationship between friends (*friendship*)
10. the state of being dependent (*dependence*)
11. the act of clearing (*clearance*)
12. the act of improving something (*improvement*)

WRITING

Portfolio Have students write descriptions about the characteristics of younger siblings or acquaintances that they most enjoy or least enjoy.

FINE ARTS

Have students research artists and musicians who displayed their talents from an early age, such as the artist Leonardo da Vinci and the composer Wolfgang Amadeus Mozart and display or play examples of such artists works, if possible.

MATH

Have students write word problems such as the following: At the Sixth-Grade Dance, tickets sold for $3.50, and 85 students attended the dance. The total cost of expenses for the dance was $112.93. What was the profit from the dance? ($184.57)

AstroWord, Suffixes. ©1998 Silver Burdett Ginn Inc. Division of Simon & Schuster.

AUDITORY LEARNERS

PARTNER Invite partners to take turns saying words ending with -*ance* or -*ence* and having the other person use the word in a sentence and spell it. Students can check disputed spellings in the dictionary.

GIFTED LEARNERS

Have students look up the suffixes -*ance*, -*ence*, -*ive*, and -*ity* in the dictionary and report to the class on their language origins.

LEARNERS WHO NEED EXTRA SUPPORT

Have students make a list of words ending in -*ance* and a list of words ending in -*ence*. Work together to make up memory sentences using as many words with the same suffix in each sentence as possible. **See Daily Word Study Practice, pages 191–192.**

Lesson 60

 **Reading** **Writing**

Reviewing Suffixes

INFORMAL ASSESSMENT OBJECTIVES

Can students

✔ read a story that contains words with suffixes?

✔ write a compare-and-contrast paragraph and a story?

Lesson Focus

READING

- Ask students to describe their experiences with eye examinations.

- On the board, write the words *favorable, nervous, examination, upward, disagreeable, dangerous, ailment, realize,* and *thoughtful.* Ask students to identify the base and suffix in each word and to explain what each word means.

- Tell students that they will read these and other words with suffixes in the story about a visit to the optometrist's office, on page 131. After reading the passage, have them recall details to write ways the brothers are alike and different.

WRITING

- On page 132, students will write a follow-up story about the brothers. The questions on page 132 will help. Remind students to include words from the box.

- As they revise and proofread their stories, students should review the original selection to be sure their sequels follow it logically.

Name _____

 Reading ▶ Read the story. Then write your answer to the question at the end of the story.

The Wrong Brother

Devon and his brother Jake were in an optometrist's waiting room. Devon's last report card had not been favorable. His parents wondered if his poor educational performance was due to bad eyesight.

"Look at this cool picture of snow boarders," said Jake, pointing to a magazine.

"I can't. I'm too nervous," said Devon.

An assistant called Devon's name, and he followed her into the examination room.

The optometrist's name was Dr. Carson. She told Devon to sit in a special chair and look upward. She put some drops in his eyes and said, "For a while these drops will make sunlight seem much brighter, but the effect will wear off in a few hours."

She conducted mysterious tests, shining lights into Devon's eyes and asking questions. She was likable, but Devon found the process disagreeable. He was sure that she would say he suffered from some dangerous ailment. However, when the examination was over, Dr. Carson went out to tell Devon's mother that his eyesight was perfect. "I didn't realize you had another son," said Dr. Carson. "Why are you squinting at that magazine, young man? Do your eyes hurt when you read?"

"Sometimes," said Jake in a thoughtful tone. "But I don't really mind."

Their mother sighed with exhaustion and made an appointment for Jake.

Compare and contrast Devon and Jake based on the information in this story.

_____
_____
_____
_____
_____
_____

FOCUS ON ALL LEARNERS

ENGLISH LANGUAGE LEARNERS/ESL

Ask students what they know about the meaning of the words *optometrist, optics,* or *optical.* Explain that all of these words come from the Greek word for *eye.*

 VISUAL LEARNERS

INDIVIDUAL Write on the board all of the suffixes covered in Unit 5. Have students look for and circle words containing these suffixes as they reread the story on page 131.

 VISUAL LEARNERS

LARGE GROUP Write ten words with suffixes on the overhead projector. Give students a few minutes to study the words. Turn off the projector and have students write as many words as they recall.

Write a story about Jake's trip to the optometrist's office. Make sure your story fits with what you have learned so far about Jake, Devon, and Dr. Carson. Use words from the word bank in your story.

smaller	responsible	blurriest
humorous	conversation	adjustable
downward	confidence	information
realize	activity	payment
careful	upward	impressive
readable	clearer	persistence

• How does Jake feel during the eye examination?
• What does Dr. Carson say?
• How does Devon react?

Helpful Questions

132 Lesson 60
Review suffixes: Writing

 AUDITORY LEARNERS

PARTNER Have one partner read aloud words from the story containing suffixes. Have the other partner define those words.

GIFTED LEARNERS

Have students add more detail to the original story, seeing how many words with suffixes covered in this unit they can insert into the original version.

LEARNERS WHO NEED EXTRA SUPPORT

Talk about the meaning of unclear words from the box on page 132 before students begin to write. **See Daily Word Study Practice, pages 191–192.**

CURRICULUM CONNECTIONS ✳ ●◆■ ◆●

SPELLING

Use the following words and dictation sentences as a posttest for the spelling words in the second half of Unit 5.

1. **neighborhood** Welcome to the **neighborhood.**
2. **friendship** This ring is a sign of **friendship.**
3. **improvement** My handwriting needs **improvement.**
4. **breakable** Wrap **breakable** gifts carefully.
5. **digestible** When you're sick, eat foods that are easily **digestible.**
6. **connection** There is no **connection** between the two buildings.
7. **presentation** Everyone clapped at the end of the **presentation.**
8. **addition** The **addition** of some mustard made the sandwich tastier.
9. **clearance** The **clearance** of the field caused trouble in town.
10. **dependence** The team feels **dependence** on the coach.
11. **sincerity** We could hear the **sincerity** in the doctor's voice.
12. **impressive** Jenna's speech was very **impressive.**

SCIENCE

Portfolio Have students study references for information on the human eye. Invite them to draw and label a diagram.

HEALTH

Ask students to find out how often people should have routine eye examinations.

MATH

Have students calculate the percentage of classmates who wear eyeglasses or contact lenses.

Technology AstroWord, Suffixes. ©1998 Silver Burdett Ginn Inc. Division of Simon & Schuster.

Lesson 61

Pages 133–134

Unit Checkup

Reviewing Suffixes

Lesson Focus

PREPARING FOR THE CHECKUP

- On the board, list the suffixes -er, -or, -ist, -est, -ous, -al, -ward, -en, -ize, -ful, -ness, -hood, -ship, -ment, -able, -ible, -ion, -ation, -ition, -ance, -ence, -ive, and -ity. Congratulate students for learning about so many suffixes.

- Invite students to write words on the board containing any of the suffixes studied in the unit and tell what they mean and/or use them in sentences.

USING THE PAGES

Have volunteers read the directions for each of the sections on pages 133 and 134 and then explain them in their own words. Model examples similar to the ones in the Checkup if you feel it is necessary. After the assessment, review suffixes and spelling rules for students that may benefit from more practice.

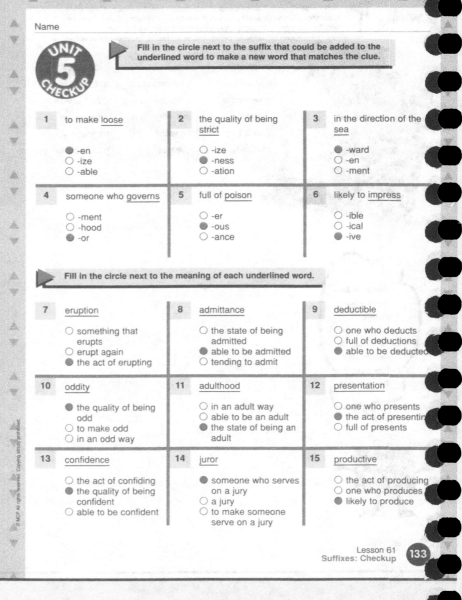

UNIT 5 CHECKUP

Name _____

▶ Fill in the circle next to the suffix that could be added to the underlined word to make a new word that matches the clue.

1 to make <u>loose</u> ● -en ○ -ize ○ -able	**2** the quality of being <u>strict</u> ○ -ize ● -ness ○ -ation	**3** in the direction of the <u>sea</u> ● -ward ○ -en ○ -ment
4 someone who <u>governs</u> ○ -ment ○ -hood ● -or	**5** full of <u>poison</u> ○ -er ● -ous ○ -ance	**6** likely to <u>impress</u> ○ -ible ○ -ical ● -ive

▶ Fill in the circle next to the meaning of each underlined word.

7 eruption ○ something that erupts ○ erupt again ● the act of erupting	**8** admittance ○ the state of being admitted ● able to be admitted ○ tending to admit	**9** deductible ○ one who deducts ○ full of deductions ● able to be deducted
10 oddity ● the quality of being odd ○ to make odd ○ in an odd way	**11** adulthood ○ in an adult way ○ able to be an adult ● the state of being an adult	**12** presentation ○ one who presents ● the act of presenting ○ full of presents
13 confidence ○ the act of confiding ● the quality of being confident ○ able to be confident	**14** juror ● someone who serves on a jury ○ a jury ○ to make someone serve on a jury	**15** productive ○ the act of producing ○ one who produces ● likely to produce

Lesson 61
Suffixes: Checkup **133**

FOCUS ON ALL LEARNERS ✹ • ♦ ■

ENGLISH LANGUAGE LEARNERS/ESL

Review the instructions for the Checkup individually with students. If necessary, compose a sample item in each format or work on the assessment as a group exercise.

VISUAL LEARNERS
INDIVIDUAL Have students write one word containing each suffix on separate slips of paper. Use the words for the following activity.

KINESTHETIC LEARNERS

LARGE GROUP **Materials:** three boxes

Label each of three boxes *Nouns, Verbs,* or *Adjectives.* Have students read the words they have written for the previous activity and file them in the correct boxes. Read the words from each box and ask students to determine if all the words are correctly filed.

133

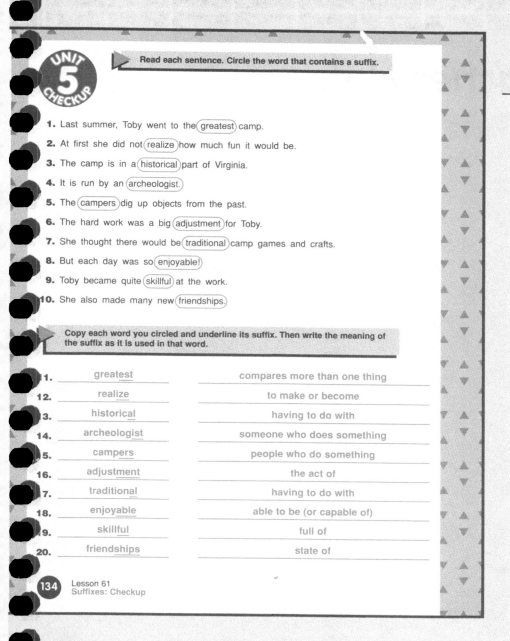

ASSESSING UNDERSTANDING OF UNIT SKILLS ✳ • ◆ ▪ • ◆ •

UNIT 5 CHECKUP

▶ Read each sentence. Circle the word that contains a suffix.

1. Last summer, Toby went to the (greatest) camp.
2. At first she did not (realize) how much fun it would be.
3. The camp is in a (historical) part of Virginia.
4. It is run by an (archeologist.)
5. The (campers) dig up objects from the past.
6. The hard work was a big (adjustment) for Toby.
7. She thought there would be (traditional) camp games and crafts.
8. But each day was so (enjoyable!)
9. Toby became quite (skillful) at the work.
10. She also made many new (friendships.)

▶ Copy each word you circled and underline its suffix. Then write the meaning of the suffix as it is used in that word.

11.	great**est**	compares more than one thing
12.	real**ize**	to make or become
13.	historic**al**	having to do with
14.	archeolog**ist**	someone who does something
15.	camp**ers**	people who do something
16.	adjust**ment**	the act of
17.	tradition**al**	having to do with
18.	enjoy**able**	able to be (or capable of)
19.	skill**ful**	full of
20.	friend**ships**	state of

134 Lesson 61
Suffixes: Checkup

ASSESSING UNDERSTANDING OF UNIT SKILLS

Student Progress Assessment You may wish to review the observational notes you made as students worked through the activities in this unit. Your notes will help you evaluate the progress students made with suffixes.

Portfolio Assessment Review the materials students have collected in their portfolios. Talk with students individually to discuss their written work and the progress they have made since the beginning of the unit. As you review students' work, evaluate how well they use the unit word study skills.

Daily Word Study Practice For students who need additional practice with any of the topics in this unit, quick reviews are provided on pages 191–192 in Daily Word Study Practice.

Word Study Posttest To assess students' mastery of skills covered in this unit, use the posttest on pages 111g – 111h.

SPELLING

Use the following dictation sentences as a review for the spelling words in Unit 5.

1.	**editor**	Send in your article to the magazine **editor.**
2.	**wearier**	After the hike, I was **wearier** than my dad.
3.	**courageous**	**Courageous** people do what they think is right.
4.	**comical**	The performers were **comical**.
5.	**homeward**	The pioneers were **homeward** bound.
6.	**legalize**	For what age would you **legalize** driving?
7.	**improvement**	The landscape is an **improvement** to the house.
8.	**digestible**	Rice is a very **digestible** food.
9.	**presentation**	The **presentation** was long.
10.	**clearance**	We bought a sofa at the **clearance** sale.
11.	**sincerity**	Friends trust you because of your **sincerity.**
12.	**impressive**	An **impressive** amount of work went into your report.

SMALL GROUP

AUDITORY LEARNERS

Have volunteers take turns choosing words filed in the boxes from the previous activity to read and define.

GIFTED LEARNERS

Have small groups work together to create a board game or card game featuring words with suffixes covered in this unit.

LEARNERS WHO NEED EXTRA SUPPORT

Encourage students to find one example word for each suffix taught in this unit. The word they choose should be very familiar to them. They should use this word as a reminder of the suffix's meaning. **See Daily Word Study Practice, pages 191–192.**

Teacher Notes

INTRODUCING

Unit 6

Suffixes, Plurals, and Syllables

Student Performance Objectives

In Unit 6, students will review and extend their understanding of the rules for adding suffixes to words. They will practice forming irregular plurals of words and recognizing syllables in words. Students will be introduced to the poetic form *haiku*. They will also develop letter-writing skills. As students practice applying concepts involving suffixes, irregular plurals, and syllables, they will be able to

◆ Add suffixes to words that double the final consonant

◆ Add suffixes to words that end in *e*

◆ Recognize words with more than one suffix

◆ Add suffixes to words ending in *y* or *le*

◆ Form the plurals of words ending in *f, fe,* or *o*

◆ Recognize irregular plural forms

◆ Recognize the number of syllables in words

Contents

UNIT 6 RESOURCES
Assessment Strategies   135c
   Overview   135c
   Unit 6 Pretest   135e–135f
   Unit 6 Posttest   135g–135h
   Unit 6 Student Progress Checklist   135i
Spelling Connections   135j–135k
Word Study Games, Activities, and Technology   135l–135o
Home Connection   135p–135q

TEACHING PLANS
Unit 6 Opener   135–136
Lesson 62: Words that Double the Final   137–138
       Consonant to Add a Suffix
Lesson 63: Words that Drop the Final *e*   139–140
       to Add a Suffix
Lesson 64: Words with More than One Suffix   141–142
Lesson 65: Adding Suffixes to Words Ending in *y*   143–144
Lesson 66: Adding Suffix *-ly* to Words Ending   145–146
       in *y* or *le*
Lesson 67: Plural Forms for Words Ending in   147–148
       f and *fe*
Lesson 68: Plural Form for Words Ending in *o*   149–150
Lesson 69: Other Plural Forms   151–152
Lesson 70: Syllables   153–154
Lesson 71: Syllables   155–156
Lesson 72: Review Suffixes, Plurals, Syllables   157–158
Lesson 73: Unit 6 Checkup   159–160

Assessment Strategy Overview

In Unit 6, assess students' ability to understand the rules for adding suffixes to words, forming irregular plurals of words, and dividing words into syllables. There are various ways to assess students' progress. If desired, encourage students to evaluate their own work and participate in setting goals for their own learning.

FORMAL ASSESSMENT

The Unit 6 Pretest on pages 135e–135f helps to assess a student's knowledge at the beginning of the unit and to plan instruction.

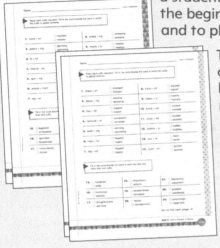

The Unit 6 Posttest on pages 135g–135h helps to assess mastery of unit objectives and to plan for reteaching, if necessary.

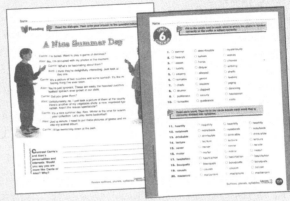

INFORMAL ASSESSMENT

The Reading & Writing pages and Unit Checkup in the student book are an effective means of evaluating students' performance.

Skill	Reading & Writing Pages	Unit Checkup
Add Suffixes to Words that Double the Final Consonant	157–158	159–160
Add Suffixes to Words that End in e	157–158	159–160
Words with Multiple Suffixes	157–158	159–160
Add Suffixes to Words that End in y	157–158	159–160
Add Suffix -ly to Words Ending in y or le	157–158	159–160
Plurals of Words Ending in f and fe	157–158	159–160
Plurals of Words Ending in o	157–158	159–160
Unusual Plural Forms	157–158	159–160
Syllables	157–158	159–160

PORTFOLIO ASSESSMENT

Portfolio This logo appears throughout the teaching plans. It signals opportunities for collecting students' work for individual portfolios. You may also want to collect the following pages.

❖ Unit 6 Pretest and Posttest, pages 135e–135h

❖ Unit 6 Reading & Writing, pages 157–158

❖ Unit 6 Checkup, pages 159–160

STUDENT PROGRESS CHECKLIST

Use the checklist on page 135i to record students' progress. You may want to cut the sections apart to place each student's checklist in his or her portfolio.

Administering and Evaluating the
Pretest and Posttest

DIRECTIONS

To help you assess students' progress in learning Unit 6 skills, tests are available on pages 135e–135h. Administer the Pretest before students begin the unit. The results of the Pretest will help you identify each student's strengths and needs in advance, allowing you to structure lesson plans to meet individual needs. Administer the Posttest to assess students' overall mastery of skills taught in the unit and to identify specific areas that will require reteaching.

PERFORMANCE ASSESSMENT PROFILE

The following chart will help you identify specific skills as they appear on the tests and enable you to identify and record specific information about an individual's or the class's performance on the tests.

Depending on the results of the tests, refer to the Reteaching column for lesson-plan pages where you can find activities that will be useful for meeting individual needs or for daily word study practice.

PERFORMANCE ASSESSMENT PROFILE

Skill	Pretest Questions	Posttest Questions	Reteaching Focus on All Learners	Reteaching Daily Word Study Practice
Add Suffixes to Words that Double the Final Consonant	3, 5, 7	3, 5, 7	137–138, 157–158	192–194
Add Suffixes to Words that End in e	2, 4, 6, 8	2, 4, 6, 8	139–140, 157–158	192–194
Add Suffixes to Words that End in y	9, 10, 11, 13	9, 10, 11, 13	143–144, 157–158	192–194
Words with Multiple Suffixes	15–23	15–23	141–142, 157–158	192–194
Add Suffix -ly to Words Ending in y or le	9, 12	9, 12	145–146, 157–158	192–194
Plurals of Words Ending in f and fe	24, 27, 29, 34	24, 27, 29, 34	147–148, 157–158	192–194
Plurals of Words Ending in o	25, 32	25, 32	149–150, 157–158	192–194
Unusual Plural Forms	26, 28, 30, 31, 33, 35–39	26, 28, 30, 31, 33, 35–39	151–152, 157–158	192–194
Syllables	40–51	40–51	153–158	195

> Read each suffix equation. Fill in the circle beside the word in which the suffix is added correctly.

1. sharp + en
- ○ sharppen
- ○ sharpen

8. trace + ed
- ○ traceed
- ○ traced

2. dance + ing
- ○ dancing
- ○ danceing

9. heavy + ly
- ○ heavily
- ○ heavyly

3. trap + ed
- ○ trapped
- ○ traped

10. funny + est
- ○ funnest
- ○ funniest

4. compute + er
- ○ computeer
- ○ computer

11. study + ed
- ○ studied
- ○ studyed

5. swim + ing
- ○ swiming
- ○ swimming

12. bubble + ly
- ○ bubbly
- ○ bubbley

6. hope + ful
- ○ hopeful
- ○ hopful

13. lazy + er
- ○ lazer
- ○ lazier

7. big + est
- ○ biggest
- ○ bigest

14. quick + er
- ○ quicker
- ○ quickier

> Fill in the circle beside the word in each box that has more than one suffix.

15.
- ○ hardened
- ○ softly

18.
- ○ importance
- ○ actions

21.
- ○ frightening
- ○ enjoyment

16.
- ○ humorous
- ○ tearfully

19.
- ○ peacefulness
- ○ tomatoes

22.
- ○ greatest
- ○ needlessly

17.
- ○ thoughtfulness
- ○ admiring

20.
- ○ busier
- ○ courageously

23.
- ○ surprisingly
- ○ happiness

Go to the next page. →

▶ Fill in the circle beside the plural form for the first word in each box.

24. scarf
- ○ scarves
- ○ scarfs

32. potato
- ○ potatos
- ○ potatoes

25. solo
- ○ soloes
- ○ solos

33. man
- ○ men
- ○ mans

26. trout
- ○ treat
- ○ trout

34. roof
- ○ rooves
- ○ roofs

27. knife
- ○ knives
- ○ knifes

35. tooth
- ○ teeth
- ○ tooves

28. mouse
- ○ mousies
- ○ mice

36. child
- ○ childs
- ○ children

29. puff
- ○ puffs
- ○ puffes

37. foot
- ○ feet
- ○ foots

30. ox
- ○ oxes
- ○ oxen

38. scissors
- ○ scissores
- ○ scissors

31. spaghetti
- ○ spaghetti
- ○ spaghetties

39. moose
- ○ mooses
- ○ moose

▶ Read each word. Then fill in the circle beside the number that tells how many syllables are in the word.

40. tennis
○ 2 ○ 3 ○ 4

43. flowerpot
○ 2 ○ 3 ○ 4

46. repetition
○ 2 ○ 3 ○ 4

49. congratulations
○ 3 ○ 4 ○ 5

41. paper
○ 2 ○ 3 ○ 4

44. napkins
○ 2 ○ 3 ○ 4

47. melon
○ 2 ○ 3 ○ 4

50. determination
○ 3 ○ 4 ○ 5

42. blanket
○ 2 ○ 3 ○ 4

45. shopkeeper
○ 2 ○ 3 ○ 4

48. strawberries
○ 3 ○ 4 ○ 5

51. abilities
○ 3 ○ 4 ○ 5

Possible score on Unit 6 Pretest is 51. Number correct _____

Read each suffix equation. Fill in the circle beside the word in which the suffix is added correctly.

1. moist + en
- ○ moistten
- ○ moisten

8. praise + ing
- ○ praiseing
- ○ praising

2. glance + ing
- ○ glancing
- ○ glanceing

9. hearty + ly
- ○ heartily
- ○ heartyly

3. fit + ed
- ○ fitted
- ○ fited

10. silly + est
- ○ sillyest
- ○ silliest

4. reduce + ed
- ○ reduceed
- ○ reduced

11. pry + ed
- ○ pried
- ○ pryed

5. spin + ing
- ○ spining
- ○ spinning

12. possible + ly
- ○ possibly
- ○ possibley

6. amaze + ment
- ○ amazement
- ○ amazment

13. scary + er
- ○ scaryer
- ○ scarier

7. jog + er
- ○ jogger
- ○ joger

14. slick + er
- ○ slicker
- ○ slickier

Fill in the circle beside the word in each box that has more than one suffix.

15.
- ○ legalized
- ○ annoyance

18.
- ○ chiefs
- ○ adoptions

21.
- ○ sharpening
- ○ scratchiness

16.
- ○ operation
- ○ foolishness

19.
- ○ mysteriously
- ○ hazardous

22.
- ○ torpedoes
- ○ fearlessly

17.
- ○ miraculously
- ○ dizzier

20.
- ○ puppeteer
- ○ delightfully

23.
- ○ longingly
- ○ healthiest

Go to the next page. →

Fill in the circle beside the plural form for the first word in each box.

24. wolf
- ○ wolves
- ○ wolfes

32. tornado
- ○ tornados
- ○ tornadoes

25. radio
- ○ radioes
- ○ radios

33. alumnus
- ○ alumni
- ○ alumnies

26. salmon
- ○ salmons
- ○ salmon

34. belief
- ○ believes
- ○ beliefs

27. life
- ○ lives
- ○ lifes

35. crisis
- ○ crises
- ○ crisises

28. moose
- ○ meese
- ○ moose

36. grandchild
- ○ grandchilds
- ○ grandchildren

29. cliff
- ○ cliffs
- ○ clives

37. woman
- ○ women
- ○ womans

30. bacterium
- ○ bacteries
- ○ bacteria

38. series
- ○ serious
- ○ series

31. zucchini
- ○ zucchini
- ○ zucchinus

39. aircraft
- ○ aircraft
- ○ aircrafts

Read each word. Then fill in the circle beside the number that tells how many syllables are in the word.

40. igloos
○ 2 ○ 3 ○ 4

43. illegal
○ 2 ○ 3 ○ 4

46. distribution
○ 2 ○ 3 ○ 4

49. geographical
○ 3 ○ 4 ○ 5

41. lettuce
○ 2 ○ 3 ○ 4

44. windowpane
○ 2 ○ 3 ○ 4

47. corporation
○ 2 ○ 3 ○ 4

50. inseparable
○ 3 ○ 4 ○ 5

42. quickened
○ 2 ○ 3 ○ 4

45. scorekeeper
○ 2 ○ 3 ○ 4

48. pronunciation
○ 3 ○ 4 ○ 5

51. inefficient
○ 3 ○ 4 ○ 5

Possible score on Unit 6 Posttest is 51. Number correct _____

Student Progress Checklist

Make as many copies as needed to use for a class list. For individual portfolio use, cut apart each student's section. As indicated by the code, color in boxes next to skills satisfactorily assessed and mark an X by those requiring reteaching. Marked boxes can later be colored in to indicate mastery.

STUDENT PROGRESS CHECKLIST
Code: ■ Satisfactory   ☒ Needs Reteaching

Student: _____ _____ Pretest Score: _____ Posttest Score: _____	Skills ❏ Suffixes ❏ Plurals ❏ Syllables	Comments / Learning Goals
Student: _____ _____ Pretest Score: _____ Posttest Score: _____	Skills ❏ Suffixes ❏ Plurals ❏ Syllables	Comments / Learning Goals
Student: _____ _____ Pretest Score: _____ Posttest Score: _____	Skills ❏ Suffixes ❏ Plurals ❏ Syllables	Comments / Learning Goals
Student: _____ _____ Pretest Score: _____ Posttest Score: _____	Skills ❏ Suffixes ❏ Plurals ❏ Syllables	Comments / Learning Goals
Student: _____ _____ Pretest Score: _____ Posttest Score: _____	Skills ❏ Suffixes ❏ Plurals ❏ Syllables	Comments / Learning Goals

Spelling Connections

INTRODUCTION

The Unit Word List is a comprehensive list of spelling words drawn from this unit. The words are grouped by suffix additions to words and by plural formations of words. To incorporate spelling into your word study program, use the activity in the Curriculum Connections section of each teaching plan.

The spelling lessons utilize the following approach for each set of words.

1. Administer a pretest of the words that have not yet been introduced. Dictation sentences are provided.

2. Provide practice.

3. Reassess. Dictation sentences are provided.

A final test is provided in Lesson 73 on page 160.

DIRECTIONS

Make a copy of Blackline Master 46 for each student. After administering the pretest for each word study element, give each student a copy of the appropriate word list.

Students can work with a partner to practice spelling the words orally and identifying the appropriate phonetic spelling rule for each word. They can also make and use letter cards to form the words on the list. You may want to challenge students to identify other words that have the same phonetic elements. Students can write words of their own on *My Own Word List* (see Blackline Master 46).

Have students store their list words in an envelope or plastic zipper bag in the back of their books or notebooks. Alternatively, you may want to suggest that students keep a spelling notebook, listing words with similar patterns. You could also invite students to build word-wall displays in the classroom. Each section of the wall can focus on words with a single word study element. The walls will become a good spelling resource when students are writing.

UNIT WORD LIST

Words that Double the Final Consonant or Drop the Final *e* to Add a Suffix, Words with More than One Suffix, Suffixes for Words Ending in *y*, Adding *-ly* to Words Ending in *y* or *le*

jogging

swimmers

changing

hesitation

peacefulness

generosity

studies

scariest

possibly

luckily

Plural Forms for Words Ending in *f*, *fe*, and *o*; Other Plural Forms; Syllables; Syllabicating Words with Prefixes and Suffixes

knives

chiefs

potatoes

tornadoes

scissors

series

misunderstanding

apologized

appreciated

unfortunately

Name _____

 **S**pelling

UNIT 6 WORD LIST

Words that Double the Final Consonant or Drop the Final e to Add a Suffix, Words with More than One Suffix, Suffixes for Words Ending in y, Adding ly to Words Ending in y or le

jogging	generosity
swimmers	studies
changing	scariest
hesitation	possibly
peacefulness	luckily

Plural Forms for Words Ending in f, fe, and o; Other Plural Forms; Syllables; Syllabicating Words with Prefixes and Suffixes

knives	series
chiefs	misunderstanding
potatoes	apologized
tornadoes	appreciated
scissors	unfortunately

My Own Word List

Word Study Games, Activities, and Technology

The following collection of ideas offers a variety of opportunities to reinforce word study skills while actively engaging students. The games, activities, and technology suggestions can easily be adapted to meet the needs of your group of learners. They vary in approach so as to consider students' different learning styles.

● **TO DOUBLE OR NOT**

Write these sentences on the chalkboard, as they appear at the right. Ask volunteers to complete the sentences by adding suffixes to the words in parentheses. They should read the sentences aloud, spelling the new words, and explain why they did or did not double the final consonant. Call on others to identify the suffixes in the underlined words and explain the rule for adding suffixes that applies in each case.

> Alex is (plan) a garden. He is (plant) tomatoes, corn, and marigolds <u>cheerfully</u>.
> The <u>scarily</u> loud sound of the lightning (stun) us. Its force (stunt) the growth of the tree it hit.
> Craig is a <u>surprisingly</u> complete baseball (play). He is a good (hit) as well as a fine fielder.
> Sara (grin) at first. Then she (laugh) <u>uproariously</u>.
> Snowball is the (big) horse in the race. <u>Amazingly</u>, he is also the (fast).

▲ **FOLLOW THAT RULE**

Invite students to play a game of "follow that rule." Arrange them in groups of three or four. Give each group a number cube. Tell group members to take turns rolling the cube and saying a word that matches the number shown. Players rolling a one or a two must say and spell a word that follows the rule for doubling the consonant. A three or a four requires a word that follows the rule for dropping the final *e*; a five or a six, for changing *y* to *i*. Each word counts as one point; the first player to reach six points wins.

◆ **TOM SWIFTIES**

Introduce the class to Tom Swifties, in which Tom's statements are turned into jokes by adding adverbs ending in *-ly* to make jokes. First note that one such joke is a Tom Swifty. Two or more are Tom Swifties. Ask a volunteer to identify the rule that applies in forming the plural. Then give these examples.

"Look at the fireflies," Tom said *glowingly*. "That was a difficult exam," Tom said *testily*.

Invite students to work in pairs to create Tom Swifties using adverbs whose base words end in *-y*. Suggest that they illustrate their work in individual books, or collect the pages in a class joke book that can be displayed for everyone's enjoyment.

■ ANIMAL GROUPS

Discuss words that are used to identify different groups of animals. You might prompt students to name commonly known terms such as a *herd* of cattle; a *pack* of wolves; a *pride* of lions. If possible, display a copy of the book *An Exaltation of Larks* by James Lipton. If not, write on the chalkboard several examples from that book of unusual words for identifying groups of animals. Examples could include a *skulk* of foxes; a *gaggle* of geese (on land or on water); a *skein* of geese (in flight); a *crash* of rhinoceroses; a *leap* of leopards; a *parliament* of owls. Ask pairs of students to list the singular and plural forms of animal names, and challenge them to create interesting names that might be used to identify these groups of animals.

✳ ADDING *-LY* TO WORDS

Write the following words on the chalkboard: *hasty, hearty, lucky, possible, noble, simple.* Call on volunteers to add the suffix *-ly* to each word and tell which rule applies to the new word. (*Rule 1: hastily, heartily, luckily; Rule 2: possibly, nobly, simply.*)

● A MUSIC REVIEW

Provide partners with a printed copy of the paragraph shown at right. Tell them to rewrite the paragraph by adding suffixes according to the rules or by substituting the correct plural form for each of the words in parentheses. When they finish, ask volunteers to read the rewritten sentences aloud, spelling the new words and explaining the changes. You might challenge the class to write two sentences that could be added to the review, following the format of the original.

> A sellout crowd (fill) the concert hall. They (clap) enthusiastically for the musicians playing the (violin) and (piccolo). The audience also (hum) along with the singer performing the (solo), but they saved their (big) response for the (drum). They (snap) their fingers in time with the beat, and (tap) their feet (quick) when he switched to a more upbeat tempo. They (marvel) at how he (strut) his stuff by (jam) without any preparation after the scheduled performance ended.

▲ FORMING PLURALS

Tell students to list and form plurals for as many words as they can that end in *o.* Have them list their words in two columns: one for words that form the plural by adding *-s;* the other for words that add *-es.* Challenge them to use the plural forms of their words in sentences. Ask volunteers to read selected sentences aloud, then spell the *o* word correctly and define it. You might extend the activity by applying it to *f* and *fe* words and to words with *oo.*

◆ FORMING NEW WORDS

Write *loveableness, hopefully, fearlessness,* and *cheerfulness* on the chalkboard. Ask students to read each word and write the base word. Then have them form new words by adding two different suffixes to each base word. Encourage students to share their words with a partner, working at the chalkboard or on paper at their seats.

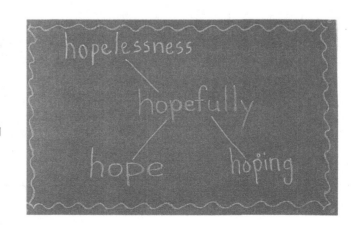

■ A VEGETARIAN MENU WITH PLURAL FORMS

Tell students to create a menu for a restaurant that serves vegetables whose plural forms are words discussed in this unit, such as zucchini, spinach, and radishes and other vegetables that follow the same rule. Encourage them to be creative and include other ingredients such as herbs and spices. Challenge them to add lively descriptions of each menu item, using words that follow various suffix rules from this unit.

Specials

Stuffed Avocados
Broiled Tomatoes
Broccoli with Lemon
Scalloped Potatoes
Baked Zucchini

✽ SYLLABLE BASEBALL

Blackline Master 47 features the outline of a baseball diamond with home plate and first, second, and third bases. This can be used as a game board on which partners can play "syllable baseball." Make enough copies to distribute to pairs of students. Students take turns playing the roles of the pitcher and the batter. The pitcher says a base word containing one syllable. The batter writes the base word on a separate sheet of paper and adds as many syllables as he or she can to form a new word. After counting the number of syllables in that word, the batter moves a paper token that many bases and stays there. Players switch roles and repeat the process. Each player gets nine at-bats, advancing the token one base for each syllable in every new word he or she forms. Each time the batter crosses home plate, one run is scored. The player with the most runs after nine at-bats wins.

● CREATING HAIKU THEMES

Tell students that a brief scene from nature is traditionally the subject in haiku. You might suggest the following themes as examples: a robin sitting in a tree, a kitten stalking a ball, snow silently falling on the ground. Have students work individually or in small groups to come up with other momentary scenes from nature that could serve as the subject of a haiku poem. You might allow them to look at pictures in magazines for ideas. After they finish, ask groups to share their best examples with the class.

Technology

The following software products are designed to develop students' grammar skills.

Ace Publisher   Students in grades 6 and up edit stories themselves or have a friendly android help them by using the editor's handbook. Punctuation, spelling, and grammar skills are emphasized.
** Mindplay
  160 West Fort Lowell Street
  Tucson, AZ 85705
  (800) 221-7911

Grammar Baseball   A baseball game format offers students in grades 2–12 opportunities to practice grammar as they alternate between being pitchers and batters. Skill emphasis is on identifying correct usage in short paragraphs.

**GAMCO Educational Materials
  P.O. Box 1911
  Big Spring, TX 79721
  (800) 351-1404

Grammar Games   An introductory quiz assesses grammar skills and then places students into various activities accordingly. Four games offer practice in correcting fragmented sentences, using correct noun and verb forms, and punctuation.
**Davidson & Associates, Inc.
  19840 Pioneer Avenue
  Torrance, CA 90503
  (800) 545-7677

Name _____

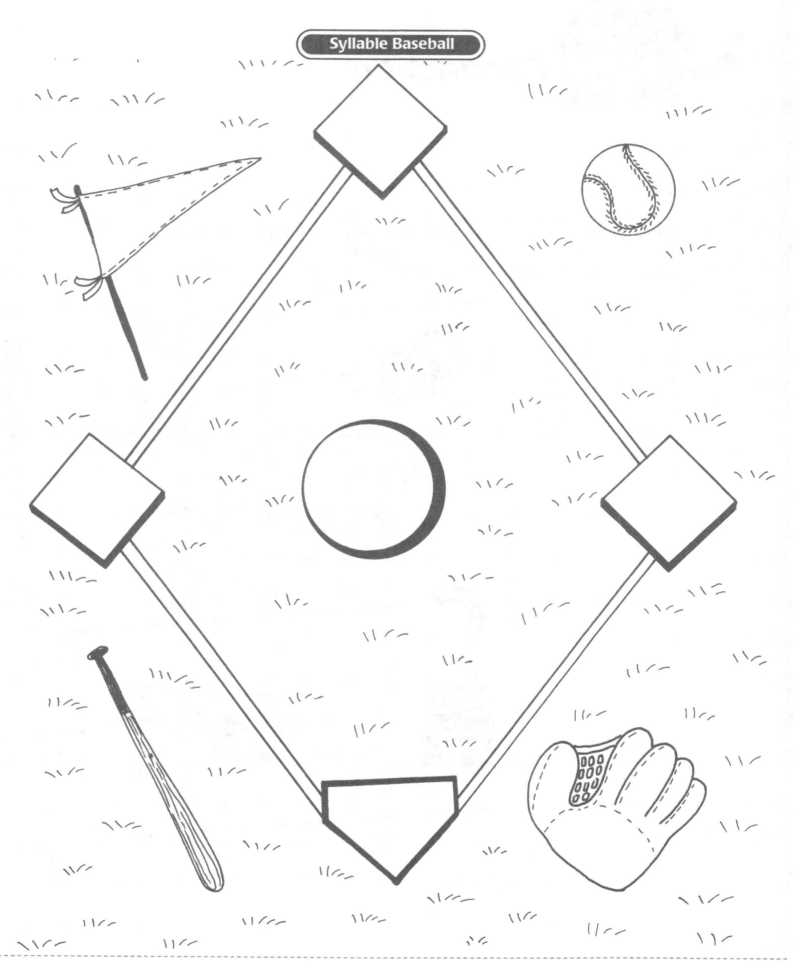

Syllable Baseball

Home Connection

HOME LETTER

A letter is available to be sent home at the beginning of Unit 6. This letter informs family members that students will be learning more about suffixes, words with multiple suffixes, plural forms of words, unusual plural forms, and the rules of syllabication. The suggested home activity revolves around "Animal Oddities." After finding suggested suffixes and plurals, the family discusses the subject of the poem. The child is also encouraged to collect unusual facts about other animals. This activity promotes interaction between child and family members while supporting the student's learning of reading and writing words with the targeted word study skills. A letter is also available in Spanish on page 135q.

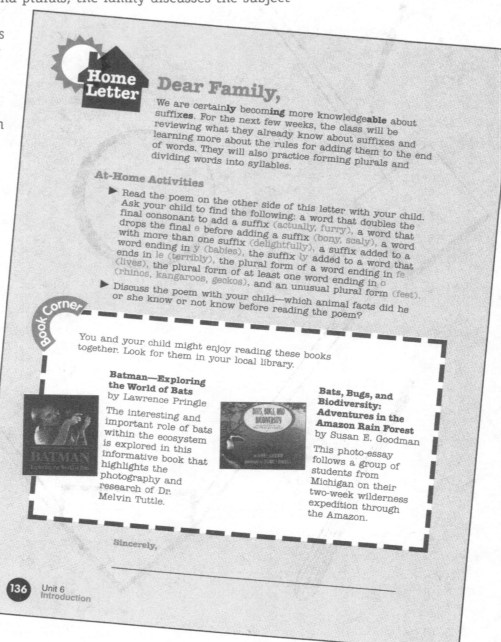

Home Letter

Dear Family,

We are certainly becoming more knowledgeable about suffixes. For the next few weeks, the class will be reviewing what they already know about suffixes and learning more about the rules for adding them to the end of words. They will also practice forming plurals and dividing words into syllables.

At-Home Activities

▶ Read the poem on the other side of this letter with your child. Ask your child to find the following: a word that doubles the final consonant to add a suffix (actually, furry), a word that drops the final e before adding a suffix (bony, scaly), a word with more than one suffix (delightfully), a suffix added to a word ending in y (babies), the suffix ly added to a word that ends in le (terribly), the plural form of a word ending in fe (lives), the plural form of at least one word ending in o (rhinos, kangaroos, geckos), and an unusual plural form (feet).

▶ Discuss the poem with your child—which animal facts did he or she know or not know before reading the poem?

Book Corner

You and your child might enjoy reading these books together. Look for them in your local library.

Batman—Exploring the World of Bats
by Lawrence Pringle

The interesting and important role of bats within the ecosystem is explored in this informative book that highlights the photography and research of Dr. Melvin Tuttle.

Bats, Bugs, and Biodiversity: Adventures in the Amazon Rain Forest
by Susan E. Goodman

This photo-essay follows a group of students from Michigan on their two-week wilderness expedition through the Amazon.

Sincerely,

Carta para la casa

Estimada familia,

En las próximas semanas, la clase va a repasar lo que ya conoce sobre los sufijos, y aprenderá más acerca de las reglas para añadirlos al final de las palabras en inglés. También va a practicar la formación de plurales y la división de palabras en sílabas.

Actividades para hacer en casa

He aquí algunas actividades que su hijo/a y ustedes pueden realizar juntos.

▶ Lean el poema en la página 135 con su hijo/a. Pídanle que encuentre lo siguiente: una palabra que dobla la consonante final para añadir el sufijo (**actually, furry**); una palabra que quita la **e** final antes de añadir el sufijo (**bony, scaly**); una palabra con más de un sufijo (**delightfully**); un sufijo añadido a una palabra que termina en **y** (**babies**); el sufijo **ly** añadido a una palabra que termina en **-le** (**terribly**); la forma plural de terminar una palabra en **o** (**rhinos, kangaroos, geckos**); y una forma inusual de plural (**feet**).

▶ Comenten las cosas "raras" con su hijo/a: ¿Qué datos él o ella conocía antes de leer el poema?

▶ Animen a su hijo/a a reunir una serie de datos raros sobre animales y úsenlos para impresionar a amigos y familiares.

Rincón del libro

Su hijo/a y ustedes pueden disfrutar juntos de la lectura de estos libros. Búsquenlos en la biblioteca de su localidad.

Batman—Exploring the World of Bats
por Lawrence Pringle

Este libro informativo, que destaca las fotografías y la investigación del Dr. Merlin Tuttle, explora el papel interesante e importante de los murciélagos dentro del ecosistema.

Bats, Bugs, and Biodiversity: Adventures in the Amazonian Rain Forest
por Susan E. Goodman

Este ensayo fotográfico sigue a un grupo de estudiantes de Michigan en una expedición de dos semanas por la selva del Amazonas.

Atentamente, _____

Unit 6
Pages 135–136

Suffixes, Plurals, and Syllables

> ### ASSESSING PRIOR KNOWLEDGE
>
> To assess students' prior knowledge of suffixes, plurals, and syllables, use the pretest on pages 135e–135f.

Unit Focus

USING THE PAGE

- Have a volunteer read "Animal Oddities" aloud as classmates follow along.
- Invite students to restate facts about each of the animals described.
- Which of the animals mentioned in the poem do students find most interesting, and why?
- **Critical Thinking** Encourage students to tell new things they learned in response to the question at the bottom of the page.

BUILDING A CONTEXT

- Write the words *terribly* and *bony* on the board. Have volunteers write the base word under each. (*terrible, bone*) Ask how each base was changed to spell the suffix form. (Final e was dropped before adding -*ly* and -*y*.)
- Write *rhino* and *rhinos*. Note that the plural is formed by adding -*s*. Ask students how to form plurals for other words that end in *o*, such as *hero*. (*heroes*)
- Write *feet* on the board. Ask how this plural form is special. (*The plural is formed with a vowel change instead of adding* -s.)
- Write the words *manatee, mermaid,* and *mealworms*. Ask volunteers how they would divide each word into syllables.

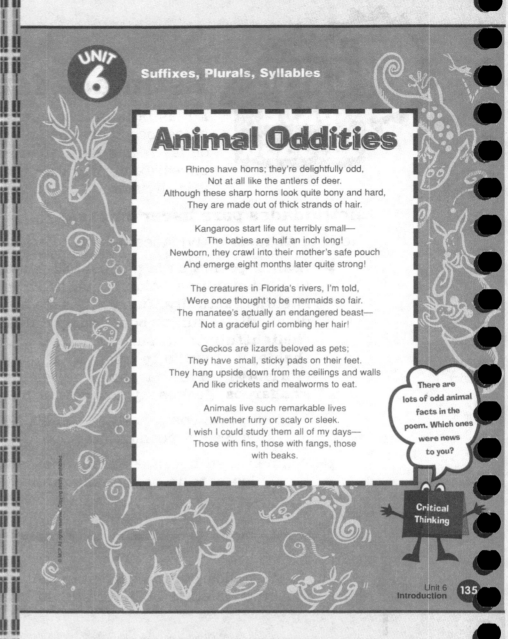

Animal Oddities

Rhinos have horns; they're delightfully odd,
Not at all like the antlers of deer.
Although these sharp horns look quite bony and hard,
They are made out of thick strands of hair.

Kangaroos start life out terribly small—
The babies are half an inch long!
Newborn, they crawl into their mother's safe pouch
And emerge eight months later quite strong!

The creatures in Florida's rivers, I'm told,
Were once thought to be mermaids so fair.
The manatee's actually an endangered beast—
Not a graceful girl combing her hair!

Geckos are lizards beloved as pets;
They have small, sticky pads on their feet.
They hang upside down from the ceilings and walls
And like crickets and mealworms to eat.

Animals live such remarkable lives
Whether furry or scaly or sleek.
I wish I could study them all of my days—
Those with fins, those with fangs, those
with beaks.

> There are lots of odd animal facts in the poem. Which ones were news to you?

Critical Thinking

Unit 6
Introduction   135

UNIT OPENER ACTIVITIES

DISCUSSING UNIQUE ANIMALS

Reread the poem together. Invite students to talk about other odd or interesting animal facts they know related to the animals in the poem or the animal world in general.

CHECK THAT FACT!

Challenge students to document the facts in the poem. Small groups might each focus on one of the animals. Have students list evidence they find in nonfiction books, references materials, and nature magazines to substantiate the poem's curious facts. Encourage them to add other information they discover also.

YOU AND YOUR GECKO

Geckos are popular pets. Have students contact a pet store for information about the cost, habits, requirements, and life span of these reptiles.

Home Letter

Dear Family,

We are certain**ly** becom**ing** more knowledg**eable** about suffix**es**. For the next few weeks, the class will be reviewing what they already know about suffixes and learning more about the rules for adding them to the end of words. They will also practice forming plurals and dividing words into syllables.

At-Home Activities

▶ Read the poem on the other side of this letter with your child. Ask your child to find the following: a word that doubles the final consonant to add a suffix (actually, furry), a word that drops the final e before adding a suffix (bony, scaly), a word with more than one suffix (delightfully), a suffix added to a word ending in y (babies), the suffix ly added to a word that ends in le (terribly), the plural form of a word ending in fe (lives), the plural form of at least one word ending in o (rhinos, kangaroos, geckos), and an unusual plural form (feet).

▶ Discuss the poem with your child—which animal facts did he or she know or not know before reading the poem?

Book Corner

You and your child might enjoy reading these books together. Look for them in your local library.

Batman—Exploring the World of Bats
by Lawrence Pringle

The interesting and important role of bats within the ecosystem is explored in this informative book that highlights the photography and research of Dr. Melvin Tuttle.

Bats, Bugs, and Biodiversity: Adventures in the Amazon Rain Forest
by Susan E. Goodman

This photo-essay follows a group of students from Michigan on their two-week wilderness expedition through the Amazon.

Sincerely,

_____

BULLETIN BOARD

Display a collection titled "Remarkable Animal Oddities." Invite students to draw pictures or display photographs of the animals in the poem on page 135. Have students add captions describing curious facts about each animal and underline the suffixes and plural forms.

Remarkable Animal Oddities

Rhinos have horns made out of thick hair.

Kangaroos start life out terribly small.

Geckos have sticky pads on their feet.

● The Home Letter on page 136 will familiarize family members with the phonics skills covered in this unit. Students should take home the page and complete the activities with a family member. Encourage them to look for one or both of the book suggestions in the library to read together.

● The Home Letter can also be found on page 135q in Spanish.

CURRICULUM CONNECTIONS ✳

WRITING

Have students write a letter to federal representatives, urging them to enact legislation protecting the manatee. Ask students to spend time adding thoughts to a draft of a whole-class letter. Before it is sent, display the letter on a chart or with an overhead projector and have students work together to edit and proofread a final version. Require students to back up their requests and comments with researched facts.

LITERATURE

Some students will enjoy reading folk tales, poetry, or other literature about mermaids. Have volunteers use library subject guides to gather materials that can be placed in the center for others to share.

SCIENCE

Make available resources that students can use to research the question of how lizards adapt to extreme temperature variations in the deserts, where many of them live. Students can expand their research to include adaptations of other desert animals or animal adaptations in different environments.

Lesson 62

Pages 137–138

Words That Double a Final Consonant to Add a Suffix

✳ ◆ ● ◆ ● ◆ ✳ ◆ ● ◆ ■ ◆ ●

Lesson Focus

INTRODUCING THE SKILL

- Write the following base words and suffixes on the board: *plan, clip, shop;* *-ed, -ing,* and *-er.*

- Invite volunteers to add the suffixes to each base word and write new words on the board. Ask how the spelling of each base word changed. (*The final letter was doubled before the suffix was added.*)

- Invite volunteers to add *-est* and *-ness* to the words *mad* and *dark.* (*maddest, madness, darkest, darkness*)

- Have students explain the spelling change for *maddest.* (*When a short vowel word ends in a single consonant, the consonant is usually doubled before adding a suffix that begins with a vowel.*)

USING THE PAGES

Review the Rule on page 137 and have students apply it to *mad* and *maddest.* Read the directions for pages 137 and 138. Afterward, discuss what students learned about adding a suffix to base words.

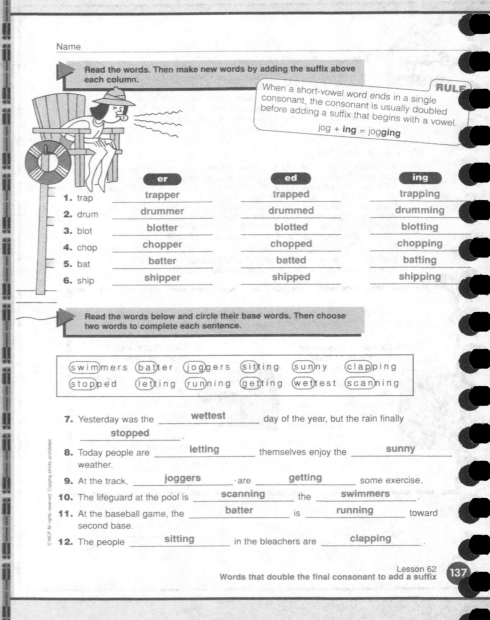

Name _____

Read the words. Then make new words by adding the suffix above each column.

> **RULE**
> When a short-vowel word ends in a single consonant, the consonant is usually doubled before adding a suffix that begins with a vowel.
>
> jog + **ing** = jog**ging**

		er	**ed**	**ing**
1.	trap	trapper	trapped	trapping
2.	drum	drummer	drummed	drumming
3.	blot	blotter	blotted	blotting
4.	chop	chopper	chopped	chopping
5.	bat	batter	batted	batting
6.	ship	shipper	shipped	shipping

Read the words below and circle their base words. Then choose two words to complete each sentence.

swim mers	bat ter	jog gers	sit ting	sun ny	clap ping
stop ped	let ting	run ning	get ting	wet test	scan ning

7. Yesterday was the ____**wettest**____ day of the year, but the rain finally ____**stopped**____.

8. Today people are ____**letting**____ themselves enjoy the ____**sunny**____ weather.

9. At the track, ____**joggers**____ are ____**getting**____ some exercise.

10. The lifeguard at the pool is ____**scanning**____ the ____**swimmers**____.

11. At the baseball game, the ____**batter**____ is ____**running**____ toward second base.

12. The people ____**sitting**____ in the bleachers are ____**clapping**____.

Lesson 62
Words that double the final consonant to add a suffix **137**

FOCUS ON ALL LEARNERS ✳ ● ◆ ■

ENGLISH LANGUAGE LEARNERS/ESL

Practice distinguishing between short and long vowels in words ending with single consonants in order to know when to double a final consonant. Have students add *-ing* to *clean, tap, float,* and *ship.* (*cleaning, tapping, floating, shipping*)

VISUAL LEARNERS

LARGE GROUP Write *-er, -ing,* and *-ed* on the board. Point out one of the suffixes and have students name base words to which that suffix can be added. List the base words and ask whether or not the base word changes when the suffix is added, and if so, how.

VISUAL LEARNERS

SMALL GROUP Have groups of students add suffixes *-er* and *-est* to adjectives *big, hot, tall, wet, cold,* and *fast* and use the words in factual sentences. Two groups can check the accuracy of one another's facts.

Circle each base word that ends in a single consonant. Then form new words by putting the base words and suffixes together.

(slip)	slipper	er	slipping	ing	slipped	ed
(bag)	bagger	er	baggage	age	bagged	ed
(glad)	gladly	ly	gladness	ness	gladdest	est
(scrub)	scrubber	er	scrubbing	ing	scrubbed	ed
(big)	bigger	er	biggest	est	bigness	ness
(jog)	jogger	er	jogged	ed	jogging	ing
(slim)	slimming	ing	slimmer	er	slimmest	est
arm	armful	ful	armed	ed	arming	ing
(mad)	madden	en	madder	er	madness	ness
pack	packed	ed	packing	ing	packer	er
(ship)	shippers	ers	shipped	ed	shipping	ing
(fit)	fitter	er	fitful	ful	fitting	ing
(can)	canned	ed	canning	ing	canner	er
rent	renter	er	rented	ed	renting	ing
(rip)	ripped	ed	ripping	ing	ripper	er
(flap)	flapping	ing	flapped	ed	flapper	er
chill	chilly	y	chilling	ing	chilled	ed
sharp	sharper	er	sharpen	en	sharpness	ness
(map)	mapped	ed	mapping	ing	maps	s
(clean)	cleaner	er	cleanest	est	cleaning	ing
(drop)	dropping	ing	dropped	ed	dropper	er
wild	wildly	ly	wilder	er	wildest	est
(flat)	flatter	er	flattest	est	flatten	en
(fog)	fogged	ed	fogging	ing	foggy	y
(slug)	slugging	ing	slugger	er	slugged	ed

(138) Lesson 62
Words that double the final consonant to add a suffix

AUDITORY LEARNERS

PARTNER Invite pairs if students to call out words from page 138 for one another to spell aloud.

GIFTED LEARNERS

Materials: newspapers

Invite students to circle words in a news article or in headlines in which final consonants appear to be doubled before a suffix. Have them list the words and their bases.

LEARNERS WHO NEED EXTRA SUPPORT

After students have completed page 138, review their answers and identify each feature of the base word and the suffix that must be considered when determining whether or not the final consonant of the base word is doubled. **See Daily Word Study Practice, pages 192-194.**

CURRICULUM CONNECTIONS

SPELLING

Use the following words and dictation sentences as a pretest for the first group of spelling words in Unit 6.

1. **jogging**   **Jogging** is good for your health.
2. **swimmers** The **swimmers** raced to the end of the pool.
3. **changing** The leaves are **changing** colors.
4. **hesitation** After a moment's **hesitation**, the driver turned left.
5. **peacefulness** A car horn disturbed the morning's **peacefulness**.
6. **generosity** Thanks to people's **generosity** the school has a new soccer field.
7. **studies**   Mark **studies** in the library.
8. **scariest** Lightning is the **scariest** part of a storm.
9. **possibly** It could not **possibly** snow.
10. **luckily** **Luckily**, the watch was found.

WRITING

Portfolio Have students pick ten of the base words plus suffixes from page 138. Have them use the words in a short story, perhaps about their favorite type of weather.

SOCIAL STUDIES

Have students use a map of South America to create questions to ask one another. Their questions might compare the size of South American countries, ask about the highest mountain range or the longest river, or the countries that are farthest from and closest to the U.S.

PHYSICAL EDUCATION

Have students learn and demonstrate some of the stretches that are recommended before running or jogging. Discuss the advantages of stretching before exercising.

Technology   AstroWord, Base Words & Endings. ©1998 Silver Burdett Ginn Inc. Division of Simon & Schuster.

Lesson 63

Pages 139–40

Words That Drop Final e to Add a Suffix

INFORMAL ASSESSMENT OBJECTIVE

Can students

✔ apply the spelling rules for adding suffixes to base words ending with *e*?

Lesson Focus

INTRODUCING THE SKILL

- On the board, write the words: *making, purely, closest,* and *receivable.*

- Call on a volunteer to name the base word and suffix for each word. (*make, -ing; pure, -ly; close, -est; receive, -able*)

- Ask which base words required a spelling change. (*make, close, receive*)

- Explain that the final *e* in *pure* was not dropped when the suffix was added because the suffix begins with a consonant.

- Invite students to read the rule on page 139 and apply it to the words on the board.

USING THE PAGES

Remind students to refer to the rule when doing the exercises on both pages. After students have completed the pages, review what they have learned about dropping final *e*.

Name _____

▶ Form new words by adding the suffixes.

> **RULE**
> When a word ends in a final **e**, usually the **e** is dropped before adding a suffix that begins with a vowel. Usually the **e** is not dropped when adding a suffix that begins with a consonant.
>
> change + **ing** = chang**ing**

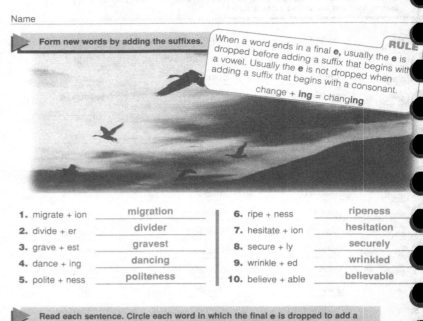

1. migrate + ion   migration
2. divide + er   divider
3. grave + est   gravest
4. dance + ing   dancing
5. polite + ness   politeness

6. ripe + ness   ripeness
7. hesitate + ion   hesitation
8. secure + ly   securely
9. wrinkle + ed   wrinkled
10. believe + able   believable

▶ Read each sentence. Circle each word in which the final e is dropped to add a suffix. Then write the base word of each circled word on the lines.

11. The (latest) grade Gary (received) in math wasn't very good.   late   receive
12. He (decided) it was (desirable) to work harder.   decide   desire
13. He (hoped) to do better and (believed) he could do it.   hope   believe
14. Everyone was (amazed) at his (determination.)   amaze   determine
15. Mr. Martin, his teacher, (praised) him as he (improved.)   praise   improve
16. Gary (derived) great pleasure from his continued (success.)   derive   continue

Lesson 63
Words that drop the final e to add a suffix   139

FOCUS ON ALL LEARNERS ✳ ● ◆ ■

ENGLISH LANGUAGE LEARNERS/ESL

Help students understand that the focus of this lesson is on the spelling of certain words with suffixes, rather than on the meaning of the suffixes.

VISUAL LEARNERS

PARTNER   Instruct pairs of students to divide a sheet of paper into two columns labeled *Final e Dropped* and *No Change.* Challenge students to think of ten words containing suffixes that fit a theme and write them in the appropriate column on the paper.

KINESTHETIC LEARNERS

SMALL GROUP   **Materials:** letter tiles

Have students obtain letter tiles from a commercial board game. Have them assemble the tiles into base words ending in *e* and then add suffixes, removing the final *e* when necessary. A point is earned for each letter in a word spelled correctly.

Form new words by adding suffixes. Remember, usually the final e is dropped if the suffix begins with a vowel.

1. startle + ing   **startling**
2. have + ing   **having**
3. mobile + ity   **mobility**
4. elevate + or   **elevator**
5. write + ing   **writing**
6. blue + est   **bluest**
7. compute + er   **computer**
8. sincere + ly   **sincerely**
9. hope + ful   **hopeful**
10. appreciate + ed   **appreciated**
11. decide + ed   **decided**
12. describe + able   **describable**
13. practice + ed   **practiced**
14. improve + ment   **improvement**
15. forgive + ness   **forgiveness**
16. guide + ance   **guidance**

Complete each sentence with one of the words you wrote.

17. Sarah helped Sue learn to use her new **computer** .
18. Sue wanted to use it for **writing** school papers.
19. She **appreciated** Sarah's help and wanted to do something for her in return.
20. She knew Sarah played softball but was **having** trouble with her hitting.
21. If Sarah could show an **improvement** , she might make the team.
22. Sue was the team's best hitter, so she **decided** to help Sarah.
23. She was **hopeful** that Sarah could do it.
24. The two girls **practiced** together every day.
25. With Sue's **guidance** , Sarah worked hard and made the team.

140

Lesson 63
Words that drop the final e to add a suffix

LARGE GROUP

AUDITORY LEARNERS

Challenge students to choose a base word and base word with suffix from pages 139 or 140 to use in a sentence; for example, *I use the computer to compute mathematical equations.*

GIFTED LEARNERS

Encourage students to give clues for words from pages 139 and 140 for a partner to guess and write the word.

LEARNERS WHO NEED EXTRA SUPPORT

List the following suffixes on the board: *-ing, -ly, -est, -able.* Have pairs of students make up a nonsense word that ends with *e*, such as *pote, duttle,* or *smake.* Help them determine whether or not the final *e* is dropped when each of the suffixes is added to the nonsense word. **See Daily Word Study Practice, pages 192-194.**

CURRICULUM CONNECTIONS ✳ ● ● ■ ◆ ●

SPELLING

Provide a list of spelling words: *jogging, swimmers, changing, hesitation, peacefulness, generosity, studies, scariest, possibly, luckily.*

Invite students to use a spelling word to complete the following analogies orally or in writing on the board.

1. Painter: paints as student: ____. (*studies*)
2. Cruelty: kindness as stinginess: ____. (*generosity*)
3. Dancer: dancing as jogger: ____. (*jogging*)
4. Soon: late as unfortunately: ____. (*luckily*)
5. Stage: actors as pool: ____. (*swimmers*)
6. Longer: longest as scarier: ____. (*scariest*)
7. Joy: happiness as calm: ____. (*peacefulness*)
8. Recognize: recognition as hesitate: ____. (*hesitation*)
9. Responsible: responsibility as possible: ____. (*possibility*)
10. Write: writing as change: ____. (*changing*)

WRITING

Portfolio

Have students write a Title-Down poem, in which the first letter of each line, when read vertically, spells out the subject of the poem. Encourage students to use suffix words built on base words with final *e*'s in the titles and the lines of their poems.

SCIENCE

Have students research important events in the history of computers. Have them look into how the first computers were invented and when home computers first became popular.

SOCIAL STUDIES

Have each student "score a run" by contributing one fact of baseball trivia to a class discussion. Students might find out places in the world where baseball is popular, locations of professional and Little League halls of fame, and milestones in the history of baseball.

Technology

AstroWord, Base Words & Endings. ©1998 Silver Burdett Ginn Inc. Division of Simon & Schuster.

140

Lesson 64

Pages 141–142

Words With More Than One Suffix

INFORMAL ASSESSMENT OBJECTIVES

Can students

✔ recognize multiple suffixes in words?

✔ apply spelling rules to add multiple suffixes to base words?

Lesson Focus

INTRODUCING THE SKILL

- Explain that many words have more than one suffix. Write *tearfully* on the board and ask a volunteer to name its base word. *(tear)* Point out that the word *tearfully* has two suffixes. The first is *-ful* and the second is *-ly*.

- Write these headings on the board: *Base Word, Suffix 1, Suffix 2*. List the following words and have volunteers fill in the base word and suffixes: *powerlessness, heartening, hardened, rigorously*.

- Allow time for students to suggest additional words with more than one suffix and add the words to the chart.

USING THE PAGES

Read and discuss the instructions for pages 141 and 142. After students have completed the pages, invite them to discuss what they learned about working with multiple suffixes.

Name

Mix and match these base words and suffixes. Decide which can go together to make new words with more than one suffix. You may use a suffix more than once. Write the words you make, and tell what each word means.

> **RULE**
> Many words have more than one suffix. Additional suffixes are added according to the rules you have learned.

ion
ful
moist
ive
ed
ish
en
thought
mystery
ness
vacate
act
peace
ly
ous
ing
courage
create
s
fool

Answers will vary. Possible answers are given.

	Word	Meaning
1.	peacefulness	state of being full of peace
2.	peacefully	in a way that is full of peace
3.	courageously	in a way that is brave
4.	foolishness	state of being silly
5.	moistened	made moist or damp
6.	moistening	making moist or damp
7.	thoughtfulness	state of being full of thought
8.	thoughtfully	in a way that is full of thought
9.	actions	things that are done
10.	actively	in a way that shows much action
11.	vacations	times spent free of school or work
12.	mysteriously	in a way that is full of mystery
13.	creations	things that are created
14.	creatively	in a way that is inventive

FOCUS ON ALL LEARNERS

ENGLISH LANGUAGE LEARNERS/ESL

Tell students that they can identify words with multiple suffixes by looking for familiar base words or roots in longer words. Help them determine whether the letters added to bases in a selection from one of their texts make up one or more suffixes.

VISUAL LEARNERS

LARGE GROUP Write the following suffixes and base words on the board: *-ed, -ing, -ly, -s, -en, -ness, -less, -ful, -able; enjoy, profit, care, law, mean, question, fear, thank, trust, quick, remark, pain*. Have students use the elements to create words with more than one suffix.

KINESTHETIC LEARNERS

INDIVIDUAL Have students write words with more than one suffix on separate slips of paper and then fold each strip to divide the word into its component parts.

> Combine each base word with two suffixes.

1. thought + ful + ness — **thoughtfulness**
2. sharp + en + ed — **sharpened**
3. awake + en + ed — **awakened**
4. fear + ful + ness — **fearfulness**
5. truth + ful + ness — **truthfulness**
6. celebrate + ion + s — **celebrations**
7. amaze + ing + ly — **amazingly**
8. power + less + ness — **powerlessness**
9. thank + ful + ness — **thankfulness**
10. cheer + ful + ly — **cheerfully**
11. wide + en + ing — **widening**
12. favor + able + ly — **favorably**
13. fright + en + ing — **frightening**
14. hope + ful + ly — **hopefully**
15. vacate + ion + s — **vacations**
16. disturb + ing + ly — **disturbingly**

> Use the words you wrote to complete the following sentences.

17. A person who never lies or cheats has the virtue of ___truthfulness___.

18. A synonym for *happily* is ___cheerfully___.

19. An antonym of *powerfulness* is ___powerlessness___.

20. The alarm clock ___awakened___ everyone at six o'clock this morning.

21. A synonym for *scary* is ___frightening___.

22. A pencil with a broken point needs to be ___sharpened___.

23. The traffic had to follow a detour because the road crews were ___widening___ the street.

24. There were many ___celebrations___ in our town when the high school football team won the championship.

25. Someone who is afraid is in a state of ___fearfulness___.

26. To be in agreement with something means to react ___favorably___ to it.

27. The two families took their summer ___vacations___ at the same time.

28. Their ___thoughtfulness___ in sending flowers was greatly appreciated.

(142) Lesson 64
Words with more than one suffix

AUDITORY LEARNERS

LARGE GROUP

As you call out each of the following words, ask for volunteers, in turn, to identify and spell the base word and the suffixes: *lessened, dictators, connections, gratefulness, migrations, hastened, cheerfulness, amazingly, container*.

GIFTED LEARNERS

Have students work in small groups to pick a letter and see how many words they list in three minutes that begin with that letter and have more than one suffix.

LEARNERS WHO NEED EXTRA SUPPORT

Materials: newspaper or magazine articles

Have students skim newspapers or magazines, circling words that have more than one suffix. Review their choices for accuracy and completeness. **See Daily Word Study Practice, pages 192-194.**

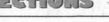

SPELLING

Have students complete the sentences with a spelling word: *jogging, swimmers, changing, hesitation, peacefulness, generosity, studies, scariest, possibly, luckily.*

1. Even good (*swimmers*) must be cautious in the ocean.
2. The mayor thanked Mrs. Jones for her (*generosity*) in donating land for a park.
3. Ben had to leave the room during the (*scariest*) part of the movie.
4. Dad bought new shoes for (*jogging*).
5. The bus can't (*possibly*) be late; I saw it leave school on time.
6. After a moment's (*hesitation*), Dad agreed to let me have a kitten.
7. The actors are (*changing*) into their costumes.
8. The family sat back to enjoy the (*peacefulness*) of the quiet summer night.
9. (*Luckily*) Jack found the dollar bill he had dropped.
10. My cousin (*studies*) Spanish in Mexico every summer.

WRITING

Portfolio Have students write about an occasion in which someone showed them unusual thoughtfulness. Have them describe what happened and analyze both the causes and effects of the person's special actionss.

LANGUAGE ARTS

Have students find examples of poems written in celebration of something, such as a holiday, a famous historic event, a heroic action, or a beautiful scene and present them to the class.

SCIENCE

Encourage students to find information about amazingly unique inventions and how they can be created.

Technology **AstroWord**, Base Words & Endings; Suffixes. ©1998 Silver Burdett Ginn Inc. Division of Simon & Schuster.

Lesson 65

Pages 143–144

Adding Suffixes to Words Ending in -y

INFORMAL ASSESSMENT OBJECTIVE

Can students

✔ understand and apply the spelling rules for adding suffixes to base words ending with -*y*?

Lesson Focus

INTRODUCING THE SKILL

- On the board, write the words *decoys, supplies, multiplied, multiplying,* and *destroyer.*

- Ask volunteers to spell the base word for each word and tell if there was or was not a spelling change when the suffix was added.

- Read the following rules and have students identify the word on the board that applies:

1. If a word ends in -*y* preceded by a vowel, make it plural by adding -*s*.
2. If a word ends in *y* preceded by a consonant, make it plural by changing the *y* to *i* and adding -*es*.
3. If a word ends in *y* preceded by a consonant, change the *y* to *i* before adding any suffix except -*ing*.
4. If a word ends in *y* preceded by a vowel, just add the suffix.

USING THE PAGES

You may wish to work through the first four items on the page together. Review the directions for the remaining sections of pages 143 and 144. Later, review students work.

Name _____

> Study the examples. Then complete the rules for adding suffixes to words ending in **y**.

Forming Plurals		Adding Other Suffixes	
study—studies	valley—valleys	funny—funnier	occupy—occupying
story—stories	bay—bays	heavy—heaviest	obey—obeyed

1. If a word ends in **y** preceded by a consonant, make it plural by changing the **y** to _____i_____ and adding the letters _____es_____ .
2. If a word ends in **y** preceded by a vowel, make it plural by adding _____s_____ .
3. If a word ends in **y** preceded by a consonant, change the letter _____y_____ to _____i_____ before adding any suffix except **ing**.
4. If a word ends in **y** preceded by a _____vowel_____ , just add the suffix.

> Combine each base word and suffix. Then write the new word to complete each sentence.

5. Mike and Jeff went to the carnival and (stay + ed) _____stayed_____ until closing time.
6. Mike went on more rides than Jeff, so he felt (dizzy + er) _____dizzier_____ .
7. They both agreed that a new ride, the Tornado, was the (scary + est) _____scariest_____ .
8. They (try + ed) _____tried_____ their luck at the games and won some prizes.
9. Mike and Jeff both had a very (enjoy + able) _____enjoyable_____ time.
10. There were so many (activity + s) _____activities_____ , they wished they could stay longer.
11. They made plans to return in a few (day + s) _____days_____ .

Lesson 65
Adding suffixes to words ending in y   **143**

FOCUS ON ALL LEARNERS

ENGLISH LANGUAGE LEARNERS/ESL

Before beginning page 143, ask if students have ever been to a carnival. Can they describe or remember the names of the rides they went on? Discuss different rides at fairs and amusement parks.

VISUAL LEARNERS

LARGE GROUP Brainstorm words whose base words end in *y*, such as *beautiful, decoys, enjoyable, parties,* and *trying.* Write the words on the board and call on volunteers to identify the rule applied for adding each suffix.

KINESTHETIC/VISUAL LEARNERS

SMALL GROUP Have students work together to create another crossword or other word puzzle using words from the lessons. Copies can be made for classmates to solve.

> **Make new words by adding the suffixes.**

1. turkey + s   turkeys
2. occupy + es   occupies
3. pry + ed   pried
4. canary + es   canaries
5. lazy + er   lazier
6. healthy + est   healthiest
7. sky + es   skies
8. spy + es   spies
9. bossy + er   bossier
10. study + ed   studied
11. sentry + es   sentries
12. dirty + er   dirtier

> **Use the words you wrote to complete the crossword puzzle.**

Across

2. tried to learn
4. lives in
6. guards
9. more covered with grime than another
10. large birds that are eaten by many people on Thanksgiving Day

Down

1. having the best health of all
2. people who keep secret watch on the actions of others.
3. more fond of telling others what to do than another
5. small yellow birds that sing sweetly
7. the heavens
8. raised, moved, or forced with a lever

AUDITORY LEARNERS

PARTNER Have pairs of students read the four rules on page 143 aloud to each other, one at a time, and think of examples for each one.

GIFTED LEARNERS

Have learners copy the crossword puzzle on page 144 and then try to expand it, adding at least three new words that end in -y and have suffixes. They should write the clues as well.

LEARNERS WHO NEED EXTRA SUPPORT

Have pairs of students review the words used to complete the crossword puzzle on page 144. Have them identify the word ending in -y to which each ending has been added. **See Daily Word Study Practice, pages 192-194.**

CURRICULUM CONNECTIONS

SPELLING

Divide the class into two teams to hold a spelling bee. Each time you say a spelling word, the first person in line calls out the first letter, the second member calls out the second letter, and so on. The spelling words are *jogging, swimmers, changing, hesitation, peacefulness, generosity, studies, scariest, possibly, luckily.*

WRITING

Portfolio Have students write a short story about spies. The story should have clear problems and solutions, a vivid setting, and clearly defined characters. Encourage students to use words that end in -y and have suffixes.

MATH

Have students research what makes different people happy. Have them work together to produce and conduct a "happiness survey." After conducting the survey, they should present the results in chart form. Who are the happiest people?

SCIENCE

Have students look up information about domestic and wild turkeys and create a chart or diagram to compare and contrast the features of the two types.

AstroWord, Base Words & Endings; Suffixes. ©1998 Silver Burdett Ginn Inc. Division of Simon & Schuster.

Lesson 66

Pages 145–146

Adding Suffix -ly to Words Ending in -y or -le

INFORMAL ASSESSMENT OBJECTIVE

Can students

✔ understand and apply the spelling rules for adding the suffix *-ly* to base words ending with *-y* or *-le*?

Lesson Focus

INTRODUCING THE SKILL

- Write the following words on the board: *gently, dreamily, creepily, terribly,* and *nobly*. Invite students to identify each base word and tell how each was changed when the suffix *-ly* was added.

- As you read the following rules, ask students to apply them to the words on the board.

1. When a word ends in *-le*, drop the *le* before adding *-ly*.
2. When a word ends in *-y* preceded by a consonant, change the *y* to *i* before adding *-ly*.

USING THE PAGES

Relate the words in the box on page 145 to the rules below them and the examples on the board. Be sure students understand the goal of each exercise on pages 145 and 146. After they have completed the exercises, encourage them to discuss what they have learned about adding the suffix *-ly*.

Name _____

▶ **Study the examples. Then complete the rules.**

heavy + ly = heavily	wobble + ly = wobbly
cheery + ly = cheerily	feeble + ly = feebly

1. When a word ends in **y** preceded by a consonant, follow this rule to add the suffix **ly**:
   Change the letter ___y___ to ___i___ before adding **ly**.

2. When a word ends in **le**, follow this rule to add the suffix **ly**:
   Drop the letters ___le___ and add **ly**.

▶ **Add the suffix ly to each word. Then complete the sentences, using words you formed.**

3. easy ___easily___   4. possible ___possibly___   5. lucky ___luckily___
6. simple ___simply___   7. happy ___happily___   8. noble ___nobly___
9. bubble ___bubbly___   10. hearty ___heartily___   11. hasty ___hastily___
12. sleepy ___sleepily___   13. thrifty ___thriftily___   14. wiggle ___wiggly___

15. Jenny wasn't fully awake yet, so she ___sleepily___ got out of bed.

16. She realized she had overslept and ___hastily___ tried to get ready.

17. She couldn't ___possibly___ be late for school today.

18. ___Luckily___, the school bus was a little late so she caught it in time.

19. Jenny is such a good speller that she ___easily___ won the spelling bee.

20. She ___simply___ took her time spelling each word.

21. She smiled ___happily___, glad that she had been on time.

Lesson 66
Adding suffix ly to words ending in y or le   **145**

FOCUS ON ALL LEARNERS ✳ ◦ ◆ ■

ENGLISH LANGUAGE LEARNERS/ESL

Explore with students the ways in which the modifications made when adding *-ly* to words ending in *-y* or *-le* effect the pronunciation of the resulting words.

VISUAL LEARNERS

PARTNER   Invite pairs of students to look through fiction books in the classroom to find words ending in *-ly* built on base words ending with *-y* or *-le*. Have them log the words on paper.

KINESTHETIC LEARNERS

SMALL GROUP   Have students write words from page 146 on the board as word equations for classmates to solve, such as *heavy + ly = (heavily)*.

Choose a word from the box that fits each clue and write it on the line. Then circle each word you wrote in the puzzle below. Some of the words in the puzzle go across, and others go down.

heavily	ably	pebbly	nimbly	crackly	dizzily
wobbly	busily	easily	creepily	nobly	feebly
simply	prickly	sleepily	sparkly	angrily	lazily
greedily	saucily	happily	sloppily	drizzly	wiggly

1. __angrily__ in an angry way
2. __drizzly__ weather that is damp and misty
3. __pebbly__ the way an ocean beach filled with small stones looks
4. __lazily__ in a lazy way
5. __busily__ in a busy way
6. __wobbly__ like a chair that would move from side to side if you sat on it
7. __sparkly__ how fireworks look
8. __crackly__ how fire sounds
9. __greedily__ in a greedy way
10. __easily__ in an easy way
11. __ably__ the way a competent person does something
12. __sleepily__ in a sleepy way
13. __simply__ in a simple way

A N B R G W O B B L Y D S S
S A N G R I L Y D E P R I L
P B A E E C P D F W A I M E
A U A A E I E A B L Y Z P E
R S G S D R B L S D I Z L P
K I U I I P B W B L M L Y I
L L G L L B L A Z I L Y T L
Y Y H Y Y Z Y C R A C K L Y

146 Lesson 66
Adding suffix -ly to words ending in y or le

AUDITORY LEARNERS

LARGE GROUP

Read aloud the words *scary*, *jumpy*, *drizzle*, *twinkle*, *single*, and *hungry*. Ask students to pronounce and then spell each word after adding the suffix *-ly*.

GIFTED LEARNERS

Challenge pairs of students to write as many pairs of antonyms as they can that end with the suffix *-ly*.

LEARNERS WHO NEED EXTRA SUPPORT

Have students write sentences using the words they circled in the puzzle at the bottom of page 146. **See Daily Word Study Practice, pages 192-194.**

SPELLING

Use these words and dictation sentences as a posttest for the first group of spelling words for Unit 6.

1. **generosity** Few people know about Aunt Martha's **generosity**.
2. **scariest** The **scariest** part of the accident was when Alan fainted.
3. **jogging** My dog and I go **jogging** each day.
4. **luckily** **Luckily** I found the information on the Internet.
5. **peacefulness** The music created a mood of **peacefulness**.
6. **changing** The students are **changing** classes.
7. **studies** Jed's mom **studies** computer programming.
8. **possibly** No one could **possibly** rake all those leaves in an hour.
9. **hesitation** Jesse solved the problem without any **hesitation**.
10. **swimmers** **Swimmers** are not allowed in this part of the river.

WRITING

Portfolio Have students write a letter to a friend describing a real or imaginary fireworks display. The letter may be informal in style, but should use correct grammar, spelling, and mechanics. Encourage students to use words that add the suffix *-ly* to words ending in *-y* or *-le*.

SCIENCE

Have students research the history of fireworks and safety precautions needed for their manufacture and use.

SOCIAL STUDIES

Challenge students to list and share as many discoveries or inventions made in China as they can.

Technology

AstroWord, Base Words & Endings. ©1998 Silver Burdett Ginn Inc. Division of Simon & Schuster.

Lesson 67

Pages 147–148

Plural Forms for Words Ending in -f or -fe

INFORMAL ASSESSMENT OBJECTIVE

Can students

✔ apply the spelling rules for forming plurals of words ending with -f, -ff, or -fe?

Lesson Focus

INTRODUCING THE SKILL

- On the board, write the words *lives, shelves,* and *whiffs.*

- Point to the words *lives* and *shelves* and ask how the base words were changed when the suffix -es was added. Ask if the base word *whiff* was changed when the suffix -es was added. (*no*)

- Have students write on the board the plurals of *chief, belief, reef,* and *roof.* (*chiefs, beliefs, reefs, roofs*)

- Have students turn to page 147 and read the rule in the box at the top of the page. Then invite volunteers to apply the rule to each word on the board.

USING THE PAGES

Identify the pictures on page 148 and review the directions for both pages. After students have completed the exercises, discuss what they have learned about the plural forms of words ending in -f, -ff, or -fe.

Name _____

▶ Write the plural form of each word on the lines below.

1. wolf	wolves	2. elf	elves	
3. cuff	cuffs	4. hoof	hooves	
5. thief	thieves	6. knife	knives	
7. muff	muffs	8. puff	puffs	
9. calf	calves	10. scarf	scarves	
11. roof	roofs	12. reef	reefs	
13. sniff	sniffs	14. cliff	cliffs	
15. staff	staffs	16. chief	chiefs	
17. sheaf	sheaves	18. life	lives	

RULES

If a word ends in **f** or **fe**, usually change the **f** or **fe** to **v** and add **es** to make the word plural. Exceptions to this rule are *chief, belief, reef,* and *roof.* A word that ends in **ff** is made plural by adding **s**.

wolf—wol**ves**   cliff—cliff**s**
knife—kni**ves**   chief—chief**s**

▶ For each clue or definition below, write the correct plural word.

19. __wolves__ — wild animals, similar to dogs
20. __hooves__ — horses' feet
21. __calves__ — baby cattle
22. __knives__ — cutting instruments
23. __chiefs__ — heads of tribes
24. __sniffs__ — what your nose does
25. __roofs__ — tops of houses
26. __thieves__ — outlaws who steal
27. __cuffs__ — bands around the wrists
28. __elves__ — tiny imaginary folk
29. __scarves__ — cloths worn on the head or neck
30. __reefs__ — ridges of rocks in an ocean or lake, often made of coral
31. __cliffs__ — steep sides of rocks
32. __puffs__ — short bursts of smoke or steam
33. __staffs__ — sticks or poles used for support when walking

Lesson 67
Plural form for words ending in f or fe   **147**

FOCUS ON ALL LEARNERS

ENGLISH LANGUAGE LEARNERS/ESL

Explain that it is necessary to memorize the exceptions to the first rule, which you wrote on the board, because there is no general rule to cover them. (In other words, to memorize examples such as *chiefs* and *roofs.*)

VISUAL LEARNERS

SMALL GROUP

Tell students to write six sentences using the plural form of words that end in -f, -fe, and -ff. Then suggest that they exchange papers with a partner. Have each partner underline the plural form of each word and write the singular form.

KINESTHETIC LEARNERS

LARGE GROUP

Invite students to scramble the letters of plural forms of words from the lesson for classmates to rewrite.

Write the plural word that describes each picture.

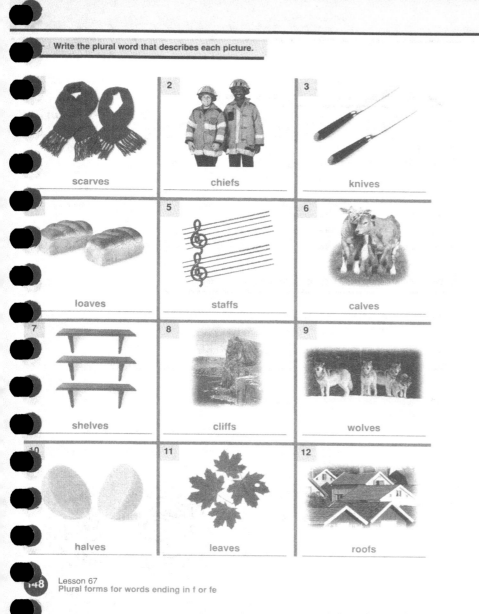

1. scarves	2. chiefs	3. knives
4. loaves	5. staffs	6. calves
7. shelves	8. cliffs	9. wolves
10. halves	11. leaves	12. roofs

Lesson 67
Plural forms for words ending in f or fe

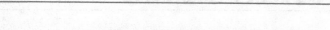

AUDITORY LEARNERS

PARTNER Suggest that pairs of students work together having one student name a base word from the lesson for a partner to spell the plural form. Partners can then switch roles.

GIFTED LEARNERS

Have students create riddles, the answers to which are plural forms of words ending in -f or -fe.

LEARNERS WHO NEED EXTRA SUPPORT

Have students write the singular form of each word they wrote for the exercise on page 148. **See Daily Word Study Practice, pages 192-194.**

CURRICULUM CONNECTIONS ✳ ● ◆ ■ ◆ ●

SPELLING

Use the following words and dictation sentences as a pretest for the second group of words in Unit 6.

1. **knives**   This store will sharpen dull **knives**.
2. **chiefs**   The photo shows Native American **chiefs**.
3. **potatoes**   Pierce the skins of the **potatoes** before baking.
4. **tornadoes**   **Tornadoes** are dangerous storms.
5. **scissors**   These **scissors** are rusty.
6. **series**   The library has a **series** of books about famous disasters.
7. **misunderstanding** You and I had a **misunderstanding**.
8. **apologized**   No one could **possibly** rake all those leaves in an hour.
9. **appreciated** The coach **appreciated** the team's hard work.
10. **unfortunately Unfortunately**, Alex had already seen the movie.

WRITING

Portfolio Ask students to write their own dictionary definition for each term they wrote on the lines on page 148, including singular and plural forms of the word.

SOCIAL STUDIES

Have students research the responsibilities of *chief of staff*. Then ask them to locate references to the current White House Chief of Staff in the newspaper or television news.

SCIENCE/SOCIAL STUDIES

Have half the class look up facts about the characteristics and habits of wolves, while the other half looks up stories and myths about these animals. Have each group share their findings and compare features of the animals expressed in the different forms.

Technology

AstroWord, Base Words & Endings. ©1998 Silver Burdett Ginn Inc. Division of Simon & Schuster.

Lesson 68
Pages 149–150

Plural Form for Words Ending in -o

INFORMAL ASSESSMENT OBJECTIVE

Can students

✔ apply the spelling rules for forming plurals of words ending with -o?

Lesson Focus

INTRODUCING THE SKILL

- Explain to students that if a word ends in -o, -s is usually added to make the word plural. Exceptions such as *tomato, potato, hero, echo,* and *torpedo* are made plural by adding -es.

- Have students generate a list of nouns that end with -o and write each word on the board.

- Have volunteers select a word on the board and add the suffix that is used to form its plural. Tell students to write each newly formed word on a sheet of paper.

USING THE PAGES

Ask a volunteer to read the rule on page 149. Have students apply it to the sample words in the box and words written on the board. Be sure students understand the directions for the exercises on pages 149 and 150. After they have finished these exercises, discuss what they have learned about plural forms of words ending in -o.

Name _____

▶ Form the plural of each word by adding s or es.

1. stereo **s**   2. solo **s**
3. hero **es**   4. tempo **s**
5. photo **s**   6. poncho **s**
7. rodeo **s**   8. tomato **es**
9. avocado **s**   10. domino **s**
11. piccolo **s**   12. burro **s**
13. piano **s**   14. radio **s**
15. tuxedo **s**   16. kangaroo **s**

> **RULE**
> If a word ends in **o**, an **s** is usually added to make the word plural. For some exceptions, the plural is formed by adding **es**.
>
> potato—potato**es**   echo—echo**es**
> buffalo—buffalo**es**   hero—hero**es**
> torpedo—torpedo**es**   tornado—tornado**es**

▶ Write a plural word from above to complete each sentence.

17. At the outdoor cafe, Maria and Tim ordered tuna salad with juicy red _____ tomatoes _____.

18. It was chilly out, so they were glad they had worn their _____ ponchos _____.

19. Maria brought her camera and hoped to get some _____ photos _____ of the concert.

20. They had listened to the musicians on their _____ stereos _____ but had never seen them.

21. They arrived just as two men in black _____ tuxedos _____ came on stage.

22. The men sat at _____ pianos _____ and played several duets.

23. Then they took turns playing _____ solos _____.

24. Later they were joined by a quartet of flutes and _____ piccolos _____.

25. Tim enjoyed the ballads, but Maria liked the songs with livelier _____ tempos _____.

Lesson 68
Plural form for words ending in o   **149**

FOCUS ON ALL LEARNERS

ENGLISH LANGUAGE LEARNERS/ESL

Review with students the list of words at the top of page 150 that will be used to do the puzzle.

VISUAL LEARNERS

SMALL GROUP

Have students choose plural forms of words ending with -o to use with adjectives to write descriptive phrases, such as *vine-ripened tomatoes, crispy fried potatoes,* and *dangerously destructive tornadoes.*

KINESTHETIC LEARNERS

INDIVIDUAL Materials: newspapers, scissors

Have students search through newspaper adds to cut out and highlight base words and plural forms of words ending in -o.

The plural forms of the words in the word bank will help you answer the questions. Use the plural words to complete the crossword puzzle.

photo	soprano	rodeo	solo	piano	tornado
potato	tomato	avocado	sombrero	kangaroo	torpedo

Across

1. What are red and juicy and used in making spaghetti sauce?
3. What are hopping animals found in Australia called?
7. What can a photographer take?
9. What are violent, whirling, funnel-shaped clouds with high winds?
10. What are pieces of music for one voice or one instrument called?
11. In what kinds of contests do contestants ride horses bareback for 10 seconds?

Down

2. What are cigar-shaped missiles used under water called?
4. What do you call broad-brimmed hats that tie under the chin?
5. What are pear-shaped fruits with large pits in the middle?
6. Who are people with the highest singing voices?
7. Which vegetables taste good baked, mashed, French fried, or scalloped?
8. For which instruments did Mozart and Chopin write music?

Across/Down answers in crossword:
TOMATOES, KANGAROOS, PHOTOS, TORNADOES, SOLOS, RODEOS, PIANOS, SOPRANOS, TORPEDOES, SOMBREROS, AVOCADOS, POTATOES

AUDITORY LEARNERS

LARGE GROUP

Read aloud riddles or definitions of words that end in -o. Form the clue to lead to a plural answer. Have students correctly spell each plural form; for example, *We are the highest kind of women's singing voice.* (sopranos)

GIFTED LEARNERS

Have pairs of learners trace the etymology of selected words that end in -o, such as *potato, tomato, avocado, rodeo,* and *tornado.*

LEARNERS WHO NEED EXTRA SUPPORT

Have partners create lists of words that end in *o*. Have them drill each other on how to spell the plurals of these words until they are satisfied they have mastered each example. **See Daily Word Study Practice, pages 192-194.**

CURRICULUM CONNECTIONS

SPELLING

Suggest that each student choose the plural form of a word that ends in -o to dictate for the class to write. As each word is given, the student should also use it in a sentence. Begin with words from the spelling list:

potatoes   We like mashed **potatoes** best.

tornadoes   **Tornadoes** can suck up and destroy almost anything in their path.

WRITING

Portfolio Invite students to get together with a partners to write riddles using words that end with -o. Display the riddles on a bulletin board and have classmates solve them.

SCIENCE/SOCIAL STUDIES

Have students find books or articles about Australia and read about animals, plants, and environments unique to that continent. Ask them to report briefly on what they have learned.

FINE ARTS

Encourage students who play the piano to prepare and play piano duets for the class.

Technology

AstroWord, Base Words & Endings. ©1998 Silver Burdett Ginn Inc. Division of Simon & Schuster.

Lesson 69
Pages 151–152

Other Plural Forms

INFORMAL ASSESSMENT OBJECTIVE

Can students

✔ write the plural forms of irregular nouns?

Lesson Focus

INTRODUCING THE SKILL

- Display the following on the board.

Singular	_Plural_
sheep	sheep
salmon	salmon
crisis	crises
child	children
tooth	teeth

- Call on a volunteer to read the singular and plural forms of each word. Lead students to the conclusion that some words change in their plural form while others remain the same.

- Give students an opportunity to suggest additional examples, writing the singular and plural forms of the words on the board. Have students use the words in sentences.

USING THE PAGES

- Have students read and discuss the two boxed rules and the sample words on page 151. Review the directions for both pages. Afterward, ask students to summarize what they know about irregular plural forms.

- **Critical Thinking** Invite students to respond to the question on page 152.

151

Name _____

▶ The words in the word bank are the same in their singular and plural forms. Choose one of the words to complete each pair of sentences.

> **RULE** Some words do not change at all in their plural form.

sauerkraut	aircraft	spinach	spaghetti	oatmeal
salmon	broccoli	trout	zucchini	scissors
series	moose	wheat		

1. The _____**moose**_____ had large antlers.
   The herd of _____**moose**_____ was headed toward the lake.
2. A small, two-engine _____**aircraft**_____ just landed.
   Three jet _____**aircraft**_____ took off within the last ten minutes.
3. She picked a _____**zucchini**_____ from the garden.
   The recipe called for three _____**zucchini**_____

▶ Complete each phrase by writing the plural of the word in parentheses. You may use your dictionary.

> **RULE** A few words change completely in their plural form. Other plural forms may not be familiar because they come from other languages.
> tooth—teeth   crisis—crises
> ox—oxen   phenomenon—phenomena

4. six wild _____**geese**_____ (goose)
5. three lovely _____**women**_____ (woman)
6. four watery _____**oases**_____ (oasis)
7. five generous _____**alumni**_____ (alumnus)
8. six tiny _____**mice**_____ (mouse)
9. two dangerous _____**bacteria**_____ (bacterium)
10. two tired _____**feet**_____ (foot)
11. six annoying _____**lice**_____ (louse)
12. five handsome _____**men**_____ (man)
13. eight noisy _____**children**_____ (child)

Lesson 69
Other plural forms **151**

FOCUS ON ALL LEARNERS ✳ • ◆ ▪ ◆

ENGLISH LANGUAGE LEARNERS/ESL

Ask students if they can think of any words in their first language whose plurals are formed other than with -s or -es.

VISUAL LEARNERS

LARGE GROUP Write these words on the board: _woman, parentheses, mice, bacteria, curriculum, macaroni, oxen,_ and _scissors._ Have students label each word _singular, plural,_ or _both._

KINESTHETIC LEARNERS

PARTNER Challenge pairs of students to design a word-search puzzle using plurals. Have them create a clue for each word.

Complete the sentences with the plural forms of the words in parentheses.

1. The Smiths and the Carters were going to the college's _____alumni_____ picnic.
   (alumnus)

2. That morning, the Carters' daughter lost two loose _____teeth_____.
   (tooth)

3. Mrs. Smith saw two _____mice_____ in her basement while getting the picnic basket.
   (mouse)

4. Despite these _____crises_____, both families were ready to leave on schedule.
   (crisis)

5. The picnic ground was near the woods, and they saw some _____deer_____.
   (deer)

6. There was a lake nearby with more _____geese_____ than they had ever seen.
   (goose)

7. The _____women_____ had made sandwiches and brought _____popcorn_____
   (woman)   (popcorn)
   for snacks.

8. Their husbands had made a salad of _____spinach_____, _____zucchini_____,
   (spinach)   (zucchini)
   and tomatoes.

9. After lunch, some of the _____men_____ and _____women_____ decided to take
   (man)   (woman)
   advantage of the fishing.

10. They had fished for _____salmon_____ but had never fished for _____trout_____.
    (salmon)   (trout)

11. The _____children_____ hiked through the woods
    (child)

    until their _____feet_____ hurt.
    (foot)

> What besides the scenic flights would you consider a "highlight" of the picnic, and why?

12. They were sure they had spotted two
    _____moose_____ with big antlers.
    (moose)

13. They were told that they probably had seen
    _____elk_____
    (elk)

14. The highlight was scenic flights over the lake in two
    _____aircraft_____.
    (aircraft)

Critical Thinking

152 Lesson 69
     Other plural forms

AUDITORY LEARNERS

LARGE GROUP

Read aloud the answers to the exercise on page 152 and ask volunteers to identify whether each word is singular, plural, or both.

GIFTED LEARNERS

Challenge students to use phrases from page 151 or phrases of their own to write rhyming couplets; for example, *A disgusting bacterium has invaded my aquarium.*

LEARNERS WHO NEED EXTRA SUPPORT

Have students write sentences using the singular and plural forms of words from this lesson. Remind them that some forms will be the same. **See Daily Word Study Practice, pages 192-194.**

CURRICULUM CONNECTIONS ✳ ● ◆ ■   ● ◆

SPELLING

As you read the following word equations aloud, have students write or spell aloud the answer. Use:

knife x 2 (*knives*)
chief x 2 (*chiefs*)
potato x 2 (*potatoes*)
tornado x 2 (*tornadoes*)
scissors x 2 (*scissors*)
series x 2 (*series*)
mis + understanding (*misunderstanding*),
apologize + ed (*apologized*)
appreciate + ed (*appreciated*)
un + fortunate + ly (*unfortunately*).

WRITING

Portfolio Have students write a nonsense poem for younger children that uses as many of the types of plural forms highlighted in this lesson as possible. Have them illustrate their poems and share them with students in primary grades or with younger siblings.

SCIENCE

Have students research game such as deer and fish to learn if they live in the local area, how large the population is, and when hunting is allowed.

HEALTH

Have students identify what lice are, how they are transmitted, how to avoid catching them, and how to end an infestation if one should occur.

Technology

AstroWord, Base Words & Endings. ©1998 Silver Burdett Ginn Inc. Division of Simon & Schuster.

152

Lesson 70

Pages 153–154

Syllables

INFORMAL ASSESSMENT OBJECTIVES

Can students

✔ identify the number of syllables in words?

✔ divide compound words and words that end in *-le* into syllables?

Lesson Focus

INTRODUCING THE SKILL

- Write the following words on the board: *scramble, speckle, rattlesnake, notebook, grandmother, driveway, rowboat, snapshot, table, thimble,* and *wiggle.*

- State the following rules: When a compound word is made up of two single-syllable words, it is divided between the words that make up the compound (otherwise, it follows the regular rules of syllabication); words that end in *-le* preceded by a consonant are divided before the consonant.

- Have volunteers divide each word on the board into syllables according to the rules.

USING THE PAGES

Read the directions for pages 153 and 154 and review the rules and examples on page 154. Introduce the poetry form *haiku*. When students have completed the activities, have them check their work to assess what they know about syllables.

Name _____

▶ Write a word from the word bank to complete each sentence. Then list each word under the correct heading.

| apologized | misunderstanding | disagreements | unfairly | appreciated |
| endangered | unfortunately | sympathetic | unpleasant | understood |

1. Sometimes friends have serious __disagreements__ .
2. __Unfortunately__ , it happened to John and Carlos.
3. For two days, there were __unpleasant__ feelings between them.
4. Then John realized that he had treated Carlos __unfairly__ .
5. He knew he had __endangered__ their friendship.
6. He wanted to clear up the __misunderstanding__ .
7. He __apologized__ to Carlos for misjudging him.
8. Carlos __understood__ how John could have made the mistake.
9. John __appreciated__ Carlos's understanding.
10. It was good to have a friend who was so __sympathetic__ .

Three syllables

| endangered | unfairly |
| unpleasant | understood |

Four syllables

disagreements

apologized

sympathetic

Five syllables

unfortunately

misunderstanding

appreciated

Lesson 70
Syllables **153**

FOCUS ON ALL LEARNERS

ENGLISH LANGUAGE LEARNERS/ESL

Use word examples to review the difference between vowels and vowel sounds. For example, *actually* has four vowel sounds and four syllables; *breathing* has three vowels but only two vowel sounds.

VISUAL LEARNERS

PARTNER Suggest that pairs of students make a list of words with an increasing number of syllables. The first word will have one syllable, the second word two, and so on. A sample list might begin with *snow, asleep, butterfly, traditional, unbelievable,* and so on.

KINESTHETIC LEARNERS

LARGE GROUP Invite students to list antonym word pairs on the board that include twp-syllable words with *-le.* Students can take turns demonstrating the meaning of a word pair for the others to guess Include *giggle, frown; still, trembling; strong, feeble; nimble, lazy; tumble, rise; proud, humble; agree, quibble.*

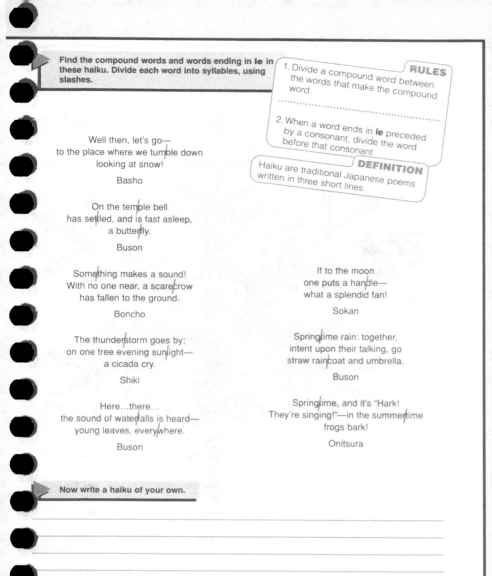

Find the compound words and words ending in **le** in these haiku. Divide each word into syllables, using slashes.

RULES
1. Divide a compound word between the words that make the compound word.
2. When a word ends in **le** preceded by a consonant, divide the word before that consonant.

DEFINITION
Haiku are traditional Japanese poems written in three short lines.

Well then, let's go—
to the place where we tum/ble down
looking at snow!

Basho

On the tem/ple bell
has set/tled, and is fast asleep,
a but/ter/fly.

Buson

Something makes a sound!
With no one near, a scare/crow
has fallen to the ground.

Boncho

The thunder/storm goes by;
on one tree evening sun/light—
a cicada cry.

Shiki

Here…there…
the sound of water/falls is heard—
young leaves, every/where.

Buson

If to the moon
one puts a han/dle—
what a splendid fan!

Sokan

Spring/time rain: together,
intent upon their talking, go
straw rain/coat and umbrella.

Buson

Spring/time, and it's "Hark!
They're singing!"—in the summer/time
frogs bark!

Onitsura

Now write a haiku of your own.

_____

_____

_____

AUDITORY/VISUAL LEARNERS

LARGE GROUP

As students read aloud the poems on page 154, have them count the number of syllables in each haiku. 17 syllables is the traditional count.

GIFTED LEARNERS

Call out a number from three to five and see how many words with that number of syllables students, in turn, can say in 30 seconds or a minute.

LEARNERS WHO NEED EXTRA SUPPORT

Read aloud with students the haiku on page 154. Help students hear the number of syllables in each line. If necessary, have them repeat lines several times. **See Daily Word Study Practice, page 195.**

CURRICULUM CONNECTIONS

SPELLING

List the spelling words on the board: *knives, chiefs, potatoes, tornadoes, scissors, series, misunderstanding, apologized, appreciated, unfortunately.* Have students add a spelling word to each of the following groups of words.

1. leaders, heads, (_chiefs_)
2. confusion, bewilderment, (_misunderstanding_)
3. sadly, unluckily, (_unfortunately_)
4. carrots, turnips, (_potatoes_)
5. admired, enjoyed, (_appreciated_)
6. lists, numbers, (_series_)
7. spoons, forks, (_knives_)
8. storms, hurricanes, (_tornadoes_)
9. needle, thread, (_scissors_)
10. wrong, sorry, (_apologizes_)

WRITING

Portfolio Point out that even though most traditional haiku describe scenes in nature, it is possible to write haiku about a variety of subjects. Have students write haiku about an urban landscape, a school activity, or a favorite pastime.

FINE ARTS

Bring to class children's art books that show reproductions of Japanese art. Have students try to find examples that could be used to illustrate the haiku on page 154.

HEALTH

Have students research bicycle safety rules and create a simple poster or pamphlet explaining those rules. Encourage them to share their posters with primary grade classrooms.

Technology

AstroWord, Multisyllabic Words. ©1998 Silver Burdett Ginn Inc. Division of Simon & Schuster.

Lesson 71

Pages 155–156

Syllables

INFORMAL ASSESSMENT OBJECTIVES

Can students

✔ identify the number of syllables in words?

✔ divide words according to specific rules of syllabication?

Lesson Focus

INTRODUCING THE SKILL

- Read the syllabication rules on pages 155 and 156 with students. Study the sample words that apply to each rule.

- Write these words on the board: *rapid, constant, reduce, magazine, fingerprint, compute, magnetic, windowpane, silver, razor, shutters, publication,* and *waterfall.* Ask for volunteers to divide the words into syllables using vertical lines and identify the rule to which the word applies.

- Challenge students to suggest other words for each rule to write on the board and divide into syllables.

USING THE PAGES

- Read the directions for pages 155 and 156 together. Remind students to refer to the syllabication rules printed on the pages or on their printed lists as they complete the exercises.

- **Critical Thinking** Ask students to read and share their ideas about the question concerning the picnic on page 155.

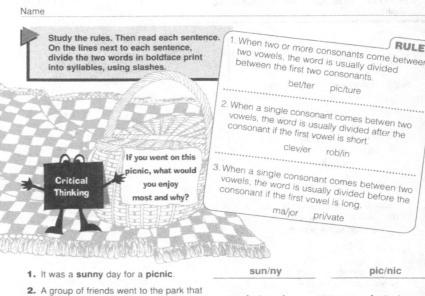

Name _____

Study the rules. Then read each sentence. On the lines next to each sentence, divide the two words in boldface print into syllables, using slashes.

RULES

1. When two or more consonants come between two vowels, the word is usually divided between the first two consonants.

    bet/ter   pic/ture

2. When a single consonant comes betwen two vowels, the word is usually divided after the consonant if the first vowel is short.

    clev/er   rob/in

3. When a single consonant comes between two vowels, the word is usually divided before the consonant if the first vowel is long.

    ma/jor   pri/vate

If you went on this picnic, what would you enjoy most and why?

1. It was a **sunny** day for a **picnic**.	sun/ny	pic/nic
2. A group of friends went to the park that was **beyond** the **forest**.	be/yond	for/est
3. Jack had **never** been there **before**.	nev/er	be/fore
4. Jane said to **follow** her through the **tunnel**.	fol/low	tun/nel
5. Maria and Adam brought their **tennis rackets**.	ten/nis	rack/ets
6. Jane spread out the **yellow blanket**.	yel/low	blan/ket
7. Adam was **hungry** and opened the **basket**.	hun/gry	bas/ket
8. He took out the **napkins** and **paper** plates.	nap/kins	pa/per
9. They had cheese sandwiches with **lettuce** and **olives**.	let/tuce	ol/ives
10. For dessert they ate some **melon** that had a very sweet **flavor**.	mel/on	fla/vor

Lesson 71
Syllables **155**

FOCUS ON ALL LEARNERS ✴ ◦ ◆ ⬛ ◆

ENGLISH LANGUAGE LEARNERS/ESL

Point out to students that understanding the number of syllables in a word will help them pronounce and spell the word correctly.

VISUAL LEARNERS

LARGE GROUP   Write the following words on the board and have students explain the rule that is used to syllabicate each word: *con-stant, cub-by-hole, chalk-board, fin-ger-print, re-duce, rap-id, no-ble, e-go.*

KINESTHETIC LEARNERS

PARTNER   Have students take turns calling out a word on page 156 for a partner to write on the board and divide into syllables. Students can consult the rules and check each other.

Write the number of syllables you hear in each word. Then write the word and use slashes to divide it into syllables.

flowerpot

1. expertly	3	ex/pert/ly	2. expression	3	ex/pres/sion
3. disbelief	3	dis/be/lief	4. inefficient	4	in/ef/fi/cient
5. determination	5	de/ter/mi/na/tion	6. kangaroos	3	kan/ga/roos
7. strawberries	3	straw/ber/ries	8. shopkeeper	3	shop/keep/er
9. inseparable	5	in/sep/a/ra/ble	10. quickened	2	quick/ened
11. illegal	3	il/le/gal	12. drizzled	2	driz/zled
13. distribution	4	dis/tri/bu/tion	14. corporation	4	cor/por/a/tion
15. windowpane	3	win/dow/pane	16. scorekeeper	3	score/keep/er
17. igloos	2	ig/loos	18. shredding	2	shred/ding
19. operations	4	op/er/a/tions	20. irreversible	5	ir/re/vers/i/ble
21. football	2	foot/ball	22. decided	3	de/cid/ed
23. gratefully	3	grate/ful/ly	24. abilities	4	a/bil/i/ties
25. battery	3	bat/ter/y	26. geographical	5	ge/o/graph/i/cal
27. proceeded	3	pro/ceed/ed	28. congratulations	5	con/grat/u/la/tions
29. improper	3	im/prop/er	30. idea	3	i/de/a
31. showboat	2	show/boat	32. puppeteer	3	pup/pet/eer
33. repetition	4	rep/e/ti/tion	34. oneself	2	one/self
35. windowpane	3	win/dow/pane	36. fingerprint	3	fin/ger/print

AUDITORY LEARNERS

LARGE GROUP

Invite students to take turns saying a multisyllabic word and calling on a volunteer to say another word that begins with the same letter and has the same number of syllables.

GIFTED LEARNERS

Call out a number of syllables and challenge students to see how many words with that many syllables they can write in 30 seconds. Then time them to see how long it takes them to correctly divide their words into syllables.

LEARNERS WHO NEED EXTRA SUPPORT

Work with students individually to explain exactly how the syllabication rules reviewed in this lesson apply to specific words. Encourage them to ask questions. **See Daily Word Study Practice, page 195.**

CURRICULUM CONNECTIONS

SPELLING

Call out each of the spelling words *knives, chiefs, potatoes, tornadoes, scissors, series, misunderstanding, apologized, appreciated, unfortunately.* After each word, have a volunteer say aloud a two-word phrase using the spelling word with the same number of syllables; for example, *wise chiefs, powerful tornadoes.* Then have them write the phrase on the board.

WRITING

Portfolio Challenge students to write a description of an outdoor event using as many multisyllabic words as possible. Then tell them to edit their writing, using synonyms in place of the words they originally wrote. Which version do they prefer, and why?

HEALTH

Have students look in cookbooks or other sources for safety guidelines on packing foods for picnics, school lunches, and so on. What foods need to be kept cool, how cool must they be kept, and what are the best methods for keeping them cool?

SOCIAL STUDIES

Have students obtain lists and maps of the state parks and recreation areas in their state or region. Discuss what recreational activities are available at these areas (such as boating, swimming, hiking, and camping), routes for getting to the areas, when the parks are open, and any fees for using the parks.

Technology

AstroWord, Multisyllabic Words. ©1998 Silver Burdett Ginn Inc. Division of Simon & Schuster.

Lesson 72

Pages 157–158

Reading **Writing**

Suffixes, Plurals, Syllables

INFORMAL ASSESSMENT OBJECTIVES

Can students

✔ read a dialogue that contains words that involve spelling changes when suffixes are added and words whose plurals are formed in various ways?

✔ write an advice column?

Lesson Focus

READING

- Write the word *dominoes* and *mice* on the board. Review the different ways of forming the plural of words.

- Then write the words *delightfully*, *fascinating*, and *easily*. Ask how each base word was changed when the suffix was added. Ask students to divide each word into syllables.

- Have students read the dialogue silently and then ask volunteers to assume the roles of Carrie and Alex for reading. Have students respond to the writing prompt that follows it.

WRITING

Explain to students that they will write an advice-column letter to the characters Carrie and Alex. Students should think about what they know about how friends with very different personalities can learn to get along. Remind them to use words from the word box in their column.

Name

 Reading ▶ Read the dialogue. Then write your answer to the question below.

A Nice Summer Day

Carrie: I'm bored. Want to play a game of dominos?

Alex: No, I'm occupied with my photos at the moment.

Carrie: What's so fascinating about them?

Alex: I think they're delightfully interesting. Just look at this one.

Carrie: It's a picture of two zucchini and some spinach. It's the most boring thing I've ever seen.

Alex: You're just ignorant. These are easily the heaviest zucchini and leafiest spinach ever grown in our state.

Carrie: Did you grow them?

Alex: Unfortunately, no. I just took a picture of them at the county fair. Here's another of my vegetable shots: a new, improved type of radish. Aren't the leaves spectacular?

Carrie: It's a nice summer day, Alex. Winter is the time for scanning your collection. Let's play some basketball!

Alex: Just a minute. I need to put these pictures of geese and mice into my animal album.

Carrie: I'll be swimming down at the park.

Contrast Carrie's and Alex's personalities and interests. Would you say you are more like Carrie or Alex? Why?

_____
_____
_____
_____
_____
_____

Lesson 72
Review suffixes, plurals, syllables: Reading **157**

FOCUS ON ALL LEARNERS ✳ • ◆ ▪

ENGLISH LANGUAGE LEARNERS/ESL

To familiarize students with the concepts on these pages, discuss the word *personality*. Also, to make sure that students understand what is meant by the term *advice columns*, you might want to bring in and discuss age-appropriate examples.

VISUAL LEARNERS

INDIVIDUAL **Materials:** newspapers or magazines

Distribute printed matter for students to skim through and tell them to look for examples of compound words. Have them copy the words onto a piece of paper and divide the words into syllables.

KINESTHETIC LEARNERS

PARTNER Invite partners to act out the scene involving the characters Carrie and Alex. Encourage students to add to the dialogue.

Writing ▷

Imagine that you are someone who writes an advice column for young people. Carrie and Alex have written you a letter saying they are good friends but they cannot think of any activities they both enjoy. Write them a letter suggesting some activities that might suit both their personalities. Also suggest ways in which a friendship can be valuable even when it is between people who have very different interests. Use words from the word bank in your letter.

getting
beliefs
received
decided
determination
simply
thoughtfully
agreeably
carefully
crises
tried
disagreements
possibly
radios
children

Helpful Hints
- Refer to Carrie and Alex's letter.
- Use a sympathetic, positive tone.
- Give specific, practical suggestions.

158 Lesson 72
Review suffixes, plurals, syllables: Writing

SPELLING

Use the following words and dictation sentences as a posttest for the second group of words in Unit 6.

1. **knives** — Wash the dirty **knives**, please.
2. **chiefs** — The **chiefs** of police spoke to the journalists.
3. **potatoes** — Jane washed and peeled the **potatoes**.
4. **tornadoes** — Some scientists study **tornadoes**.
5. **scissors** — Put the **scissors** away when you finish using them.
6. **series** — Our teacher read us a **series** of books by the same author.
7. **misunderstanding** — The two friends argued because of a **misunderstanding**.
8. **apologized** — The little girl **apologized** for breaking the vase.
9. **appreciated** — I **appreciated** the card you sent when I was sick.
10. **unfortunately** — **Unfortunately**, the traffic was very heavy.

SCIENCE

Plant scientists are constantly working to introduce new and better types of fruits and vegetables. Have students pick a certain example, such as apples, tomatoes, potatoes, or corn, and contact their state agricultural extension agency for information on different hybrids.

HEALTH/PHYSICAL EDUCATION

Explain that although not everyone enjoys or is able to play competitive sports, it is important for everyone to get some sort of regular physical exercise. Have students discuss and make a list of alternative methods of getting exercise, for example: jumping rope, swimming, walking, dancing, and doing gymnastics.

Technology

AstroWord, Multisyllabic Words; Suffixes; Base Words & Endings. ©1998 Silver Burdett Ginn Inc. Division of Simon & Schuster.

AUDITORY LEARNERS

PARTNER Have one partner say aloud a singular noun for which the plural is formed irregularly. Examples are *moose, goose, louse, child, man,* and *woman.* Have the partner give the plural form for each word.

GIFTED LEARNERS

Have students write additional dialogue for Carrie and Alex, using more examples of the word study elements covered in this unit and keeping the dialogue consistent with the two characters' personalities.

LEARNERS WHO NEED EXTRA SUPPORT

Review with learners the concept of inferring characters' personalities from what they say and do and also from what other characters say about them. **See Daily Word Study Practice, pages 192–195.**

Lesson 73

Pages 159–160

Unit Checkup

Reviewing Suffixes, Plurals, Syllables

Lesson Focus

PREPARING FOR THE CHECKUP

- On the board, write the following word equations: *sled + ing = ?, bake + ed = ?, juicy + est = ?, grumpy + ly = ?,* and *possible + ly = ?* Ask volunteers to solve each equation by writing the word and explaining the rule behind each spelling change.

- On the board write the words *delightfully, gladly,* and *foolishness.* Have volunteers underline each suffix.

- Write *loaf, life, tomato, potato,* and *man* on the board. Ask students to spell the plural of each.

- Write *coffeepot, speckle, whimper, never,* and *loner* on the board. Ask students to divide the words into syllables.

USING THE PAGES

Have students read the directions for the Checkup pages. After students finish the pages, take time to discuss items that were sources of common errors.

159

Name _____

Fill in the circle next to each word in which the plural is formed correctly or the suffix is added correctly.

1. ○ swimer	○ describeable	● mysteriously
2. ○ heavyly	○ turkies	● wolves
3. ● oases	○ heros	○ chieves
4. ● luckily	○ dirtyier	○ writeing
5. ○ stoping	● obeyed	○ shelfs
6. ○ tomatos	● geese	○ feebley
7. ● chiefs	○ likeable	○ joging
8. ○ drumer	● clapped	○ danceing
9. ● politeness	○ securly	○ hesitateion
10. ○ tornados	○ guideance	● roots

Read each word. Then fill in the circle beside each word that is correctly divided into syllables.

11. heartily	● heart/i/ly	○ hear/ti/ly	○ heart/ily
12. notebook	○ not/e/book	○ notebo/ok	● note/book
13. drinkable	○ drin/ka/ble	○ drink/able	● drink/a/ble
14. lecture	● lec/ture	○ lect/ure	○ le/cture
15. never	○ ne/ver	● nev/er	○ ne/v/er
16. motor	● mo/tor	○ mot/or	○ moto/r
17. hesitation	○ hes/it/a/tion	○ hes/i/tat/ion	● hes/i/ta/tion
18. bouquets	● bou/quets	○ bo/uq/uets	○ bo/uquets
19. cousin	○ cou/sin	● cous/in	○ co/usin
20. macaroni	○ ma/ca/ro/ni	● mac/a/ro/ni	○ ma/car/on/i

FOCUS ON ALL LEARNERS ✳ • ◆ ■

ENGLISH LANGUAGE LEARNERS/ESL

To build background for the sentences on page 160, discuss with students what a *flea market* is. Once the term has been defined, ask whether students have ever been to a flea market or similar kind of marketplace.

LARGE GROUP

VISUAL LEARNERS

Write on the board the syllabication rules from Lesson 71, pages 155–156. Beneath each rule, have students write a word that demonstrates the rule, with the relevant phonetic element(s) underlined.

PARTNER

KINESTHETIC LEARNERS

Materials: newspapers

Have learners look through newspapers and circle words that end in final *e.* Have them add suffixes to the words, writing the new words on paper. Partners can check one another's spelling of the words.

UNIT 6 CHECKUP

 Read each sentence. Write the plural form of each underlined word on the lines below. Use slash marks to divide each word that has more than one syllable.

1. Jeanette bought a great <u>scarf</u> at the flea market.
2. It shows a dancing red <u>tomato</u> against a green background.
3. She also bought a stuffed animal—a <u>moose</u>.
4. Jeanette's mother purchased a fuzzy <u>poncho</u>.
5. Jeanette's father tried on a snazzy <u>tuxedo</u>.
6. Jeanette's father decided to buy a <u>stereo</u> instead.
7. One dealer at the market displayed an antique <u>muff</u>.
8. Another dealer was offering a charming porcelain <u>elf</u>.
9. A <u>child</u> stared at a collection of cuckoo clocks.
10. He had never seen so many clocks in his <u>life</u>.
11. Jeanette's little brother saw the cutest fire <u>chief</u> doll.
12. One dealer featured an antique <u>knife</u> collection.
13. For lunch, Jeanette's family ate <u>spaghetti</u>.
14. After lunch, a <u>woman</u> recommended that they look at a collection of old beads.
15. The dealer had a <u>shelf</u> filled with only blue beads.
16. Jeanette bought some beads to sew onto the <u>cuff</u> of a sweater.

17.	scarves	18.	to/ma/toes
19.	moose	20.	pon/chos
21.	tux/e/dos	22.	ster/e/os
23.	muffs	24.	elves
25.	chil/dren	26.	lives
27.	chiefs	28.	knives
29.	spa/ghet/ti	30.	wom/en
31.	shelves	32.	cuffs

160 Lesson 73
Suffixes, plurals, syllables: Checkup

AUDITORY LEARNERS

PARTNER Have one partner call out the singular form of words from Lessons 67–69 and the other partner call out and spell the plural form. Then have the partners switch roles.

GIFTED STUDENTS

Have one student call out a word that has changed the base word before adding a suffix. See how quickly other students can call out an explanation of how the base word was changed; for example, *Dropped the final* e.

LEARNERS WHO NEED EXTRA SUPPORT

Help students create a list of the phonics rules covered in Unit 6, with selected examples to illustrate each rule. **See Daily Word Study Practice, pages 192-195.**

ASSESSING UNDERSTANDING OF UNIT SKILLS

Student Progress Assessment You may wish to review the observational notes you made as students worked through the activities in this unit. Your notes will help you evaluate the progress students made with adding suffixes, making words plural, and dividing words into syllables.

Portfolio Assessment Review the materials students have collected in their portfolios. Talk with students individually to discuss their written work and the progress they have made since the beginning of this unit. As you review students' work, evaluate how well they use the unit word study skills.

Daily Word Study Practice For students who need additional practice with any of the topics in this unit, quick reviews are provided on pages 192–195 in Daily Word Study Practice.

Posttest To assess students' mastery of skills covered in this unit, use the posttest on pages 135g–135h.

SPELLING

Use the following dictation sentences to review the spelling words in Unit 6.

1. **jogging** — All the **jogging** shoes are on sale.
2. **swimmers** — **Swimmers** must shower before entering the pool.
3. **changing** — The caterpillar is **changing** into a butterfly.
4. **peacefulness** — The **peacefulness** of the inn pleased all the guests.
5. **generosity** — Everybody was amazed by the woman's **generosity**.
6. **studies** — Lily **studies** ballet three afternoons a week.
7. **possibly** — We may **possibly** go to the movies on Friday.
8. **knives** — Expensive **knives** were on display in the kitchen store.
9. **chiefs** — The fire **chiefs** voted on the year's most heroic rescue.
10. **potatoes** — The **potatoes** were undercooked and lumpy.
11. **apologized** — The kids **apologized** for making so much noise.
12. **unfortunately** — **Unfortunately**, the restaurant was out of apple pie.

Teacher Notes

INTRODUCING

Unit 7

Alphabetizing, Using the Dictionary, Multi-meaning Words, Homographs

Contents

Student Performance Objectives

In Unit 7, students will review dictionary skills in the use of guide words, entry words, the pronunciation key, respellings, and definitions. Students will apply these skills in various reading and writing activities. As these skills are developed, students will be able to

◆ Recognize alphabetical order

◆ Recognize and understand the function of guide words

◆ Recognize and understand the pronunciation key and the use of dictionary respellings

◆ Recognize and understand multiple meanings of words

◆ Proofread to check written work

UNIT 7 RESOURCES
Assessment Strategies   161c
   Overview   161c
   Unit 7 Pretest   161e–161f
   Unit 7 Posttest   161g–161h
   Unit 7 Student Progress Checklist   161i
Spelling Connections   161j–161k
Word Study Games, Activities, and Technology   161l–161o
Home Connection   161p–161q

TEACHING PLANS
Unit 7 Opener   161–162
Lesson 74: Alphabetizing and Guide Words   163–164
Lesson 75: Dictionary Pronunciation Key   165–166
Lesson 76: Dictionary Respellings and Looking   167–168
       Under the Correct Word Form
Lesson 77: Multi-meaning Words, Homographs   169–170
Lesson 78: Review Alphabetizing, Dictionary Skills,   171–172
       Multi-meaning Words, Homographs
Lesson 79: Unit 7 Checkup   173–174

161b

Assessment Strategy Overview

Throughout Unit 7, assess students' ability to use the dictionary to find information about words and their meanings. There are various ways to assess students' progress. You may also want to encourage students to evaluate their own work and participate in setting goals for their own learning.

FORMAL ASSESSMENT

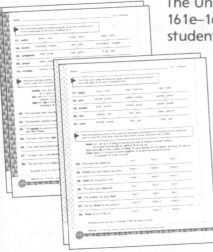

The Unit 7 Pretest on pages 161e–161f helps to assess a student's knowledge at the beginning of the unit and to plan instruction.

The Unit 7 Posttest on pages 161g–161h helps to assess mastery of unit objectives and to plan for reteaching, if necessary.

INFORMAL ASSESSMENT

The Reading & Writing pages and Unit Checkup in the student book are an effective means of evaluating students' performance.

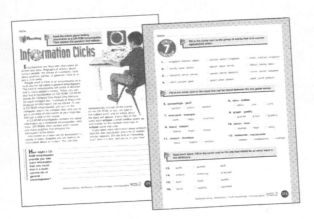

Skill	Reading & Writing Pages	Unit Checkup
Alphabetizing	171–172	173–174
Identifying Guide Words	171–172	173–174
Dictionary Pronunciation Key	171–172	173–174
Dictionary Respellings	171–172	173–174
Understanding Entry Words	171–172	173–174
Multimeaning Words	171–172	173–174
Homographs	171–172	173–174

PORTFOLIO ASSESSMENT

 This logo appears throughout the teaching plans. It signals opportunities for collecting students' work for individual portfolios. You may also want to collect the following pages.

❖ Unit 7 Pretest and Posttest, pages 161e–161h

❖ Unit 7 Reading & Writing, pages 171–172

❖ Unit 7 Checkup, pages 173–174

STUDENT PROGRESS CHECKLIST

Use the checklist on page 161i to record students' progress. You may want to cut the sections apart to place each student's checklist in his or her portfolio.

Administering and Evaluating the
Pretest and Posttest

DIRECTIONS

To help you assess students' progress in learning Unit 7 skills, tests are available on pages 161e–161h. Administer the Pretest before students begin the unit. The results of the Pretest will help you identify each student's strengths and needs in advance, allowing you to structure lesson plans to meet individual needs. Administer the Posttest to assess students' overall mastery of skills taught in the unit and to identify specific areas that will require reteaching.

PERFORMANCE ASSESSMENT PROFILE

The following chart will help you identify specific skills as they appear on the tests and enable you to identify and record specific information about an individual's or the class's performance on the tests.

Depending on the results of the tests, refer to the Reteaching column for lesson-plan pages where you can find activities that will be useful for meeting individual needs or for daily word study practice.

ANSWER KEYS

Unit 7 Pretest, page 161e (BLM 49)

1. close, closet, clothes
2. swallow, swam, switch
3. pail, pain, pale
4. came, cane, care
5. fanciful, fancy, fantasy
6. compliment, connect, conquest
7. steppe, stride, string
8. treason, treasure, tremble
9. people, plentiful, presentation
10. mark, marker, marking

11. civic
12. eighty
13. exhale
14. decade
15. error
16. heritage

Unit 7 Pretest, page 161f (BLM 50)

17. luxury / mail
18. perfect / perish
19. bunk / burner
20. fashion / fate
21. care / cast

22. foul-4
23. finish-1
24. twist-1
25. foul-1
26. foul-3
27. finish-4
28. twist-3

Unit 7 Posttest, page 161g (BLM 51)

1. flaunt, flaw, flourish
2. guard, guest, guilt
3. stain, stale, stare
4. image, imagine, imitate
5. school, science, score
6. misery, mistake, misunderstood
7. office, official, officiate
8. treason, treasure, tremble
9. practical, practice, prayer
10. camper, campground, campsite

11. mandate
12. meaning
13. prune
14. decide
15. fancy
16. athletics

Unit 7 Posttest, page 161h (BLM 52)

17. twine / ulcer
18. cow / crab
19. X-ray / yap
20. pronounce / prose
21. inch / include

22. light-1
23. jam-1
24. handle-2
25. light-3
26. jam-4
27. handle-1
28. jam-3

PERFORMANCE ASSESSMENT PROFILE

Skill	Pretest Questions	Posttest Questions	Reteaching Focus on All Learners	Reteaching Daily Word Study Practice
Alphabetizing	1–10	1–10	163–164, 171–172	194–195
Guide Words	17–21	17–21	163–164, 171–172	194–195
Pronunciation Key	11–16	11–16	165–166, 171–172	194–195
Dictionary Respellings	11–16	11–16	167–168, 171–172	194–195
Multimeaning Words	22–28	22–28	169–172	194–195
Homographs	22–28	22–28	169–172	194–195

▶ Fill in the circle under the group of words that is in correct alphabetical order.

1. close, closet, clothes ○ | clothes, closet, close ○ | closet, close, clothes ○

2. swam, swallow, switch ○ | switch, swam, swallow ○ | swallow, swam, switch ○

3. pale, pail, pain ○ | pail, pain, pale ○ | pain, pail, pale ○

4. came, cane, care ○ | care, came, cane ○ | care, cane, came ○

5. fancy, fanciful, fantasy ○ | fanciful, fantasy, fancy ○ | fanciful, fancy, fantasy ○

6. compliment, conquest, connect ○ | connect, compliment, conquest ○ | compliment, connect, conquest ○

7. steppe, stride, string ○ | string, stride, steppe ○ | steppe, string, stride ○

8. treason, treasure, tremble ○ | tremble, treason, treasure ○ | treason, treasure, tremble ○

9. people, presentation, plentiful ○ | people, plentiful, presentation ○ | people, presentation, plentiful ○

10. marker, marking, mark ○ | marking, marker, mark ○ | mark, marker, marking ○

▶ Fill in the circle under the word that the dictionary respelling stands for.

11. siv´ ik — civic ○ | civil ○ | several ○

12. āt´ ē — ate ○ | eighty ○ | eat ○

13. eks hāl´ — exhale ○ | exhaust ○ | exclaim ○

14. dek´ ād — deck ○ | decayed ○ | decade ○

15. er´ ər — ear ○ | err ○ | error ○

16. her´ i tij — heredity ○ | heritage ○ | hearsay ○

Pronunciation Key
ā ape
e ten
ē me
i fit
ə e in agent
ə u in circus
d dog
h help
j jump
k kiss
l leg
m meat
r red
s see
t top
v vast
sh she

Go to the next page. →

> ▶ Fill in the circle under the dictionary guide words that could be found on the same page as the word in boldface print.

17. magic

luxury / mail
○

loud / machine
○

mall / mask
○

18. peril

pocket / prison
○

patent / peace
○

perfect / perish
○

19. bunker

bunk / burner
○

bruise / bump
○

boost / bundle
○

20. fast

fashion / fate
○

fate / feast
○

fable / fashion
○

21. cash

cement / cereal
○

blue / call
○

care / cast
○

> ▶ Read the dictionary entries. Then read the sentences and decide which meaning of each boldfaced word is used. Fill in the circle under the word and its correct dictionary entry number.

finish (fin´ ish) **v. 1.** to bring or come to an end **2.** to give a certain surface **3.** to give final touches to; perfect **4.** to use up

foul (foul) **adj. 1.** dirty, smelly, or rotten **2.** very wicked, evil **3.** stormy, not clear **4.** not fair

twist (twist) **v. 1.** to wind or twine together **2.** to give the wrong meaning on purpose **3.** to turn around

22. The player hit a **foul** ball.

foul-1
○

foul-2
○

foul-4
○

23. Finish your work before you leave.

finish-1
○

finish-3
○

finish-4
○

24. Twist the string into a ball.

twist-1
○

twist-2
○

twist-3
○

25. The plant has a **foul** odor.

foul-1
○

foul-3
○

foul-4
○

26. The weather has been **foul**!

foul-2
○

foul-3
○

foul-4
○

27. Did you **finish** all the peanuts?

finish-2
○

finish-3
○

finish-4
○

28. Twist the lid off the jar.

twist-1
○

twist-2
○

twist-3
○

Possible score on Unit 7 Pretest is 28. Number correct _____

▶ Fill in the circle under the group of words that is in correct alphabetical order.

1. flaw, flaunt, flourish ○   flourish, flaw, flaunt ○   flaunt, flaw, flourish ○

2. guard, guest, guilt ○   guest, guilt, guard ○   guard, guilt, guest ○

3. stain, stare, stale ○   stale, stare, stain ○   stain, stale, stare ○

4. imagine, image, imitate ○   image, imagine, imitate ○   image, imitate, imagine ○

5. school, score, science ○   science, score, school ○   school, science, score ○

6. misery, mistake, misunderstood ○   misunderstood, mistake, misery ○   mistake, misery, misunderstood ○

7. officiate, official, office ○   office, official, officiate ○   office, officiate, official ○

8. treason, treasure, tremble ○   tremble, treason, treasure ○   treasure, treason, tremble ○

9. practice, practical, prayer ○   prayer, practical, practice ○   practical, practice, prayer ○

10. campground, campsite, camper ○   camper, campground, campsite ○   campground, camper, campsite ○

▶ Fill in the circle under the word that the dictionary respelling stands for.

				Pronunciation Key
11. man´ dāt	manly ○	mandate ○	manage ○	a cat
12. mēn´ iŋ	meanly ○	meaning ○	moment ○	ā ape e ten
13. pro͞on	proud ○	prove ○	prune ○	ē me i fit
14. di sīd´	decide ○	decayed ○	deceased ○	ī ice oͦo tool
15. fan´ sē	fence ○	fancy ○	fans ○	d dog f fall
16. ath let´ iks	athletes ○	lettuce ○	athletics ○	k kiss l leg

Pronunciation Key
a cat
ā ape
e ten
ē me
i fit
ī ice
oͦo tool
d dog
f fall
k kiss
l leg
m meat
n nose
p put
r red
s see
t top
ŋ ring
th thin, truth

Go to the next page. →

> Fill in the circle under the dictionary guide words that could be found on the same page as the word in boldface print.

17. twitch	twine / ulcer ○	turkey / twain ○	turtle / twist ○
18. coyote	courtyard / coveys ○	cow / crab ○	counterplan / coupled ○
19. xylophone	wind / X-ray ○	yap / yearn ○	X-ray / yap ○
20. proper	profit / prone ○	pronounce / prose ○	protect / prove ○
21. incident	income / incite ○	in / incense ○	inch / include ○

> Read the dictionary entries. Then read the sentences and decide which meaning of each boldfaced word is used. Fill in the circle under the word and its correct dictionary entry number.

handle (han´ dəl) n. **1.** a part that is designed to be grasped by the hand **2.** a name or title **3.** the feel of a fabric or textile

jam (jam) n. **1.** a crowded mass **2.** a difficult state of affairs **3.** a music session **4.** a food made by boiling fruit and sugar to a thick consistency

light (līt) adj. **1.** having little weight **2.** of little importance; trivial **3.** easily disturbed **4.** easily digested

22. The suitcases were very **light**.	light-1 ○	light-2 ○	light-3 ○
23. The accident caused a bad traffic **jam**.	jam-1 ○	jam-2 ○	jam-4 ○
24. The **handle** he used on the radio was Red Pepper.	handle-1 ○	handle-2 ○	handle-3 ○
25. The baby was a very **light** sleeper.	light-2 ○	light-3 ○	light-4 ○
26. They were eating toast and **jam**.	jam-2 ○	jam-3 ○	jam-4 ○
27. The door had a gold **handle**.	handle-1 ○	handle-2 ○	handle-3 ○
28. The rock band had a **jam** session.	jam-1 ○	jam-2 ○	jam-3 ○

Possible score on Unit 7 Posttest is 28. Number correct _____

Student Progress Checklist

Make as many copies as needed to use for a class list. For individual portfolio use, cut apart each student's section. As indicated by the code, color in boxes next to skills satisfactorily assessed and mark an X by those requiring reteaching. Marked boxes can later be colored in to indicate mastery.

STUDENT PROGRESS CHECKLIST

Code: ■ Satisfactory   ☒ Needs Reteaching

Student: _____ _____ Pretest Score: _____ Posttest Score: _____	Skills ❑ Alphabetizing ❑ Dictionary Skills ❑ Multi-meaning Words ❑ Homographs	Comments / Learning Goals
Student: _____ _____ Pretest Score: _____ Posttest Score: _____	Skills ❑ Alphabetizing ❑ Dictionary Skills ❑ Multi-meaning Words ❑ Homographs	Comments / Learning Goals
Student: _____ _____ Pretest Score: _____ Posttest Score: _____	Skills ❑ Alphabetizing ❑ Dictionary Skills ❑ Multi-meaning Words ❑ Homographs	Comments / Learning Goals
Student: _____ _____ Pretest Score: _____ Posttest Score: _____	Skills ❑ Alphabetizing ❑ Dictionary Skills ❑ Multi-meaning Words ❑ Homographs	Comments / Learning Goals
Student: _____ _____ Pretest Score: _____ Posttest Score: _____	Skills ❑ Alphabetizing ❑ Dictionary Skills ❑ Multi-meaning Words ❑ Homographs	Comments / Learning Goals

Spelling Connections

A final test is provided on page 174.

INTRODUCTION

The Unit Word List is a comprehensive list of spelling words drawn from units throughout this text. These words reflect a variety of phonetic elements presented to students.
To incorporate spelling into your word study program, use the activity in the Curriculum Connections section of each teaching plan.

The spelling lessons utilize the following approach.

1. Administer a pretest of these words. Dictation sentences are provided.

2. Provide practice.

3. Reassess. Dictation sentences are provided.

A final test is provided on page 174.

DIRECTIONS

Make a copy of Blackline Master 54 for each student. After administering the pretest, give each student a copy of the word list.

Students can work with a partner to practice spelling the words orally and identifying the phonetic element for each word. They can also make and use letter cards to form the words on the list. You may want to challenge students to identify other words that have the same phonetic element. Students can write words of their own on *My Own Word List* (see Blackline Master 54).

Have students store their list words in an envelope in the back of their books or notebooks. You may want to suggest that students keep a spelling notebook, listing words with similar patterns. You could also invite students to build word wall displays in the classroom. Each section of the wall can focus on words with a single phonetic element. The walls will become a good spelling resource when students are writing.

UNIT WORD LIST

Review of Phonetic Skills

opaque
ancient
leisure
automobile
incredible
triangular
contradict
manufacture
collector
appointment
accidentally
spaghetti

Name _____

 **S**pelling

UNIT 7 WORD LIST

Review of Word Study Skills

opaque	contradict
ancient	manufacture
leisure	collector
automobile	appointment
incredible	accidentally
triangular	spaghetti

My Own Word List

My Own Word List

My Own Word List

Word Study Games, Activities, and Technology

The following collection of ideas offers a variety of opportunities to reinforce word study skills while actively engaging students. The games, activities, and technology suggestions can easily be adapted to meet the needs of your group of learners. They vary in approach so as to consider students' different learning styles.

● DICTIONARY RESPELLINGS

Write the following words on the chalkboard: *annoyance, censorious, draught, hysterical, convenience, enchantment, habitat, interference, catcher, energize, permanent.*
Have students copy the words. Then tell students to find each word in a dictionary. Ask volunteers to write the dictionary respelling under each word on the board, divide the word into syllables, indicate the accented syllable, and pronounce the word correctly.

▲ FINDING ENTRY WORDS

You might create a word wall from entry words that students find in their outside reading. Select students by alphabetical order to be the class entry-word "volunteer for a day." Each day a different student should write a new entry word on the word wall. Call on volunteers to suggest or look up other words for which the word on the wall is the entry word. These words can also be added to the word wall that day.

◆ YOU CAN LOOK IT UP!

Divide the class into groups of four. Then write the following words on the chalkboard: *exercise, civilizations, resistance, angle, dessert, guiltily, capitol,* and *building.* Challenge groups to find each word in the dictionary and arrange them in alphabetical order. The first group to find the words, arrange the words in alphabetical order, and take turns pronouncing each correctly wins.

■ A NOTEBOOK DICTIONARY

Invite students to collect the new words they learn. Using a notebook, students can create a personal dictionary by listing unfamiliar words as they are encountered. Encourage students to look each word up in another dictionary and create a complete entry including respelling, pronunciation, and primary definition(s). Suggest that they devote a double page to each starting letter and leave enough room between entries on a page to maintain alphabetical order. Encourage students to add illustrations as appropriate. Challenge them to use these new words in class and in their homework assignments.

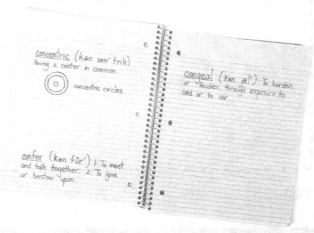

✳ ACRONYMS

Point out the etymology part of a dictionary entry and tell students that there are interesting stories behind the origins of many words. Sometimes, words are *acronyms*. An acronym is a word formed from the first letter or letters of each word in a compound term. Write these words on the chalkboard: *scuba, radar, sonar, laser*. Have students look up the words in a dictionary and ask volunteers to write on the board the full description for each word. Then have students work with a partner to find out more about these acronyms or other acronyms of their own choosing. Encourage use of reference works other than the dictionary. Have student partners write a paragraph about each acronym, illustrate their work, and share what they learn with the class.

● PROOFREADING

You might consider having partners exchange paragraphs and proofread one another's work before it is collected. If classroom dictionaries contain a list of proofreaders' marks, suggest students find the symbols for period, comma, capitalization, lowercase letters, and indenting a paragraph and use them in their proofreading. If not, write the information as shown at right on the chalkboard and model the use of these symbols.

Proofreading Marks

capital letter	≡
small letter	/
add comma	⌃
add period	⊙
indent paragraph	¶
check spelling	◯

▲ NEW WORDS WITHIN NEW WORDS

Discuss with students that sometimes when they look up the definition of an unfamiliar word, they may find that there are other words within the definition whose meaning they must also look up to understand the original word. Write these words on the chalkboard: *civilization, paleontology, crystal, phantom,* and *phonemics*. Challenge students to look up the words, write their meanings, and also look up and write the meanings of other words in the definition of the original word.

◆ GUIDE-WORD CHALLENGE

Have groups of three or four students play "guide-word challenge." Read a pair of guide words from one page in the dictionary and have each group copy the words. Then have groups brainstorm for a set period of time to list as many words as they can that could appear on the same page as the guide words. Afterward, compare the entries in the dictionary with the groups' lists. The group with the most words wins.

■ HOMOGRAPH SENTENCES

Write the following homographs on the chalkboard: *leave, close, tender, duty, tire, scale, loaf,* and *prune.* Tell students to find each spelling in the dictionary. Have them define each homograph, indicating that homographs are two words with the same spelling and pronunciation but different meanings. Challenge students to use both meanings of each word in a single sentence, as shown in the examples at the right. Students may enjoy humorously illustrating their sentences.

✳ DICTIONARY MULTIPLEX

Make enough copies of Blackline Master 55 to distribute one to each student. Briefly discuss the concept of movie-theater multiplexes or the idea of a number of small theaters in one building. Tell students to imagine that the BLM shows a floor plan of a "Dictionary Multiplex." Remind students that some words in a dictionary are accompanied by illustrations. Explain to students that in each of their theaters, they should draw a picture illustrating one word. Then they should write a complete dictionary entry for that word in the space provided. This should include the word, the dictionary respelling, the part of speech, the derivation (if it applies), and the specific definition that applies to that illustration. When students have finished, encourage them to fold their "Multiplex" in half (like a greeting card). On the outside, they might print the words *Now Showing* and list the words inside in alphabetical order. You might wish to display the finished projects on your word wall.

Technology

The following software products are designed to provide practice in dictionary skills.

Macmillan Dictionary for Children This multimedia dictionary for students (ages 6–12) features over 12,000 words, 1,000 pictures, and 400 sound effects. Some pages include hyperlinks that offer connections to semantically related words or word derivations. Several word games are included.
** Simon & Schuster Interactive
   P.O. Box 2002
   Aurora, CO 80040-2002
   (800) 910-0099

Reading Blaster Through hundreds of word-skill games, students in third through sixth grade can practice alphabetizing, spelling, recognizing synonyms and antonyms, and following directions.

** Davidson & Associates, Inc.
   19840 Pioneer Avenue
   Torrance, CA 90503
   (800) 545-7677

Merriam-Webster's Dictionary for Kids Students can use this online dictionary to find the meanings of 20,000 words and play a variety of word games.
** Mindscape
   88 Roland Way
   Novato, CA 94945
   (800) 234-3088

Dictionary Multiplex

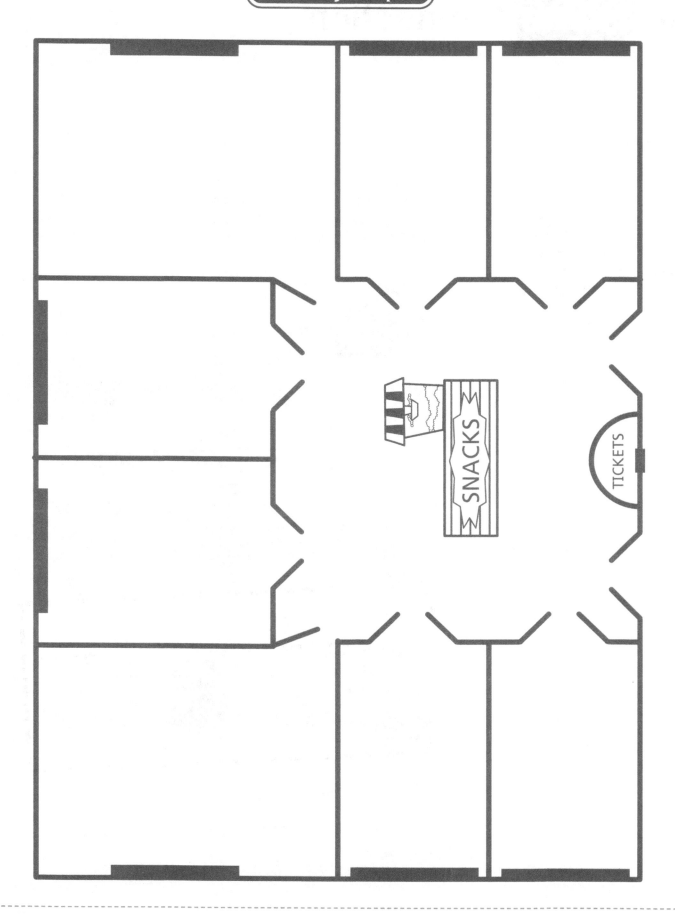

Home Connection

HOME LETTER

A letter is available to be sent home at the beginning of Unit 7. This letter informs family members that students will be reviewing dictionary skills as a basis for good research skills. The suggested home activity involves interpreting, creating, and writing definitions for nonsense words to reinforce dictionary skills. This activity promotes interaction between child and family members while supporting the student's learning of reading and writing words with the targeted word study skills. A letter is also available in Spanish on page 161q.

Home Letter

Dear Family,

Dictionary skills form the basis of good research skills. Over the next few weeks, your child will be reviewing dictionary skills, including recognizing alphabetical order, using guide words, understanding how to read a pronunciation key, and understanding words with multiple meanings.

At-Home Activities

▶ With your child, read the poem and the nonsense words and definitions on the other side of this letter. Ask your child to write a paragraph using some of the words from the poem.

▶ Ask your child to make up a few nonsense words of her or his own and write dictionary definitions for these words. You may also wish to encourage your child to write an original poem, using the nonsense words.

▶ Encourage your child to keep a vocabulary notebook and include new words and definitions.

Book Corner

You and your child might enjoy reading these books together. Look for them in your local library.

How I Came to Be a Writer

by Phyllis Reynolds Naylor

Naylor writes openly about the experiences and influences that led her to a literary career.

Poetry From A to Z — A Guide for Young Writers

by Paul B. Janeczko

Poets comment candidly on their work in this useful and encouraging resource for beginning poets.

Sincerely,

162   Unit 7
Introduction

CARTA para la casa

Estimada familia,

Saber usar el diccionario es la base para lograr buenas destrezas de investigación. En las próximas semanas, su hijo/a va a repasar las destrezas del uso de diccionarios, incluyendo reconocer el orden alfabético, uso de palabras guías, entender cómo leer la clave de la pronunciación y entender las palabras con significado múltiple.

Actividades para hacer en casa

He aquí algunas actividades que su hijo/a y ustedes pueden realizar juntos.

▶ Con su hijo/a, lean el poema y las palabras sin sentido y las definiciones en la página 161. Pídanle que escriba un párrafo usando algunas de las palabras del poema.

▶ Pídanle a su hijo/a que invente algunas palabras sin sentido y que escriba definiciones de diccionario para ellas.

▶ Animen a su hijo/a a mantener un cuaderno de vocabulario para incluir nuevas palabras y definiciones.

Rincón del libro

Su hijo/a y ustedes pueden disfrutar juntos de la lectura de estos libros. Búsquenlos en la biblioteca de su localidad.

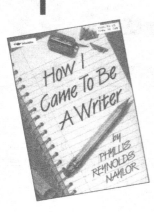

How I Came to Be a Writer
por Phyllis Reynolds Naylor

Naylor escribe con franqueza acerca de las experiencias e influencias que la condujeron a una carrera literaria.

Poetry from A to Z—A Guide for Young Writers
por Paul B. Janeczko

Unos poetas comentan con franqueza su trabajo en este útil y animado recurso para poetas principiantes.

Atentamente, _____

Unit 7

Pages 161–162

Alphabetizing, Dictionary Skills, Multi-meaning Words, Homographs

ASSESSING PRIOR KNOWLEDGE

To assess prior knowledge of alphabetizing, dictionary skills, multi-meaning words, and homographs, use the pretest on pages 161e–161f.

Unit Focus

USING THE PAGE

- Ask students to read "The Awkward Type" to themselves. What do they notice about the poem? *(Several nonsense words appear.)*

- Have students reread the poem, checking the sample dictionary page for the meanings of the unknown words.

- Invite students to write or tell the poem in prose, substituting real words for the nonsense words; for example; *I am not the graceful type who dances vaguely around a highly polished dance floor in a gauzy dress.*

- **Critical Thinking** Invite students to answer the question at the bottom of the page.

BUILDING A CONTEXT

- Ask students in what order the words in the nonsense dictionary are arranged. (alphabetically)

- Ask why the words *bloof* and *emert* appear at the top of the dictionary page. (They are the first and last entry words on the page.)

- Have students identify the entries that have more than one meaning. *(bloof, bufongo, closilious)*

- Invite volunteers to use the respellings to pronounce the nonsense words.

161

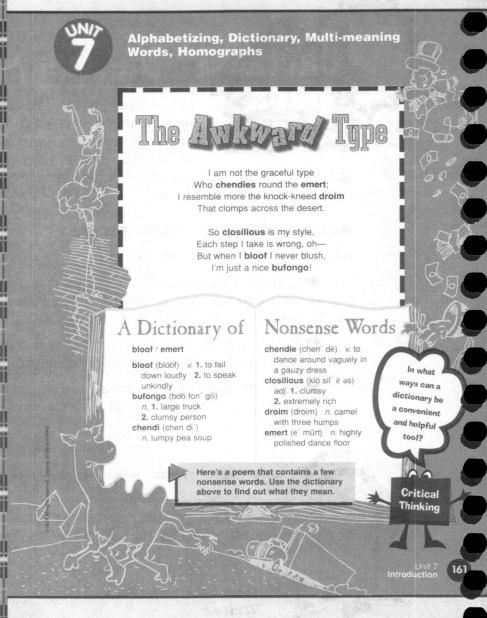

UNIT 7
Alphabetizing, Dictionary, Multi-meaning Words, Homographs

The Awkward Type

I am not the graceful type
Who **chendies** round the **emert**;
I resemble more the knock-kneed **droim**
That clomps across the desert.

So **closilious** is my style,
Each step I take is wrong, oh—
But when I **bloof** I never blush,
I'm just a nice **bufongo**!

A Dictionary of — Nonsense Words

bloof / emert

bloof (blōōf) *v.* **1.** to fall down loudly **2.** to speak unkindly
bufongo (bōō fon′ gō) *n.* **1.** large truck **2.** clumsy person
chendi (chen di′) *n.* lumpy pea soup
chendie (chen′ dē) *v.* to dance around vaguely in a gauzy dress
closilious (klō sil′ ē əs) *adj.* **1.** clumsy **2.** extremely rich
droim (droim) *n.* camel with three humps
emert (ē′ mûrt) *n.* highly polished dance floor

In what ways can a dictionary be a convenient and helpful tool?

Here's a poem that contains a few nonsense words. Use the dictionary above to find out what they mean.

Critical Thinking

Unit 7 Introduction 161

UNIT OPENER ACTIVITIES

LISTEN FOR FUN

Read the poem aloud to the class, conveying its humor and meaning through your expression. Discuss whether the poem is easier to understand now. Why? Ask if the poem's title is appropriate. Why or why not?

SILLY STYLE

Make available to students samples of nonsense verse by such writers as Edward Lear, Eve Merriam, Lewis Carroll, and Jack Prelutsky. Encourage them to bring in poetry books they may own. Invite students to read several of the poems and perhaps recite some of their favorites aloud.

THE LATEST THING

Point out that slang expressions are made up, just like the poem's nonsense words. Have students list examples of current slang words or phrases. Ask them to work with partners to compose dictionary entries for these words, listing pronunciations, parts of speech, and definitions and then arrange the entries in alphabetical order with guide words.

Home Letter

Dear Family,

Dictionary skills form the basis of good research skills. Over the next few weeks, your child will be reviewing dictionary skills, including recognizing alphabetical order, using guide words, understanding how to read a pronunciation key, and understanding words with multiple meanings.

At-Home Activities

► With your child, read the poem and the nonsense words and definitions on the other side of this letter. Ask your child to write a paragraph using some of the words from the poem.

► Ask your child to make up a few nonsense words of her or his own and write dictionary definitions for these words. You may also wish to encourage your child to write an original poem, using the nonsense words.

► Encourage your child to keep a vocabulary notebook and include new words and definitions.

You and your child might enjoy reading these books together. Look for them in your local library.

How I Came to Be a Writer
by Phyllis Reynolds Naylor
Naylor writes openly about the experiences and influences that led her to a literary career.

Poetry From A to Z — A Guide for Young Writers
by Paul B. Janeczko
Poets comment candidly on their work in this useful and encouraging resource for beginning poets.

Sincerely,

_____

BULLETIN BOARD

Ask students to pretend they are artists who have been hired to create illustrations for "The Awkward Type!" Display a copy of the poem along with students' artwork. Students may also enjoy writing and illustrating poems with nonsense words. Published poems using nonsense words can serve as models as students write.

THE AWKWARD TYPE !

I am not the graceful type
Who **chendies** 'round the **emert**;
I resemble more the knock-kneed **droim**
that clomps across the desert.

So **closilious** is my style,
Each step I take is wrong, oh—
But when I **bloof** I never blush,
I'm just a nice **bufongo**!

● The Home Letter on page 162 is intended to acquaint family members with the dictionary skills students will be studying in the Unit 7 lessons. Students can take the page home, complete the activities with a family member, and look for the books pictured on the page when they visit the library.

● The Home Letter can also be found on page 161q in Spanish.

CURRICULUM CONNECTIONS ✳

WRITING

Have students write journal entries describing times they have felt like the *bufongo* who narrates "The Awkward Type!"

SCIENCE

Provide students with reference sources in which they can discover if real camels are awkward animals and how many humps they have. Provide maps or a globe for locating places where camels are found.

MUSIC

Have students listen to several different music selections, each having a different tempo and mood. Ask each student to vote for the one he or she thinks is most appropriate for *chendieing*. Have them add a few words explaining their choice.

Lesson 74

Pages 163–164

Alphabetizing; Guide Words

INFORMAL ASSESSMENT OBJECTIVES

Can students

✔ alphabetize words to the fourth letter?

✔ identify words that fall between specific guide words?

Lesson Focus

INTRODUCING THE SKILL

- Write the following groups of words on the board: *limit, limb, limp, lime; cowboy, coward, cowl, cows; molasses, mold, molt, mollusk; humor, humble, human, humidity*. Ask volunteers to rewrite each set of words in alphabetical order. *(limb, lime, limit, limp; coward, cowboy, cowl, cows; molasses, mold, mollusk, molt; human, humble, humidity, humor)*

- Ask students which letter of each word they had to look at in order to alphabetize the words. *(fourth)*

- Remind students that the dictionary, like other reference books, uses guide words to help locate entries. If available, show two different dictionary formats, one with two guide words per page and another with two guide words for the two-page spread.

USING THE PAGES

Have students read the hints and directions on pages 163 and 164. After students complete the pages, discuss the dictionary skills they have practiced in this lesson.

Name _____

▶ Read the words in each group and write them in alphabetical order.

> **HINT**
> In a dictionary the **entry words** are arranged in alphabetical order. When words begin with the same letter or letters, look at the next letter to decide the alphabetical order.

1	tiger table today that teach
	table
	teach
	that
	tiger
	today

2	circle cabin claim chalk ceiling
	cabin
	ceiling
	chalk
	circle
	claim

3	indeed illusion imagine imitate inflate
	illusion
	imagine
	imitate
	indeed
	inflate

4	habit hadn't hammer hall hair
	habit
	hadn't
	hair
	hall
	hammer

5	paddle panel painter palace pants
	paddle
	painter
	palace
	panel
	pants

6	rear realize realist ready realm
	ready
	realist
	realize
	realm
	rear

▶ Number the words in each group to show the correct alphabetical order.

7.			8.			9.		
bungalow	3		locker	3		caricature	3	
bundle	2		locality	1		carve	5	
bunt	5		locket	4		carnival	4	
bunk	4		locomotive	5		carbon	2	
bunch	1		locate	2		caravan	1	

Lesson 74
Alphabetizing **163**

FOCUS ON ALL LEARNERS

ENGLISH LANGUAGE LEARNERS/ESL

Before beginning, direct students' attention to a posted English alphabet or have volunteers write one on the board. Talk about how this alphabet is the same and/or different from others students know.

VISUAL LEARNERS

PARTNER

Materials: dictionaries

Write the following words on the board: *fabulous, philosopher, cinnamon, trapeze, barometer, khaki, turbulent, minority, liberty*. Have each pair of students list the words in alphabetical order and write the guide words for the page containing each word.

KINESTHETIC LEARNERS

PARTNER Each pair of students can draw a tic-tac-toe grid on paper and write a word of their choice in each of nine spaces. To play, students take turns choosing a word and naming a word that would come before and after it in alphabetical order. If correct, an X or 0 can be written on the word.

Read the guide words and entry words in each column. Circle any entry words that would *not* be on the same page as those guide words. Then number the rest of the words in the column in alphabetical order.

> **HINT**
> In the dictionary the **guide words** at the top of the page show the first and last entries on the page. All the other entries on that page are in alphabetical order between those words.

1. ascend / auditorium

4	attack
1	asleep
3	athlete
2	astonish
___	(artist)

2. macaroni / make

(manager)	___
machinery	1
made	2
majestic	4
magnify	3

3. swallow / swung

swoop	3
switch	2
(symphony)	___
swam	1
(survey)	___

Find four words in the box that would be on the dictionary page with each pair of guide words. Write those words in alphabetical order below the guide words.

4. club / coil

clump
coal
coast
cocoa

dance	coal	level	limp
coast	coin	dark	decide
date	clump	cocoa	dahlia
lift	liberty		

5. daily / deep

dance
dark
date
decide

6. lesson / listen

level
liberty
lift
limp

(164) Lesson 74
Guide words

AUDITORY/VISUAL LEARNERS

LARGE GROUP

Write each of the following pairs of guide words on the board in turn: *candy, canon; forever, form; serve, set; wear, wedding.* Invite students to name words that would appear on the pages headed by each set of guide words. Have them list the words alphabetically on the board.

GIFTED LEARNERS

Materials: dictionaries

Challenge students to locate the following dictionary entries: *MD, D-day, un–,* and *ice age.* Ask them to name the words preceding and following each entry and indicate the relevant guide words.

LEARNERS WHO NEED EXTRA SUPPORT

Give students a collection of words beginning with the same letter. Have students first find any words with the same second letter, then those with the same initial three letters, and finally any with the same initial four letters. Help students alphabetize the words. **See Daily Word Study Practice, pages 194–195.**

SPELLING

Use the following words and dictation sentences as a pretest for spelling words in Unit 7.

1. **opaque** — The glass in the window is **opaque**.
2. **ancient** — The necklace is a copy of an **ancient** design.
3. **leisure** — Some people do not know how to relax in their **leisure** time.
4. **automobile** — A new coat of paint made the **automobile** look brand new.
5. **incredible** — The owl has **incredible** hearing.
6. **triangular** — The island is roughly **triangular**.
7. **contradict** — Please do not **contradict** me.
8. **collector** — Every weekend, the shell **collector** searches the beach.
9. **manufacture** — My great-grandfather invented a way to **manufacture** that product.
10. **appointment** — The storm prevented me from getting to my **appointment**.
11. **accidentally** — I **accidentally** broke the vase.
12. **spaghetti** — There are many delicious sauces for **spaghetti**.

WRITING

Portfolio Prompt pairs of students to choose dictionary pages at random. Have them then write a paragraph, story, or poem using at least six words from the page.

SCIENCE

Remind students that encyclopedias use guide words to organize articles much as dictionaries use them to organize words. Assign students animal subjects to research in encyclopedias. Ask them to find their subjects and name the guide words on the page(s). Have students share some of the data they find.

MUSIC

Help students create a musical alphabet. Assign each student a letter of the alphabet. Then invite students to name a piece of music whose title begins with their letter. Students might get ideas from the radio, the library, or the school music teacher.

Lesson 75

Pages 165–166

Dictionary Pronunciation Key

INFORMAL ASSESSMENT OBJECTIVES

Can students

✔ use a pronunciation key to identify symbols used in dictionary respellings?

✔ identify words based on their respellings?

✔ understand the use of accent marks in respellings?

Lesson Focus

INTRODUCING THE SKILLS

- Have students look at the dictionary pronunciation key on page 165. Call attention to the letters associated with the symbols and the key words that provide examples of the different sounds.

- On the board, write the words: *April, boil, truly, thistle, western, trim, long, reach, this, treasure,* and *round.* Have students use the pronunciation key to identify the symbols and key words that match the sounds of the underlined letters.

- Write the words *treasury, medicine, inspire,* and *society* on the board. Ask volunteers to identify the syllables that are said with more stress (accented).

USING THE PAGES

Read the hint on page 165 and the rule on page 166 together. Review the directions for both pages and provide help as needed as students work.

Name _____

Study the pronunciation key. Then look at the words in the word bank and read and say each symbol below the box. Write the word from the word bank that has the sound that symbol stands for. The key words in the pronunciation key will help you.

HINT
The dictionary respelling beside each entry word helps you pronounce that word. The dictionary's pronunciation key shows the symbols used in the respelling.

Vowels				Consonants			
Symbol	**Key Words**	**Symbol**	**Key Words**	**Symbol**	**Key Words**	**Symbol**	**Key Words**
a	cat	oo	look, pull	b	bed	s	see
ā	ape	o͞o	tool, rule	d	dog	t	top
ä	cot, car	ou	out, crowd	f	fall	v	vat
e	ten, berry	u	up	g	get	w	wish
ē	me	ʉ	fur, shirt	h	help	y	yard
i	fit, here	ə	a in ago	j	jump	z	zebra
ī	ice, fire		e in agent	k	kiss, call	ch	chin, arch
ō	go		i in pencil	l	leg	ŋ	ring, drink
ô	fall, for		o in atom	m	meat	sh	she, push
oi	oil		u in circus	n	nose	th	thin, truth
				p	put	th	then, father
				r	red	zh	measure

1. g _____ gallop
2. o͞o _____ school
3. ā _____ pail
4. th _____ thrift
5. zh _____ treasure
6. ē _____ people
7. oi _____ spoil
8. sh _____ should
9. ŋ _____ sting
10. th _____ those
11. ä _____ chart
12. ʉ _____ spurt

spurt	thrift
spoil	should
sting	treasure
school	pail
those	gallop
people	chart

Lesson 75
The dictionary pronunciation key **165**

FOCUS ON ALL LEARNERS

ENGLISH LANGUAGE LEARNERS/ESL

Invite students to share a word from their primary language that sounds different than its spelling suggests. Explain that English contains many such words and that dictionary respellings help readers determine how words should sound.

VISUAL LEARNERS

SMALL GROUP

Materials: dictionaries

Ask each group to locate one of these words in the dictionary: *aphid, chisel, tiara, foist,* and *ruse.* Have volunteers from the groups write each word's respelling on the board, including accent marks. Have students "teach" each other the correct pronunciations.

KINESTHETIC LEARNERS

PARTNER

Materials: dictionaries

One student can write the dictionary respelling of an unusual word and then have the partner write the word represented by the respelling. A dictionary can be used to confirm.

Use the pronunciation key and accent marks to help you say each respelled word. Then read the word that goes with the respelling. Circle the letter or letters in each word that stand for the schwa sound.

1. mōt´ ər bōt — motorboat
2. nes´ ə ser´ ē — necessary
3. sul´ fər — sulfur
4. jen´ ər ə lē — generally
5. im bal´ əns — imbalance
6. kən surn´ — concern
7. en si´ klə pē´ dē ə — encyclopedia
8. sim plis´ ə tē — simplicity
9. ed´ it ər — editor
10. ə plôd´ — applaud

Use the pronunciation key and accent marks to help you say each respelled word below. In front of each respelling, write the word from the word bank that is represented by the respelling.

11. exercise — ek´ sər siz
12. officiate — ə fish´ ē āt
13. currency — kur´ ən sē
14. misunderstand — mis´ un dər stand´
15. presentation — prē sən tā´ shən
16. megaphone — meg´ ə fōn
17. effective — ə fek´ tiv
18. plentiful — plen´ ti fəl
19. kerosene — ker´ ə sēn

Word Bank

misunderstand
effective
officiate
megaphone
exercise
presentation
currency
plentiful
kerosene

AUDITORY LEARNERS

LARGE GROUP

Materials: dictionaries

Read the following words aloud, using a combination of correctly and incorrectly placed accents: *diagonal, necessity, miniature, sergeant, stucco, minnow, mileage, accustomed, tundra.* Ask students if the stress is correct in each word. Have them use dictionaries to confirm responses.

GIFTED LEARNERS

Have students use the pronunciation key on page 165 to try writing respellings for multisyllabic words. Students can use a dictionary to check their work.

LEARNERS WHO NEED EXTRA SUPPORT

Say words from the lesson, placing heavy stress on the accented syllable(s). Ask students to repeat the words and to identify the stressed syllable. **See Daily Word Study Practice, pages 194–195.**

CURRICULUM CONNECTIONS

SPELLING

On the board, write the following word sets. Then call out the spelling words *opaque, ancient, leisure, automobile, incredible, contradict, manufacture, collector, appointment, accidentally* and *spaghetti.* Invite a volunteer to write each word in the appropriate word set and explain the relationship of the words.

1. argue, disagree *(contradict)*
2. buyer, saver *(collector)*
3. mistakenly, by chance *(accidentally)*
4. fun, relaxation *(leisure)*
5. transparent, clear *(opaque)*
6. old, aged *(ancient)*
7. truck, van *(automobile)*
8. make, form *(manufacture)*
9. square, round *(triangular)*
10. date, meeting *(appointment)*
11. amazing, unbelievable *(incredible)*
12. macaroni, noodles *(spaghetti)*

WRITING

Portfolio Invite students to write a short rhyming poem. Then have them rewrite the poem so that the rhyming words are shown with their phonetic respellings. Encourage volunteers to exchange phonetic versions with a partner, who must then read aloud the poem.

MATH

Ask students to write dictionary respellings for the unit's spelling words and several others from the lesson. Have them organize the words according to the stressed syllable. Challenge students to graph the results on a bar graph. What, if any, conclusions can students draw about the frequency in English of various syllable stresses?

LANGUAGE ARTS

Prompt students to develop a research topic from one of the words on the pages. For example, they might read about *exercise* equipment, *kerosene* or other fuels, foreign *currencies,* or *treasure* hunts. Tell students to list five unfamiliar words from their research, look up the words in a dictionary, and use the respellings to help them pronounce the words. Encourage them to present their research findings to the class.

Lesson 76

Pages 167–168

Dictionary Respellings; Looking Under the Correct Word Form

INFORMAL ASSESSMENT OBJECTIVES

Can students

✔ identify words based on their respellings?

✔ identify and locate dictionary entry forms of words?

Lesson Focus

INTRODUCING THE SKILLS

- Write the following dictionary respellings and sets of words on the board: fan tas´ tik, plak ´ət, and līk´ wīz. Tell students to use the pronunciation key on page 167 to identify the word represented by each respelling. *(fantastic, placket, likewise)*

- Remind students that dictionaries list entry words in their simplest form, without suffixes, verb endings, and spelling changes.

- Read these words and ask students which form of the word they would look up in the dictionary: *colliding (collide), resentful (resent), courses (course), happily (happy), astonishment (astonish).*

USING THE PAGES

Discuss the hints on pages 167 and 168. Be sure students understand the directions for both pages. Later, review the exercises with students and the dictionary skills they have learned.

Name _____

▶ Read each sentence. Use the pronunciation key and accent marks to pronounce the respelled word in the sentence. Then fill in the circle beside the word that is represented by the respelling.

> **HINT**
> Many dictionaries have a short pronunciation key on every page or every other page.

a	cat	ō	go	ʉ	fur	ə	a in ago
ā	ape	ô	fall, for	ch	chin		e in agent
ä	cot, car	oo	look	sh	she		i in pencil
e	ten, berry	ōō	tool	th	thin		o in atom
ē	me	oi	oil	*th*	then		u in circus
i	fit, here	ou	out	zh	measure		
ī	ice, fire	u	up	ŋ	ring		

1. Scientists believe that the earliest (in hab´ i tənts) of China lived in caves.
   ○ inhibitions ● inhabitants ○ inheritance

2. Later, scientists think, these people began to farm and keep (do mes´ tik) animals.
   ● domestic ○ domesticated ○ docile

3. Several ancient settlements have been (di skuv´ ərd) in China.
   ○ disclosed ● discovered ○ discouraged

4. Scientists have (eg sam´ ind) the ruins of these settlements.
   ● examined ○ examination ○ excavated

5. Some of the oldest of these settlements are located in the rich (val´ ē) of the Hwang Ho River.
   ○ valid ● valley ○ value

   CHINA

6. These settlements, say the scientists, were (kən struk´ tid) as long ago as 2000 B.C.
   ○ erected ○ construction ● constructed

7. The people of these settlements developed a form of strong (guv´ ərn mənt).
   ○ governor ● government ○ governing

8. They also were able to make (brānz) tools.
   ● bronze ○ bronzed ○ brass

9. In time the settlements were united into city-states and (em´ pīrz).
   ○ umpires ○ employs ● empires

Lesson 76
Dictionary respellings **167**

FOCUS ON ALL LEARNERS ✳ ◆ ▪ ◻

ENGLISH LANGUAGE LEARNERS/ESL

Read through the pronunciation key with students. For each sound, ask them to select a word from their primary language or a familiar English word that contains the sound. Work together to assemble a personal pronunciation key.

VISUAL LEARNERS

PARTNER **Materials:** index cards

Have students write "What is it?" or "What am I?" riddles on one side of index cards. The answers should appear on the other side of the cards, written as a dictionary respelling. Students can have partners decipher the respellings to answer the riddles.

KINESTHETIC LEARNERS

LARGE GROUP Write the following words on the board: *faster, facts, effectively, leaping, closest, wrinkled, leaves,* and *tiniest.* Invite students to come to the board and write the correct dictionary entry form for each word, erasing and/or adding letters as necessary.

Read each word. Beside it, write the entry word you would look for in the dictionary.

HINT
Entry words do not usually have the suffixes and spelling changes that words can have when we use them in sentences. Most spelling changes appear at the beginning or at the end of the entry.

1. striding — stride
2. compliments — compliment
3. enraged — enrage
4. guiltily — guilt
5. resistance — resist
6. geese — goose

7. connected — connect
8. driving — drive
9. sang — sing
10. jetties — jetty

Read the paragraphs. Notice the numbered words in boldface print. Write each numbered word as you would find it as a dictionary entry word.

Mongolia is **located** east of the Chinese
11
province of Sinkiang. Within Mongolia is the Gobi
Desert, one of the **largest** desert areas in
12
the world. Large plains, or **steppes**, where most
13
of the population live, surround the Gobi. For
centuries the people of Mongolia have **kept**
14   15
herds of livestock on these steppes.
Present-day Mongolians live mostly by tending
herds. Their **ancestors,** the Mongols, were
16
among the **world's** most **feared** warriors. In the
17   18
1100s and 1200s, their leader, Genghis Khan,
and his **successors led** these warriors on
19   20

military **conquests** that reached from Europe to
21
Southeast Asia to the Middle East. In fact, the
famous Great Wall of China was **built** in an
22
unsuccessful attempt to keep the Mongol
warriors out of China.

11. locate
12. keep
13. successor
14. large
15. ancestor
16. lead
17. steppe
18. world
19. conquest
20. century
21. fear
22. build

CURRICULUM CONNECTIONS

SPELLING

Call out each spelling word: *opaque, ancient, leisure, automobile, incredible, contradict, manufacture, collector, appointment, accidentally* and *spaghetti*. Have volunteers spell each word and use it in a sentence.

WRITING

Portfolio Have students write a series of postcards from a trip through China's history. Urge them to use data from the lesson pages, with additional research if they wish. Ask students to use at least two or three spelling words in their postcard messages.

HISTORY/LANGUAGE ARTS

Read aloud the quotations below. Have students identify the dictionary entry form for each underlined word, then locate each word in a dictionary. Ask volunteers to use the respellings to pronounce the word. Have students define each word in context. Discuss the meaning of each statement

"Good resolutions are easier made than executed." (Benjamin Franklin)

"Newspapers are the world's mirrors." (James Ellis)

"To read without reflecting is like eating without digesting." (Edmund Burke)

SOCIAL STUDIES

Provide a selection of age-appropriate books about Chinese history and contemporary China. Encourage students to compare and contrast life in ancient China with life in China today.

AUDITORY LEARNERS

LARGE GROUP Stage a dictionary bee in which students take turns saying and spelling the correct dictionary entry form for each word you give. Students are eliminated when they give an incorrect answer.

GIFTED LEARNERS

Challenge students to think of words with irregular plurals, verb tenses, comparatives, or other inflections. Then have partners tell the correct dictionary entry form for each irregular word.

LEARNERS WHO NEED EXTRA SUPPORT

Remind students that dictionary entry words are usually in their simplest form. When students encounter inflected forms, encourage them to say or write the base word before looking it up in the dictionary. **See Daily Word Study Practice, pages 194–195.**

Lesson 77
Pages 169–170

Multiple-meaning Words; Homographs

Lesson Focus

INTRODUCING THE SKILLS

- Write these sentences on the board
  The city pool opens today.
  There was a large pool of applicants for the job.
  Ask students to define *pool* in each sentence.

- Write the word *homograph* on the board. Explain that homographs are words that are spelled the same but have different meanings and origins.

- As students look up *pool* in the dictionary, point out the raised number that follows each entry. This number shows there is another word with the same spelling but a different meaning and a different word history.

- Explain that some words have only one dictionary entry but multiple meanings. Have students look up the word *draw* and discuss its different meanings.

USING THE PAGES

Read the rules and the directions on pages 169 and 170. Call on volunteers to explain what to do in their own words. Later, discuss what students have learned.

169

Name

Read the article, and notice the words in boldface print. Then read the dictionary entries for each of those words, and underline the definition that fits the article.

RULE
In the dictionary, when there is more than one meaning for an entry word, numbers identify the different definitions. The meaning listed first is usually the most commonly used.

A Most **Unlikely** Hero

An unlikely hero today prevented a freak **accident** in our state's **capital** from turning into a disaster. The event occurred shortly after 9:00 A.M. at the corner of Weston and LaPlace Streets near the city **center**.
   Construction workers were engaged in replacing one of the massive stone tigers that flank the **building** at 101 LaPlace Street. Just as a crane was putting the recently repaired statue back on its pedestal, a truck hurtled around the corner of Weston Street. The truck was loaded with manufactured **goods** for the **port**, just a few blocks away. When the driver made the turn onto LaPlace Street, he lost control of his vehicle.
   As the truck headed toward the crane, all except one of the workers scattered. Haley Cooper was standing next to the pedestal directing the crane operator when the truck slammed into the crane. The crane jerked forward and might have crushed Ms. Cooper. However, as the cables from the crane loosened, the tiger slipped gently sideways and down, landing in front of Ms. Cooper and shielding her from the crane.
   "It was a miracle!" proclaimed the truck driver

---

accident (ak´ si dənt) *n.* **1.** a happening that is not expected or planned **2.** an unfortunate happening or instance of bad luck that causes damage or injury **3.** chance

building (bil´ diŋ) *n.* **1.** anything that is built with walls and a roof; a structure, such as a house, factory, or school **2.** the act or work of one who builds

capital (kap´ it'l) *n.* **1.** the same as capital letter **2.** a city where the government of a state or nation is located **3.** money or property that is put into a business or that is used to make more money

center (sen´ tər) *n.* **1.** a point inside a circle or sphere that is the same distance from all points on the circumference or surface **2.** the middle point or part, the place in the middle **3.** a person whose position is at the middle point

construction (kən struk´ shən) *n.* **1.** the act of constructing or building **2.** the arrangement of words in a sentence

goods (goodz) *pl.n.* **1.** things made to be sold; wares **2.** personal property that can be moved

port (pôrt) *n.* **1.** a harbor **2.** a city with a harbor where ships can load and unload

---

FOCUS ON ALL LEARNERS

ENGLISH LANGUAGE LEARNERS/ESL

Explain that figuring out which meaning of a homograph or multiple-meaning word is being used in a given sentence depends on studying the context of the sentence. Demonstrate, using context clues in a sample sentence.

VISUAL LEARNERS

LARGE GROUP

Materials: dictionaries

   Write *pitcher, estate, fortune, graze, tender, duty,* and *dissolve* on the board. Tell students to look up each word in a dictionary and tell how many entries it has. If it has one entry, ask how many definitions are under the entry.

KINESTHETIC LEARNERS

PARTNER

Materials: dictionaries

Have partners take turns giving one another a word to find in the dictionary to determine if the word is a homograph or a multiple-meaning word.

Read these entries. Decide which word to use to complete each sentence below. Write the word and its number on the line in the sentence. You may need to add a suffix to the entry word.

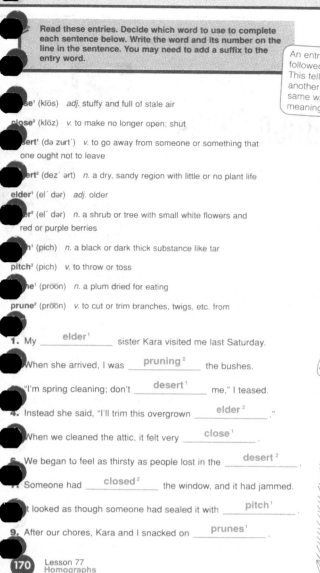

close¹ (klōs) *adj.* stuffy and full of stale air

close² (klōz) *v.* to make no longer open; shut

desert¹ (də zurt´) *v.* to go away from someone or something that one ought not to leave

desert² (dez´ ərt) *n.* a dry, sandy region with little or no plant life

elder¹ (el´ dər) *adj.* older

elder² (el´ dər) *n.* a shrub or tree with small white flowers and red or purple berries

pitch¹ (pich) *n.* a black or dark thick substance like tar

pitch² (pich) *v.* to throw or toss

prune¹ (prōōn) *n.* a plum dried for eating

prune² (prōōn) *v.* to cut or trim branches, twigs, etc. from

1. My _____ elder¹ _____ sister Kara visited me last Saturday.

2. When she arrived, I was _____ pruning² _____ the bushes.

3. "I'm spring cleaning; don't _____ desert¹ _____ me," I teased.

4. Instead she said, "I'll trim this overgrown _____ elder² _____."

5. When we cleaned the attic, it felt very _____ close¹ _____.

6. We began to feel as thirsty as people lost in the _____ desert² _____.

7. Someone had _____ closed² _____ the window, and it had jammed.

8. It looked as though someone had sealed it with _____ pitch¹ _____.

9. After our chores, Kara and I snacked on _____ prunes¹ _____.

CURRICULUM CONNECTIONS

SPELLING

Have pairs of students create two- (or three-) word phrases consisting of one spelling word plus another word beginning with the same letter, for example *slimy, slurpy spaghetti; conscientious collector.*

WRITING

Have students look up the word *pun* in the dictionary. Discuss the meaning together. Then ask students to make up their own puns, using multiple-meaning words or homographs.

SCIENCE

One of the major threats to auto safety is driving at excessive speeds. Have students contact their state or the federal Department of Transportation for information on the importance of obeying speed limits.

SOCIAL STUDIES

Have students use a classroom globe or map to identify the major ports of the United States. Then invite small groups of students to pick a specific port, locate information about its history, and share their findings.

Technology

AstroWord Vocabulary.
©1998 Silver Burdett Ginn Inc.
Division of Simon & Schuster.

AUDITORY/VISUAL LEARNERS

INDIVIDUAL   **Materials:** index cards

Ask students to collect homographs they hear or come across in reading. Have them write the homographs and their meanings on the cards. Keep the completed cards in alphabetical order.

GIFTED LEARNERS

Ask students to think of ways that multiple-meaning words might be used incorrectly. Have them discuss the importance of referring to dictionaries in order to better understand the meanings of words.

LEARNERS WHO NEED EXTRA SUPPORT

Sit down with students and help them skim through several pages of a dictionary, looking for homographs and multiple-meaning words. See if they can put the different definitions into their own words.
See Daily Word Study Practice, pages 194–195.

Lesson 78

 **Reading** **Writing**

Reviewing Alphabetizing, Dictionary Skills, Multi-meaning Words, Homographs

---

INFORMAL ASSESSMENT OBJECTIVES

Can students

✔ read a how-to article that refers to concepts covered in the unit?

✔ write an encyclopedia article?

Lesson Focus

READING

- Have students write a definition for the word *encyclopedia* . Then ask students to share their ideas to create the most accurate definition they can.

- Ask students what a CD-ROM is and what kinds of information are available in this format. If there are CD-ROM encyclopedias in the classroom or school library, ask students who have used them to describe how to access information on them.

- Invite students to read the article that describes how to use a CD-ROM encyclopedia and to respond to the question following the article.

WRITING

Explain that on page 172, students are to compose an article on a subject of their choice for a new CD-ROM encyclopedia. Remind them that while the text may be similar to that in a standard written report, they can enhance their article with audio and video features. Remind them to use words from the box.

Name _____

 Reading ► Read the article about finding information in a CD-ROM encyclopedia. Then answer the question that follows.

Information Clicks

Encyclopedias are filled with information on almost any topic. Biographical articles about famous people, the stories of inventions, facts about gophers, games, or galaxies—they're all just a click away.

People used to think of an encyclopedia as a multi-volume set called a general encyclopedia. This kind of encyclopedia still exists in libraries and in many people's homes. Today, you can also find encyclopedias on CD-ROM. CD-ROM stands for Compact Disc-Read Only Memory. On each compact disc, hundreds of thousands of pieces of information can be stored. To use a CD-ROM encyclopedia, just turn on the computer, pop in the compact disc, and you've got a universe of information at your fingertips with just a click of the mouse.

A CD-ROM encyclopedia contains the same information as a traditional encyclopedia—and more. CD-ROMs often contain short movies and many graphics that enhance the information in the article.

Information on a topic can be accessed in a variety of ways. Suppose you are looking for information about an eclipse. You can look alphabetically through all the entries on the CD-ROM, or you can type in the subject word, and an article about the topic will appear. If you click on the entry word **eclipse** a small window opens up, and entries for the multiple meanings of **eclipse** come into view.

If you need more information about eclipses, click the *See also* button and a list of related articles appears. Did you find an interesting one? Give it a click, and you're on your way!

How might a CD-ROM encyclopedia provide you with more information than you could find in a multi-volume set of general encyclopedias?

_____
_____
_____
_____
_____
_____
_____

Alphabetizing, dictionary, multimeanings, homographs: Reading

---

FOCUS ON ALL LEARNERS ✳ ● ◆ ■

ENGLISH LANGUAGE LEARNERS/ESL

To make it easier for students to comprehend the article on page 171, discuss the meanings of the words *encyclopedia, compact disc, traditional, graphics, accessed,* and *eclipse.*

VISUAL LEARNERS

SMALL GROUP If possible, demonstrate (or have a volunteer demonstrate) how to use a CD-ROM encyclopedia for students. Click on each feature described in the encyclopedia article.

KINESTHETIC LEARNERS

INDIVIDUAL If the technology is available, have students actually operate a CD-ROM encyclopedia as described in the article on page 171.

A company is planning a new CD-ROM encyclopedia. You have been invited to write a short article for use in the encyclopedia on a subject of your choice. Include a reference to another article that would contain information, as well as an audio or video description of some aspect of your topic. Use words from the word bank. Here are some guidelines to help you write.

claim	close	correct	direct
form	general	measure	prefer
procedure	various	size	symbol
system	unit	pronunciation	

Assume your reader knows nothing about your subject.

Define any special terms.

List different aspects of your subject and cover each one.

Include the most important facts.

Leave out insignificant details.

Helpful Hints

Lesson 78
Alphabetizing, dictionary, multi-meanings, homographs: Writing

---

AUDITORY/VISUAL/KINESTHETIC LEARNERS

Have partners read the article on page 171 aloud to each other and create a flowchart showing the steps involved in accessing information on a CD-ROM encyclopedia.

GIFTED LEARNERS

Challenge students to expand the article on page 171 by looking up a real topic in a CD-ROM encyclopedia (or a traditional encyclopedia) and describing the steps they took to find information and what they learned.

LEARNERS WHO NEED EXTRA SUPPORT

Using sample reference sources as models, remind students that it is important to understand how reference sources are organized in order to effectively access the information they contain. **See Daily Word Study Practice, pages 194–195.**

CURRICULUM CONNECTIONS ✳ ● ● ■ ● ◆

SPELLING

Write the spelling words on slips of paper: *opaque, ancient, leisure, automobile, incredible, contradict, manufacture, collector, appointment, accidentally,* and *spaghetti*. Hand individual words to students and challenge them to use props and classmates to act out a mini-skit that will convey the word to the others. The student who guesses the word can spell it aloud.

LANGUAGE ARTS

Portfolio Have students write a persuasive letter to the principal or parent organization explaining why a CD-ROM encyclopedia would be a useful addition to their classroom, school, or local public library. Have them support their opinions with facts.

MATH/SOCIAL STUDIES

Have student groups work together to research a chosen topic, such as a historical event or a famous person. Instruct half the group to use traditional print resources and the other half to use a CD-ROM encyclopedia. Have them keep track of the number of references they find, and also have them classify the types of references (text, photo, audio, video). Finally have them present to the class a chart or graph comparing the number and types of references they found. Discuss the pros and cons of each form of research.

SCIENCE

Have students use balls or other spheres to create a simple model demonstrating how a lunar or solar eclipse takes place. Encourage them to research the topic of eclipses in a traditional or CD-ROM encyclopedia.

Lesson 79

Pages 173–174

Unit Checkup

Reviewing Alphabetizing, Dictionary Skills, Multi-meaning Words, Homographs

INFORMAL ASSESSMENT OBJECTIVES

Can students

✔ recognize words in correct alphabetical order?

✔ identify words that fall between specific guide words?

✔ identify the forms of words that would be used as entry words?

✔ use a dictionary pronunciation key?

✔ distinguish among definitions of multi-meaning words in given sentences?

Lesson Focus

PREPARING FOR THE CHECKUP

- On the board, write the guide-word pairs *elf, emerge* and *emit, ending* and the entry words *enable, elm, empty, embassy, encounter,* and *elope*. Have volunteers write each entry word in alphabetical order under the correct guide words.

- Write the words *order, totem,* and *atom*. Have students use a dictionary pronunciation key to identify how the letter *o* is pronunciation in each word.

- Write *blind* on the board. Have students look it up and tell its different meanings.

USING THE PAGES

Read the directions for each section on pages 173 and 174. Later have students check their work

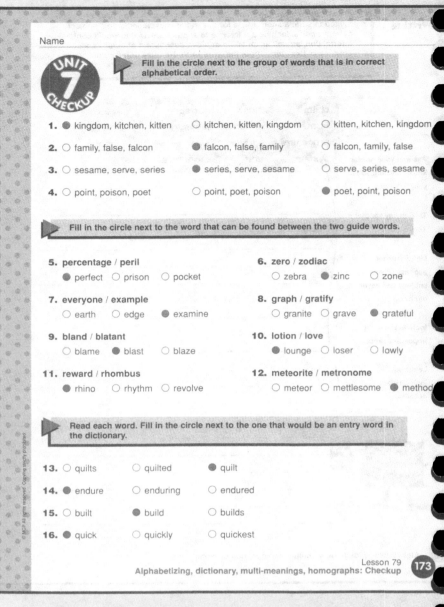

Name _____

Fill in the circle next to the group of words that is in correct alphabetical order.

1. ● kingdom, kitchen, kitten ○ kitchen, kitten, kingdom ○ kitten, kitchen, kingdom
2. ○ family, false, falcon ● falcon, false, family ○ falcon, family, false
3. ○ sesame, serve, series ● series, serve, sesame ○ serve, series, sesame
4. ○ point, poison, poet ○ point, poet, poison ● poet, point, poison

Fill in the circle next to the word that can be found between the two guide words.

5. **percentage / peril**
   ● perfect ○ prison ○ pocket

6. **zero / zodiac**
   ○ zebra ● zinc ○ zone

7. **everyone / example**
   ○ earth ○ edge ● examine

8. **graph / gratify**
   ○ granite ○ grave ● grateful

9. **bland / blatant**
   ○ blame ● blast ○ blaze

10. **lotion / love**
    ● lounge ○ loser ○ lowly

11. **reward / rhombus**
    ● rhino ○ rhythm ○ revolve

12. **meteorite / metronome**
    ○ meteor ○ mettlesome ● method

Read each word. Fill in the circle next to the one that would be an entry word in the dictionary.

13. ○ quilts ○ quilted ● quilt
14. ● endure ○ enduring ○ endured
15. ○ built ● build ○ builds
16. ● quick ○ quickly ○ quickest

Lesson 79 **173**
Alphabetizing, dictionary, multi-meanings, homographs: Checkup

FOCUS ON ALL LEARNERS

ENGLISH LANGUAGE LEARNERS/ESL

Remind students to make sure they completely understand the directions in the Unit Checkup before trying to answer any questions. Work with students as necessary and help them to recheck their work as they finish.

AUDITORY/VISUAL LEARNERS

LARGE GROUP Project or copy onto the board a dictionary pronunciation key. Go through the key, sound by sound, pronouncing each example and asking students for other examples to illustrate the sound-letter relationships.

KINESTHETIC LEARNERS

INDIVIDUAL Materials: index cards

Copy onto index cards sets of guide words from a dictionary and sample entry words that appear under each set. Scramble the cards and have students match the entry words that go with each set of guide words.

UNIT 7 CHECKUP

▶ **Read the dictionary entry. Then answer the questions that follow.**

a	cat	ō	go	u	up
ā	ape	ô	fall, for	ʉ	fur
ä	cot, car	ȯȯ	look	ə	a in ago
e	ten	ōō	tool		e in agent
ē	me	oi	oil		i in pencil
i	fit	ou	out		o in atom
ī	ice				u in circus

poach¹ (pōch) *v.* to cook in water that is almost boiling

poach² (pōch) *v.* to hunt or catch fish illegally on someone else's land

pocket (päk´ət) *n.* **1.** a small bag sewn into a piece of clothing **2.** a hollow place, sometimes filled with something **3.** a small group

podiatry (pə dī´ə tre) *n.* the branch of medicine that deals with problems of the foot

podium (pō´ dē əm) *n.* a raised platform, usually used by a speaker

point (point) *n.* **1.** the sharp end of something **2.** a moment in time **3.** a purpose *v.* to aim

1. According to the pronunciation key, the **e** in pocket is pronounced like the **e** in what other word? _____ **agent** _____

2. What is a podium? _____ **a raised platform** _____

3. What does **point** mean in the following sentence? When asked for directions, the police officer pointed her finger at the street sign. _____ **aimed** _____

4. What does the word **poach** mean in the following sentence? Sam was arrested for poaching salmon from Mr. Lord's stream. _____ **hunting or fishing illegally** _____

5. Write a one-syllable word that rhymes with the second syllable of podium. _____ **Answers will vary. Example: be** _____

6. What does the word **point** mean in the following sentence? The point of the pencil ripped the damp piece of paper. _____ **sharp end** _____

7. What does the word **pocket** mean in the following sentence? Workers found a pocket of silver in the rock. _____ **hollow place filled with something** _____

8. According to the pronunciation key, which syllable in podiatry receives the primary accent? _____ **di/the second syllable** _____

9. Which meaning of **pocket** is used in the following sentence? A pocket of French speakers live in that region of Maine. _____ **small group** _____

10. What does the word **point** mean in the following sentence? What is the point of writing all your letters in code? _____ **a purpose** _____

(174) Lesson 78
Alphabetizing, dictionary, multi-meanings, homographs: Checkup

---

AUDITORY LEARNERS

LARGE GROUP Read aloud different forms of words, such as *thinks, thinking, thought, think.* Ask volunteers to identify the word that would be the correct form for a dictionary entry.

GIFTED LEARNERS

Materials: dictionaries

Have students look up selected words in different dictionaries, such as a student dictionary, a college edition, and an unabridged volume. Ask students to compare and contrast the kinds and amounts of information they find.

LEARNERS WHO NEED EXTRA SUPPORT

Discuss the information provided by the pronunciation key and dictionary entries on page 174 before students begin the checkup. **See Daily Word Study, pages 194–195.**

CURRICULUM CONNECTIONS ✳ ● ◆ ■ ◆ ●

Student Progress Assessment You may wish to review the observational notes you made as students worked through the activities in this unit. Your notes will help you evaluate the progress students made with dictionary skills.

Portfolio Assessment Review the materials students have collected in their portfolios. Talk with students individually to discuss their written work and the progress they have made since the beginning of the unit. As you review students' work, evaluate how well they use the unit skills.

Daily Word Study Skills For students who need additional practice with any of the topics in this unit, quick reviews are provided on pages 194–195 in Word Study Practice.

Word Study Posttest To assess students' mastery of skills covered in this unit, use the posttest on pages 161g–161h.

SPELLING

Use the following words and dictation sentences as a posttest for spelling words in Unit 7.

1. **opaque** — Jean wore **opaque** green tights as part of her costume.
2. **ancient** — My cousin visited the **ancient** pyramids in Egypt.
3. **leisure** — My father builds bird houses in his **leisure** time.
4. **automobile** — An **automobile** assembly line is interesting to see.
5. **incredible** — Some people have **incredible** memories.
6. **triangular** — The diamond pendant has a **triangular** shape.
7. **contradict** — Millie is too polite to **contradict** her host.
8. **collector** — The **collector** donated his masks to the museum.
9. **manufacture** — My great-grandfather invented a way to **manufacture** that product.
10. **appointment** — Emily's mom made an **appointment** for a haircut.
11. **accidentally** — She **accidentally** put salt instead of sugar in the recipe.
12. **spaghetti** — Home-made **spaghetti** is my favorite dish.

Teacher Notes

Teacher Notes

Daily Word Study Practice

Contents

UNIT 1 (LESSONS 1–10, 12–13)

Consonant Variants, Consonant Combinations,   180
Vowel Combinations

UNIT 2 (LESSONS 14–27)

Vowel Pairs, Vowel Digraphs, Diphthongs   183

UNIT 3 (LESSONS 28–41)

Word Parts, Prefixes   186

UNIT 4 (LESSONS 42–50)

Roots, Compounds, Possessives, Contractions   189

UNIT 5 (LESSONS 51–61)

Suffixes   191

UNIT 6 (LESSONS 62–73)

Suffixes, Plurals   192

UNIT 7 (LESSONS 74–79)

Alphabetizing, Dictionary Skills, Multi-meaning   194
Words, Homographs

UNITS 1–2, 4, 6 (LESSONS 11–13, 25–27, 48–50, 70–73)

Syllables   195

UNIT 1 LESSONS 1–13
Consonant Variants, Consonant Combinations, Vowel Combinations

◆ Write these words on the board: *banquet, kettle, chorus, unique, kingdom, fickle, opaque, strike, meek, cannibal, trick, talk, antique*. After volunteers read them aloud, have students copy them and underline the letters that stand for the *k* sound.

◆ On the chalkboard ledge display these words on index cards: *queen, quilt, quail, quiz, quarterback, quicksand*. After students pronounce the words and identify the letters that stand for the initial sound, pose simple riddles like the following and have students identify the mystery word: *What word names a small brown bird?* (quail)

◆ Draw a three-column chart with these headings: /ch/, /sh/, and /k/. Display these word cards and have students pronounce the words, listening for the sound that the letters *ch* stand for: *echo, chef, chart, catch, orchid, brochure, chauffeur, cheap, character*. Have volunteers tape each card in the correct chart column.

◆ Play "name that word" by giving these clues and asking students to write answers beginning with /n/: *You do this with yarn.* (knit) *This is another word for* backpack. (knapsack) *This is a body part.* (knee) *You cut meat with this.* (knife) Ask students to underline the silent letter that begins each word.

◆ Write the letters *k, ck, que, qu, ch,* and *kn* on the board. Give students ten minutes to look for and record words containing these letters. Have them compare lists with a partner and identify the sound each letter or group of letters represents.

◆ Distribute cards with words containing the hard and soft sounds of *c* and *g*, for example, *juicy, licenses, course, decades, guest, gazebo, rage, tragedy, pledge, judge, bridge*. Designate the four corners of the room with these signs: /k/, /s/, /g/, and /j/. Have students hold the cards and stand in the appropriate corners.

◆ Flash these words and have students clap their hands if the words contain the hard sound of *c* or snap their fingers if the words contain the soft sound of *c*: *cement, cake, celery, circus, cymbal, century, common, became, cardboard, audience*.

◆ Display these words and have students stamp their feet if the words contain the hard sound of *g* or tap their desks if they contain the soft sound of *g*: *region, pledge, gallop, gymnasium, garden, disgust, gentle, stagehand, judge, guest, sponge*.

◆ Write these words on the board and have students copy them: *physical, forty, puff, rough, follow, enough, cliff, photograph, afflict,* and *trophies*. Have students use a colored marker to underline the letter or letters representing the *f* sound.

◆ Remind students that the letters *gh* can be silent or stand for the *f* or *g* sound. Label a chart with these three headings and then display these word cards: *ghost, tough, neighbor, brought, ghoul, thought, coughed*. Have students read each word, identify the sound of *gh*, and tape the card in the correct column.

◆ Ask students to name words in which *f, ph, ff,* or *gh* stand for the *f* sound. Record the words on the board. Then have students work with partners to use the words to construct crossword puzzles. Have them exchange puzzles with another pair.

Daily Word Study Practice

◆ Have students write these sounds on four index cards: /s/, /z/, /sh/, and /zh/. Then write these words on the board and have each one read aloud: *usually, unsure, enclosure, miser, treasure, noisy, suddenly, music, ensure, solid.* Have students display the card that corresponds to the sound of *s* in each word.

◆ Have students make up riddles for words in which *s* stands for /z/, /sh/, or /zh/ and share them with a partner. For example, for the word *treasure,* the clue might be *The letter* s *stands for* /zh/ *in a word that names something valuable.*

◆ Write these words on cards and place them around the room: *treasure, posy, tense, leisure, because, surprise, sand, please, selfish, measure, satisfy, insurance, research, hasty, trousers, usually.* Divide students into four treasure-hunting teams and have them locate the words in which *s* stands for /s/, /z/, /sh/, or /zh/.

◆ Have students copy words, using a green marker for words where *wh* has the *hw* sound and a red marker for words where *wh* has the *h* sound. You might use these words: *whale, whetstone, whenever, wheeze, whip, why, whom, white, whiz, whoop, whoosh, whirl, whose.*

◆ Give students cards and have them work with partners to write words in which *w* has the sound *h* or *hw.* Have them exchange words with another pair of students and then sort the word into two piles based on the sound of *w.*

◆ Read these words and have students put a finger to their lips each time they hear a word that contains the *sh* sound: *marsh, circle, suspicion, satisfy, relation, shudder, snore, summer, patient, stroll, ancient, shaped, superstition, ocean.*

◆ Write these words on the board and ask volunteers to underline the letters that represent the *sh* sound in the words: *negotiate, special, partial, ocean, shouted, accomplished, magician, harsh, commercial, potential, starfish, sufficient.*

◆ Play an opposites game in which students name antonyms that contain the sound of *sh.* For example, *the opposite of* kind (harsh), *the opposite of* ordinary (special), *the opposite of* onshore (offshore), *the opposite of* hasty (patient).

◆ Have the group brainstorm a list of words in which the letter *s* represents the sounds of *s, z, sh,* and *zh.* Write their suggestions on the board. Then ask volunteers to underline the *s* in each word and identify the sound it stands for.

◆ Write the key words *soccer, rose, sure,* and *treasure* as headings on the board. Then write these words to the side: *casual, assure, sample, Russia, leisure, insurance, solve, noise, nose, secret, issue, silent.* Have students read each word and write it under the key word in which *s* stands for the same sound.

◆ Divide students into two teams, the "Thunders" and the "Rhythms." Have each team pronounce its name and listen for the sound that *th* represents. Then say these words and have each team signal when *th* has the same sound as in their name: *enthusiasm, weather, nothing, marathon, healthful, brother, theater, mother, faithful, father.*

◆ Write the key words *thin* and *then* on two paper bags. Then give students cards with words containing the letters *th.* Have them read the words and sort the cards into the bags based on the sound of *th.*

◆ Play a word scramble game with words containing *th*, for example, *threw, thin, their, moth, them*. Write the letters of the words in random order and then have students work with a partner to write the letters in the correct order. Once a word has been written, ask students to identify the sound of *th*.

◆ Give three volunteers cards labeled with the sounds of *s*, *sk*, and *sh* and have them stand. Give the rest of the group cards with words containing the letters *sc*. Have students read their words, listening for the sound of *sc* and joining the appropriate line behind a volunteer with that sound card.

◆ Work with students in brainstorming three lists of *sc* words with the sounds *s*, *sk*, and *sh*. After reviewing the words in each list, ask each student to select one word from each list and combine them in a single sentence. For example, *We were conscious of the scent of the scarlet flowers.*

◆ Give students cards with the following words and have them pantomime or act out the words: *scowled, scampered, scanned, luscious, scythe, sculpt, conscious*. Once a word is guessed, have a volunteer write it on the board and then have students identify the sound of the letters *sc*.

◆ Write these words on the board and have students pronounce them: *design, gnat, assign, gnome, sign, resign, cologne*. Have students use colored chalk to underline any silent consonants in the words.

◆ Write the words *ki___en, wa___, fe___, ca___ing, di___, sti___ed* on the board and have students copy them, supplying the missing consonant combination (*tch*) for each. Have students pronounce each word and use it in an oral sentence that illustrates its meaning.

◆ Lead students in brainstorming words containing the consonant combination *wr*. Write the words on the board. Give students grid paper and have them work with a partner to make up word-search puzzles using these words. Have them exchange puzzles with another pair.

◆ Challenge students to make up rhythmic rhymes about a rhinestone-wearing rhinoceros in a rhubarb patch. Encourage them to illustrate their rhymes. Invite students to share their rhymes and drawings with the group so that others can identify all of the words with the *r* sound.

◆ Write the consonant combinations *ch, ck, kn, ph, wh, sh, th, sc, gn, tch, rh,* and *wr* on the board. Ask volunteers to come to the board and list words containing each combination. Have others in the group read each word, identify the consonant combination, and identify the sound it represents.

◆ Have students repeat the following words, listening for the vowel sound: *heard, wear, fear, bear, earn, gear*. Say the words again and have them point to their ears if they hear /ear/, point to the earth if they hear /ur/, and point up in the air if they hear /air/.

◆ Divide the class into three teams and assign each team one of the three sounds represented by the letter combination *ear*. Set a timer for five minutes and have students list as many words as they can that contain the specified sound. To turn the activity into a race, award 1 point for each correct word.

Daily Word Study Practice

◆ Write the phonograms *-are* and *-air* as heads for two columns. Work with students to develop lists of words containing each phonogram. Point out homophones that occur in the lists and discuss their meanings. Some possibilities include *pare, pair; fare, fair; stare, stair;* and *hare, hair.*

◆ Write the phonograms *-ild, -ind,* and *-ost* on pieces of tagboard and give them to three volunteers to hold. Have each student think of a word containing one of the phonograms and join the correct line. Then have students pronounce their words, identify the vowel sounds, and use the words in sentences.

◆ Pronounce words with long and short vowel sounds. Have students raise their right hands if the sound is long and their left hands if the sound is short. In your list, include words with the letter combinations *ild, ind, ost,* and *old*—for example, *wild, wind, cost, mold, gold, host, sold,* and *hind.*

UNIT 2   LESSONS 14–27
Vowel Pairs, Vowel Digraphs, Diphthongs

◆ Assign pairs of students to work together to play a game of *ai-ay* ping-pong. Have them alternate writing words containing these vowel pairs on a piece of paper folded in half. Continue the game until one student cannot think of any more words.

◆ Write these and other words containing *ai* or *ay* on cards and place them in a box: *braid, play, daisy, train, relay, delay, replay, mayor, stay.* Have students select a word and pantomime clues to help others guess the word. As each word is guessed, have a volunteer write it on the board and identify the vowel sound.

◆ Write the following words on the board, omitting the vowel pairs *ai* or *ay* in each word: *train, daisy, jail, complain, repayment, stay.* Call on volunteers to complete each word with the correct vowel pair. Then have them read the word and use it in a sentence.

◆ Write these words on the board: *succeed, either, leisure, pedigree, protein, receive, receipt, wheel, steeple, proceed.* Ask each student to select a word and give a clue to it. For example, *My mystery word means "to go ahead."* (proceed) Invite the rest of the class to guess each mystery word.

◆ Have students fold a sheet of paper into eight sections. In each section, have them draw a picture of an object whose name contains the vowel pair *ee* or *ei.* Encourage students to exchange papers and write labels for the pictures. Have them underline the vowels that stand for the long *e* sound. Examples include *tree* and *receipt.*

◆ Challenge students to create sentences that contain at least two words with the vowel pairs *ee* and *ei.* To help them get started, you may wish to share this example: *Eek, I see three spiders on the ceiling!*

◆ Write the following words on cutouts of ten bowling pins: *boast, crow, stow, arrow, coach, boast, toaster, elbow, goal, oboe.* Place the pins in random order and have students take turns reading the words. Those who can read all ten words correctly score a strike.

◆ Have pairs of students brainstorm a list of sports-related words containing the vowel pairs *oa, oe,* and *ow*—for example, *bowling, arrow, goal, throw, coach, row, snowshoe, snow board, boat.* Then have them work together to write a brief sports article using as many of these words as possible.

Daily Word Study Practice

◆ Have students fold their papers into three columns and head each column with the vowel pairs *oa, oe,* and *ow.* Then dictate these words and have students write them in the correct column, based on the spelling of the long *o* sound: *toe, row, boat, goal, slow, toad, soap, hoe.*

◆ Divide students into groups of seven and have each group form a circle. Give each group a sheet of paper with these vowel pairs: *ai, ay, ee, ei, oa, oe,* and *ow.* Have students pass the paper around the group. Each student in turn will add a word containing one of the vowel pairs.

◆ Write words containing the vowel pairs *ai, ay, ee, ei, oa, oe,* and *ow* on the board. Call on volunteers to pronounce each word, underline the vowel pair, and identify the vowel sound associated with the vowel pair.

◆ Divide students into small teams. For each team, post a sheet of chart paper on the board with these vowel pairs: *ai, ay, ee, ei, oa, oe,* and *ow.* Have students on each team take turns writing a word with one of the vowel pairs in the appropriate column. The first team to write words for all seven vowel pairs wins the round.

◆ Have each student write the terms *long* a, *long* e, and *short* e on three index cards. Then read these words and have them hold up the correct card to identify the first vowel sound heard in each word: *great, pleasant, preacher, breakfast, break, weather, sweater, greasy, eagles, beaver, beagle, leash, steak.*

◆ Have students work with a partner to brainstorm a list of animal names that include the *ea* digraph, such as *beaver, pheasant,* and *bear.* Then have them circle words that contain the long *a* sound, underline words with the long *e* sound, and draw a box around words with the short *e* sound.

◆ Have students write sentences with words that have the three sounds represented by the *ea* digraph. To help students get started, you may wish to provide this example: *The team had whole wheat muffins, steak, and peaches for breakfast.* Have students exchange sentences and identify words with the *ea* digraph.

◆ Pronounce these words: *steak, feather, deaf, mean, steady, break, east.* For each word have students identify if the vowel digraph *ea* represents the long *e,* the long *a,* or the short *e* sound.

◆ Have students write the words *field* and *pie* on either side of an index card. Then say these words and have students display the word that has a corresponding vowel sound: *niece, notify, believe, yield, cries, shriek, shield, fierce, tries, retrieve, spied, reprieve.*

◆ Draw a large pie and a shield on the board and divide each into ten sections. Call some volunteers to the board and have them write words containing the digraph *ie* in the drawing that corresponds to the vowel sound heard in each word.

◆ Give students cards with words containing the vowel pairs *ee, ei,* and *ie.* Possible words include *receive, cheek, seize, steep, deceive, ceiling, green, knee, modified, collie, chief, tried, fried,* and *believe.* Have each student display the card, read the word, and identify the vowel sound.

◆ Read the following words and have students point to the sky each time they hear the long *i* sound and point to their feet each time they hear the long *e* sound: *chief, lied, field, believe, tried, relief, shield, disbelief.*

Daily Word Study Practice

◆ Write these words on the board and have students copy them, using a red marker to write the letters that stand for the long *a* sound heard in each word: *rein, sleigh, vein, obey, survey, reindeer, convey, freight, neighbor, weigh, hey.*

◆ Write the names of these household objects on cards and distribute them to students: *automobile, shawl, laundry, faucet, lawnmower.* Have these students give clues about the identity of their mystery objects for others in the group to guess.

◆ Write sets of three words that contain the vowel digraphs *ea, ey, ie,* and *ei.* Two words in each set should have the same vowel sound, for example, *head, bean, feather.* Have students underline the two words in which the vowel digraph represents the same sound.

◆ Display two large cutouts of a foot and a boot. Have students brainstorm lists of words that contain the vowel digraph *oo* and write them on the shape that corresponds to the vowel sound heard in each word.

◆ Have pairs of students use a paper plate, brad, and larger paper clip to make a spinner with these key words: *goose, look,* and *blood.* After each spin, have students name a word in which *oo* has the same vowel sound as the key word.

◆ Write *shampoo, wood,* and *flood* on large cards and post them in separate areas of the room. Then say these words and have students point to the word card where the vowel digraph *oo* represents the same sound: *snoop, took, foolish, raccoon, bloodhound, bookworm, groom, crooked, flood.*

◆ On each side of an index card, have students draw a picture of a biscuit and a fruit. Have them say each picture name, listening for the sound represented by the *ui* digraph. Then say these words and have them display the picture whose name has the same vowel sound: *cruise, quilt, recruit, suitable, pursuit, nuisance, rebuilt, guitar.*

◆ Label two small paper bags with /i/ and /$\overline{oo}$/. Then present students with these word cards and have them sort the cards according to the sound of the vowel digraph: *mannequin, pursuit, exquisite, building, cruiser, guitar, circuit, guilty, quiver, nuisance.*

◆ Assign students to groups of seven. Tape seven papers to the board and label them with the letters *oo, ui, au, aw, ea, ei, ey,* and *ie.* Have each group choose a paper. Each group member should record at least one word containing the group's vowel digraph on the chart. Students can work together to read the words and identify the vowel sounds heard in the words.

◆ Write the words *boy* and *boil* on the board and have students identify each diphthong and the sound they represent. Then write these words on the board, omitting the diphthong: *foil, point, broil, moist, poison, toy, annoy, corduroy.* Have students supply each missing diphthong to write the whole word.

◆ Work with students in brainstorming words that contain the diphthongs *oi* and *oy* and write them on the board. Ask student volunteers to select a mystery word from the list and give clues to the rest of the class. Once the word is guessed, erase the word from the list. Continue until all the words have been erased.

◆ Assign students to work in pairs and have them create scrambled word puzzles with words containing the diphthongs *ou* and *ow.* For example, the word *grow* could be written as "wgor." Once students have created five or six puzzles, have them exchange puzzles with another pair and decode the scrambled words.

◆ Write these words on cards and have students read them aloud: *prow, journey, renown, powder, row, journey, touch, out, owe, plow, four, flown*. Have students crook their fingers like horns when they hear a word with the same vowel sound as *cow*.

◆ Have pairs of students take turns composing oral sentences that contain at least one word with the diphthong *ou* or *ow*. Have the partner who is listening write the *ou* or *ow* word, read it aloud, and circle the diphthong.

◆ Draw a treasure chest on the board. Have each student add a "jewel" to the chest by writing a word that contains the diphthong *ew*. When everyone has contributed a jewel, randomly point to the words and have the group read them aloud.

UNIT 3   LESSONS 28–41
Word Parts, Prefixes

◆ Write the terms *base word, root, prefix,* and *suffix* in a column on the board. In another column, write a brief definition for each term, using the information found in Lesson 28. Have students draw lines matching each term with its definition.

◆ Write a number of base words and roots on separate index cards. Then write prefixes and suffixes on other cards. Give a small group of students the cards and challenge them to make as many words as possible by combining the cards. Have students use each word in an oral sentence.

◆ Write these headings on the board: *Base Word, Prefix,* and *Suffix.* Then say or write these words and ask students to list their component parts in the correct columns: *unwholesome, unsuccessful, recounted.* Repeat this activity, using the headings *Root, Prefix,* and *Suffix* and these words: *important, transportable, autographed.* Encourage students to add their own words to these charts.

◆ Write the prefixes *ir-, im-, il-,* and *in-* on a spinner made from a paper plate, a large paper clip, and a metal brad. Have students work in small groups to take turns spinning the spinner. Have them give words beginning with the designated prefix.

◆ Write these prefixes on the board: *ir-, im-, il-, in-.* Then distribute cards with these words: *visible, patient, logical, correct, regular, possible, literate, perfect, expensive.* Have volunteers read each word and then match it with a prefix on the board to make a new word.

◆ Play an opposites game by saying these words and asking students to respond with antonyms formed by adding prefixes: *responsible, efficient, patient, exact, literate, rational, effective, regular, legible.*

◆ Write the words *embodied, immerse,* and *immature* on the board. Then share these sentences, omitting the words in parentheses: *We will (immerse) the lettuce in water. Democratic ideals are (embodied) in our history. The toddler is too (immature) for a camping trip.* Have students complete each sentence with one of the words.

◆ Assign students to work in pairs and have them play several rounds of "im-em tic-tac-toe." To move, one student writes a word beginning with the prefix *im-* in a game grid while the other writes a word beginning with the prefix *em-*. The first player to get three words with *im-* or *em-* in a row wins the round.

Daily Word Study Practice

◆ Write these words on the board and have students read them aloud: *immigrant, empowered, embed, impatience, improbable, impure*. Have volunteers define each word, using the meanings of the prefixes *im-* and *em-*. Then call on other students to use the words in oral sentences.

◆ Have students label each side of a coin or a chip with the prefixes *mis-* and *mal-*. Then have partners take turns flipping the coin and giving a word that begins with the designated prefix.

◆ Write these base words on cards and turn them face down on a table: *understand, function, treat, quote, spell, read, nutrition, pronounce, name*. Have students take turns selecting a word, adding the prefix *mal-* or *mis-* to create a new word, and then using this new word in an oral sentence that illustrates its meaning.

◆ Write these words on the board: *malnutrition, discontent, irregular, misadventure, imperfect, incapable*. For each word, write a clue on the board such as *To not be perfect is to be ___*. Ask volunteers to fill in each missing word, underline the base word, and circle the prefix.

◆ Write these categories on the board: *Health, Vehicles, Politics*. Challenge pairs of students to write words beginning with the prefixes *anti-* and *counter-* that they associate with each of these categories. For example, the terms *antifreeze, antilock, antiknock, antitheft*, and *antipollution* might be associated with the category *vehicles*.

◆ Write these words on the board and have them read aloud: *countermove, antilock, antipathy, antisocial, countersign, counterpart*. Ask volunteers to circle the prefix in each word. Then ask other students to use the words in sentences.

◆ Display these words on cards and have them read aloud: *descend, depart, defrost, dehumidify, deplane, dethrone*. Have students analyze the meaning of the prefix *de-* in each word. Have them place the words where *de-* means "down" in one pile and where *de-* means "away" in another pile.

◆ Assign students to work in pairs. Have them collaborate to write as many words as possible in five minutes that begin with the prefix *de-*. Have each pair compare their list with another pair and circle any words that are exclusive to their list.

◆ On the chalkboard ledge, display these words on index cards: *forenoon, postscript, forehead, postgraduate, forecast*. After students read the words and identify the prefixes, pose riddles like the following and have students identify the mystery word: *What word names a brief message appearing at the end of a letter?* (postscript)

◆ Say the following words and have students write an antonym for each that contains either the prefix *fore-* or *post-*: *undergraduate, afternoon, background, prewar*.

◆ Write these words on the board: *freeze, social, centralize, control, date, clockwise, part, ground*. Tell students to add the prefix *de-, anti-, counter-, fore-*, or *post-* to these words to form new words. Encourage them to check their answers in a dictionary.

◆ Review the two meanings of the prefix *over-*, the two meanings of the prefix *ultra-*, and the three meanings of the prefix *super-*. Challenge students to find at least one word that illustrates each of these prefix meanings.

◆ Divide the class into small groups. Allow five minutes for the groups to brainstorm a list of words that contain the prefixes *over-, ultra-*, and *super-*. Ask them to use as many of their words as they can in a paragraph.

187

◆ Have students describe powers that a superhero might have with words that have the prefixes *over-*, *ultra-*, and *super-*. For example, a superhero might have *ultrasensitive* hearing, might be immune to the dangers of *ultraviolet* light, and might fly at *supersonic* speeds. Have students create cartoons with captions using these words.

◆ Write these words in a column on the board: *dowdy, unemotional, reckless, overweight, confident*. Have students copy the words and next to each write an antonym that contains the prefix *over-*, *ultra-*, or *super-*.

◆ Mention to students that many advertisements contain words that begin with the prefixes *ultra-* and *super-*. Have students look at ads in newspapers and magazines for words containing these prefixes. Students can also write original ads using words beginning with *ultra-* and *super-*.

◆ Write these words on the board: *semiannual, transverse, transpire, semicolon, semitropical, transition, transmigration, translation*. Have students copy the words and underline those in which a prefix is added to a base word and circle those in which the prefix is added to a root.

◆ Have students recall the three different meanings of the prefix *trans-* and the two meanings of the prefix *semi-*. Have students give at least one example of a prefixed word that illustrates each meaning. For example, the prefix *trans-* in *transcontinental* means "across a continent."

◆ Have students work with a partner to make up a secret code. For example, they might use numerals to represent letters of the alphabet. Then have them write five or six words with the prefixes *trans-* and *semi-* and give them to another pair of students to translate.

◆ To help students understand words that incorporate the prefix *semi-*, ask questions like the following: *What's the difference between a circle and a semicircle? a colon and a semicolon? a finalist and a semifinalist? a professional and a semiprofessional?*

◆ Read aloud these words and have volunteers write them on the board: *subsoil, midnight, submerged, sublet, midtown, midpoint*. Ask other students to circle the prefixes in the words. Then have students use the words in oral sentences.

◆ Write the category headings *Time* and *Place* on the board. Then lead students in brainstorming words in each category that begin with the prefix *mid-*. For example, words for time might include *midday, midnight, midyear, midsummer,* and *midwinter*.

◆ Challenge students to draw a scene that includes things whose names contain the prefixes *sub-* and *mid-*. For example, students might draw a *suburb* connected by a *subway* to a city. Above the city, they might show a plane in *midair*, and they could also show a *submarine submerged* in *midstream*.

◆ Hold up one, two, and then three fingers and have students identify the prefix associated with each number. Then display these fingers in random order and have students respond with the names of vehicles. For example, if two fingers are displayed, students might respond by naming a bicycle or a biplane.

◆ Talk about the meaning of the terms *monolingual, bilingual,* and *trilingual,* and ask students into which category they fall. Graph the results and have students identify the different languages they speak.

◆ Have students fold a paper in fourths. Have them head each part with one of these prefixes: *uni-, mono-, bi-, tri-*. Have them draw and label four pictures whose names contain these prefixes, such as a unicycle, monorail, bicycle, and tricycle.

◆ Review *uni-, mono-, bi-*, and *tri-* by asking questions such as the following: *How many tracks does a monorail have? How many horns does a unicorn have? What base do you go to if you hit a triple? How many issues a year does a bimonthly magazine have?*

UNIT 4   LESSONS 42–50
Roots, Compounds, Possessives, Contractions

◆ Write these words on the board: *portable, repulsive, deposited, propellers, eject*. Ask volunteers to read the words. Then have other students underline the roots and use their meanings to help them define the words.

◆ Head five sheets of chart paper with the roots *pos, pel, pul, port*, and *ject*. Have each student visit each chart and write a word that contains the root. Then randomly point to the recorded words and have students read and use them in oral sentences that illustrate their meanings.

◆ Using the charts created in the previous activity, student partners can play a mystery word game. One student selects a word and gives clues about its meaning, so his or her partner can guess the mystery word.

◆ Read the following words: *audience, dictate, edict, auditorium, audition, dictionary, audible*. Have students cup their hands behind their ears if the root means "hear." Have them cup their hands around their mouths if the root means "say."

◆ Display these words on cards and have each read aloud: *captive, intercept, capable, receptionist, receive, receipt, receptacle*. Call on volunteers to identify the root in each word and define it based on the meaning of this root.

◆ Draw a large pair of glasses on a piece of tagboard. Label one lens *spec* and the other lens *spect*. Have students write words containing these roots on each lens. Then have volunteers randomly point to these words and call on others to define and use them in sentences.

◆ Write these roots on index cards and place them in a bag: *pos, pel, pul, port, ject, aud, dict, cap, cept, ceipt, spec, spect, mit, miss, man*. Have students take turns selecting a card from the bag, reading the root and giving its meaning. Then have them give one or more words containing the root.

◆ Write the words *manicure, dismissal, omit, speculate*, and *inspector* on the board. Challenge students to identify the root in each word. Have them use the words in oral sentences.

◆ Give students categories such as tools, clothing, furniture, and sports. Have them work in small groups to select a category and brainstorm compound words that belong in this category. Have students share their words and their meanings with the class.

UNIT 4

◆ Have students make up "puniddle" puzzles by drawing two pictures that represent a compound word. For example, pictures of a pine tree and an apple could represent the word *pineapple*. Have students exchange puzzles with a partner and attempt to solve them.

◆ Have students write some wacky explanations to explain how some compound words were formed. For example, they might describe how the words *flapjack* or *dragonfly* came to be. Encourage students to be creative and humorous in their descriptions.

◆ Students can play "I'm thinking of a word" by defining a compound for others to guess. For example, a clue for the compound word *sweatshirt* might be *This is a good shirt to wear when you're exercising.*

◆ Have each student write two component words of a compound on two index cards. Collect all the cards and mix them up. Then redistribute two cards to each student. Have students circulate around the room, looking for the missing halves of their compounds. Continue until all the words have been matched.

◆ Challenge students to write a menu by using only foods that are compound words. Have them share their menus with a partner or in a small group.

◆ Write the following sentence on the board: *As soon as my grandmother sees the first snowflake, she makes me wear a turtleneck and an overcoat.* Have volunteers underline each compound. Then have students write their own sentences about seasons, using compound words.

◆ Write each of the three rules governing the formation of possessives on separate sheets of chart paper and tape them to the board. Have students do a "walkabout" to visit each chart and record an example of a word that follows the rule on the chart.

◆ Select examples of words that illustrate the three rules for forming singular and plural possessives and randomly write them on the board. Have each student select one word, tell whether it refers to one or to more than one, and then use it in an oral sentence.

◆ Have students develop a list of plural words that do not end in *s*, for example, *men, women, children, oxen, geese, mice, deer, moose, elk, trout, salmon.* Then have them write the plural possessive form of each word.

◆ Have students look for book titles that contain both singular and plural possessive words. Have them underline the singular possessive forms and circle the plural possessive forms.

◆ Give students ten index cards. Have them think of ten nouns that name animals. Tell them to write the singular possessive form on one side of the card and the plural possessive form on the other side. Have them share their cards with a partner.

◆ Have each student write a sentence that contains both a singular and a plural possessive. Assign partners and have them exchange and then illustrate each other's sentences.

◆ Have students look through trade books to find examples of dialogue and record the contractions used in these excerpts. Beside each contraction, have them write the two words that were combined to form the contraction.

◆ Have students listen for contractions in everyday classroom conversation. Encourage them to keep a contraction log for a day or two in which they record the contractions they hear.

Daily Word Study Practice

Suffixes

◆ Play a game of "careers" in which students pantomime the work of a photographer, an organist, a geologist, a farmer, and so on. Once an occupation is guessed, have a volunteer write it on the board. Then ask students to identify the base word and the suffix.

◆ Have students write the letter *S* on one side of a card and *W* on the other side. Then read these words and have students display the letter *S* if the word ends with a suffix or the letter *W* if the word is without a suffix: *advance, beginner, choir, permissible, reliance, detective, item, homeward.*

◆ Work with students in brainstorming a list of adjectives to which the suffixes *-er* and *-est* can be added. Develop a three-column chart with these words. Then have each student select an adjective and use all three forms in oral sentences that illustrate their meaning.

◆ Write these headings on three pieces of chart paper and tape them to the chalkboard: *Drop the* e; *Change* y *to* i, *Double the Final Consonant.* Have students write adjectives ending with *-er* and *-est* that illustrate each rule.

◆ Distribute a page from a newspaper or magazine to each student. Review the definition of a suffix. Remind students that some words look as if they have suffixes, but they do not, for example, *romance.* Tell students to skim their page for suffixes and circle any they find. Have students share their results in small groups.

◆ Remind students that when adding the suffixes *-ous* and *-al* to base words, sometimes the spelling of the base word changes. Have students make a list of five words that illustrate these spelling changes, write each word on the board, and explain the change.

◆ Read these definitions and have students write a word containing the suffix *-ward, -en,* or *-ize* that matches each definition: "to make standard" *(standardize),* "to make short" *(shorten),* "in the direction of the sea" *(seaward),* "to become sad" *(sadden).*

◆ List these words on the board and have students write an antonym containing the suffixes *-ward* or *-en* for each word: *backward, tighten, lengthen, downward.* Then challenge students to write a sentence that contains an antonym pair.

◆ Write these suffixes on the board: *-al, -er, -ize.* Then display cards with these base words: *provide, region, symbol, paint, option, standard.* Have students read each base word and identify its part of speech. Then have a volunteer hold the word card beside a suffix to form a new word. Have students identify the part of speech of each new word and use it in a sentence.

◆ Read these words and ask students to identify the base word and the suffix: *whiteness, spoonful, painful, kindness, harmful, willful, drawerful, fitness.* Call on volunteers to explain how the meaning of each base word was changed by the suffix.

◆ Ask pairs of students to choose the suffix *-ful* or *-ness.* Suggest that they use dictionaries, spelling books, or other resources to compile a list of words containing the suffix. Have them share their completed list with a pair of students who chose the other suffix.

◆ Play a "guess my word" game in which you think of a word and students guess it by asking questions that contain words with *-ful* or *-ness,* such as *Is it healthful? Will it benefit my fitness? Will it be painful?* Whoever guesses the answer starts another round by choosing a new mystery word.

UNIT 5

◆ Draw eleven large circles on chart paper and explain that they are flower centers. Write one of these suffixes inside each center: *-or, -ist, -er, -est, -ous, -al, -ward, -en, -ize, -ful, -ness*. Have students write words ending with these suffixes on paper flower petals and tape them to the corresponding flower center.

◆ Have students write the letter *S* on a card. Read these sentences and have them hold up the *S* each time they hear a word with a suffix: *The advertisement said the trip would be enjoyable and mysterious, not perilous. The actor told many humorous stories of the happiest memories of his wonderful childhood.*

◆ Distribute cards with *-hood, -ship,* and *-ment*. Have students pass the cards until you give a stop signal. Those holding a card should say a word ending with the suffix. Have the student sitting to the left or the right identify the part of speech.

◆ Pairs of students can create word equations. Write this formula on the board and ask students to explain its meaning: *base word + suffix = new word*. Have students use the formula to write lists of words containing the suffixes *-hood, -ship,* and *-ment*. For example, *neighbor + hood = neighborhood*.

◆ Have students write these suffixes on opposite sides of an index card: *-ible, -able*. Say these words and have each defined: *disagreeable, responsible, convertible, flexible, breakable, enjoyable, reproducible*. Have students identify the suffix by displaying the correct side of the card.

◆ Place cards with these words on the chalkboard ledge: *unbearable, misjudgment, imported, transcontinental*. Ask volunteers to select a word. Then have them identify the prefix, the root or base word, and the suffix. Call on other students to define each word and use it in a sentence.

◆ Write these words on the board: *information, population, vibration, obstruction, composition, demotion, relation*. Have students copy these words in a column. Beside each word have them write the base word. Have them underline any dropped letters.

◆ Have pairs of students create riddles for words with the suffixes *-ance, -ence, -ive,* and *-ity*. For example, *What word has the suffix -ance and describes a final sale at a store?* (clearance). Encourage students to share their riddles with the class.

◆ Form two teams. Have one team choose 15 suffixes and write them on index cards. Have the other team write 30 base words to which suffixes can be added. Have the base-word team display a word. A member of the suffix-team then holds up a suffix and says the new word. Continue until all base words have been used.

UNIT 6   LESSONS 62–73

Suffixes that Alter Base-Word Spellings, Plurals

◆ Write these headings on two charts and tape them to the board: *Double Final Consonant, No Change*. Discuss when it is necessary to double a base word's final consonant when adding a suffix. Then ask each student to think of at least three words containing suffixes for each category and write them on the appropriate chart.

Daily Word Study Practice

◆ Display these suffix equations and have students complete them: 1. ___ + *en* = *flatten*, 2. *rip* + *ing* = ___, 3. ___ + *er* = *jogger*, 4. ___ + *y* + *foggy*, 5. *chill* + *ed* = ___. Encourage students to make up their own equations to share with a partner.

◆ Dictate these words and have students write them: *guidance, practiced, cleaning, politeness, migration, bluest, deciding, securely*. Have students circle each word in which the final *e* was dropped from the base word when the suffix was added.

◆ Read these riddles and tell students that the answers will be words that drop the final *e* or double the final consonant before adding a suffix. *I am a person who loves to spend my time in stores. Who am I?* (shopper) *I am the time of year when students do not go to school. What am I?* (vacation) Have students write their answers.

◆ Read aloud these words and have students hold up their fingers to indicate how many suffixes they hear in a word: *cheerfulness, surprisingly, thoughtfulness, saddened, handsomely, acceptances, truthfulness, powerlessness, softener, lawlessness*.

◆ Give each student a card on which you have written a word that has more than one suffix. Have students remove each suffix so that only the base word is left. Have them note any spelling changes that occurred as a result of the suffixes.

◆ To play "suffix hunt," give each student a page from a newspaper or magazine. Challenge students to skim the pages for words with more than one suffix. Suggest that students write the words and then underline the first suffix and circle the second suffix.

◆ On separate sheets of chart paper, write the four spelling rules found in Lesson 65 for adding suffixes to words ending in *y*. Have students look for words that illustrate each spelling rule and write them under the rule. Post the charts as a spelling aid.

◆ Write these words on cards and place them in a bag: *hastily, possibly, sloppily, feebly, sparkly, lazily, happily, busily, merrily*. Have students take turns selecting a card and identifying the base word and the suffix. Then have them state the rule that was used when the suffix was added to the base word.

◆ Play a "spell checker" game. Make cards for words ending with *y* or *le* to which suffixes have been added. Some of these words should be deliberately misspelled. Display each card and have students act as spell checkers by identifying and correcting each misspelled word.

◆ Write these words on the board: *admirable, politely, shipped, wiggled, supplies, monkeys*. Call on volunteers to identify each base word and write it on the board. Then have students identify whether a spelling change in the base word occurred when the suffix was added.

◆ To help students remember the exception to the rule for forming the plural of words ending in *f*, have them make up a humorous sentence that incorporates the words *chief, belief, reef*, and *roof*. For example: *The chiefs climbed upon some roofs to discuss their beliefs about reefs*.

◆ Write these words on the board: *cliff, sheaf, chief, loaf, shelf, half, leaf, roof, wolf, puff, scarf*. Have students fold a paper in half and label the columns *Change to* v and *No Change*. Have them write the plural form of each word in the appropriate column.

◆ Have students brainstorm lists of words ending with *f, fe*, and *ff* and record them on chart paper. Then have them play the "one and one" game, using the words by saying *one shelf + one shelf = two shelves* or *one cliff + one cliff = two cliffs*.

◆ Have students write -s and -es on opposite sides of an index card. Then say these words and have students display either -s or -es to show how they would form the plural: *potato, hero, rodeo, tuxedo, torpedo, kangaroo, echo, piano, domino, hero, tornado.*

◆ Have students draw and label pictures of objects or people whose names end in *o* and form the plural by adding -es. These names could include *tomatoes, potatoes, heroes, torpedoes,* and *tornadoes.*

◆ Prepare cards with the following words and display one card at a time: *half, muff, rodeo, wharves, autos, lives, dominos, chief, whiff, wife, thief, scarves, staffs, tomatoes, avocado.* Have a volunteer read the word and identify it as singular or plural. Then ask another student to give the other form of the word.

◆ Say these words aloud and have students hold up their right hands if the form stated is singular, their left hands if it is plural, and both hands if it is both singular and plural: *women, alumnus, mouse, salmon, children, chili, people, oases, man, goose, aircraft, elk, oxen.*

UNIT 7   LESSONS 74–79
Alphabetizing, Dictionary Skills, Multi-meaning Words, Homographs

◆ Select ten words from a dictionary page and write them in a column on the board. Ask students to work against the clock to write the words in alphabetical order. Repeat this activity several times over a few days and challenge students to improve their individual times.

◆ Remind students that entries for letters *A–C* are in the first fourth of a dictionary, entries for *D–L* are in the second fourth, entries for *M–R* are in the third fourth, and entries for *S–Z* are in the last fourth. Say words and have students identify the section of the dictionary in which the entry would be found.

◆ Write two guide words from a dictionary page on the board. Then list eight words, four of which do not appear on the page. Have students identify those words that would be on the dictionary page with the guide words. Have them tell whether the other words would come before or after this page in the dictionary.

◆ Have half the class write their last names on cards and display them on the chalkboard ledge. Then have students write the names in alphabetical order. Repeat this procedure, using the first names of the other half of the class.

◆ Lead the class in brainstorming a list of words that end with the suffixes -er, -est, -s, -es, -ed, and -ing. Write the words on the board. Then next to each word, have volunteers write the dictionary entry for the word.

◆ Encourage students to think of a "What is it?" or "What am I?" riddle, and write it on a card. Have them write the answer as a dictionary respelling on the other side. Invite students to exchange riddles with a partner. After the students answer the riddles, challenge them to decipher the respellings to check if their answers are correct.

◆ Have pairs of students use a dictionary to locate at least five homographs. Have them write a sentence for one of the definitions under each entry. Ask them to share their sentences with another pair of students, who can then look up the homograph in the dictionary and write the correct definition for the word as it is used in the sentence.

Daily Word Study Practice

◆ Distribute a newspaper or magazine article to each student. Have students skim their articles, searching for at least three unfamiliar words. Have them record the words and then look up their meanings in a dictionary. Have them identify the definition that corresponds to the meaning of the word as it is used in the article.

UNITS 1–2, 4, 6   LESSONS 11–13, 25–27, 48–50, 70–73

Syllables

◆ Have students repeat words after you, clapping hands or snapping fingers to mark each syllable. Possible words to use include *cabin, music, patient, lizard, conscientious, optimistic, overwhelmed, uncomfortable, ridiculous, reprimanded, defective,* and *distrustful.*

◆ Ask pairs of students to select a book of their choice. Challenge them to go on a word hunt to find at least five words that are one syllable, two syllables, and three syllables in length. You may wish to award bonus points if students locate any four-syllable words.

◆ Write these words on the board and have students underline the vowels with colored chalk: *photo, father, razor, rapid, smaller, finish, sentence, pities, comic, melon, appear.* Then have students divide each word into syllables and identify the syllabication rule that applies.

◆ Ask volunteers to copy the four syllabication rules found in Lesson 11 onto chart paper. Then challenge students to find at least ten words to illustrate each rule. Have them write the words under the rules and post the charts in the classroom for reference.

◆ Distribute old magazine and newspaper pages and invite students to hunt for words that contain the diphthong *ew,* like in *few.* Have them copy each word they find and then write the number of syllables heard when they pronounce the word.

◆ Have students review the four syllabication rules presented in Unit 1. Then have them select ten words from Lesson 25 and apply these rules to divide these words into syllables.

◆ Have students recall the syllabication rules presented in Lesson 48 and record them on four sheets of chart paper as they are dictated. Ask each student to find at least one word that illustrates each rule and write it on the appropriate chart. Display the charts for reference in the classroom.

◆ Play a game of "syllabication baseball." The pitcher gives words that each batter divides into syllables. To score a home run, the batter must correctly divide the word and identify which syllabication rule or rules apply.

◆ On chart paper, write the six syllabication rules presented in Lesson 71 and post them in different areas of the room. After reviewing the rules on the charts, have students form small groups, visit each chart, and add words to the chart that illustrate the rule.

◆ Have each student review the syllabication rules presented in Lesson 71 and select the rule that he or she finds most difficult to apply. Have the students work with a partner to search for at least five words that follow this rule. Have students copy the words and use a colored marker to divide them into syllables.

Teacher Notes

Teacher Notes

Teacher Notes

Teacher Notes